STORM OF THE CENTURY
The Labor Day Hurricane of 1935

Revised Edition

WILLIE DRYE

Guilford, Connecticut

An imprint of The Rowman & Littlefield Publishing Group, Inc.
4501 Forbes Blvd., Ste. 200
Lanham, MD 20706
www.rowman.com

Distributed by NATIONAL BOOK NETWORK

British Library Cataloguing in Publication Information available

Library of Congress Cataloging-in-Publication Data

Names: Drye, Willie, author.
Title: Storm of the century : the Labor Day hurricane of 1935 / Willie Drye.
Description: Revised edition. | Guilford, Connecticut : Lyons Press, [2019] |
    Includes bibliographical references and index.
Identifiers: LCCN 2019007989 (print) | LCCN 2019008556 (ebook) | ISBN
    9781493037988 (e-book) | ISBN 9781493037971 (pbk. : alk. paper)
Subjects: LCSH: Labor Day Hurricane, 1935. | Florida Keys
    (Fla.)—History—20th century. | Hurricanes—Florida—Florida
    Keys—History—20th century. | World War, 1914-1918—Veterans—United
    States—Employment. | Veterans—Florida—Florida Keys—History—20th
    century.
Classification: LCC F317.M7 (ebook) | LCC F317.M7 D79 2019 (print) | DDC
    975.9/41063—dc23
LC record available at https://lccn.loc.gov/2019007989

♾™ The paper used in this publication meets the minimum requirements of American National Standard for Information Sciences—Permanence of Paper for Printed Library Materials, ANSI/NISO Z39.48-1992.

Printed in the United States of America

Contents

Notes and Acknowledgments for the Second Edition iv
Foreword to the Second Edition by Kerry Emanuel, PhD viii
Prologue: Sunday, September 1, 1935 x

CHAPTER ONE: A Remote Paradise 1
CHAPTER TWO: Forgotten Men 21
CHAPTER THREE: A Wind Stirs in the Atlantic 56
CHAPTER FOUR: It's Blowing Like Hell Down Here 89
CHAPTER FIVE: In the Heft of the Hurricane 109
CHAPTER SIX: A Terrible Sunrise 134
CHAPTER SEVEN: Just a Catastrophe 143
CHAPTER EIGHT: An Act of God 161
CHAPTER NINE: Regret to Inform You 184
CHAPTER TEN: For the Record 209
CHAPTER ELEVEN: The Illusion of Remoteness 236
CHAPTER TWELVE: Time Borrowed from the Wind 269

Notes. 297
Select Bibliography. 355
Index 358

NOTES AND ACKNOWLEDGMENTS
FOR THE SECOND EDITION

I've always thought that Franklin Roosevelt was a good president.

When I made that statement many years ago to a hostess in Florida who'd invited me to lunch before a book signing for *Storm of the Century: The Labor Day Hurricane of 1935*, her facial expression changed like the sun going behind a dark cloud, and I thought, *Well, Drye, you won't be invited here again.*

Some time later I came across a review of *Storm* on the website of a big-box bookstore. The reviewer was affiliated with a well-known, respected university in Pennsylvania. She said many complimentary things about my book, but she wasn't pleased that I'd explained in some detail the political maneuvering and blame dodging by members of Roosevelt's administration that followed the deaths of the veterans in the hurricane. She apparently thought that my purpose for writing the book was to tarnish FDR's historical image, and so she ended her otherwise flattering comments with the caveat "even though the author has an obvious political agenda."

There's an old newsroom axiom that says that if you've annoyed both sides when you write about a controversial issue, you probably got the story right. I'd like to think that the anecdotes I've cited above are an indication that I came somewhere close to getting the story of this long-ago tragedy right.

I say all this to assure the reader that my purpose in writing *Storm of the Century: The Labor Day Hurricane of 1935* was to tell the story that the facts presented. My agent, Jeanne Fredericks, and Globe Pequot executive editor Rick Rinehart made the deal for the new edition, and I'm very grateful to both of them for giving me the opportunity to re-tell and add to this remarkable tale.

Cathy Keller, owner of Hooked on Books bookstore in Islamorada, Florida, repeatedly urged me to do a new edition of *Storm* because customers keep asking her for copies of the book, which has been out of print for some time.

Gayle Butters of Archer, Florida, and Jim Walton of Stephenville, Texas, provided documents that gave dramatic, firsthand accounts of the hurricane. Butters, the granddaughter-in-law of the late Fern Butters, gave me a copy of Fern's unpublished memoir of the storm. Walton, a retired meteorologist, sent me a copy of the letter that trainmaster George Branch wrote to his daughter detailing the ill-fated rescue train's harrowing journey from Miami to Islamorada.

I'm also grateful to the many meteorologists who have reviewed—and when necessary corrected—my work over the past 20 years and let me pester them with questions. They include the late William Gray of Colorado State University; his protégé and successor at CSU, Phil Klotzbach; Kerry Emanuel of Massachusetts Institute of Technology, a member of the National Academy of Sciences; Keith Blackwell of the University of South Alabama's Coastal Weather Research Center; many meteorologists who are or were with NOAA, including Chris Landsea, Sam Houston, Wilson Shaffer, and Brian Jarvinen; Jeff Masters of the website Weather Underground.

I owe special thanks to NOAA meteorologist and hurricane historian Neal Martin Dorst, who tracked down additional information about Leonard Povey's historic hurricane hunting flight on September 2, 1935, and who gave me perspective and insight on many of the events discussed in the book. And former Weather Channel meteorologist Bryan Norcross, who's now the hurricane specialist at WPLG-TV in Miami, was always willing to answer questions and offer encouragement.

Brad Bertelli, curator at the Florida Keys History and Discovery Center in Islamorada, helped with new facts about the hurricane and reviewed the new chapter about Hurricane Irma. And I'd also like to thank the center's executive director, Jill Miranda-Baker, and the board of directors for making a permanent home in the center's research library for the crates of documents and boxes of books I accumulated while researching the story of the 1935 hurricane.

Dan Baker, who was an editor at the *Macon Telegraph* when I worked there back in the 1980s, edited the first draft of the Hurricane Irma chapter.

Mary Barley allowed me to use her guest house in Islamorada when I needed a place to stay while doing research.

I started an enduring friendship with Jerry and Mary Lou Wilkinson in Tavernier when I started digging into Jerry's files in 1998.

Dr. Dean Hawley, professor of forensic pathology at the Indiana University School of Medicine, helped me visualize the awful conditions that rescuers faced immediately after the hurricane. Dr. Michael Higginbotham also provided helpful medical information.

Tom Beard of Port Angeles, Washington, provided information about the untimely death of U.S. Coast Guard Lieutenant William Clemmer.

The late Herbert Saffir—who helped devise the Saffir-Simpson Scale for rating a hurricane's intensity and destructive potential—offered invaluable insights about the nature of powerful storms.

Chester "Bo" Morgan, now a professor of history at the University of Southern Mississippi, advised me on New Deal–era politics in the South, while David Sansing, emeritus professor of history at the University of Mississippi, provided some colorful facts about U.S. Representative John Rankin.

Author Tom Knowles, now retired from his distinguished career at Florida State University, graciously shared some of his research on the 1935 hurricane.

Librarians and archivists, those unsung caretakers of our accumulated knowledge, were invaluable. I want to thank Michael Cotter at East Carolina University; John McMinn and Esperanza DeVarona at the University of Miami; and the staffs at the P.K. Yonge Library of Florida History at the University of Florida in Gainesville; the University of Wyoming library in Laramie; and the Franklin D. Roosevelt Presidential Library in Hyde Park, New York. I'm also indebted to the research assistants at the Mariner's Museum in Newport News, Virginia; the MacArthur Memorial Library in Norfolk, Virginia; and the Pigeon Key National Historic District in Marathon, Florida.

Tom Hambright, who's now retired from his former position as historian at the Monroe County Public Library in Key West, provided invaluable insights into the history of the Florida Keys. The late Jim Clupper at the Islamorada branch of the library provided Red Cross records and other documents related to the storm.

Lieutenant Commander Glen Freeman, Lieutenant Paul Lange, and Warrant Officer Dave Umberger of the U.S. Coast Guard told me about storms at sea, and attorney John McAfee of McCotter, McAfee, and Ashton in New Bern, North Carolina, helped me understand the political aspects of this story.

Colonel D. J. Kieley, USMC (Ret.) of the National Naval Aviation Museum in Pensacola, Florida, provided helpful contacts and details about 1930s-era aircraft.

Sarah Duran, now an attorney in Seattle, took on research missions when she lived in South Florida. Author and former *Macon Telegraph* colleague Ed Grisamore provided news clips, and Alan Snel, now producer of LVsportsbiz.com in Las Vegas, let me use his home as a base for research at the FDR library when he lived in New Paltz, New York.

Historian Paul George of Miami convinced me that my topic was worth writing a book and helped with early planning. The late Wright Langley of Key West offered encouragement, advice, and documents about the storm, and Larry Wiggins gave me copies of Homestead newspapers from the mid-1930s.

Phyllis Mitchell, Bob Mitchell, Patty Lodge, and Bob Lodge talked about their experiences in Hurricane Irma and also provided warm hospitality. Richie Russell invited me into his home to talk about his ancestors' awful experience in the Labor Day Hurricane of 1935 and his own family's experience in Hurricane Irma.

Lisa Thomas pulled the proposal that became *Storm of the Century* off the slush pile at National Geographic in 2001, saw some potential there, and got the first edition of the book greenlighted for publication.

And finally, the hard work and high competence of my wife, Dr. Jane Morrow, have meant that I've always had a place to work in good times and bad.

Wilmington, North Carolina
February 14, 2019

FOREWORD TO THE SECOND EDITION

By Kerry Emanuel, PhD, Professor of Atmospheric Science, Massachusetts Institute of Technology; member, National Academy of Sciences; member, American Academy of Arts and Sciences; named one of the 100 most influential people by Time *magazine in 2006*

Nothing captures the imagination like a good storm. Perhaps our fascination with storms stems from their continued challenge to civilization in the face of substantial progress in science and technology. As vastly improved forecasts have eliminated the element of surprise, arrogance has replaced ignorance as the main source of our suffering. From a mayor who, for fear of losing business, refuses to evacuate his city in the face of certain destruction to a resident who insists she can ride out the storm because she always has, natural selection now seems to target the proud over the ignorant. Yet, as has always been the case, it is the poor who suffer most at the hands of the proud, the ignorant, and the greedy. Hurricanes Katrina and Sandy are recent reminders that despite all our progress we remain far from invulnerable to Mother Nature.

Each region and each culture has a distinctive storm lore, whether it be the Blizzard of 1888, the Hurricane of 1938, or the Great Gale of 1703. These are tales of the struggle between man and nature, and there are villains, victims, and heroes aplenty. Take Hurricane Katrina of 2005. Forecasters had nailed the track and intensity of the storm days in advance, and the head of the National Hurricane Center had the courage to violate his agency's protocol by directly phoning the mayor of New Orleans, warning him that his city was in imminent danger. But the mayor postponed evacuating the city to give his lawyers time to ascertain whether he could be sued by local businesses if the evacuation proved unnecessary. Thus thousands of mostly poor residents became trapped by rising water, as there was not enough time to organize their evacuation. Yet scores of individuals and several agencies, some acting without mandate, managed to save thousands.

The Labor Day Hurricane of 1935, the most intense hurricane ever to have struck the U.S., also served, as with most natural cataclysms, as a stage upon which human frailty and magnificence both played out. Its story is here wonderfully told by Willie Drye, a reporter with decades of experience and a real knack for exploring the human dimensions of a natural disaster. If your experience is anything like mine, you will find yourself entranced and riveted by this account of a vicious hurricane pitted against a fragile community reeling from the Great Depression. From the heroic but ultimately ineffective efforts to locate and gauge the storm to the bungling incompetence and cowardice of some and the valiant efforts of others charged with moving a work crew of veterans out of harm's way, to individual stories of suffering, love, and compassion, this is the saga of mankind as revealed by the encounter of a single natural phenomenon with a small community. It is a story that has played out over and over again in our history and, alas, is destined to be repeated.

Cambridge, Massachusetts
February 20, 2017

PROLOGUE:
SUNDAY, SEPTEMBER 1, 1935

In the waning days of the summer of 1935, a patch of bad weather—thunderstorms, wind, and rain—blew off the west coast of Africa and rumbled across the Atlantic Ocean. As the weather system approached The Bahamas in late August, it picked up a counterclockwise circulation imparted by the rotation of the Earth, drew energy from saltwater that had baked for months beneath the blazing summer sun, and evolved into a tropical storm.

It was the time of year when such storms often form in that part of the world, although the 1935 season had been relatively quiet. The summer's first hurricane hadn't formed until August 18 a few hundred miles east of Puerto Rico. It had stayed well offshore from the United States as it churned northward, weakened as it reached the cool North Atlantic, and plowed into Newfoundland with 60-mile-per-hour (mph) winds.

There was something different about the second storm of the season, however. This one would become a small hurricane of tremendous power that would cause havoc far out of proportion to its diminutive size. It would strike the Florida Keys with a force beyond any human standard of measurement. Hurricanes weren't named in 1935, but the storm that formed off The Bahamas in late August would become the most powerful hurricane ever to strike the United States. This anonymous killer would spread grief throughout the country. Its aftermath would reverberate for months through the highest government offices in Washington, DC, and then it would quickly fade from the nation's collective memory.

But when the storm crossed Andros Island in The Bahamas during the evening of Saturday, August 31, 1935, it did little more than rustle trees and snap some branches. Steering clear of shipping lanes and eluding the primitive, porous hurricane detection system of that era, the storm slipped quietly into the Straits of Florida, within easy striking distance of Florida or Cuba.

On August 31, Grady Norton, the U.S. Weather Bureau's chief hurricane forecaster in Jacksonville, told the Associated Press that the storm was "a small one and has no hurricane winds yet—we have been able to watch it so short a time we cannot be sure what it will do."

Unknown to Norton and the Weather Bureau, however, the storm found perfect conditions for strengthening in the straits, and its energy exploded overnight.

It was exactly the kind of hurricane one might expect to form in the middle of the Great Depression, when so many forces—economic, political, even natural—seemed to be aligning solely for the purpose of punishing those least capable of protecting themselves. In 1935 the United States was in the grip of a bewildering paradox of poverty in the midst of plenty. In the cities, hungry men got into fistfights over garbage discarded by restaurants, and people lined up for blocks to receive a cup of soup or a sandwich. Meanwhile, farmers slaughtered livestock, poured out milk, and burned grain because no one could buy what they produced. Then the banks foreclosed on the farms, forcing the bankrupt farmers off their land. Farmers who managed to hold on to their property didn't fare much better. A prolonged drought put hundreds of thousands of people on the brink of starvation and made dust of the topsoil in the Midwest. The prairie winds whipped the dust into thick, choking clouds that towered over the land and turned midday to dusk.

About two million men roamed the country seeking work that wasn't there.

"On the highways the people moved like ants and searched for work, for food," author John Steinbeck later wrote in *The Grapes of Wrath*. "And the anger began to ferment."

The misery wasn't confined to the United States. As poet W. H. Auden noted, "[W]aves of anger and fear" encircled the globe during the 1930s. In Germany, a mediocre landscape artist who'd found a brilliant new career in politics steadily strengthened his grip on the German people, built horrible new weapons of war, and started hatching one of history's vilest schemes for world conquest. In Japan, ambitious military warlords seized power and plotted a brutal campaign to dominate Asia and the Pacific Ocean. In Italy, the posturing buffoon who controlled the government dreamed of creating a new Roman Empire as he prepared to unleash mechanized warfare on a poor African nation that had been a cradle of civilization but now could barely feed its people.

The malignancies bedeviling the world seemed to feed this storm. How else could it have acquired such awful power? And when this witches' brew of wind and water had achieved an unearthly strength, it found hundreds of down-and-out men who'd been ground beneath the heel of the Depression and were completely unprotected from its onslaught, and it steered straight for them.

The U.S. Weather Bureau had been issuing advisories on the storm for two days. But in 1935 there were no weather satellites watching from the heavens to pinpoint a tropical weather system so that meteorologists knew its exact location at any given moment. There were no hurricane-hunting airplanes to penetrate to the heart of the storm to obtain invaluable information about whether it was weakening or strengthening. Meteorologists relied on reports from ships at sea for much of their information about violent storms, but when a hurricane was roaming the ocean, captains were trying to put as much distance as they could between their ships and the bad weather.

Considering the primitive conditions under which U.S. Weather Bureau forecasters worked, they could be forgiven if their hurricane forecasts and warnings weren't always spot-on accurate. But in July 1935, the Weather Bureau had, with considerable fanfare, made a very public statement about its forecasting abilities that far exceeded its capabilities.

The bureau had paid for a full-page advertising supplement in newspapers across the nation announcing that hurricanes threatening the southern U.S. coast during the coming peak of the hurricane season "are going to find it 'tough going' from now on."

The ad was formatted to look like a news story, complete with blaring headlines—"Storm Warning—Hurricane Coming!"—dramatic photos, and the byline of John L. Frazier. Many readers no doubt thought it was a news story when they saw it in their local newspapers.

"Uncle Sam has perfected his hurricane service for this area, perfected it to the extent of putting a decided crimp in their stealthy approach," Frazier wrote.

The key to this new efficiency was decentralizing the Weather Bureau's warning system so that information on developing storms went to Weather Bureau offices in New Orleans, Jacksonville, and San Juan instead of its main office in Washington, DC. And hurricane advisories would now be issued from those offices instead of Washington, Frazier wrote.

Reorganizing the bureau for more efficiency and accuracy was a public service. Making public claims that the new system was virtually infallible was very foolish, and the deadly proof of that foolishness was already prowling the seas barely two months after the bureau's very public boasting.

It was another of the harsh ironies of the time that the men in the path of this vicious storm were put there because their government was trying to help them. They were American military veterans, and they were very much on Ed Sheeran's mind at daybreak on Sunday, September 1, 1935. The men—most of whom had served in what was then called the Great War—were sleeping in shacks all around Sheeran as the sun crept above the horizon of the Atlantic Ocean and began its spectacular ascent into the heavens above the Florida Keys.

The Weather Bureau hadn't said yet that the disturbance posed a direct threat to the Keys, but that meant nothing to Sheeran. He trusted his own observations and judgment more than those of men sitting in offices hundreds of miles away.

Sheeran had already been at work for several hours. It didn't matter to him that it was Labor Day weekend or that he'd intended to spend the holiday with his wife in their comfortable home in the Miami suburb of Coral Gables. A bad storm was prowling the seas somewhere east of the Keys, and from Sheeran's point of view only a fool would sit still and do nothing when he knew trouble might be heading his way.

Sheeran was 65 years old, but advancing age had done little to diminish his energy. The Wisconsin native had spent most of his adult life working in South Florida and the Keys. In September 1935 he was supervising the construction of a highway bridge that would finally link the Lower Keys with the Upper Keys and the mainland. The project was part of a New Deal effort to help Depression-wracked Key West, whose 12,000 residents were trying to survive on an average income of $7 per month. Some of the veterans worked for Sheeran, although the federal officials in charge of the vets camps had created so many regulations about their work hours it was difficult to get much use out of them.

Sheeran had served as a combat engineer in France during World War I, and he'd learned to keep his wits about him, establish his priorities, and focus on his work in difficult situations. He was wounded when he refused to stop working on a bridge simply because the Germans were shooting at him. His stubborn dedication to his job had earned him a Purple Heart, a promotion from captain to major, and a citation for bravery from General Pershing himself.

He had weathered many hurricanes and developed a skill for detecting them that was almost a sixth sense. A distant hurricane telegraphs its approach in a subtle but unmistakable code that is written in the clouds, the sea, and the air. Sheeran had learned to recognize these subtleties, and on

September 1, 1935, he was dead certain of two things: This was a bad storm and it was headed his way.

Months earlier Sheeran had prepared for the possibility of a hurricane when he ordered his crew to dig a 1,000-foot canal at the southern tip of Lower Matecumbe Key. He was responsible for a lot of expensive floating construction equipment that, if left in exposed waters, would easily be destroyed by a hurricane. As the sun came up Sunday morning, Sheeran and his men were moving the equipment into the canal, where the sheltered water and surrounding mangroves would provide some protection from the winds and rough seas he was certain would be upon them in another day or two.

But he was powerless to do anything about the 400 or so men dozing in the flimsy shacks of the three work camps that had been established in the Upper Keys a few months earlier. Few of the veterans had any idea of the power of a hurricane or how vulnerable the slender, low-lying Keys were to these storms.

As Sheeran worked, horrible memories of a tragedy that occurred 29 years earlier in an identical setting kept flashing through his mind. In 1906 he was working on the construction crew building the famous Key West Extension of the Florida East Coast Railway from Miami to Key West. Hundreds of men hired for the massive project were housed in work camps and houseboats in the Keys. Most of them had never been in the tropics and knew nothing of the danger of the storms that sometimes come roaring off the ocean in late summer and early fall.

In mid-October the Keys natives—known as Conchs after the tough shellfish that was a staple of their diet—told railroad construction supervisors that a powerful storm was headed their way. The Conchs pleaded with the bosses to evacuate the workers, but their warnings were ignored. The hurricane struck the Keys with winds of more than 130 mph on the morning of October 18, 1906.

At least 130 workers were killed. Many died when the hurricane yanked a houseboat from its moorings at Long Key and hauled it out to sea. The storm pulled the houseboat far beyond any hope of rescue and then methodically smashed the vessel and spilled the doomed occupants into the churning ocean.

Corpses washed up on beaches for days afterward.

Now Sheeran feared another slaughter was in the making. He knew the veterans' poorly built wooden shacks would be useless in the face of a hurricane's fury. The only way to protect the men was to load them aboard a train and get them off the islands. But Sheeran was employed by the Florida State Highway Department and didn't have the authority to order a special train for the vets. Evacuation was up to the federal officials in charge of the work camps, and he wondered if they were taking the threat seriously.

At least one of them was. Sam Cutler, an assistant administrator, had been gathering information about the storm since the previous afternoon. At age 59 he had never been in a hurricane, but he was cautious by nature, and his training as a safety engineer had reinforced this tendency. Cutler was in temporary command of the work camps during the holiday weekend because his boss, 45-year-old Ray Sheldon, had decided to take a brief honeymoon in Key West with his wife of one week. Cutler wanted to evacuate the veterans immediately, but that decision would have to be made by still another administrator, Fred Ghent, who was in charge of the veterans work program in Florida.

Fred Ghent's office was almost 500 miles up the coast in Jacksonville. He had a lot more on his mind that weekend than simply what was going on in the Keys.

When he was hired only five months earlier as administrator for the work program, Ghent seemed perfect for the job. He was compassionate and wanted to help the veterans get their lives back on track. But officials in Washington had decided to terminate the program, and in early August Ghent was told he'd soon be out of a job. The news was a bitter surprise, and he planned to get his mind off things for a while by spending Sunday, September 1, on a Jacksonville golf course.

At the same time Sheeran was moving his equipment into sheltered waters, Fred Ghent sleepily answered his ringing telephone. It was Ray Sheldon calling from Key West. Sheldon said he'd just talked to the U.S. Weather Bureau's office there, and the meteorologist had suggested he might want to take the next ferry back to the work camps in the Upper Keys. The storm that had crossed The Bahamas the night before might make the waters too rough for the ferry in a day or two. Ghent hated to interrupt Sheldon's brief honeymoon, especially since he didn't think this storm would amount to much. But someone had to be there to take charge. Ghent reluctantly ordered his assistant to return to the camps. Soon Sheldon and his bride were on their way out of Key West to catch the 8 a.m. ferry at No Name Key.

In the camps, many veterans continued sleeping until the oppressive heat of the late summer day slowly baked them into the bleary and painful wakefulness that accompanies a nasty hangover. They rolled out of their bunks and lined up at barrels of ice water to slake the intense thirst that always follows a night of boozing. As they waited their turns they greeted others who joined them in line, calling many of them by their nicknames, such as "Chain Gang," "Big Boy," "Mad Dog," and "Slim."

The men sipped cups of water and discussed the events of the previous evening with wry humor. They chatted about the storm they heard had formed somewhere out there over the Atlantic. All summer, they had been hearing warnings that a hurricane was coming, and they wanted to see one, although they doubted that it would amount to much. They had faced real danger in France 18 years ago, they reminded each other, and they sure as hell weren't afraid of a little wind and rain. Besides, it would cool things off and blow away the damned mosquitoes for a few days.

The men living in the Keys work camps in the summer of 1935 represented a cross section of America's Depression casualties. Many were well-trained professionals who'd been earning good livings and raising families before the economic crash threw them out of work. Others had been bouncing from job to job for a decade or more since their discharge from the military, unable to stay with one job and put down roots. Some of the men in the Keys were making a genuine effort to turn their lives around. A few even brought their families down to the islands, rented cottages, planted gardens, and seemed settled for the first time in years.

But drinking and despondency were serious problems in the work camps. Many vets felt they had landed at the end of the world in the isolated, sparsely populated Florida Keys and had nothing more to lose. One veteran who worked on the bridge construction crew told friends he intended to make his tomb in one of the concrete support arches. When the crew started pouring concrete for pier number 61—his payroll number—he planned to leap into the wet cement and be buried alive.

For the vets, drinking was an escape from the ruins of their lives. They were, in a very real sense, the dregs of the "Lost Generation"—men who had been profoundly changed by their experiences in World War I.

Most of the men in the Keys work camps had been members of the American Expeditionary Force. When they boarded troopships for Europe in April 1917, they were the United States' contribution to the massive conflict that had been greedily swallowing lives by the millions for three years.

The world simply hadn't been prepared for the astonishing death toll of the Great War. Dramatic improvements in weapons in the late nineteenth and early twentieth centuries made the slaughter inevitable. Author Donovan

Webster noted that warfare hadn't changed much in almost 1,000 years until Alfred Nobel's invention of dynamite in 1866 "boosted the bloody art of war from bullets and bayonets to long-range high explosives."

Despite the staggering loss of life after three years of fighting, the Allies—Great Britain, France, and Italy—and the Central Powers—Germany, Austria-Hungary, and Turkey—were still locked in a stalemate when the Americans arrived.

The American Expeditionary Force commander, General John Pershing, kept his green troops in training camps for the better part of a year getting them ready for the fight. The Americans saw their first real combat in June 1918 at Chateau-Thierry and Belleau Wood in northern France and immediately distinguished themselves as fierce and daring fighters. When U.S. Marine artillery under Colonel Manus McCloskey arrived near the scene of a German advance, a French officer told him Allied troops had been ordered to retreat.

"Retreat?" McCloskey growled. "Hell no! We just got here." The colonel's Marines dug in, sighted their guns, and stopped the Germans with devastatingly accurate fire.

But the Americans also faced the Germans' murderously effective weaponry, and they paid a terrible price. At Belleau Wood, where American soldiers fought in bitter trench warfare, "masses of earth, chunks of rock, splinters of trees leaped into the air as the shells exploded," recalled Lieutenant Colonel Frederick Wise. "Machine-gun and rifle bullets thudded into the earth unendingly."

When the fighting ended in November 1918, American casualties stood at more than 364,000 dead, wounded, and missing. American losses didn't begin to compare with the staggering death toll suffered by the European belligerents, but it was a bloody toll for less than a year of actual fighting. Still, the Americans' brief participation tipped the balance in the Allies' favor, forcing the Central Powers to surrender.

The Western world rejoiced at the capitulation of Germany and its allies. But the horrible experience of combat left permanent psychological scars on many members of the American Expeditionary Force, who discovered they couldn't easily settle back into civilian life. Many years later this condition would be called post-traumatic stress disorder. In 1919 it was known as shell shock.

Like their counterparts in Europe whose lives had been shattered, many American servicemen had seen their beliefs destroyed by the brutality of modern warfare. The wholesale, indiscriminate slaughter and destruction of the war crushed any conviction that humanity was progressing toward a peaceful, benevolent civilization. Many who survived the conflict were certain their lives were meaningless.

That sense of purposelessness increased after the vets returned from France. The American economy struggled to absorb millions of discharged vets into the workforce. The nation underwent a brutal readjustment as it made the transition from war to peace. In January 1920 the United States slumped into a severe recession. Millions of vets who'd found jobs soon after their return lost them.

The nation came out of the recession by the summer of 1921, and the economic recovery was dramatic. Soon the Roaring Twenties swept the United States into unprecedented prosperity, and bad times seemed gone forever. The distractions of the 1920s helped some people forget the horrors of the Great War. Americans largely ignored Prohibition while making millionaires of the gangsters who sold them watered-down drinks at outrageously inflated prices in illegal speakeasies.

When they weren't drinking gin and dancing, they amused themselves with fads such as crossword puzzles and flagpole sitting—and everyone seemed to be getting rich in the stock market. For a while it was easy to believe Republican presidents Warren Harding, Calvin Coolidge, and Herbert Hoover when they said the United States had entered a new era of perpetual prosperity that would permanently eliminate poverty.

In Florida, real estate speculation soared to unheard-of heights as millions of people—including celebrities, sports stars, and politicians—flocked there thinking all they had to do to become wealthy was to buy a few acres of land.

The decade that followed the war was a time of empty euphoria, however, when many Americans pursued pleasure and wealth because there seemed to be nothing else to do and no reason to look for anything more. And no one seemed to notice or care that the machinery of commerce was becoming dangerously unbalanced.

The stock market crash in 1929 and the ensuing Depression came just as veterans were entering what were supposed to be their most productive years. Now, instead of building careers and raising families, hundreds of vets were sweating, swatting mosquitoes, drinking bootleg whiskey, and building a bridge in the remote Keys for a dollar a day plus food and housing—if the term "housing" could be applied to a 10-by-20-foot cabin with a canvas roof where four men slept.

But they were on a payroll, and in that respect they were a lot better off than the millions who'd long ago lost hope of finding jobs. Federal officials in Washington regularly received letters from unemployed veterans who'd heard about the work program and would gladly have endured the discomfort and isolation of the Keys in exchange for a regular paycheck.

By September 1935 the Depression was approaching the end of its sixth year. President Franklin D. Roosevelt's many New Deal programs had rescued millions from the brink of ruination. Harry Hopkins, appointed director of the Federal Emergency Relief Administration by Roosevelt, was motivated by a simple but powerful objective. "I'm here to see that people don't starve," he said.

But America's economy was still in shambles. *Fortune* magazine estimated in 1932—when President Hoover was still in the White House—that 34 million Americans had no income. That was more than one-quarter of the nation's population of 127 million. By 1935 almost 20 percent of the nation's workforce was still unemployed, and many of those who had jobs were working in unhealthful or dangerous conditions for bare subsistence wages.

Still, Americans mired in the middle of the Great Depression managed to find some distractions from the grimness of the times. In the summer of 1935, many people were enjoying the illusion of wealth and power by buying expensive real estate—with play money—and trying to bankrupt their opponents in a wildly popular new board game called Monopoly.

Sports entered a new era when lights were erected at Cincinnati's Crosley Field, and on May 24, 1935, the hometown Reds beat the visiting Philadelphia Phillies 2-1 in the first Major League Baseball game played at night. And in August a struggling bandleader named Benny Goodman electrified an audience in Los Angeles when he and his bored musicians suddenly cut loose with blaring brasses, wild improvisations, and throbbing drums while playing for a dance. The moment marked the birth of a new genre of popular music that came to be called Swing.

Humorist Will Rogers kept Americans chuckling during the hard times with his bipartisan barbs at politicians of all stripes. "There is something about a Republican that you can only stand him just so long," he once observed, "and on the other hand, there is something about a Democrat that you can't stand him quite that long."

As the Labor Day weekend of 1935 approached, however, Americans were mourning the loss of Rogers's homespun, incisive wit. He had been killed in a plane crash in Alaska on August 15. Millions of Americans learned details of Rogers's death in the weekly newsreels that preceded feature films in theaters across the nation.

Hollywood was cranking out a steady stream of movies intended to take America's collective mind off the problems of the day, and they had a huge audience. There were around 17,000 movie theaters in the nation. More than half the nation's population went to those theaters at least once a week. A frothy new comedy called *Top Hat* featuring Fred Astaire and Ginger Rogers had been released just in time for the Labor Day weekend of 1935.

As audiences were lining up to watch Astaire and Rogers dance cheek to cheek on Saturday evening, August 31, the S.S. *Dixie* left its berth in New Orleans and set sail for New York. The liner carried 233 passengers who hadn't been as troubled by the Depression as many other Americans. Aboard the liner were several doctors, a newly minted Yale University professor with a fondness for playing poker and the piano, a movie actress, a group of young women from Pennsylvania who had won a three-week trip across the United States and Mexico, a Catholic priest, honeymooners, and a young woman who was bored almost beyond endurance. As the ship sailed across the placid waters of the Gulf of Mexico, Charlotte Evans could find nothing better to do than write a letter to her mother in Philadelphia. "It's the quietest crowd I ever saw," Evans complained, "and there's no excitement."

Captain Einar Sundstrom commanded the *Dixie*, and he hoped the voyage stayed boring. The *Dixie* was due in New York Harbor on Thursday, September 5, and Sundstrom looked forward to spending a few days with his wife and two daughters in his trim, two-story brick house in the Long Island village of Little Neck.

As the sun came up Sunday morning, September 1, the *Dixie* was steaming southeast in the Gulf toward the tip of the Keys. Soon Sundstrom would take the ship around Key West and swing her northeast into the Straits of Florida and the Gulf Stream.

He knew rough weather had been reported around The Bahamas, and he knew the serious danger of entering the Straits of Florida when a hurricane was in the neighborhood. A ship in the Straits has only about 50 miles of maneuvering room—not nearly enough to avoid a hurricane. But Sundstrom had sidestepped many storms during his 34 years at sea and figured he could outwit this one. He'd been a sailor since he was a boy. He'd commanded tankers and freighters before being given command of the *Dixie*, and he'd brought many ships through storms and disasters at sea. He also had a reputation for never having failed during an emergency.

But Sundstrom didn't expect much trouble on this trip. According to the U.S. Weather Bureau, the storm was well to the south of him and moving in the opposite direction of his ship.

Cuban army meteorologists also were following the storm and reported Sunday night that the center of the hurricane was about 180 miles east of Havana.

Hurricane forecasters in Cuba had for some time been an annoyance to the U.S. Weather Bureau for a simple reason—their forecasts often were more accurate than the Weather Bureau's. The tension between the Weather Bureau and Cuban meteorologists dated back 35 years, when the Weather Bureau had banned weather data from Cuba being transmitted to U.S. Weather Bureau offices. Shortly after the ban, the savage hurricane of September 8, 1900, ripped into unprepared Galveston, Texas, and killed nearly 10,000 people.

Scorn and criticism were piled high on the Weather Bureau after the spectacular destruction and huge death toll in Galveston—so high that Willis Moore, director of the bureau, defended his agency by publishing distorted and false claims about the accuracy of the Weather Bureau's forecasts.

Cuban forecasters initially thought the storm that had just crossed The Bahamas on September 1, 1935, would strike Havana or stay just offshore from the Cuban capital as it moved into the Gulf of Mexico. But during the day Sunday, barometers in Havana started rising, an indication that the storm's center was no longer headed in their direction. During the day Monday, forecasters at Cuba's Belen Observatory determined that the hurricane was moving very slowly and had become an extremely powerful storm.

As Cuban army forecasters studied the data and pondered how to interpret it, a transplanted American who was a favorite of the de facto ruler of Cuba was looking over their shoulders.

Leonard James Povey—"Len" to his friends back in the United States—was known as "El Phenomena" to Colonel Fulgencio Batista, the strongman who was the real power behind a succession of puppet presidents in Cuba in the 1930s.

Povey had made a colorful, if unlikely, journey to Havana.

When he was a teenager, young Len Povey wanted more than anything to learn to fly. So he left his home in New Hampshire at the age of 15 and

lied about his age to join the Canadian army air force. He was in pilot training for several weeks when his true age was discovered and he was kicked out.

Determined to become a pilot, Povey went to Toronto, enlisted again,
landed at the same training camp, was recognized and again kicked out.

When he turned 18 in 1922, he enlisted in what was then known as the
U.S. Army Air Service and finally fulfilled his dream of learning to fly. After
his discharge he became a stunt pilot and earned a reputation as a true daredevil, living by his wits, his remarkable reflexes and hand-eye coordination,
and the motto "God hates a coward." Twice he'd avoided certain death, even
bringing a biplane in for a miraculous landing after a midair collision with
another plane sheared off about four feet of his plane's upper wing.

In 1934 Povey impulsively performed some of his most daring aerobatic
stunts as he approached an airport in Miami. He knew such stunting was
illegal so close to an airport, but it was a beautiful day and he was in a buoy-
ant mood. When he landed he was met by a federal aviation inspector who'd
seen his spectacular stunts.

The inspector told Povey he'd violated federal regulations and had the
choice of either paying a $500 fine or losing his pilot's license for a month.
Povey had only $50 to his name. After he handed over his license, the inspec-
tor complimented his aerobatics.

But Povey had greatly impressed a Cuban army officer who also happened to witness his performance. The officer persuaded him to come to
Cuba to train pilots for Colonel Batista.

As Povey discussed the hurricane's mysterious movements with Cuban
forecasters, the architect of the programs that had given jobs in the Keys to
the needy veterans finally escaped the withering heat of Washington. As the
rising sun bathed the Hudson River Valley in its soft, elegant light, President
Roosevelt's special train pulled into the station at Highland, New York. FDR
was helped into a waiting car for the short drive across the Hudson River to
Springwood, his estate in Hyde Park.

It had been a long and busy summer for the president. The first session
of the 74th Congress had lasted 235 days, the longest since 1922. Congress
had also spent a record $10.25 billion.

The marathon assembly was part of Democratic strategists' careful preparation for the upcoming political season. An election year was only a few
months away, and politicians were feeling the primal urge to begin that odd
courtship ritual with voters known as campaigning. With that in mind, leaders
of the overwhelmingly Democratic Congress kept lawmakers in the capital

through the summer hoping to resolve all controversial legislation so Republicans would have less ammunition to use against Democratic candidates.

They'd nearly succeeded in clearing the decks of potentially troublesome issues. They hit a snag in the last hours, however, when Senator Huey Long, the renegade Democrat who'd turned his home state of Louisiana into a personal fiefdom and been labeled a "madman" by a U.S. senator from his own party, began a filibuster against the last piece of New Deal legislation.

Long didn't think the bill provided enough funding for loans to cotton and wheat farmers and vowed to prevent the Senate from voting on it. His windy blustering blocked action on the bill that also would have provided funding for one of FDR's New Deal centerpieces—Social Security. When the gavel fell to end the first session, Long dashed out a side door of the Senate chamber and boarded a train for New York. There he told a reporter that Congress was "a bunch of cowards" for knuckling under to FDR and boasted he'd be elected president in 1936 on a third-party ticket if the Republicans again nominated Hoover and Roosevelt was the choice of the Democrats.

Roosevelt planned to spend several weeks at Hyde Park, but he wouldn't be idle. He also had his eye on the 1936 election.

The president hadn't said whether he would seek a second term, but he was going to work on a series of speeches about the accomplishments of the New Deal that would lay the groundwork for that announcement. He intended to deliver the speeches in late September during a cross-country trip that would have the appearance and trappings of a fall campaign tour.

More than 80 years after FDR's smashing win in the 1936 election—he won 46 of 48 states—it seems absurd to question whether there was ever any doubt that he'd be reelected. But in the late summer of 1935, even his most ardent backers were a little uneasy.

Roosevelt would need at least 266 electoral votes to win another term in the White House. As the election year approached, Roosevelt supporters and campaign strategists jotting down numbers and projections on scratch pads and the backs of envelopes were 30 or 40 votes shy of that total.

FDR and his strategists knew they'd be facing opposition from both sides of the political spectrum. Some Americans—such as Long—were convinced that Roosevelt's policies hadn't done enough to pull the nation out of the Depression and wanted a more radical shift to the left. But many businessmen were weary of New Deal regulations on industry and wanted a conservative Republican president at the helm of American government. The Republican leadership also was desperate to avoid a repeat of the 1934 elections when Democrats nearly chased them out of Washington by winning about 70 percent of the combined total of seats in the U.S. Senate and House of Representatives.

Roosevelt knew the political waters would soon be heating up. But as he joined his wife, Eleanor, and his mother, Sara, for breakfast at Springwood on Sunday morning, September 1, 1935, he had no idea that a potentially serious political problem was brewing for him 1,200 miles to the south in the warm waters of the Straits of Florida. And FDR's legendary charm and political shrewdness would be powerless against the forces fueling this problem.

CHAPTER ONE

A Remote Paradise

When Bernard Russell was a boy walking to school, he'd sometimes take off his shoes, tie the laces together, and toss them across his shoulder. Then he'd walk barefoot for about a mile down the sandy beach to the Matecumbe Graded School in the seaside village of Islamorada in the Florida Keys.

Russell's occasional choice of routes was part schoolboy whimsy and part convenience. In the 1930s much of the Keys was still covered with dense underbrush. Walking along the beach was easier, and he could also study the Atlantic Ocean, which laps at the shores of Upper Matecumbe Key. The turquoise waters often resemble a giant saltwater lake, thanks to the coral reefs that parallel the Keys and act as a breakwater, keeping the breakers four miles or so offshore.

The Alligator Reef Lighthouse stands guard over the reefs. The 136-foot-tall lighthouse rises above the remains of the U.S.S. *Alligator*, which wrecked on the reef in November 1822. The lighthouse's unique nighttime signal—five consecutive flashes of a white light and one flash of a red light at intervals of five seconds—had warned mariners of the reef since 1873.

At high tide the Atlantic was only about 100 feet from the front door of the two-room schoolhouse that Russell attended. In June 1935 Russell was 16 years old and part of the largest graduating class that Matecumbe Graded School had ever produced. Nine students received diplomas for completing the nine grades the school offered. In the remote, sparsely populated Keys, parents who wanted their children to finish their secondary education had to send them to live with friends or relatives in Key West or Homestead to attend high school.

That summer Russell had become friends with schoolmate Laurette Pinder, who was 17 and lived at the other end of the island. There was something a little special about this friendship, and both teenagers realized it.

The 48-star American flag that snapped in the sea breeze in front of the Matecumbe Graded School identified Islamorada as part of the United States. But in many ways Islamorada was much farther removed from the mainland—and mainstream America—than the 40 miles or so of coral and saltwater that separated the village from the tip of the Florida peninsula. Automobiles, telephones, and a few other early twentieth-century technological advances had found their way to Islamorada by the summer of 1935. But the people on the islands between Key West and the peninsula still lived much as their grandparents had in the previous century.

Key West, 75 miles to the south over land and water, had a population of about 12,000, but fewer than 1,000 residents inhabited the islands between Key West and the mainland. Two small electric plants—one at Tavernier north of Islamorada and the other at Marathon to the south—provided electricity for the few residents in those villages, but the other communities outside Key West were without power. At nightfall, Islamorada residents lit their kerosene lanterns.

Islamorada and the other tiny communities on the string of coral islands that make up the Keys did have a link of solid steel connecting them to the mainland and the modern world—the Key West Extension of the Florida East Coast Railway (FEC). In 1935 the daily arrival of the southbound passenger train from Miami to Key West—the southernmost island in the 130-mile chain—was a major event in Islamorada. When the snorting, smoking, steam-powered locomotive chuffed to a stop around 9:30 a.m. at the Islamorada station, village residents gathered to greet passengers, pick up packages, board the train, or just watch the commotion.

On most mornings a few residents were likely to be coming and going at the post office, where Bernard's father, John Russell, was postmaster. The building housing the post office was literally a stone's throw from the train station. After checking their mail they might step around to the small store that John Russell and his brother Clifton owned in the rear of the same building. They could buy a soft drink for a nickel and sip it as they stood on the post office porch, shaded from the tropical sun by an overhang supported by three columns. It had been built in 1928 of native coral salvaged from the tailings left behind after the island's first road had been graded. Bernard Russell, 10 years old at the time, had driven a Model T dump truck slowly along the road while others picked up chunks of coral and tossed them onto the back of the truck.

When the daily train arrived, the post office idlers often stepped off the porch and strolled up unpaved DeLeon Street to join the other onlookers at the depot.

A passenger gazing out the coach window during the brief stop at Islamorada might have wondered why anyone would want to live there. Even with the railroad and the highway linking the Upper Keys to the mainland, the remoteness of the islands was unsettling to many outsiders. The slender, sun-drenched outcroppings that divide the Atlantic Ocean and Florida Bay are so unlike any other place on Earth that first-time visitors a century ago often found the Keys eerie and foreboding. In 1908 writer Ralph Paine described the islands as "worthless, chaotic fragments of coral reef, limestone and mangrove swamp . . . aptly called the sweepings and debris which the Creator hurled out to sea after He finished shaping the Florida peninsula."

For the most part, the rest of the world ignored the Keys. "There were never enough people on those Keys to really make big news, or anything like that, and a lot of it has never had any attention paid to it," said William Johns, a reporter for the *Miami Daily News* who was based in Homestead in 1935.

The nearest doctors and dentists—and other securities and advantages of civilization—were many miles away. Other than the train, the only way to get to Key West was to drive onto a ferry at Lower Matecumbe Key, seven miles south of Islamorada, for a four-hour boat ride to No Name Key. From there it was a 45-mile drive to Key West. Or you could go by sailboat. If luck and the wind were on your side, you could sail to Key West in a few days. If the wind was against you or the weather suddenly turned bad, the trip could take much longer.

The railroad right-of-way had been hacked through a dense tropical jungle, and much of Upper Matecumbe and the other Keys were still covered by a thick tangle of ferns, buttonwood, mangrove, poisonwood, and palm trees. Over the years Islamorada residents had worn a series of foot trails through the underbrush, but in 1935 there still were places on the island where you couldn't see the sun.

The train passenger might have noticed the outdoor privies in Islamorada. In 1935 the number of outhouses far exceeded the number of telephones on Upper Matecumbe Key. Indoor toilets wouldn't have been of much use anyway because a plentiful supply of fresh water was required to flush them. Fresh water doesn't occur naturally on the Keys, and rainwater for drinking was collected in large cisterns. Every drop was far too precious to be used for indoor plumbing.

The islanders kept a close watch on their cisterns. Pools of fresh water inevitably became a hatchery for mosquitoes. Avoiding the stinging insects was all but impossible. They were everywhere, especially during the summer rainy season. Many residents kept a small pot of pyrethrum burning near their doors. The fumes—a natural insecticide—discouraged mosquitoes from coming into their houses. Anyone venturing outside—especially after dark during the summer—would be surrounded within seconds by a cloud of the buzzing bloodsuckers. The islanders slept with mosquito netting around their beds, and when they went outside they often wore hats with fine mesh netting that covered their faces. They also wore clothing that nearly covered their bodies despite the heat. Men typically wore denim overalls over a long-sleeved shirt. Women often wore long-sleeved dresses and an old-fashioned sunbonnet.

Living in the middle of the Atlantic meant constantly watching the weather—especially from August to November, when hurricanes were often forming somewhere beyond the horizon. The U.S. Weather Bureau tried to monitor hurricanes and issue reasonably accurate advisories and warnings, but keeping track of a hurricane in 1935 was a tricky job. Meteorologists relied heavily on information about weather conditions from ships at sea and trained weather observers stationed along the coast who sent information several times a day about wind speed, barometric pressure readings, and other details to the U.S. Weather Bureau. Forecasters did the best they could with the tools and information they had, but sometimes they were just wrong about where a hurricane was and where it was heading.

Island residents knew the only storm warning they could really count on was their barometers and their own knowledge of the natural indicators that told them when a hurricane was heading their way.

"My dad lived by the barometer," Bernard Russell said. "He read that every day, like he did his Bible."

Despite the isolation and inherent dangers, life on the isolated Keys offered some benefits not known elsewhere. Crime was almost nonexistent, and many residents of the close-knit Keys communities didn't bother locking their doors when they left their homes. And while millions of Americans in other parts of the country struggled to put food on their tables during the 1930s, the Keys were surrounded by a sort of saltwater pantry that helped mitigate the cruelest effect of the Depression—hunger.

Lobster—which the locals called crawfish—was abundant on the Atlantic side of the islands, and queen conchs were plentiful farther south.

Pompano, tuna, grouper, and snapper could be reeled in farther offshore. The deeper waters teemed with big game fish, such as sailfish, swordfish, tarpon, and amberjack, and many islanders augmented their seafood diets with small produce gardens.

Of the fewer than 1,000 people who lived on the Keys outside Key West, most lived in the Upper Keys, the segment of islands stretching southward from Key Largo to Long Key. Tomato gardens and key lime groves dotted the interior of the Upper Keys. Some residents used the railroad to ship their produce to markets on the mainland. Others made a living by plucking sponges from the surrounding waters and selling them in Key West.

The Middle Keys—the islands between Conch Key and Pigeon Key—and the Lower Keys, which encompassed the southernmost islands outside Key West, were virtually uninhabited in 1935.

Islamorada's only church—Matecumbe Methodist—stood next to the oceanfront school. In the summer of 1935, Reverend Robert Carlson, 39, and his wife, Maude, 35, were newcomers to Islamorada. The couple had come to the Keys in June from LaBelle, a small town on the peninsula about halfway between Fort Meyers and the western shore of Lake Okeechobee, and they were still getting to know their new congregation. The couple lived in a one-story wood-frame house near the church.

Many of the pioneers who settled the Keys in the mid-nineteenth century rested in a small cemetery next to the Methodist church. The most prominent grave was that of Etta Pinder, a 14-year-old girl who drowned in 1914. Her grief-stricken parents stationed a marble angel at the head of their daughter's grave to watch over her eternal slumber.

Life moved mostly to the rhythms and whims of the sea. Islamorada residents lived on or near the beach, but their modest houses bore no resemblance to the oceanfront mansions that line much of Florida's coast today. In 1935 air-conditioning was decades away from being commonplace. In Islamorada, homes, the school, and the church were built on the beach to take advantage of the cool breezes blowing off the ocean.

Sometimes in the summer, those cooling winds come in the form of a sudden storm. The oppressive heat cooks up a squall that sweeps across the islands from the Atlantic or Florida Bay. Rising winds sway the palms and rustle their fronds, and across the water the horizon no longer separates the ocean and the sky. The rain begins with a few big drops that slam heavily into the ground and raise little puffs of dust. Soon it is coming down in dense silvery sheets, visibility drops to a couple hundred feet, and the turquoise waters are pocked by a million tiny splashes.

Occasionally the grim-looking clouds spit out a brilliant, jagged lightning bolt that briefly illuminates everything with an eerie bluish tinge. Sudden sharp cracks of thunder shake the earth. The temperature plummets and the wind gusts suddenly to maybe 30 or 40 mph. It can all seem quite impressive—and perhaps a bit frightening—to a newcomer who has never seen one of these garden-variety summer storms. But it usually doesn't last very long. The squall lumbers away as quickly as it came and the wind dies back down, and pretty soon it's so still and stiflingly hot, that fierce little storm seems like a fleeting dream.

The houses on the beach were sturdy enough to easily withstand these brief, intense blows, but Keys residents had no illusions about whether their homes would endure the fury of a hurricane. Many had built even sturdier shelters near the center of the island where they rode out the hurricanes that occasionally visited the islands.

The shelter that John Russell built for his family was typical of the structures erected by his neighbors. The buildings were constructed with thick timbers that often were held together by long, heavy-duty railroad bolts. Russell had even anchored his to the coral island with long steel screws. The postmaster wasn't one to belittle the power of a hurricane, but he thought his hurricane house would stand up to most anything the sea could throw at it.

Russell and his neighbors were less certain, however, about how they would protect themselves from problems they feared the railroad would eventually cause when an especially bad hurricane came their way.

When the Key West Extension—more popularly known as the Overseas Railroad—was completed in 1912, it joined the slender strand of islands like a string of pearls and, for the first time, threw them open to the outside world. But the seafaring Conchs complained loudly when workers started building the roadbed for the railroad. Instead of constructing bridges across the shorter spans between the islands, Henry Flagler's engineers decided to support the tracks by building causeways. Unlike bridges supported by a series of piers, the solid causeways blocked the tidal flows. In some places the causeways were elevated as much as 13 feet above normal low tide. The natives shook their heads in dismay. To them the railroad looked like nothing more than a giant dike, and they feared that one day a hurricane would pile up water against it until it was well above their heads. "It'll drown us like rats," they muttered.

Still, the railroad brought many benefits to the islands, and the 110-mile train trip down the Keys was a thrilling ride. The rails crossed about two dozen islands, and a series of causeways and bridges spanned almost 18 miles of water altogether. Crossing the magnificent bridges—especially the Seven-Mile Bridge near Marathon and the spectacular steel suspension span at Bahia Honda—offered an unparalleled view of the Atlantic Ocean and Florida Bay. The bridges were just wide enough for the train tracks, so passengers looking out the coach windows saw only water beneath them and got the sensation that they were floating over the ocean.

They could see squadrons of pelicans gliding inches above the waves, following the contours of the swells. They could watch seagulls wheeling and floating in the sea breeze, and if they were lucky they might see a dolphin or a manta ray leap from the brine beneath them. Passengers on the daily northbound evening train from Key West to Miami got a special treat—they could watch the vividly colorful tropical sunset that marks the end of each day in the Keys.

The railroad was a testament to the iron will and unlimited wealth of Henry Morrison Flagler, who, with his Standard Oil Co. partner, John D. Rockefeller, amassed one of the great fortunes of the nineteenth century. Flagler made several visits to Florida between 1878 and 1883 and was so charmed by the graceful antiquity of St. Augustine that he decided to build a hotel there. He also invented Florida tourism when he bought a small group of railroads to create the Florida East Coast Railway. As he extended the line down the coast from Jacksonville, he built more hotels along the way.

By 1896 Flagler's railroad had reached Fort Dallas, a small, sleepy settlement on Biscayne Bay that would soon be called Miami. There wasn't much there except mosquitoes, alligators, swamps, and a few orange groves. Key West, 160 miles to the south, was Florida's largest and wealthiest city, and Flagler couldn't rest until he figured out a way to use his railroad to take advantage of the island city's excellent deep-water harbor. He knew that a rail terminal at Key West would be hundreds of miles closer to the planned Panama Canal than seaports on the U.S. mainland, and he figured he could make additional millions hauling the world's freight to and from the tip of the Keys. He foresaw still more profits from a "train-boat" that would transport passenger and freight cars between Key West and Havana, Cuba, only 90 miles apart across the Straits of Florida.

In 1904 Flagler took on a task that seemed impossible—building a railroad across the low-lying Florida Keys to Key West. He considered running the railroad through the Everglades to the tip of the Florida peninsula, then building a bridge to carry his trains across Florida Bay to one of the Keys. But he rejected that plan in favor of an island-hopping route across the string of low-lying islands. Work began in 1905, and Flagler pushed the project to completion despite hurricanes, labor problems, and enormous cost in both money and human lives.

The final tab for the railroad was more than $20 million—almost $510 million in 2019 dollars. That worked out to about $212,000 per mile, or around $5.5 million a mile, adjusted for inflation.

But the cost in human lives was even more staggering. About 300 construction workers died during the six years it took to build the Overseas Railroad. Many were killed in October 1906 when a powerful hurricane blasted across Cuba and struck the Keys.

The Conchs knew a storm was rising. Rufus Johnson was one of the longtime Keys residents who tried to warn construction supervisors that the hurricane was bearing down on them. "I went [at] 11 o'clock at night and asked the men to get out, when they were building the railroad there," Johnson recalled many years later. "And the bosses said, 'You don't know anything.'"

As it turned out, Johnson knew far more than the other FEC bosses realized. They ignored his warning and refused to evacuate the workers, many of whom were living aboard a large houseboat docked at Long Key. The FEC's superintendent of transportation, identified by *The Daily Miami Metropolis* as Mr. Rue, scoffed at the notion that a hurricane could harm workers. The houseboats "are perfectly safe, strongly built, and well harbored," he said.

The FEC had also built a two-story, wood-frame administration building there.

As the hurricane drew nearer to the Keys, William Saunders—who worked on the construction crew—noticed that none of the Conchs employed by the FEC had showed up for work. "I am sure that the men whose forefathers had lived on the Keys had developed some sixth sense regarding the approach of a hurricane," Saunders said.

Saunders had lived in South Florida for 15 years and experienced four hurricanes. "I thought that I had learned all there was to know about such storms," he said. "But [this] was by far the worst, and I found out a lot more about them."

Early in the morning of October 18, 1906, the winds began howling at Long Key. Around 7:30 a.m. the storm pulled the houseboat from its moorings. With perhaps 150 workers—including Saunders—aboard, the houseboat was dragged helplessly into open water, where huge waves pounded it mercilessly. Some of the men were so terrified they drank teacups of laudanum, an opium derivative used for pain relief, and lay down to die.

They didn't have long to wait. Around 9 a.m. the hurricane smashed the houseboat's upper deck. A few minutes later the wind and pounding waves shattered the remnants of the boat, spilling the workers into the furious sea.

Saunders and six others managed to grab a large piece of wreckage and ride it like a raft. "It is hard to describe the way the waves rose up some three stories, then broke over us and the raft, with tons and tons of water," Saunders said. He hung on grimly, motivated by more than a simple dread of death. He was afraid his family couldn't collect his life insurance policy if he should be lost at sea and his body never found to confirm his death.

Saunders and 48 other survivors were eventually plucked from the ocean.

The hurricane's eye passed over Pigeon Key, about 20 miles south of Long Key, where the FEC had another camp for railroad construction workers. Earle Hartridge, a construction engineer at Pigeon Key, thought he was going to die.

"We thought we would never survive it," Hartridge said. He and some friends took shelter in a warehouse on the tiny island. As the storm raged outside, the men hastily scrambled atop a large pile of cement and dug a crater there. The hurricane destroyed the warehouse, but Hartridge and his companions were safe in their makeshift shelter.

Farther up the coast, the hurricane also sank the *Saint Lucie*, a steamboat with dozens of construction workers aboard.

"Strong cables were parted like so many cords, and great, powerful crafts [*sic*] loaded with human freight were buffeted about, torn and wrecked by their fury," *The Daily Miami Metropolis* wrote. "Lives were dashed out without a moment's warning."

Survivors clung to lifeboats or wreckage and tried to keep their heads above the roiling ocean. "The sea, which had abated some, picked up again," said W. J. Grant, second officer of the *Saint Lucie*. "Great God, I have never seen it so high. The rain was blinding and beat our faces like shot. I could see nothing more until a sea pitched us out of the lifeboat and into the mangroves on the shore."

The hurricane killed about 130 FEC workers and did massive damage to the railroad. "It is wreck, wreck, wreck everywhere," *The Daily Miami Metropolis* reported.

The furious storm and death toll made a strong impression on Ed Sheeran, a 36-year-old Wisconsin native who was working on the railroad construction crew. Sheeran blamed the tragedy on the supervisors' poor judgment and ignorance about the power and danger of hurricanes. When he was given a supervisory position after the 1906 storm, he became highly skilled at detecting hurricanes. In the isolated Keys, he knew that his life and those of his workers depended on it.

"We had no communication whatsoever," Sheeran said. "No telephone, no radios, no wireless—nothing but boats from Key West, and it took 10 days to get them. We absolutely relied on our barometers. We studied them and studied the wind. We talked to the natives."

Sheeran learned how to calculate a hurricane's approximate position and direction of travel using only his barometer and subtle indicators. "If I can get the speed of the wind on each side of me, I can tell pretty well where the storm is," he said. "It follows low areas. People that have never been in those storms don't know them."

Two more hurricanes pounded the Keys before the railroad was completed in 1912, but under Sheeran's guidance only 13 men were lost because of these storms.

The first FEC train rolled into Key West in January 1912, and the railroad quickly became a boon to the islands. Besides allowing them to ship their produce to markets, the railroad in a sense finally linked the Conchs to civilization. Now Key West and Homestead were only a few hours away, and some of the hardships of living on the isolated islands were eased. An Islamorada resident could now be in Key West by noon for an appointment with a doctor or dentist and be back home at 7:45 p.m. on the northbound evening train.

The major cities of the East Coast were also linked to the Keys. A passenger could board a train in Washington, DC, and be in Key West about 40 hours later. The railroad started bringing a new kind of visitor to the Keys—one who came purely for pleasure and brought plenty of money to pay for it.

The remote tropical environment and splendid fishing appealed to well-heeled sportsmen who could afford to escape the cold winters of the Northeast and Midwest. In Islamorada a "millionaires row" was created, anchored by the Matecumbe Club, an exclusive fishing resort formed by a group of very wealthy businessmen affiliated with the New York Cotton Exchange. In 1917 club members built a handsome, two-story lodge, white with green shutters, on a palm-shaded stretch of beach on Upper Matecumbe Key. A two-story porch, supported by four columns of California redwood, overlooked the Atlantic. Inside, members relaxed on wicker furniture in a comfortable lodge after spending a day on the water. Trophy catches hung on the walls of the lounge

The rich part-time residents provided a small economic boon for the Conchs. During the winter they hired the natives as fishing guides. During the summer they paid them to look after their large, empty homes.

Ed Butters had also come to the Keys for the first time on a fishing trip in 1926, and he "loved every minute of it," said his wife, Fern. Butters moved his wife and parents to Florida in 1926 when he got a job on the construction crew building the new Dade County Courthouse in Miami. Ed and Fern opened a small inn on Key Largo in late 1926.

Thomas Edison, who had moved to Fort Myers, became a regular guest. During one of his visits, he apologized to Fern because he'd stained a beautiful hand-embroidered tablecloth. The stain wouldn't come out, but the tablecloth with the stain caused by one of the most famous men in history became one of Fern's most prized possessions.

Ed bought an old U.S. Navy lifeboat, put a motor in it, and developed a reputation as one of the best fishing guides in the Keys.

In 1932 the Butterses sold their inn on Key Largo and used the money for a down payment on the Russell Arms Hotel on Upper Matecumbe Key. They renamed it the Hotel Matecumbe.

Former millionaires who'd gone bust during the Depression came to the Keys either to forget about their losses or to try to amass new fortunes. George Merrick, who created the visionary development of Coral Gables during the outrageous Florida land boom of the early 1920s, came to the Keys after he went broke on the eve of the Depression. He opened the Caribee Colony a few miles south of Islamorada near the southern tip of Upper Matecumbe Key. The little resort featured small cottages and a restaurant that became famous for its coconut pies.

Miami businessman Roland W. Craig had built his own little village on a small island between Lower Matecumbe Key and Long Key that had been created by the FEC to support a railroad bridge. Craig ran a yacht supply business, a small grocery store, and a post office on his island, which was accessible only by boat or by the railroad. Craig also talked the FEC into letting him name the island Craig Key, and the little settlement became known as Craig.

But the most famous resort was the Long Key Fishing Camp, 17 miles down the railroad tracks from Islamorada. The visitors who stepped off the train at the small Long Key station entered a world of splendid, pampered isolation.

People had been coming to Long Key for the fishing for thousands of years. The Calusa Indians were the first, drawn to this place of crystal clear waters and abundant marine life. Spanish explorers also fished there in the seventeenth and eighteenth centuries.

Soon after the Key West Extension was completed, the railroad converted the large administration building at Long Key into a handsome, comfortable lodge with accommodations for 75, and 14 surrounding bungalows were renovated to house guests as well. The camp was open from late December to early April, when the weather in the Keys is at its most pleasant and the mosquitoes virtually disappear. During the season the yachts of some of the world's wealthiest people were anchored at the camp's marina.

A caretaker looked after the expensive amenities during the off-season. In 1935 the caretaker was James E. Duane Jr., who was also a trained observer for the U.S. Weather Bureau. Duane sent daily reports of wind speeds, barometric pressure readings, and other information to meteorologists in the bureau's Key West office.

A few members of the exclusive fishing club built their own houses at Long Key. One of the most luxurious belonged to the Countess of Suffolk, England, who'd been born in Chicago and was formerly known as Daisy Leiter, heiress to a multimillion-dollar department store fortune. The countess, now known as Lady Marguerite Hyde, had spent $25,000 (an enormous sum in an era when a six-room house with a two-car garage in Detroit was selling for about $2,800) to build a bungalow she used for only a few weeks each winter. The countess furnished her pricey tropical getaway with expensive art objects collected during her travels.

The porches of the fishing lodge and first row of bungalows overlooked a wide white-sand beach, and the buildings were shaded by a grove of coconut palm trees. Wooden walkways were woven among the palms, connecting the bungalows and linking them with the lodge.

Guests could stand on the beach, look southward, and see the famous Long Key Viaduct, which carried the railroad from Long Key across more than two miles of water to Conch Key. The seemingly endless procession of arches marching toward the horizon was so handsome that the FEC used a stylized drawing of a train crossing the viaduct as a logo for the Overseas Railroad.

Those who came to the fishing camp expected to pay handsomely for their fun, and during the early 1930s the Depression seemed to be of little or no consequence to its affluent visitors. At the same time that the average household income in the United States was $1,524—just under $30 per week—guests at the Long Key Fishing Camp were happily spending $6 to $8 per night for a room in the lodge, and those who stayed in the bungalows were paying a daily rate of $8 or $9 each. The camp also had a fleet of a dozen 34-foot cabin cruisers that guests could rent for $25 a day.

Visitors to Long Key included those with names synonymous with American capitalism—Vanderbilt, Guggenheim, and Gillette—as well as politicians and European royalty. President Herbert Hoover fished at Long Key, and so did President Franklin Roosevelt. Author Zane Grey was a regular at Long Key, and the wife of newspaper publisher William Randolph Hearst dropped in a time or two, as did baseball great Lou Gehrig.

The fishing was superb, and the camp management kept detailed records of the catches and awarded prizes to the visitors. But the fishing alone wouldn't have drawn the cream of world society to a remote island in the middle of nowhere. Long Key Fishing Camp also had a picture-perfect tropical setting.

Zane Grey, who wrote about fishing and the outdoors as well as his many Western novels, combined fishing and writing when he went to Long Key. As he was about to leave to spend the winter at Long Key in 1917, Grey said he concocted the plots for his novels while waiting for a bite.

Enchanted by Long Key, the author praised the "eternal moan out on the reefs," and wrote, "always by the glowing, hot colorful day or by the soft dark night with its shadows and whisperings on the beach, that significant presence—the sense of something vaster than the heaving sea."

A staff of 60 employees waited on the guests and went to great lengths to preserve the camp's carefree, disconnected isolation from the problems troubling the rest of the world. Radios and newspapers were prohibited, and guests could bask in the sun and escape the dreary early 1930s landscape of breadlines, hungry families, and dispirited men. But as the yachts began arriving at Long Key for the 1934–1935 season, casualties from the Depression were also appearing in the Keys like debris washing ashore from a distant shipwreck.

Only a few miles up the railroad tracks from the exclusive fishing club, weary men were stepping off the FEC train and blinking in wonder at their strange tropical surroundings. The accommodations awaiting them were a good bit less sumptuous than those at Long Key. The men were housed in tents that had been set up on hastily erected wooden platforms. Most of the men were well into middle age, and all were veterans of the U.S. military. Most had served during what was then known as the Great War or the World War, although some had fought during the Spanish-American War and others had been peacetime soldiers.

The standoffish Conchs eyed the newcomers uneasily, perhaps sensing that their presence heralded profound changes in their islands.

The events that led to the veterans' arrival in the Keys began during the summer of 1932 in Washington, when President Herbert Hoover stubbornly denied the harsh reality of the Depression and seemed determined to ignore its effects on the nation's wage earners. When the bottom fell out of the stock market in 1929 and the U.S. economy entered a free fall, Hoover insisted that the hard times were only temporary, despite an unemployment roll that increased from 1.5 million in October 1929 to at least 3.2 million by March 1930. When thousands of jobless men started selling apples on the streets of New York and oranges in New Orleans, the president said the men had left their regular jobs because they could make more money peddling fruit. During the winter of 1931, Hoover insisted that no one was starving or freezing, despite clear and growing evidence to the contrary.

The harshest effects of the Depression weren't as visible on the sparsely populated Upper Keys, but in Key West the situation was every bit as desperate as it was on the mainland. The industries that had once made Key West prosperous and populous were long gone. The city's residents got by with fishing, a little income from tourists, and occasionally bootlegging booze from nearby Cuba. And Key West had its own tropical version of the street corner fruit vendors in the larger mainland cities. Instead of selling apples and oranges, Key West's jobless residents sold coconuts and limes.

Hoover refused to abandon his staunchly Republican belief that the nation's economy eventually would right itself without government intervention and insisted that the nation adhere to its traditional economic policies. But the ranks of the unemployed steadily increased. As the 1932 election approached, *Fortune* magazine published the results of a survey that concluded that 34 million Americans—more than one-fourth of the nation's population—had no income. And *Fortune* didn't even include 11 million farm families in its survey.

While Hoover insisted that the nation's economy was fundamentally sound, others feared the deprivations caused by the Depression could have grave consequences and eventually undermine the stability of the government.

One of the staunchest advocates for change was the governor of New York, Franklin D. Roosevelt, a Democrat who persuaded his state legislature to create the Temporary Emergency Relief Administration. The program, which was directed by Harry Hopkins, provided work relief that helped jobless New Yorkers get through the winter of 1931–1932.

Roosevelt's programs attracted the attention of national Democratic leaders looking for a candidate to oppose the luckless Hoover in the 1932 presidential election. With the skillful support of Louis Howe and other advisers, Roosevelt launched his campaign for the White House on April 7, 1932, when he addressed the nation during the *Lucky Strike Radio Hour*. He called for a new approach to economic recovery—a plan that built "from the bottom up and not from the top down" and focused on "the forgotten man at the bottom of the economic pyramid."

The pledge to help the forgotten man resonated with American voters and became a major theme of Roosevelt's campaign. When he won the Democratic nomination in July, he promised to remember the "men and women forgotten in the political philosophy of government" if he became president.

Thousands of destitute veterans were among the jobless ramblers roaming the country in search of work. The ex-servicemen became more visible during the summer of 1932 when they converged on Washington seeking help. They hoped to persuade Congress and Hoover to approve early payment to them of a bonus that had been authorized in 1924, when times were good and the United States was still feeling a swell of patriotic pride for the troops who helped defeat Germany in 1918. The bonus plan called for each vet to receive about $1,000 as a reward for their wartime service. Payment was due in 1945.

But in 1932 the veterans were desperate. They came to Washington on whatever transportation they could find to demand immediate help. Some vets on the West Coast started their trip by blocking railroad tracks and climbing aboard an eastbound freight train when it was forced to stop. Others formed caravans of battered trucks and automobiles and took up collections to pay for gasoline as they passed through towns en route to the nation's capital.

Many brought their hungry families with them and set up a giant city of tents, lean-tos, and shacks in the southeastern corner of Washington.

Others moved into a row of abandoned, partially demolished buildings on Pennsylvania Avenue that were being removed to make way for new government buildings.

The vets, who became known as the Bonus Marchers, wanted Congress to give them a $500 bonus—about $9,200 in 2019 dollars—immediately instead of waiting another 13 years for the full amount. But President Hoover staunchly opposed an early payment.

Tension mounted in the capital during the spring and early summer as the ranks of vets and their families steadily increased. Washington was uneasy about the presence of the veterans, and many in positions of power were tired of the sight of the shabby former soldiers and wanted them gone. Brigadier General George Moseley proposed that the Bonus Marchers be arrested and sent to concentration camps on "one of the sparsely inhabited islands in the Hawaiian group not suitable for growing sugar." As far as the general was concerned, the vets could languish indefinitely in the distant tropics and those in authority back in Washington "would not worry about the delays in due process of law in the settlement of their individual cases."

Public opinion was critical of the Bonus Marchers. A June 1932 *Washington Post* editorial complained that the veterans "can not revert to a soldier status and secure special favors in the midst of millions unemployed." The *Courier-Journal* of Louisville, Kentucky, was even sharper. "It becomes increasingly obvious that such veterans, instead of becoming reabsorbed into the great mass of the American citizenry since the war, are drawing themselves further and further apart from the rest of the population as a specially privileged class ready at all times to bring political pressure to bear on a Government which showers them with dollars," said a *Courier-Journal* editorial.

By June about 25,000 veterans and their families had gathered in the capital. Their cause was championed by Representative Wright Patman, a Texas Democrat who introduced a bill in the House of Representatives that would authorize immediate payment of the bonus. Representative Hamilton Fish, a Republican from New York, led the opposition and classified it as a test of national character. The debt wasn't due, Fish said, and Congress could not allow itself to be "coerced by any groups" into approving the bill for early payment of the bonus.

Still, it seemed that Congress was listening to the veterans' pleas. On June 15, 1932, the House of Representatives approved Patman's bill. But two days later the Senate defeated the bill, dashing the vets' hopes for receiving their money. Many Bonus Marchers left town, but a hard-core group of about 8,000 remained, many of them vowing to stay until 1945, if necessary.

Elsewhere, the sympathies of many Americans were swinging in favor of the ex-servicemen. In Las Vegas, Vice President Charles Curtis was confronted in late July 1932 by hecklers wanting to know why the Hoover Administration didn't at least give food to the veterans still bivouacked in Washington. Curtis snarled back that he'd helped many more people than the "dirty cowards" who confronted him.

President Hoover wasn't completely unsympathetic. He allowed medical supplies and some surplus army equipment to be given to the vets, but like many others in positions of power he was getting tired of the Bonus Marchers. He had the gates to the White House grounds chained shut and erected barricades on the streets nearest the mansion. By July 28 the president's patience was gone. He ordered that U.S. Army troops be used to evacuate the veterans from their camps on the government property on Pennsylvania Avenue.

Hoover's instructions stated that the troops should "use all humanity consistent with the due execution of the order." And his orders specified that only people who were occupying government property should be removed. But General Douglas MacArthur, who was in charge of the operation, decided there was "incipient revolution in the air" and referred to the ragged gathering of vets and their families as "insurrectionists" determined to overthrow the U.S. government. His troops moved in with tanks, tear gas, and bayonets, burning the vets' makeshift camps and driving them out of the District of Columbia.

Newspaper photos of the rout horrified Americans, who stared in disbelief at pictures of U.S. troops battling bedraggled ex-servicemen while their families sought shelter on the porches of Washington homes.

Hoover's hopes of winning reelection were minimal before July 1932. MacArthur's brutal treatment of the Bonus Marchers all but guaranteed the president would be defeated. In Hyde Park, New York, Franklin Roosevelt sat on the porch of his home with Felix Frankfurter, listening to news broadcasts about the veterans' rough eviction from Washington. "Well, Felix," FDR said, "this will elect me."

Roosevelt won a landslide victory in November, and voters made it clear they wanted to give the new president a free hand in dealing with the Depression by sending overwhelming Democratic majorities to the Senate and House of Representatives.

While the president-elect pondered how he was going to tackle the difficult task ahead of him, he was reminded often of the "forgotten man" he'd promised to remember. One reminder appeared in the March 1933 edition of *Atlantic Monthly* magazine in an essay by Wilson Follett. In "The Forgotten Man to His President," Follett wrote that when Roosevelt had spoken of the forgotten man, he was referring to "us, the plain folk . . . whose votes put the rungs in your ladder." By electing Roosevelt, voters had said, "We live in America, too. It is high time someone thought of us for a change; and, mark you, we mean sooner or later to be remembered."

On March 4, 1933, Franklin Roosevelt stood beneath a gray sky on the steps of the U.S. Capitol to be sworn in as the nation's 32nd President. When the moment came for FDR to take the oath of office, he laid his left hand on his family's seventeenth-century Dutch Bible. It was opened to a verse that was very important to the incoming chief executive—the 13th verse of the 13th chapter of First Corinthians.

Roosevelt's choice of verses gave a clear indication of how he intended to confront the dire emergency awaiting him. The King James English translation reads, "And now abideth faith, hope, charity, these three; but the greatest of these is charity."

Exactly how he was going to apply these virtues, however, had not been worked out. When FDR took the reins of government, the New Deal was still "a happy phrase he had coined during the campaign, and its value was psychological," Frances Perkins, who became Roosevelt's secretary of labor, later wrote in her book, *The Roosevelt I Knew.* "It made people feel better, and in that terrible period of depression they needed to feel better."

At the core of the nebulous New Deal, Perkins said, was "the forgotten man, the little man, the man nobody knew much about." Under Roosevelt, he "was going to be dealt better cards to play with."

It was nearly too late. As Roosevelt took the oath of office, banks across the country were failing, unemployment had hit a stunning 25 percent, and thousands of jobless, homeless Americans were living in shabby encampments known as Hoovervilles.

One of the driving philosophies behind FDR's New Deal was to try something, anything, to get the nation back on track. If one solution didn't work, it was withdrawn and another was quickly substituted. His approach was reflected in the flurry of bills his administration sent to Congress between March and June 1933—the first 100 days of his new administration. The Democrat-controlled Congress passed them all, creating dozens of new federal agencies and programs aimed at resuscitating the nation's comatose economy.

"He improvised, he blundered, he failed often," CBS journalist Eric Severeid said later about FDR's approach to righting the nation's wrecked economy. "He flattered and cajoled and threatened. He finessed the deck at times, and misled. But he never showed outward signs of bitterness or defeat or hatreds. He kept at it, and at it, and at it."

Eventually, Severeid said, FDR "reassembled America's energies and sense of purpose."

Among the new agencies created by the president's flurry of legislation was the Federal Emergency Relief Administration, or FERA. The legislation that established FERA—based on the statewide Temporary Emergency Relief Administration FDR had created in New York—also appropriated $500 million to be used directly for relief for the nation's jobless. Half the money would be given directly to the states. The rest would be doled out as matching funds, with the states receiving one dollar in federal money for every three dollars they spent on relief.

Soon after FDR took office, veterans began drifting back into Washington to renew their demand for the bonus payment. The new president—who had been shocked by the brutal eviction of the Bonus Marchers only a few months earlier—seemed genuinely interested in helping the men. He rode out to the veterans' encampment, waving his hat in greeting and chatting with them. He provided tents, mess halls, showers, and other comforts and sent his wife, Eleanor, to talk to them. And he insisted that the vets be provided an endless supply of coffee. "Just let free coffee flow all the time," he said. "There is nothing like it to make people feel better and feel welcome."

Roosevelt's desire to help the veterans may have been sincere, but the man who waved his fedora and extended a friendly helping hand to the vets was also one of the shrewdest politicians ever to hold America's highest elected office. The veterans reassembling in Washington were a political liability for his fledgling administration. As he labored to somehow pull the nation out of the quagmire of the Depression, he could ill afford for Americans to again see hungry, desperate families besieging the capital to plead for help. Like his predecessor, Roosevelt opposed early payment of the veterans' bonus. But if he was going to oppose the bonus, he had to find another way to get them out of Washington and put them to work. That would be difficult, however, since most of the veterans were too old for the newly formed

Civilian Conservation Corps (CCC) that had been created to build public works projects across the United States.

As the veterans began drifting back into Washington, lyricist Al Dubin sat down to write songs for an upcoming movie musical to be produced by Warner Brothers. Dubin was deeply moved by the plight of the men who had been treated as heroes in 1918 only to be booted out of the nation's capital 14 years later when they were in desperate need of help. With this in mind, he wrote "Remember My Forgotten Man," which he described as "a plea for the United States' vast army of unemployed, so many of whom were ex-servicemen reduced to standing in breadlines."

"Remember My Forgotten Man" became the rousing finale for *Gold Diggers of 1933*, which was released in May 1933. The lyrics reminded the audience that the men who'd been heroes in 1918 were now deeply troubled and needed—and deserved—help. Etta Moten sang the lyrics as she looked down from her apartment at a street scene unfolding beneath her. A police officer, about to arrest a tramp snoozing beside the apartment step, discovers that the shabbily dressed man is wearing a war medal inside the lapel of his jacket. The cop releases the tramp.

Dubin's lyrics put a face on the "forgotten man" and became a catchy reminder that Americans who'd put their lives on the line for freedom were now suffering horribly because of the Depression. And the Roosevelt Administration tried to help them.

By the summer of 1935, the administration had found what seemed like a good solution. Hundreds of veterans who had come to Washington because they didn't know where else to turn boarded southbound trains with tickets to a place most of them had never heard of. They'd been told there would be work—a highway construction project—when they got to their destination. But when they stepped off the train on a tiny, remote, sparsely populated island in the Atlantic Ocean, they wondered whether someone was indeed remembering them or trying very hard to forget them.

CHAPTER TWO

Forgotten Men

On the evening of July 7, 1935, a violent thunderstorm rolled off the Atlantic Ocean and lashed the Upper Keys with driving rain and strong winds. The squall made an impression on John Ambrose, a war veteran from Baton Rouge, Louisiana, who rode out the rough weather in a construction camp on the beach at Lower Matecumbe Key.

Ambrose was one of the hundreds of out-of-work veterans who had been sent to the Florida Keys from Washington. Vets had been arriving by train in the Keys since November 1934. Their project, one of hundreds of New Deal construction projects under way throughout the country, was to build a highway bridge that would run parallel to the Florida East Coast Railway, establishing another link from Key West to the mainland. By the summer of 1935, the three oceanfront work camps had become rustic villages with populations larger than any of the island settlements outside of Key West.

The men also had their own weekly newspaper, the *Key Veteran News*. Ambrose, a highly skilled and talented draftsman, was the staff cartoonist for the newspaper and also wrote a weekly news column. The power of the summer storm fascinated Ambrose, and he described it in the July 13 edition.

"Shacks creaked and canvas billowed and cracked," he wrote. "Throughout the night the wind rose and fell and caused deep concern to many unfamiliar with tropical storms." The squall "threatened to develop into a mild form of hurricane," he continued, adding that the thunderstorm "was a real blessing in disguise for the mosquitoes were completely blown away."

The storm's ferocity caused an uneasy stirring among the men living in the cabins on the beach. Not long after the blow, Ambrose noted that some of his Camp 5 neighbors seemed to be expecting "a gosh-awful tornado or hurricane." The men had "buttressed, lashed, moored and supported . . . all four sides and the roof" of their little one-room home.

He couldn't resist teasing the men about the improvements they'd made to their quarters. "Everything has been anchored but the family cat," Ambrose wrote. "Wouldn't it be awful if a hurricane arrived and playfully tossed it up on the railroad track in spite of the network of fortifications surrounding it?"

Only an outsider would describe a hurricane as "playful." The Conchs feared and respected the powerful storms that the Atlantic hurled at them every year or so, and anyone with notions that hurricanes were fun had some harsh lessons to learn. But then, the strangers who had been arriving by the hundreds in the isolated islands were an odd bunch. Most of them had served in the war, and many of them had put their lives on the line in the fierce fighting in France that eventually defeated Germany. Some bore scars from bullet and shrapnel wounds, and others had permanent health problems because they had been exposed to toxic gas.

Still others had been wounded in a less obvious but perhaps more debilitating way. The intense, prolonged strain of combat had permanently altered many vets' perception of the world around them and their place in it. Even before the Depression turned everything upside down, these unhappy men realized they didn't belong in the workaday world of wives and children, careers and promotions, pensions and planned retirements. Their emotional stability had been undermined by nagging self-doubt, mistrust of others, their own failures—whether self-inflicted or beyond their control—and constant fears that something terrible could happen at any moment.

Some of them endured their alienation in a sullen, confused, and passive silence. Others were enraged that they had, in effect, been evicted from society and denied the one thing on which Americans in particular base so much of their personal identity and self-respect—a steady job.

In some ways, being sent to the isolated, sparsely populated Keys made their problems worse. Now they had a steady job, but for many that was no longer enough to banish the personal demons that hounded them. There wasn't much to do in their spare time to take their minds off their frustrations except fish, write letters home, or get drunk. Quite a few chose the last form of amusement.

But drinking didn't help them forget their fears and disappointments. Booze ignited the simmering coals of their anger, burning away the restraints that held it in check when they were sober. They became mean drunks, searching for a target for their blazing, inarticulate fury. Lots of times the only thing within reach was each other, and so drunken brawls became common in the work camps.

The first fight erupted as soon as the vets drew their first pay in early November 1934. Glenn Robertson, a lawyer from Johnson City, Tennessee, whose practice had evaporated with the Depression, described the drinking spree in a November 10, 1934, letter to a friend: "Last night was pay day, the first one, and we surely had a terrible time, worse than I ever saw in a CCC camp, or any other place—some of the men are just animals," Robertson wrote.

The drunken brawling would become a payday ritual for many of the veterans. The sober, hardworking Conchs looked on in frightened astonishment and tried to remember their Methodist teachings of tolerance and compassion, but sometimes it wasn't easy.

Farther down the islands, Key West residents were trying to understand how they had become so impoverished. Jobs and money had once been abundant there.

As the nineteenth century drew to a close, Key West was Florida's largest city and among the wealthiest in the United States. The city's 20,000 residents had prospered thanks to a collection of thriving industries.

The marine salvaging industry started the city on the road to prosperity in the mid-nineteenth century. The salvagers—known locally as wreckers—started raking in handsome profits before the Civil War by rescuing crews and cargoes from ships that ran aground on the reefs a few miles offshore. Among the many Cuban influences on the city was a cigar-making industry employing more than 11,000 workers, and 90 percent of the sponges sold in the United States at the turn of the century came from the waters around Key West. The military's presence kept still more employed. Key West also was a port of call for the Mallory Steamship Lines, and that provided several hundred more jobs. But one by one, Key West's bustling industries started going belly-up as the new century turned the corner.

Improvements in marine navigation technology meant that shippers could sail safely past the reefs that had once been such an expensive bedevilment to them, and so the wreckers were out of work. The cigar makers were lured to Tampa when that city offered them tax reductions. The spongers moved to Tarpon Springs just down the coast from Tampa, and the military started closing bases in Key West after World War I. The steamship company also closed its offices there.

By the late 1920s Key West was on the skids. Within two short decades the city's tax base and more than 14,000 jobs had vanished. Even the Florida East Coast Railway, Monroe County's largest taxpayer, was forced into bankruptcy and operated under the supervision of court-appointed receivers. And with the nation and the world sliding into a deep economic depression, there were no prospects that new industry would come to Key West anytime soon.

Those residents who could afford to, left town. But about 13,000 who were either too poor or too stubborn to move stayed and tried to scratch out a living as best they could.

A promising young writer named Ernest Hemingway found the dilapidated town charming when he and his second wife, Pauline Pfeiffer Hemingway, stepped off a passenger ship from Cuba in 1928. Three years later the couple bought a rundown Spanish colonial mansion on Whitehead Street that had been a showpiece when a wealthy wrecker built it in 1851. Pauline started fixing the place up, and her husband's growing circle of celebrity friends began finding their way to Key West.

Hemingway's stature as an author grew as he worked on his books, collected sizable royalty checks, and entertained his friends—whom he dubbed the Mob—with fishing trips on the Gulf Stream and parties in his spacious home. In the spring of 1934 he spent $3,000—money he'd been paid by *Esquire* magazine—as a down payment for a fishing yacht that he named *Pilar*. He persuaded friends at the nearly deserted U.S. Navy base near his home to let him dock the boat there.

As Hemingway prospered, happily trolling the Gulf Stream aboard *Pilar*, many of Key West's impoverished natives wondered where their next meal would come from and municipal leaders fought a losing battle to keep the city solvent.

By the summer of 1934 the city faced a bond debt of $5 million that it couldn't pay, plus another $270,000 in interest that was due. Added to that was about $150,000 in past due operating expenses and more than $113,000 in unpaid salaries to city employees. Among the unpaid workers were the garbage collectors, who showed their frustration by letting the trash pile up.

Finally city and county leaders threw in the towel. The local governments were flat broke.

On July 1, 1934, Key West and Monroe County leaders passed joint resolutions declaring that due to financial distress they were handing over the responsibilities of local government to David Sholtz, the governor of Florida. He immediately declared that the entire city of Key West was on welfare and thus subject to the jurisdiction of the Federal Emergency Relief Administration (FERA). The governor's declaration made Key West's problems the official responsibility of Julius Stone, director of the Florida Emergency Relief Administration (Florida ERA), the state agency charged with implementing the Federal Emergency Relief Administration's program in Florida.

Sholtz's declaration landed Key West's story in newspapers across the country, which was exactly what Julius Stone wanted. "I knew it didn't mean a thing," Stone said of the declaration, "but I thought it sounded pretty dramatic."

He also knew the governor's move might have been illegal because it had been Stone's suggestion. "I got away with it because we were so far off that no one knew what we were doing," Stone said. "And also because I chose a time when [Harry] Hopkins was on a long vacation."

In 1929 Stone, who held a doctorate in organic chemistry from Harvard, had been hired to work under Harry Hopkins, who was running New York's state welfare program under then-governor Franklin Roosevelt. Stone's agile mind quickly adapted itself to administration. When FDR was elected president, Hopkins became his right-hand man and the director of Roosevelt's Public Works Administration (PWA), the New Deal program created to put the nation's unemployed back to work by building federally funded projects. Hopkins then hired Stone as one of his assistants.

By August 1934 the PWA had hired about 675,000 workers and was spending $39 million per week on projects. Some were massive and far-reaching, such as the Tennessee Valley Authority, which would bring cheap electricity to much of the Southeast. On a smaller scale, dozens of court-houses, baseball parks, and other public buildings were being built across the country.

Stone received a budget of $2 million in federal money to use in Key West. Within a couple of days after being handed the keys to the city, he announced that the shabby little town would be cleaned up and repackaged as a tourist destination. Stone predicted Key West would become "the Bermuda of Florida."

The idea of converting Key West into a tropical tourist town had merit. The lowest recorded temperature in the town's history was only 41 degrees, and its winter highs were usually in the 70s, making it a perfect getaway for winter-weary residents of large northeastern cities. The turquoise waters offshore offered excellent fishing, and beneath the accumulated grime of impoverished neglect, Key West's houses were a fascinating blend of architectural styles and influences. Cuban, Bahamian, and Creole cultures had also come together to create a vibrant tropical environment in Key West.

Converting the dingy little town into a tourist attraction would take a lot of hard work, however. Among Stone's first acts was putting the city's garbage trucks back on the streets, which were clogged with weeks of accumulated garbage. Ten trucks operated 18 hours a day for several months to haul away the trash.

Stone also hired public relations specialist M. E. Gilfond, who cranked out news releases about the economic miracle occurring in Key West.

Stone made sure the nation was watching the transformation of Key West. He put the credibility and prestige of the New Deal on the line in August 1934 when he wrote an article for the *New York Times* in which he boasted that the Florida ERA's effort in Key West would become a model for solving the problems plaguing the rest of the nation.

He planned to capitalize on the unique beauty beneath the city's shabby, dilapidated exterior. "Ours is a job of preservation rather than demolition," Stone told a Miami radio audience on August 24, 1934. The city's old houses would be restored and its "romantic lanes and byways" would be preserved, he promised. "We want visitors to breathe and feel the romance and lure of the sea, and the tradition of the pirate and wrecking enterprises of old."

There were skeptics. The *Tallahassee Democrat* and other Florida newspapers doubted that Stone could make his plans work. And Key West residents took a few digs at him as well. When he moved into a rambling old nineteenth-century house in Key West, local wags soon dubbed it the "Stone Hotel" because of the parade of visitors Stone entertained there. The *Miami Daily News* reported that between mid-December 1934 and late March 1935, Stone had 140 houseguests.

The clever, resourceful, and quick-witted Stone clearly enjoyed being placed in a position of absolute authority. "With a scratch of my pen I started this work in Key West, and with a scratch of my pen I can stop it," he boasted to a reporter.

While Stone relished his new authority in Key West, FDR and his advisers in Washington, DC, were still puzzling over what to do about the desperately needy veterans who again were converging on the nation's capital seeking help. When Stone announced the plans to convert Key West to a tourism economy, a solution for the problem of what to do with the veterans suddenly materialized.

Stone and other Florida ERA officials wanted to make it quicker and easier for tourists to drive from Miami to Key West. Building a highway to replace the slow ferry at Lower Matecumbe Key would cut hours off the trip but also meant building bridges to connect the islands. An island-hopping highway running the length of the Keys had long been a dream in South Florida, but the state highway department had flatly refused to provide funding for such a project.

Stone, with a few scratches of his powerful pen and the backing of Uncle Sam's treasury, announced in October 1934 that the Florida ERA would use federal money to build the bridges and connect and improve the roads that already existed on some islands, and thus create a 150-mile Miami-to-Key West highway. And instead of using CCC labor, jobless veterans—including the remnants of the Bonus Marchers who were returning to Washington—would be sent to the Florida Keys, organized into camps, and put to work on the projects.

It would be an ambitious undertaking, perhaps not quite as spectacular as the Overseas Railroad but still a monumental project. The same long stretches of open water—such as the seven-mile span between Knight Key and Little Duck Key—would have to be bridged. There wouldn't be another highway like it in the world.

Roosevelt Administration officials didn't reveal who had suggested sending the veterans to the Keys, but Louis Howe, widely regarded as the brains behind FDR's 1932 run for the White House, was often given credit for the idea.

The plan also had the fingerprints of Harry Hopkins on it. Sending the vets to the Keys to build the road followed the boilerplate philosophy of the New Deal recovery effort: that paying jobless people to work on public projects would restore their self-respect and self-confidence and benefit the larger society. "Give a man a dole and you save his body and destroy his spirit," Hopkins said. "Give him a job and pay him an assured wage, and you save both the body and the spirit."

But the plan also had some uncomfortable similarities to the one General Moseley had suggested in 1932 for getting the Bonus Marchers out of Washington—send them to a sparsely populated warm-weather island far from the nation's capital and forget about them.

As far as President Roosevelt and his advisers were concerned, sending the veterans to the far-off Florida Keys was a best-of-both-worlds solution—it provided help for the vets and a political benefit for the Roosevelt Administration. The veterans would have employment for which they would be paid $30 a month plus housing and food, and they would be in one of the most isolated regions of the United States, more than 1,100 miles from Washington and thus out of the columns of the nation's newspapers.

More veterans work camps would be established in other parts of Florida and in rural South Carolina for other federally funded projects.

Officials said nothing publicly about the political benefits of removing the veterans from Washington. Stone said later that they were only being prudent when they decided to send the vets as far from large cities as they could. "We thought we were giving these fellows a chance to get away from the big cities with temptation to spend money," Stone said. "Here there was sunshine, fresh air, and quiet."

Not to mention boredom, isolation, and clouds of mosquitoes.

The first men sent to the Keys would be housed in two work camps supervised by Colonel G. S. Robinson for the Florida Emergency Relief Administration.

One camp would be built on the beach overlooking the Atlantic on Windley Key and the other on the beach at the foot of Lower Matecumbe Key next to the ferry dock. The camp at Windley Key was designated Camp 1. The men housed there would work in a quarry on neighboring Plantation Key that would provide fossilized coral stone for the construction projects. The other camp would be designated Camp 3, and the veterans there would work with civilians employed by the state highway department to build the three-and-a-half-mile highway bridge between Lower Matecumbe Key and what was then called Jewfish Key.

B. M. Duncan, a state highway department engineer who lived in Key West, was in charge of the bridge and highway construction project. His assistant was Lawrence Bow, a Keys native. Although the veterans would be paid with federal funds, Duncan and Bow, who were state employees, would supervise their work.

In early November 1934 about 50 vets stepped off the FEC train at Windley Key, two miles up the tracks from Islamorada. Their first task was to clear away brush and start work on Camp 1.

The men who followed were from all across the United States and all walks of life. They included Jimmy Conway, a former professional boxer whose name was a fixture on sports pages from the early 1920s into the early 1930s. In January 1920, at the age of 25, Conway slugged it out for a full 12 rounds against world welterweight champion Jack Britton. The Associated Press reported that Conway took a terrific pounding but stood up to the champ and gave him a good fight before losing on a referee's decision. Despite the loss, it looked like Conway might be on his way to an eventual championship.

But by late 1934 he was in his mid-30s and hadn't reached his goal. He'd made some money in the ring, earning around $20,000 in prize money—around $370,000 in 2019 dollars. He'd also done two hitches in the peacetime army along the way, the most recent one ending in February 1930. But while sportswriters of the 1920s had admired how Conway could take continuous punches to the head and keep fighting, 15 years of such pummeling had taken its toll, and Conway almost certainly had sustained many concussions. His prize money was long gone, and he was washed up as a professional fighter and out of options for a job.

So Jimmy Conway accepted a free train ticket to the Florida Keys to help build the highway to Key West.

Arthur Mewshaw, an attorney in Charlotte, North Carolina, had been the local campaign manager for U.S. Senator Furnifold Simmons's unsuccessful bid for reelection in 1930. John T. McNulty was a former actor who had performed on Broadway and landed parts in several movies before being wounded in the war. He resumed his career after returning from France and had been a stage manager until he lost that job. Bill Hendren had been a high school principal before landing in the Keys. Other veterans had worked at large newspapers such as the *New York Times*, *New York Herald*, and *New York World* before the Depression.

The work camps offered the men at least a theoretical chance to get their lives back on track, but the program was beset with problems from the moment the first veterans arrived on Windley Key. The friction began with the primitive living conditions. The vets were housed in tents and had no place to take a bath or relieve themselves.

"There were flies," said Albert Keith, a vet from Atlanta. "You go in to eat there would be flies, you would have to fan them out of your face and food. "And a lot of time we didn't see but one person that ever represented any religious organization, that was Father McDonald from Homestead. We didn't even have as much as a book or a movie."

B. M. Duncan and Lawrence Bow also weren't happy about being required to use the veterans on their highway construction project.

The vets—angry, alienated, out of shape, and annoyed by mosquitoes and sleeping in tents—were less than enthusiastic about doing hard labor in the muggy Keys.

Duncan and Bow were accustomed to the hot, humid weather, and to working with and supervising men who wanted the job and knew how to do it. If a man didn't want to work, they didn't have much use for him. There were too many men begging for jobs to waste time with a bunch of surly veterans. Nor did they have time to make the vets comfortable in the work camps. Duncan and Bow weren't social workers. They were construction foremen with a work schedule to meet. It didn't make sense to them that they should have to mollycoddle a bunch of grown men.

Resentment festered on both sides and would soon lead to a showdown.

A few weeks after the camps opened, a small group of angry veterans went to Miami to meet with E. J. Close, operations director for the Florida ERA. The vets told him that conditions were intolerable and asked him to come see for himself.

Close went to the Keys with several other local officials, including the city engineer of Homestead. In a brief report, Close noted that camp sanitation was "terrible" and there was no discipline. He suggested that new supervisors experienced in dealing with veterans be brought in immediately to correct the problems before they got worse.

Close's report started the wheels of bureaucracy turning, albeit very slowly. On December 3 William H. D. Hinchman, the Federal Emergency Relief Administration's assistant regional engineer for the Southeast, met with Colonel Robinson to discuss the problems in the Keys. Robinson quickly made it clear that he had a low opinion of the veterans. About 40 percent of them were "psychos," and a rule forbidding whiskey in the camps was completely ignored, he said.

Robinson acknowledged that there was very little discipline in the camps, but said that was only a serious problem on paydays. "On that day, there is nothing we can do with them, and since I have taken the stand that Washington wants these men to stay here I have put up with things that I would not stand under ordinary conditions."

Robinson's claim that the vets' drinking was a problem for only a couple days each month didn't square with what Hinchman had heard, however. FEC trains went past the camps each day, and passengers were continually seeing drunken veterans, creating a serious public image problem that had to be eliminated, he said. Hinchman and Robinson decided to build canteens for the veterans, hoping this would at least keep their drinking out of public view.

Despite having a clear picture of the problems in the camps, federal administrators moved very slowly to correct them. On Christmas Eve, Albert Keith wrote a letter to the office of the U.S. Attorney General saying that conditions were unbearable. "We have no recreation, there are no regulations and no order among the men of the camp," Keith wrote. "I have never been affiliated or connected with such a disrupted and disorganized mob. It reminds me of an insane asylum."

When Keith didn't get a response to his letter, he and three other veterans sent a telegram to Louis Howe, one of President Roosevelt's closest advisers, telling him that conditions were "desperate" and that 200 men in Camp 1 were going to leave if conditions weren't improved immediately.

With the railroad hauling dozens of veterans away from Washington every week and depositing them in the Keys, FDR was ready to publicize his position on early payment of the bonus. On New Year's Eve, 1934, he announced that he opposed paying the bonus before it was due in 1945. The veterans most in need of help were already getting federal assistance, and the government was giving "very definite and distinct preference" to hiring veterans for its relief work, the president said. Besides, he added, it would cost too much to pay the bonus ahead of schedule.

A few days later, Daniel A. Hobart, commander of the American Veterans Association, sent a telegram to FDR supporting his stand on not paying the bonus early. Hobart called the demand for early payment part of "the age-old pension racket."

Meanwhile, the Florida ERA's effort to bring tourists to Key West was already paying dividends even though work on the new bridge and highway had hardly started. Stone and his assistants organized Key West residents into work details. Brightly colored signs with the slogan "Help to All Who Help Themselves" started appearing in the windows of homes and businesses as Key West residents pitched in enthusiastically to clean up their town and repair the many shabby buildings that had been eyesores for so long.

African American women in Key West were encouraged to enroll in classes taught by the Florida ERA to learn how to work as maids.

Gilfond and his staff, which included talented graphic artists, launched a nationwide advertising campaign to lure tourists to Key West. When the visitors arrived, they were given a booklet published by the Florida ERA that included a map of the city's attractions. The shabby little city of a few months earlier was described as "a luminous island city" surrounded by "a sea of emerald waters" and "saturated in the atmosphere of a romantic history."

The effort was a rousing success. About 40,000 tourists visited Key West during the 1934–1935 season, and the city's income from tourism increased by about 43 percent. Even Dizzy Dean, the star pitcher for the St. Louis Cardinals, briefly visited the city during a cruise after his team's victory in the 1934 World Series. Dean, nattily attired in a tropical-weight suit and two-tone shoes, stepped off the cruise ship long enough to be photographed at the Key West docks.

Not everyone in Key West was happy about the newcomers, however.

No one had bothered to confer with Ernest Hemingway before putting his house on the maps that were handed out to the visitors. The author's home was listed as attraction number 18, and a fair number of those 40,000 tourists tramped onto his property and peered into the windows of his home or gawked at him from the sidewalk as he tried to relax on his porch with a drink and a cigar. One especially bold visitor opened the front door of Hemingway's home and marched into his living room as though he were walking into a museum.

Hemingway made light of the intrusions in a column in the April 1935 issue of *Esquire* magazine, describing himself as "a modest and retiring chap" with no desire to compete with the other tourist attractions listed on the map. But behind the humor the author was livid, and the fact that he was an anti–New Deal Republican who despised Julius Stone only added to his rage.

When Florida ERA leaders decided in early 1935 to replace dozens of outhouses in Key West with a modern sewer system, Hemingway saw an opportunity to regain some privacy. The streets were ripped up to lay the new pipelines, and the paving bricks that had been removed were stacked at the same navy yard where Hemingway docked his yacht. The author bought 19,000 of them for $38 and put his handyman, Toby Bruce, to work building a six-foot-tall wall around his property. He urged Bruce to get the project completed before the onset of the worst part of the hurricane season in August.

While Hemingway cursed the tourists and tried to wall them out, hundreds of vets were arriving on the islands to the north of Key West. By early February 1935 about 600 men were living in the Upper Keys and working on the road construction project.

But camp administrators still hadn't improved the substandard living conditions that had so angered Albert Keith and other veterans months earlier. The men were arriving faster than carpenters could build even minimal housing for them.

"They had to rush to get up tents of any description that they could get hold of—circus tents, squad tents—and try to cut lumber and get it as soon as they could to start building shacks for them," said Hubert Nichols, an engineer from Homestead who was working on the bridge construction project.

The hastily built housing made some veterans uneasy.

"I would like to say that they were supposed to block up the shanties but the way they were blocked it was suicide for hurricane weather," said Abraham Fox, a veteran from Los Angeles who was assigned to Camp 1. "They had sawed off trees into blocks a foot and a half or two feet long and set them on top of the ground and then the house set on these. For bracing they nailed boards down the sides of the shanties onto the blocks. That was awful . . . I laid there many a night knowing that it would be like a matchbox if a storm hit."

Keys natives weren't impressed with the work camps either. Rufus Johnson, who'd lived on the islands for more than 50 years, said the camps wouldn't withstand even strong breezes. "I saw them blown to pieces with a common north wind," he said.

Winds also frequently blew down a tent used for storage at the work camps, Johnson said. "I saw a big tent for storing things there one night, and the next morning it would be all to pieces," he said.

Johnson warned one administrator about putting the camps so close to the ocean. "I told him we had high tides in October, higher than any time of the year," he said. "I said in October the tides will put that mess hall under water. He said 'You think so?' and I said 'I know so.' He said how would it be to put a lot of boards and things around it, and I said, 'Mister, water has got more power than anything in the world.'"

But state and federal officials dithered about how to resolve the housing problems. A proposal to convert boxcars into temporary housing was dropped when officials decided that would cost too much.

In late February Joseph Hyde Pratt, a FERA regional engineer in Raleigh, North Carolina, made several inspection visits to the veterans camps. He was accompanied by others, including Fred Ghent, the director of safety for the Florida ERA. Pratt was very upset with living conditions in the camps and especially displeased by the way Duncan and Bow were running them.

The camps should have been put into "first-class condition" before the veterans started work on the bridge, Pratt said. But the camps were still filthy and were only getting worse with more men pouring in every day.

The inspectors also learned that two veterans had died from spinal meningitis—a disease caused by bacteria that can thrive and spread in crowded living conditions.

Duncan received a letter on February 26, 1935, detailing the dirty and dangerous conditions the inspectors had found in the camps and ordering him to immediately make the camps as sanitary as possible and keep them that way.

By late February the men in Camp 3 had formed a five-member grievance committee to take a list of demands to administrators. The vets wanted improved sanitation in the camps. They also were upset because they thought they had not been paid as much as promised for their work, and because B. M. Duncan and Lawrence Bow were hiring skilled workers from outside the camps instead of using veterans who had the same skills and could do the same work.

Duncan responded to their demands by ordering the five members of the grievance committee thrown in jail. He didn't bother to get a warrant for their arrest or even have them charged with a crime. The veterans were outraged. On February 25 the men in Camp 3 went on strike to protest the arrest of their comrades.

Two days later Pratt, Fred Ghent, and Sam Cutler, another engineer who was Ghent's assistant, were back in the Keys to meet with Duncan and Bow. But Duncan had gone to Miami to meet Governor David Sholtz and ride the FEC train with him to Key West.

Despite the terrible conditions in the camps, Bow said he didn't think they should give in to the veterans' demands because it would only encourage them to ask for more concessions.

Ghent and Cutler left around 5:30 p.m. When they reached Miami they stopped to buy an afternoon newspaper. They were astonished to learn that National Guard troops had been sent to Islamorada. Ghent realized that Duncan had gone behind the backs of state and federal administrators and persuaded Monroe County sheriff Karl Thompson to ask the governor to send troops to the Keys.

The strike and the presence of the National Guard attracted the press to Camp 3, and on Saturday, March 2, FERA engineer Marvin Porter went to the Keys to meet with the veterans, and then returned to Miami with Duncan for a conference with Pratt and Stone.

Porter told Duncan that his authority over the veterans would be reduced. He also concluded that the arrest of the five-member veterans grievance committee that had prompted the strike had been illegal. He ordered that the camps' sanitation must be improved immediately, and that Florida State Highway Department officials—most notably Duncan and Bow—not have any part in supervising the work camps. Every camp administrator should either be a veteran or an employee of the Florida Emergency Relief Administration, he said.

Stone, Pratt, and Porter also decided to make a major change in administering both the veterans camps and the construction project. They would divide the authority, putting the state highway department engineers in charge of the actual bridge and highway work and using Florida ERA administrators to supervise the veterans camps.

It was a decision that seemed completely practical and necessary at the time, but the division of authority would have terrible consequences in a few months.

Two days later the veterans returned to work, but the strike had made Sheriff Thompson and Keys residents nervous, and the National Guard remained. Federal officials realized they were dealing with a group of men who were so troubled and volatile that they would have to be handled very carefully. Camp administrators in the Keys should not make the bridge construction their main concern, Pratt said.

"A large percentage of these veterans are problem cases and they do not seem to be able to assume responsibility, but want to be taken care of," Pratt later wrote in a report. "Most of them when handled right are willing to work and will work diligently and well. The work of the veterans, however, should not be the main consideration, but secondary to their welfare."

Fred Ghent's assistant, Sam Cutler, remained in the Keys to supervise the veterans working on the bridge being built at Camp 3. The Harvard-educated Cutler seemed, to the FERA engineers, to be the kind of administrator they needed to supervise the unruly veterans. Those who had worked with him respected his judgment and character and considered him to be an unusually capable administrator.

"I considered [Cutler] rather an exceptional person because he had all the markings of a gentleman and he was very conscientious," said Paul Vander Schouw, an administrator in the Florida Transient Division. "At the time he made [safety] inspections he was very conscientious in his reports. He was a man who could be rigid in his official duties and still be quite agreeable in personal relationships."

But some of the people in the work camps regarded Cutler differently. His Ivy League training and cautious nature, as well as his professional background, made him an object of derision. Robert A. Ayer Jr., who was a file clerk in the camps' administrative offices, said Cutler was "a very nervous sort of fellow" who "imagines things."

"He was probably the most nervous one there," Ayer said.

As the dust began to settle from the strike and the dramatic reorganization of the camps' administrative structure, Julius Stone launched a new publicity campaign to polish up the image of the veterans work program. On March 15 Stone told the United Press that Florida had been chosen for an important "sociological experiment" to rebuild the lives of "derelict World War veterans."

Stone said that 25,000 veterans eventually would be sent to the Keys for "reconditioning."

"Restoring the men to their former selves is paramount," Stone said, adding that the Keys had been chosen for the camps because they were far removed from the temptations of the city. The men would work on construction projects in the Keys, but the work would not be their main purpose for being there, he said.

Florida officials and residents were horrified at the prospect of 25,000 jobless, homeless veterans being herded into their state, and a few days after Stone's statement an embarrassed Harry Hopkins hastily explained that the federal government had no intention of sending that many men to the Keys.

Stone's comments about a social experiment in the Keys sounded a bit too good to be true to the *Washington Post*. In late March, after Congress again failed to pass a bill allowing early payment of the veterans' bonus, the *Post* sent reporter Edward T. Folliard to the Keys to take a look at the work camps.

William Hinchman, an assistant regional engineer, took charge of the camps on March 18. His task was daunting, but he was determined to correct "the worst conditions from every angle that I have encountered during my experience with the Federal Emergency Relief Administration."

Hinchman established new priorities. He immediately pulled most of the veterans off the bridge construction project and put them to work improving the camps that had been neglected by Duncan and Bow. "These two men, on account of their former experiences [as construction engineers] were interested primarily in the construction of bridges connecting the Keys and the development of a highway extending from the Florida mainland to

Key West," Hinchman said. "The welfare and rehabilitation of the men sent to this area were never taken into consideration."

Soon after Hinchman took over, the *Washington Post* published two stories by Edward Folliard that were harshly critical of the veterans work program in the Keys. Folliard described the veterans as "working guests of Uncle Sam" who had gone on a "booze rampage" during the February strike. The work camps in the Keys were a "transplanted bonus camp." The purpose of the camps in the Keys was to rehabilitate the veterans and "make them forget about a bonus march on Washington," Folliard wrote.

Hinchman set a whirlwind of changes into motion. He had the vets clean up their camps and plant palm trees. He obtained athletic equipment for the camps and urged the men to form baseball and volleyball teams. He gave them new khaki work uniforms. He tried to appeal to their sense of self-respect. And he allowed them to start their own weekly newspaper—the *Key Veteran News*.

Although Hinchman worked hard to improve the camps, he had no intention of staying in the Keys and looked for a permanent director for all seven veterans work camps in Florida. In late March Pratt suggested several possible successors for the job. He gave an especially high recommendation for one of the men.

"You have another good man down there now—Mr. Cutler," Pratt told Hinchman. "If you can use him to advantage, permanently, in connection with the camps, I shall be glad to have you do so. I consider him a very capable man in many ways."

By the end of March, Hinchman had finished his reforms and prepared to leave the Keys. But before going he delivered speeches to the vets at both camps, telling them "bygones are bygones" and imploring them to improve their behavior. "All the veterans stationed in the Keys are getting a black eye because of your actions," he said. "They don't rate it. There are plenty of special men in these encampments."

The *Key Veteran News* published Hinchman's remarks in its first issue on March 30, 1935. The newspaper also included a front-page story saying that the National Guard was protecting the veterans from "parasites" such as bootleggers.

It was a nice gesture toward the troops. Dealing with the veterans' fondness for strong drink was becoming tiresome for the soldiers and a ceaseless frustration for guard commanders.

"The chief source of all the trouble amongst the veterans seems to be caused by liquor," Lieutenant Colonel M. R. Woodward of the Florida National Guard wrote in a memo to his superiors in April 1935. "One of the main functions of the guard is to keep out all illegal shipments of liquor. The veterans resort to drinking shoe polish, hair tonic, and other fluids that contain alcohol, and this creates a very bad condition when men become intoxicated on these drinks."

Islamorada natives were getting an eyeful of the vets' determined drinking. Bernard Russell, who was 16 in 1935, recalled that one day when he was minding the cash register at his family's small store in the rear of the post office building, a long line of veterans formed outside. The camp canteen apparently had run out of beer, and the men had lined up to buy bottles of rubbing alcohol and Coca-Cola. The teenager didn't know that the veterans were mixing the rubbing alcohol with the soft drink and drinking the noxious concoction. But when Russell's father, Postmaster John Russell, saw the men leaving the store with their purchases, he knew instantly what they were doing and stopped the sales.

The postmaster was troubled by the frequent drunkenness of the veterans. "I often thought that it was almost a crime to allow so much drinking in the camps," he said. "When they got paid they would drink until it was all gone. Then they would wait until their allowances came again to get more."

The National Guard troops tried to cut off the vets' supply of hard liquor by searching everyone who got off the trains at the camps and setting up a roadblock at Plantation Key to search automobiles for booze. But protests from indignant tourists and residents put an end to those practices. Camp administrators still hadn't figured out how to curtail the payday drinking binges. "Every payday was just a big spree," said Hubert Nichols, the engineer for the bridge project.

Drunken brawls erupted regularly. "You'd see maybe a dozen at a time throwing beer bottles at each other and hitting each other over the head," Nichols said. "It looked like they would kill each other, but they always came through all right. . . . They sure were a rough bunch down there. They drank whatever they could get."

The vets may have avoided killing each other during the brawls, but the payday fighting added to the workload of the camps' medical staff, which had converted a hotel at Snake Creek into a small hospital for the veterans. "We always had boom days then, suturing their wounds," said Dr. Lassiter Alexander, a physician who worked in the hospital.

The canteens had been intended to at least keep the drunkenness out of public view. But that wasn't working. And the vets' behavior was undermining the effort to bring tourism to the Keys. In March 1935 Roosevelt's advisor Louis Howe received a letter detailing the "disgusting experience" V. M. Ollier of Chicago had during a recent visit to the Keys with his family.

"Most of the [men] were in the most revolting stages of intoxication I've ever seen," he wrote. Some were exposing themselves. One approached Ollier's car to ask for money to get back to Washington. The angry visitor told Howe that the men didn't seem to appreciate what the government was trying to do for them.

On April 1, 1935, Fred Ghent—who'd become familiar with the veterans camps as the Florida ERA's director of safety—was named as Hinchman's replacement in charge of all veterans work camps in Florida. Ghent, an Alabama native, had lived in Florida since 1925. The *Key Veteran News* predicted that Ghent, who'd served in the U.S. Navy during World War I, would earn the veterans' respect because he had "a sympathetic understanding of their condition"—especially the circumstances that drove many of them to drink excessively.

"He believes that no man ... is a habitual imbiber of liquor through choice, but that pressure from environment, reverses, etc. may be so heavy that one finally reaches a stage of despondency to the degree of inferiority complex, then resorts to stimulants with the hope of alleviation," the *News* said.

Ghent had some quirks as an administrator, however, including a habit of convincing himself that events would always unfold according to his plans. His assumptions went beyond simple optimism. He would sometimes deny reality when it conflicted with what he wanted to believe.

It was an administrative trait that might have been harmless and even useful in different circumstances. But for the veterans under Ghent's supervision, it would be a precursor to tragedy.

Ghent's superiors in Florida weren't as impressed with his abilities as the FERA officials in Washington who appointed him. Conrad Van Hyning, director of the Florida ERA and Ghent's immediate supervisor, didn't think Ghent was the right man for the job despite his support from federal officials.

"He was probably too sentimental on the whole proposition," Van Hyning said. "He was the nervous type and likely to jump at decisions."

Another camp was established soon after Ghent took the helm of the veterans work program. The new installation, designated Camp 5, was built on the beach at the upper end of Lower Matecumbe Key. The camp was built on a narrow strip of land that was one of the lowest spots in the Keys. It was anything but an ideal place for the third camp, but it was the only land that was available.

"At Camp 5, we were on the beach, at sea level, and at high tide the tide used to come right into the kitchen," said Joseph Fecteau, a veteran from Massachusetts. "In fact, at high tide it would come in and put the fire out. We could not do any cooking there in the rainy season. . . . We [were] on the lowest part of the Keys up there, you see, between the Gulf and the Atlantic."

Work had scarcely begun on Camp 5, however, when federal officials told Ghent to stop adding new buildings to the work camps.

Still, the Florida ERA went ahead with plans to establish a headquarters for the three work camps at the Hotel Matecumbe. The deal was a windfall for hotel owner Ed Butters because it meant all his space would be occupied. The hotel's second-floor rooms would become offices and living quarters for 35 administrators and office staff, and Fern Butters and her cook would prepare three meals a day for the officials.

Meanwhile, Fred Ghent was worrying about shielding the veterans from the uncontrollable ravages of nature. In an April 9 letter to Pratt, Ghent pointed out that the Florida ERA administrators needed to make plans to protect the veterans from hurricanes.

"We do know . . . that this area is subject to hurricanes, and in view of this knowledge, it is our duty to every man employed on the Keys, in connection with this program, to furnish a safe refuge during the storm," Ghent wrote.

The islands were indeed "subject to hurricanes."

The hurricane of October 1906 that had killed so many of the workers building the FEC's Overseas Railroad was only one of many powerful storms that had raked the Keys in the previous three decades. Hurricanes in 1909 and 1910 heavily damaged the railroad, and in September 1919 the strongest hurricane on record up to that time blasted Key West as it passed into the Gulf of Mexico. The storm—which nearly leveled the city—was so fierce that Sister Louis Gabriel, a nun at the Convent of Mary Immaculate, dedicated Our Lady of Lourdes Grotto, a small shrine on the grounds of The Basilica of Saint Mary Star of the Sea Catholic Church, where Key West residents could go to pray for divine protection from hurricanes.

In 1929 a hurricane crossed the Upper Keys at Key Largo, and in 1933—one of the busiest hurricane seasons on record—three powerful storms approached the Keys but didn't make landfall in the islands.

While Ghent worked on plans to protect the veterans from hurricanes, he also tried to get to know the men, visiting the camps often during his first weeks as state administrator. During a lengthy April 24 meeting with the vets, Ghent commented on the biblical story of creation, noting that God made the Earth in six days. From somewhere in the crowd, one of the men immediately shouted, "He didn't use veterans' labor!"

Ghent made a sincere effort to form a bond with the vets and promised to do his best to help them. "I don't believe there is a man in the ranks who would be here if he wasn't a victim of the Depression and his financial condition, which was caused by something beyond his control," Ghent said.

He told the veterans he'd been in their shoes before.

"I have been along the road that most of you men have," he said. "I have been out of a job, and I have looked for a job, and I know the resistance you meet and the false promises you get when you are out looking for a job. It is the most discouraging, disappointing experience that any man can have during his lifetime.... Almost every man here has lived long enough to find that his experience has been such that he could name his friends on one hand and not use all his fingers."

Ghent promised to meet with every man in the work camps to discuss his problems, adding that he hoped the individual meetings would "restore in your minds a bit of confidence in humanity."

Ghent told the veterans he had confidence in them. "I believe that human nature will react to reason and that any man who has reached the age of 35 will listen to anything that is reasonable," he said. And he said his own fate was in their hands as well.

"Gentlemen, I represent you first," he said. "I represent the Florida Emergency Relief Administration forces second, and if we can't coordinate down here and put this show over, the first man to be fired will be me."

Ghent's sincerity apparently impressed the vets, and they settled down. On May 13 the National Guard troops were withdrawn. But while the vets' conduct had indeed improved, it was still far from angelic. The *Key Veteran News* contained frequent allusions and direct references to excessive drinking, including staff-drawn cartoons showing intoxicated and hungover veterans. And despite their military backgrounds, the men had little regard for any sort of authority.

"Now, the men didn't pay much attention to rules," said Loring Scott, a veteran from Muncie, Indiana, assigned to Camp 1. "As a matter of fact there were not many rules. They did about as they pleased in general deportment.

Of course, there were some rules they didn't question. If a man didn't work, he didn't get paid, and he was reasonable enough to understand that. It seemed to be the inclination of the captains to be very lenient as to the conduct of the camps. A sort of sensitive spirit among the men. They didn't obey rules."

As the summer progressed the vets didn't confine their carousing to the camps. On weekends, especially around their monthly paydays, the vets boarded the FEC trains for Key West and Miami. Camp officials learned that Key West police were far more tolerant of the vets' drunkenness than cops in Miami and Homestead.

"They seem to be glad to have these men come to Key West," said Colonel Robinson. "If they get drunk they put them in jail until they are sober, and if they get into trouble they get in touch with me. When we were first here, 12 men received suspended sentences of 20 days in Homestead, but since that time I have discouraged the men from going to Homestead and have encouraged them only to come to Key West."

In the saloons of Key West, Ernest Hemingway was happy to hoist a glass and swap war stories with fellow veterans. Their adventures in Key West, Miami, and Miami Beach were often reported with sardonic "boys will be boys" humor in the *Key Veteran News*. The newspaper stories often mentioned the "18th floor," an inside reference to the Dade County Jail, which was located on the 18th floor of the Dade County Courthouse in Miami.

Their disruptive behavior wasn't confined to saloons. Sometimes the men weren't willing to wait for a regularly scheduled passenger train when they wanted to travel. So they used the same tactics employed by the West Coast Bonus Marchers in 1932. They'd block the railroad tracks with logs and whatever else they could lay their hands on and wait for a freight train. When the train was forced to stop, the men climbed aboard and demanded that the train take them to their destination. If they wanted to go shorter distances and didn't feel like walking or waiting for a train, they joined hands to form a human barrier and block the highway. When a car stopped, they'd pile in and tell the driver where they wanted to go.

The vets' behavior tried the patience of the Keys natives. Some of the veterans, however, attended services at Matecumbe Methodist Church, and John Russell, the postmaster, occasionally invited some of them into his home for dinner.

Others tried to provide the veterans with something to do in their spare time besides get drunk. Homestead librarian Lily Bow—whose son Lawrence Bow had been so staunchly opposed to giving in to their demands for better living conditions—sent books and magazines to the camps and wrote stories and poems for the *Key Veteran News*. The librarian doubtless felt some empathy for the veterans living in the isolated islands. She and her two young sons had lived on sparsely populated Cudjoe Key, not far from Key West, for a couple of years.

Ghent also hired a full-time recreation director for the veterans. Joseph Huau got busy setting up volleyball courts, organizing boxing matches, and laying out baseball diamonds. He also offered a sympathetic ear and served as a troubleshooter for camp administrators. "I was called on to mix with them to see if things could not be settled to clear their minds of any hard feelings toward the government," Huau said.

One of Huau's first projects was to organize baseball teams in the work camps. The sport became an obsession among the ex-servicemen, who turned out in droves to watch games between camp teams. The vets' teams also squared off on the diamond against teams of young men from the Upper Keys.

A smattering of former professional baseball players among the vets formed the nucleus of a veterans' all-star team that was admitted to the Dade County League, which was composed of nearby amateur teams. The vets started work on a baseball park.

By mid-May 1935 Ghent's reforms had made the work camps a bit more comfortable. Most of the men had been moved out of tents and were living in small cabins, which they referred to as shacks. The cabins were arranged in neat rows. In Camp 1 the men erected facetious signs naming the unpaved streets in their camp after major thoroughfares in Washington, DC, such as Pennsylvania Avenue and Vermont Avenue. They made mascots of several stray dogs, which they named Miami, Patsy, and Bonus. When Patsy gave birth to a litter of pups in late April 1935, the Camp 1 correspondent for the *Key Veteran News* reported the event.

By the summer of 1935, more work camps for veterans had been set up in other parts of Florida. In keeping with the South's unofficial but strictly observed policy of keeping the races separated, black veterans were housed in Camp 2 on Mullet Key near St. Petersburg. Camp 4 was established near Clearwater, Camp 7 was at Welaka on the Saint John's River in northeastern Florida. Camp 9 was at Leesburg, northwest of Orlando. A temporary camp, designated Camp 6, was set up briefly on No Name Key but was quickly closed.

Ghent returned to his office in Jacksonville after spending several weeks in the Keys. But he continued searching for solutions to the vets' persistent personal problems. In May he created a special staff of advisers to help them get some relief from creditors back in their hometowns, untangle bureaucratic snarls with the Veterans Administration in Washington, and help them search for jobs. He also pressed ahead with efforts to establish some sort of hurricane protection.

A proposal to build a large, reinforced hurricane shelter for the veterans was dismissed because federal officials considered it too expensive. Ghent looked for another way to protect the men from storms.

On May 16, 1935, Ghent wrote a letter to Scott Loflin, a Jacksonville lawyer who was one of the receivers handling the FEC's bankruptcy, discussing a plan to use a special train to evacuate the veterans from the islands. Ghent said he wanted a train with five coaches, and he wanted it to be available 12 to 24 hours before a hurricane was expected to strike the Keys.

He added, however, that he would not pay to have a train standing by.

Two days after Ghent sent his letter to Loflin, the *Key Veteran News* reported on its front page that the two men had discussed hurricane evacuation, and that Loflin had told Ghent that all the vets could be removed from the Keys in four to six hours. "Evacuation in Hurricanes Assured by Railroad Co-receiver," the headline read.

Ghent also promised the veterans that they'd be taken off the islands if a hurricane threatened the camps.

"Mr. Ghent said, 'We have trains waiting for you in Miami, where we can get you out of the Keys 24 hours before any storm hits you,'" said Clyde McCain, a veteran at Camp 3 from Los Angeles.

So in his own mind, Ghent seemed to have solved the problem of protecting the veterans from nature's ravages.

But Loflin had a different perception of the evacuation arrangements.

On June 6 Loflin sent a letter to Ghent telling him that the FEC would need 12 hours to put together an evacuation train and get it to the camps after officials had requested it. Loflin added that the FEC would not start assembling the train until camp officials told them where the men would be taken and gave assurances that arrangements had been made with local officials at the destination for water and sanitation services.

Loflin said nothing in his letter about keeping an evacuation train in constant readiness to send to the Keys. But Ghent had convinced himself that the FEC would have a train waiting in Homestead.

Not long after his discussions with Loflin, Ghent was chatting with Paul Vander Schouw, the assistant director of the Florida Transient Division. Vander Schouw's office was in the same building in Jacksonville as Ghent's.

"This is a bad time of year for you men down on the Keys," Vander Schouw said to Ghent. "What are you going to do if a hurricane comes?"

"Nothing for a couple of weeks," Ghent said. "The moon is not right."

Vander Schouw was puzzled by Ghent's strange remark. "I don't think the moon has anything to do with it," he said. "But in case there is one, what are you going to do?"

"Well," Ghent said, "we have made arrangements with the railroad company. We will get a train down there and get them out. It will only take two or three hours to get them out."

Vander Schouw didn't think it would be quite that simple to load hundreds of men aboard a train and get them out of the Keys in only a few hours. But Ghent insisted that the situation was under control.

Announcements were posted on camp bulletin boards telling the veterans that a special train would evacuate them from the islands if a hurricane threatened.

The phantom train supposedly parked on a siding in Homestead was the first example of Ghent believing what was most convenient for him. It wouldn't be the last.

As the summer progressed, so did work on the bridge from Lower Matecumbe Key to Jewfish Key. By early June cofferdams were in place for the construction of the first four bridge piers. Workers started pouring the concrete for some of the piers on June 7, and a month later the work was completed. A pile-driving crew started preparations for 25 more piers. Plans called for 187 piers to be built for the highway bridge.

Ghent's approach to dealing with the veterans seemed to be paying off. He'd stopped the practice of giving the men $1 every other day, and that had reduced the drunkenness. Junius T. Wigginton, who was in charge of supplies for the construction project, said the vets were doing "wonderful work on the bridge project."

"Many of these men were fine men as long as they did not get hold of alcohol," Wigginton said.

A combination of civilian laborers and veterans was being used on the project. Ed Sheeran, the survivor of the deadly 1906 hurricane, supervised the bridge construction.

By 1935 Sheeran was 65 years old, and what was left of his dark brown hair was flecked with gray. An old man's paunch encircled his waist. But he was still intensely focused on his work, and he was fiercely loyal to his friends and the men who worked under him.

Sheeran and other construction supervisors did the best they could with the veterans who'd been assigned to work with them. But fitting the men into daily work routines wasn't easy, especially since regulations imposed by the Florida ERA made it difficult for construction supervisors to use the vets efficiently.

Civilian workers reported for duty at 8 a.m. and were ferried out to the work site on a small boat. But veterans assigned to the bridge job didn't report for work until around 8:30 a.m., and a second boat had to be used to carry them to the work area.

Sheeran assigned the vets to clear brush on shore, unload construction materials, pour concrete at the construction site, and work as general laborers. A few veterans operated construction machinery such as derricks, cranes, and pumps.

But Hubert Nichols, who worked under Sheeran, said it was "just impossible" to use the veterans because of restrictions.

"All my work was so irregular," Nichols said. "I had to go off in a boat and be gone at lunch time—had to take our lunch with us, and they were very strict about the veterans; we had to have them back at 11:30 and again at 3:30 and I just could not make it, you know."

Camp administrators insisted that the vets be back on shore promptly at 11:30 a.m. to go to lunch at their mess hall. The vets didn't return from their lunch break until around 1:30 p.m., and their workday ended at 3:30 p.m., which meant that they were available for work only about five hours per day.

Despite Ghent's improvements, the veterans still had to contend with uncomfortable living conditions that got worse with the arrival of the steamy Keys summer. Hordes of mosquitoes descended on the islands, precipitating another crisis for camp administrators.

"About the middle of June, the mosquitoes were so bad that it was almost impossible to stay there," said Loring Scott, the veteran from Indiana. "You had to stay in the house, or shack, or tent, or hut from the time it began to get dark until bright daylight. You just could not stay out there on those Keys."

Many veterans even kept their cabins darkened at night so the light wouldn't attract mosquitoes, Scott said. "That didn't happen every night, but we didn't have any light—half of those shacks were not lighted during June and July, and some nights you could not go outside of the shacks without the mosquitoes swarming all over you."

A group of vets met with Sam Cutler and told him they wanted to be transferred to other camps to get away from the relentless pests. Cutler said he couldn't do that, and the vets said they would quit if they had to stay in the mosquito-infested Keys. Camp administrators decided to bring in new weapons to fight the insects. Vets assigned to the recently created Camp 5 were given the job of mosquito control. A mosquito-control crew from Camp 5 constantly patrolled the islands. In those long-ago days before environmental consciousness, the crew sprayed puddles of standing water with oil to prevent mosquitoes from breeding there.

Meanwhile, more vets arrived in the Keys. Ira Hatch, who was from the tiny town of Savage in the northwest corner of Mississippi, was typical of the vets who came to the islands looking for a new start.

"Recently [it] got so I could not get work, could not hold a job," Hatch said. "I was cooking in Washington and working on lunch counters, worked several different places. Could not make a living, $12, $14, $16 a week, twelve hours a day and seven days a week."

Soon after the July storm that so impressed John Ambrose, Sam Cutler went to the U.S. Weather Bureau's office in Miami to have the agency verify the accuracy of three barometers that would be put at the work camps.

Barometers have been around for hundreds of years, but they still are an effective way to monitor the approach of severe weather. It's difficult to think of air as having weight, but it does, and the weight is expressed as atmospheric pressure. In the seventeenth century, Italian physicist Evangelista Torricelli discovered that changes in atmospheric pressure had an odd effect on mercury. Torricelli invented the first barometer by filling a long glass tube with mercury and then turning the tube upside down and placing its open end into a small cistern of mercury. When bad weather caused the atmospheric pressure to decrease—that is, when the air became lighter—there was less pressure exerted on the mercury in the cistern. The mercury in the cistern would rise, and this allowed the mercury in the tube to drop. By marking the glass tube to measure inches, Torricelli could accurately monitor changes in atmospheric pressure.

When the weather is calm at sea level, the column of mercury in a barometer will stay at 29.92 inches on the glass tube. Barometers quickly became standard equipment on sailing ships when mariners discovered that the approach of severe weather at sea caused the mercury in the glass tube to fall to a lower level.

The hurricanes that form over the ocean, marked by extreme low pressure, have evoked fear and respect since prehistoric times. Indians living near the Atlantic called the powerful storms of late summer "hurracan," which also was their word for "evil spirit." The powerful storms have sent countless ships to the bottom of the Atlantic. The barometer gave European sailors a chance, at least, to detect and avoid these terrible storms.

The always cautious Sam Cutler—who, like the ancient philosopher Socrates, was more focused on what he didn't know than what he knew—wanted to know more about hurricanes. While at the Weather Bureau's Miami office, he dropped in on meteorologist Ernest Carson. Cutler, true to his training as a safety officer, wanted to understand the threat hurricanes posed to the vets on the Keys. He also told Carson he wanted to receive any hurricane warnings issued by the Miami office.

Carson's Miami office was responsible for monitoring conditions from the northern end of Key Largo to West Palm Beach. Conditions in Islamorada, where the work camps were headquartered, were monitored by the Weather Bureau office in Key West, and hurricane warnings for Islamorada were issued by the Weather Bureau's office in Jacksonville. But Carson told Cutler that he'd be glad to give him copies of any warnings received by the Miami office.

Carson also passed along a weatherman's rule of thumb—a hurricane does not have to strike the Keys to cause hazardous conditions on the islands. Anytime a hurricane approaches the Keys or passes through the Straits of Florida—the narrow body of water that separates the Keys from Cuba and The Bahamas—conditions are very dangerous on the islands, Carson warned.

The information undoubtedly made an impression on Cutler, who had spent his career devising ways to minimize risks in the workplace.

The reason for the danger is simple—the Straits of Florida are only about 90 miles wide, and a hurricane can be several hundred miles wide, with hurricane-force winds of at least 74 mph extending 50 miles or more all around the eye of the storm. A hurricane in the northern hemisphere rotates counterclockwise, and the winds on the right side of the hurricane's eye are even more dangerous because they have the added force of the hurricane's forward speed. Thus, if a hurricane has 100 mph winds at its center and the storm is moving at 15 mph, the winds on the right side of the eye will be 115 mph.

Sailors refer to this part of a hurricane as the dangerous semicircle. A ship at sea will go hundreds of miles out of its way to avoid this part of a storm.

The winds on the left side of the eye are less dangerous because the storm's forward motion reduces their force. This means that the storm with 100 mph winds at its center traveling at 15 mph will have winds of only 85 mph on its left side. Sailors refer to this side of a storm as the navigable semicircle, and if a ship's captain must sail near a hurricane, he will try to position his vessel so that it is on the left side of the eye's forward motion.

A hurricane moving westward through the Straits of Florida subjects the Keys to the situation that sailors go to great lengths to try to avoid. The islands are squarely within the hurricane's dangerous semicircle. Unlike a ship at sea, however, the Keys can't maneuver away from the storm.

A hurricane in the straits is "one of the worst situations that you can get on the Florida Keys," Ivan Tannehill, assistant chief of the U.S. Weather Bureau's Forecasting Division, said in 1935. The stronger winds on the hurricane's dangerous semicircle pile up water against the islands, he said.

Weather Bureau officials had long ago realized that one of their biggest problems was crafting hurricane advisories that alerted people to danger without creating panic. It was a difficult line to walk—so difficult, in fact, that the Weather Bureau reminded meteorologists of the agency's policy of issuing warnings in bulletins sent out every summer before each hurricane season. The bulletin reminded meteorologists that when they ordered the red-and-black hurricane warning flags to be hoisted at coastal stations, they were telling residents that "there is immediate need of precautionary measures to save life and property within the area encompassed by the warning."

In other words, if you see the hurricane warning flags flying, you are in danger and it's up to you to protect yourself.

The policy clearly defined the limits of the bureau's responsibilities. Forecasters should alert coastal residents that a hurricane could be heading their way, but they couldn't take responsibility for seeing that residents heeded those warnings. Still, Weather Bureau officials assumed people living on the coast wouldn't need much prompting to take action to protect their lives and property.

"Having given the warnings to constituted authorities and advised them as to precautionary measures that may be proper, the local official has done his full duty," the Weather Bureau statement said. "Whether or not the persons so warned do actually take the necessary precautions is a matter of their own responsibility."

The Conchs weren't likely to ignore an advisory telling them a hurricane was heading in their general direction. But newcomers—especially those who had been through a hurricane or two and thought they knew all about the storms—were another matter entirely.

In the 1920s new residents poured into Miami and South Florida, and thousands of them were killed by two powerful hurricanes. In September 1926 the eye of the worst hurricane on record at that time passed over downtown Miami. When the calm eye arrived, dozens of newcomers thought the storm was over and poured into the streets to see the damage. Many of them were killed when the backside of the hurricane's eye wall—the band of thunderstorms that forms around a hurricane's center—swept across the city.

In September 1928 thousands of migrant workers—most of them black—had arrived in the small towns around Lake Okeechobee to harvest the season's crops. They were completely unprepared for a vicious hurricane that was even more powerful than the storm that hit Miami two years earlier. This hurricane shoved the huge, shallow lake's waters out of its banks and sent an eight-foot wall of water rolling across the Everglades. Around 3,000 people were killed, most of them poor black migrants.

The Weather Bureau was harshly criticized after both tragedies for not providing adequate warning. But a hurricane detection system that relied heavily on ships at sea for information about the location of storms was certain to be flawed, and any Weather Bureau bulletin that included the hurricane's location was basically an educated guess.

Yet the Weather Bureau had still boasted that no hurricane would go unnoticed as it approached U.S. shores beginning in the summer of 1935.

While Sam Cutler was learning about hurricanes, a new administrator for the Florida ERA arrived in Islamorada on August 1. Ray W. Sheldon was a Massachusetts native who'd lived in Florida since 1923. Sheldon was a construction engineer whom Ghent had hired in 1933 as director of safety for the Florida ERA in Volusia County. Sheldon had made a favorable impression on other Florida ERA administrators. His new job would be supervising the three veterans work camps in the Keys.

Sheldon's wife had died unexpectedly in November 1934. But his life seemed to be on the upswing in August 1935. Besides moving from Daytona Beach to the Keys to start a new job, he planned to get married again. His bride-to-be was Gayle Colvert, 27, who had been working as a purchasing agent in Lakeland.

Sheldon had taken on a very difficult job. He was responsible for supervising about 700 men, many of whom were sullen and had little use for authority. Managing them efficiently would require an unusual combination of skills, and Sheldon's training and experience was that of an engineer, not a social worker or psychologist.

While Sheldon had impressed his supervisors, the men who worked under him were learning that he could be a difficult boss. He was dictatorial, wouldn't listen to the advice of his subordinates, and had a compulsive need to remind those under him that he was in charge.

"I found that advice or constructive criticism was definitely out of order," said John Good, who was a storekeeper for the camps. "It seemed that in every case when we men who knew what should be done made the proper suggestion to Mr. Sheldon, we were never allowed to even finish stating the suggestion, much less being asked for advice as to what order should be given and how those orders should be carried out."

Many of the men around Sheldon decided to just keep their mouths shut.

"I thought Mr. Sheldon was the type that wouldn't listen to anybody else, and would do what he wanted to do, and what I could say would have no effect," said Wilbur Jones, an auditor for the camps. "Therefore, I would probably be better off if I just kept my opinion to myself."

Ghent's insistence on believing that everything would go as he planned and Sheldon's assertion of authority by refusing to listen to his subordinates would prove to be tragic flaws. Ghent and Sheldon were responsible for the safety of hundreds of men, yet a clear and unmistakable threat to the safety of the men in their care would be denied by one and ignored by the other.

Ghent came down to Islamorada to meet with Sheldon in early August. His instructions to the new administrator for handling the veterans were simple—"make them happy." Ghent also discussed hurricane preparation with Sheldon. He told Sheldon that they would use a special train to evacuate the veterans in the event of a storm. And he told Sheldon about the recently purchased barometers for each of the work camps to help monitor the movements of any hurricanes.

Unfortunately, the instruments couldn't foretell the approach of a serious political storm brewing just over the horizon.

On August 6, 1935, Ghent and his boss, Conrad Van Hyning, and another Florida ERA administrator, R. G. Unkrich, boarded a train for Washington, DC. The veterans work program in Florida had grown steadily since the spring, but Ghent, Van Hyning, and Unkrich were concerned because federal officials in Washington seemed to be ignoring them. Ghent was especially frustrated because he felt that he had not received any definite instructions from Washington since he'd taken the job four months earlier. The Florida administrators wanted federal officials to tell them where the vets work program was going and how it was going to achieve its goals.

While the Florida administrators tried to get some direction, *New York Times* reporter Charles McLean arrived in Kingstree, South Carolina, to look at a work camp there housing veterans who were building a public golf course in the little town about 75 miles north of Charleston.

McLean toured the camps August 8 and 9, and, like Edward Folliard of the *Washington Post*, he found little to his liking. In a biting report he called the veterans work program "one of the strangest New Deal undertakings." He described the men in the South Carolina camp as "shell-shocked, whiskey-shocked and depression-shocked," and reported that 20 of them had wrecked a floor of the county jail after they'd been arrested during a recent payday drinking binge. Their behavior kept Kingstree "continually disturbed."

F. E. Simpson, a veteran at the South Carolina camp, fired back with an open letter accusing the *New York Times* reporter of having a drinking problem of his own that was so serious it had impaired his ability to accurately report what he had seen at the camp. The letter, published in the *Key Veteran News*, said that McLean had gone on a "debauch on moonshine" during his visit. Simpson said McLean was so drunk on August 9 that a group of Kingstree businessmen who came to his hotel room for an interview refused to talk to him.

As the *Times* bashed the veterans work program, Conrad Van Hyning learned in Washington that support for the work camps was falling rapidly in the Roosevelt Administration. Federal officials had decided to make major changes in the construction work in the Keys.

"We felt that the bridge project had not turned out to be a practical project for their work on the Keys [and] the camp situation wasn't satisfactory," Van Hyning said later.

The day after the *New York Times* story was published, the Florida ERA administrators prepared to leave Washington. On the afternoon of August 12, a discouraged Fred Ghent checked out of his hotel and made reservations to catch the 11:45 p.m. train for Florida.

A few hours before he had to catch his train, Ghent met Van Hyning, who had more bad news. He told Ghent that he would not be retained by the Florida ERA after the camps were closed.

The astonished Ghent immediately canceled his train reservations, deciding instead to stay in Washington one more day to try to scrounge up some job prospects.

On August 16 WPA administrator Harry Hopkins announced that all the work camps in Florida and South Carolina would be closed November 1. The veterans would be assigned to another form of relief work or transferred to the CCC, which would take over the bridge and road construction project in the Keys.

The *New York Times* gave itself a pat on the back as it reported Hopkins's announcement. A *Times* editorial claimed that federal officials decided to close the camps after the newspaper had published stories "revealing their existence and describing conditions in them."

As the news of the closing swept through the veterans camps in the Keys, the season's first hurricane stirred in the warm waters east of Puerto Rico. The storm gained strength as it moved northwestward toward the United States, but around August 20 the hurricane made a sharp turn to the north and headed away from the mainland.

While the hurricane blew itself out over the open waters of the Atlantic Ocean, *Time* magazine gave another kick to the dying veterans work program. The August 26 edition included a story that referred to the camps as "playgrounds for derelicts." The story added that the 11 veterans work camps—7 in Florida and 4 in South Carolina—housed about 2,500 "derelicts." About half the men in the camps were "psychopaths," *Time* said.

On August 26 Ray Sheldon married Gayle Colvert in a quiet civil ceremony in Miami. He didn't have time for an immediate honeymoon, but he brought his new bride to the camps with the intention of taking off for a few days as soon as he could.

In the Keys the veterans tried to cope with the news that the camps would be closed. On Friday, August 30, many of them were morose despite the approach of a convergence of events that otherwise would have had them in high spirits. A payday had arrived, the long Labor Day weekend awaited, and their beloved baseball team would play its first road game in the Dade County League in Ojus, near Miami, on the Monday holiday.

At 11:15 Friday morning, camp officials started handing out pay envelopes to the veterans at Camp 1 under the watchful eye of Monroe County chief deputy sheriff Louis Maloney. When the pay call ended at Camp 1, the paymasters moved down the islands to the other two camps, stopping first at Camp 5 and then at Camp 3.

Many vets departed immediately. Some headed north for Miami and Miami Beach. Others left for Key West.

Predictably, the payday ritual of heavy boozing began among many vets who hadn't left the camps.

"When we finished at Camp #3, it was around 2:15 or 2:30," Maloney said. "When we got back to the camps paid off first, about 75 percent of the men were drunk. This condition continued as long as they had money—as long as they could beg, borrow, or steal."

Civilian workers in the camps started clearing out for the holiday as well. Albert Davis, the barber at Camp 1, paused on his way out to check the latest notices on the camp's bulletin board. "The bulletin board at Camp 1 showed a notice on Friday guaranteeing to remove the men from the camp within six hours after receipt of the first storm warning," Davis said.

Scarcely noticed amid the gloom, departures, and drinking was a bulletin from the U.S. Weather Bureau released at 9:30 p.m. Friday—far too late for publication in Friday's papers. Another tropical storm was brewing in the warm Atlantic.

"Conditions remain unsettled and slightly squally east of The Bahamas and north of Turks Island with evidence of a weak circulation but no strong winds," the bulletin read. "Seems to be working north-northwest or northward."

By Saturday afternoon only about 400 vets were left in the work camps. Many who remained settled down to read the August 31 edition of the *Key Veteran News*.

The newspaper tried to buck up its readers' sagging spirits by reminding them that no official orders to close the camps had been received from Washington, and until those orders were issued the men should consider Hopkins's announcement a "rumor."

Camp 5 correspondent John Ambrose also continued his mocking commentary on the hurricane season and the frequent rumors that a storm was bearing down on them.

"Every day we hear discussion and dissertation upon the subject of the big wind, that all destroying tropical hurricane which has been fast approaching for the past month," Ambrose wrote in his weekly news column. "Where is the consarned thing? Is it possible that a hurricane of the proportions reported has been lost, or simply expended its velocity upon the thin atmosphere without even considering a visit to Camp Five? Aren't we important enough for the consideration of even a decrepit, spavined has-been of a tropical zephyr? Better luck next month, boys. Seek and ye shall find!"

It was a hellish thing to wish for. Around 1 p.m. that same day another bulletin from the U.S. Weather Bureau rattled across the Teletypes in newsrooms and Coast Guard stations.

"Tropical disturbance of small diameter but considerable intensity central about 60 miles east of Long Island Bahamas apparently moving westnorthwestward attended by strong shifting winds and probably gales near center," the bulletin said. "Caution advised southeastern Bahamas and ships in that vicinity."

Unfortunately for the veterans, this "tropical disturbance" would be anything but the playful zephyr that Ambrose had described in one of his earlier columns, and it was going to do a lot more than chase away the mosquitoes for a few days.

CHAPTER THREE

A Wind Stirs in the Atlantic

When the surface temperature of the Atlantic Ocean reaches 80 degrees Fahrenheit, the water becomes a launching pad for hurricanes.

The warm water helps create rising currents of warm air, which lowers the atmospheric pressure where the air is rising. The rising air and diminished pressure pull in more air around the developing weather system, and the air currents can pick up a circular motion imparted by the rotation of the Earth.

As the air currents converge at the point where the atmospheric pressure is lowest, the rotation gains momentum. A center of circulation forms. The weather system turns faster, and the winds gradually increase their speed. As the convergence becomes stronger, the winds increase and the atmospheric pressure around the center drops a little more. This causes more air to be pulled toward the center. Then the winds increase a little more, and the pressure drops still more. Warm water can cause this process to accelerate, and the warmer the water the faster the process speeds up. When this happens, it's as though nature has cranked up a huge rotary engine that's made of water, heat, and water vapor.

As summer progresses in the northern hemisphere, the intense heat of equatorial Africa generates thunderstorms that roll off the continent's west coast and ride the easterly trade winds across the Atlantic Ocean. As these disorganized thunderstorms—known as tropical waves—browse across water that has been cooking beneath the summer sun, they can pick up the circular movement and draw tremendous energy from the warm saltwater.

The waters around The Bahamas and the tip of the Florida peninsula are often at least 80 degrees by the time the long Labor Day weekend arrives. Any tropical wave or storm that browses over this tepid water can get a jolt of energy capable of triggering a Jekyll and Hyde transformation. The moist heat from the water can quickly convert a weather system whose worst feature is some nasty squalls into a powerful, dangerous storm.

At 11 a.m. on Saturday, August 31, 1935, the surface temperature of the ocean between Florida and The Bahamas was 86 degrees. The water had become high-octane hurricane fuel.

Despite its fearsomeness, a hurricane is a surprisingly delicate thing—especially in its formative stages—and exceptionally warm water alone isn't enough to create a deadly storm. During a typical summer and fall, about 60 tropical waves blow off Africa and begin their journey across the Atlantic. Most of these waves become nothing worse than bad thunderstorms with some gusty winds.

But sometimes something more happens. Each summer anywhere from 5 to 15 tropical waves encounter conditions that allow them to develop into more violent and dangerous storms. The process starts when the disturbed weather picks up the spin from the Earth. Once set in motion, the disturbance can coil tighter and tighter as it draws energy from the warm water. Its winds grow fierce as the atmospheric pressure at its center drops and more air rushes into the vacuum.

If conditions allow, the storm continues to develop. It officially becomes a hurricane when its strongest winds reach 74 mph. If the momentum continues, the hurricane becomes stronger and stronger. A tightly coiled band of thunderstorms forms around the center of the hurricane. This band, known as the eye wall, contains the hurricane's fiercest winds. But inside the eye wall, all is calm as the rapidly converging winds hit the superheated air and spiral upward.

Even when a storm manages to become a hurricane, however, there's still only a slight chance that it will develop into what meteorologists consider a major storm—one with winds exceeding 110 mph.

A hurricane that grows into a true monster with the power to level cities—that is, one with winds exceeding 156 mph and a barometric pressure reading around 27.00 inches—is a rarity among rarities. And like so many other aspects of hurricanes, the process by which a devastating storm forms isn't fully understood.

When a hurricane does manage to reach this supernatural intensity, it usually doesn't maintain it for very long. Subtle changes in conditions can cause the hurricane to weaken quickly and dramatically. Even the strongest hurricanes can become their own worst enemies. Sometimes these storms form a second eye wall around the original one. This second eye wall acts like a noose, literally strangling the hurricane and throttling its strength, as though Mother Nature herself were resorting to some desperate last-ditch method to control her own raging creation.

The tropical disturbance that formed east of The Bahamas during the last days of August 1935 would encounter those exceedingly rare, perfect conditions that foster rapid and unhindered strengthening. After it crossed The Bahamas, the warm waters and minimal upper-level winds allowed it to coil tighter and tighter until it became, for a while at least, one of the most powerful natural forces ever to roam the planet. Unlike most hurricanes that reach this intensity, however, it would hold on to its unworldly strength long enough to unleash it against men who were almost completely helpless before its power.

But when Fred Ghent called the Florida ERA office at the Hotel Matecumbe around 10 a.m. Saturday, the disturbance wasn't much more than a minimal tropical storm as it approached The Bahamas.

Ghent called to tell Ray Sheldon that he could take a couple days off with his new wife. The newlyweds planned to take the leisurely ferry ride to No Name Key, then drive from there to Key West for the holiday weekend.

Elsewhere, others were making their own weekend plans.

In Homestead two sisters, Myrtle and Sarah Hodge, ages 15 and 13, respectively, had been given permission from their parents to visit a young friend in the Keys. Despite the summer heat, Myrtle Hodge decided to take along a sweater, and the teenager stuffed a comb and a small makeup compact into the sweater pocket.

In Islamorada, Rita Berteau, the 14-year-old daughter of FEC section foreman Paul Berteau, looked forward to the arrival of the Hodge sisters. The girls had become friends when Rita stayed with the Hodge family while attending school in Homestead. Rita planned to attend a Labor Day softball game in Islamorada with her pals.

On Saturday, August 31, Bascom Grooms Jr., 13, was trying to squeeze the last bit of fun out of the summer before the start of school on September 3. He'd spent the previous few weeks with friends in Tavernier, but now the end of his vacation was fast approaching. On Monday he would have to board the train to go back to Key West, where his father, Bascom Sr., was president of the municipal electric company and one of the city's most prominent businessmen.

Things seemed about to turn around for Bascom's older sister Rosalind, who was 21. Her impulsive marriage on August 21, 1934, to Lieutenant (j.g.)

George Palmer, a young naval officer with a bright future that she'd met in Key West, had been reported in the *Miami Daily News* as "[a] marriage of interest to friends throughout Southern Florida." She'd lived briefly with her husband in San Diego where he was stationed, but she'd suddenly returned to her hometown in the summer of 1935, months before her first anniversary.

She took a job as a court stenographer in Key West. She didn't say much about her marriage, other than it was over and she'd started divorce proceedings.

Her failed marriage hadn't discouraged her from continuing her search for true love, however. She quickly rejoined her circle of friends, and she had no difficulty finding young men to take her out. The brown-eyed, athletic brunette loved to dress well and had a special fondness for white pumps. She was considered by many to be the most attractive woman in Key West.

But Rosalind Grooms Palmer didn't take herself or her looks too seriously. Her impending divorce had only sharpened her wit, and she thought her legs were too skinny for her to be really attractive.

Soon after returning to Key West, she fell in love with George Pepper, the nephew of a prominent Tallahassee attorney named Claude Pepper, who was beginning a career that would eventually make him a legend in Florida politics. Rosalind intended to marry George Pepper as soon as her divorce was final. Pepper, who was only a few weeks away from his 20th birthday, worked as a steward at Camp 3. The fun-loving young man was known for racing up and down the narrow roads in the Keys.

In July the couple visited a photographer's studio in Miami and posed in front of a backdrop painted to look like a departing train. George draped his arm around Rosalind's shoulders, and she gazed at him with an adoring smile. From a railing resembling the observation platform of a Pullman car hung a sign: "Honeymoon Special."

On Thursday, August 29, as the Labor Day weekend approached, Rosalind sat down at her typewriter to bang out a note to her kid brother. Bascom had recently written a long letter to his family back in Key West. Rosalind's response was brief, teasing, and affectionate.

"Maybe someday I'll learn to treat the family to long letters like yours," she began.

Rosalind said she'd like to be with Bascom enjoying the mosquitoes and sand flies, "but I'm through with trips for a little while."

That was a polite fiction. She'd be spending the long weekend in the Upper Keys with George. Her boyfriend shot several photos of her standing on a dock in Tavernier, stylishly dressed in a skirt, short-sleeved high-neck top, stockings, and the ever-present white pumps. She added a bit of color to her outfit by tying a bright, multicolored scarf around her waist.

"Keep your nose clean and otherwise be a gentleman," Rosalind said in closing her note to her brother. She included 50 cents in the envelope so Bascom could buy an ice cream sundae for a young friend named Elizabeth.

In Miami, Roland Craig was doing some grocery shopping Saturday when he overheard two other customers talking about a storm that had formed near The Bahamas. Craig immediately pricked up his ears. He hurriedly finished his shopping and called the U.S. Weather Bureau's Miami office.

"I asked them if that storm continued on its present course would it strike in along around Long Key, because Long Key is only four miles from my place," Craig said. "The man from the Weather Bureau office told me it would if it kept going like the present reports."

Alarmed, Craig immediately called his store and made plans to return to the Keys early Sunday morning. He had a lot of work to do to get his property ready for the blow that he thought would arrive soon.

Sam Cutler was thinking about fishing as he drove down to Camp 3 Saturday morning. His job as an assistant administrator had required him to stay in the camps every Sunday since May, and he was hoping this would be the weekend when he'd finally get a break. He'd been invited to go on an overnight fishing trip Sunday and had mentioned this to Ray Sheldon, hoping his boss would take the weekend duty so he could get away. But Sheldon had been noncommittal, and Cutler knew Sheldon was thinking about going to Key West for the weekend with his new bride.

Around 12:30 p.m. Saturday, Cutler left Camp 3 to return to the Hotel Matecumbe. He was thinking again of his fishing invitation during the short drive back to headquarters when he saw a familiar looking car approaching from the opposite direction. It was Sheldon's Chevrolet. As the car passed him, Cutler saw Gayle and Ray Sheldon in the automobile. Cutler knew they were headed to the foot of Lower Matecumbe Key to catch the ferry to Key West. He disconsolately resigned himself to spending yet another weekend in the camps.

At 1 p.m. Sheldon drove his car aboard the ferry, which was scheduled to arrive at No Name Key around 5:30 p.m. From there Sheldon would have a 43-mile drive to Key West.

As the ferry pulled out of its berth, the Weather Bureau issued another advisory on the developing storm. Using information from weather stations and observers and ships at sea, the advisory reported that the small "tropical disturbance" had attained "considerable intensity" and was about 60 miles east of The Bahamas.

This advisory was waiting for Cutler when he walked into the camps' administrative offices at the Hotel Matecumbe. The disappointment about his canceled fishing trip vanished as he studied the bulletin, which said the storm was "moving west-northwestward attended by strong shifting winds and probably gales near center. Caution advised southeastern Bahamas and ships in that vicinity."

Cutler went to a map on the wall and carefully placed a thumbtack at the approximate position of the hurricane. Then he sat down at his desk and started making phone calls. He stayed at the desk well into the night, carefully putting more thumbtacks into the map each time he received new information.

As Cutler fretted over the map, the usual payday weekend drinking binge was well under way among the 400 or so men who'd decided to stay in the work camps during the holiday. But the recent announcement that the camps would soon close gave the vets more sorrows than usual to drown.

"These men who didn't leave the camp for the holidays were drinking more heavily than I had seen them over a period of about a year since the camp began," said John Good, the storekeeper for the work camps.

By Saturday afternoon the storm advisories had gotten the attention of newspapers. The *Miami Daily News*, an afternoon paper, carried the U.S. Weather Bureau's 1 p.m. advisory in a small box on its front page.

The *Key West Citizen* also was an afternoon newspaper, and as the departing sun sank slowly into the Gulf of Mexico and bathed the island city in its soft, flattering light, author Ernest Hemingway put down his pencil and settled into a chair on his porch to sip a drink and read the local paper—in private.

Handyman Toby Bruce had recently finished the six-foot-tall brick wall around the writer's property. It was a curious structure because the paving bricks Bruce used for the wall hadn't been intended for such a purpose, and besides, Bruce never claimed to know anything about bricklaying. He'd done the best he could, but the courses of brick were not straight. They rose and fell slightly, and the mortar between them was smeared on instead of smoothly applied and pointed.

But Bruce's effort more than satisfied Hemingway. At last the author could relax on his porch without enduring the prying eyes of tourists, and he hoped that his disappearance from public view would also diminish his appeal as a tourist attraction.

Hemingway also was happy with the day's work he'd completed in his large studio behind his home. He'd finished one short story and started work on another.

But he was jolted out of his self-satisfaction when a small headline near the bottom of the *Citizen's* front page caught his eye. "Storm Warning," it read. Beneath the headline was the U.S. Weather Bureau's 1 p.m. advisory saying that a "tropical disturbance" had formed east of The Bahamas. The *Citizen* reported that Gerald S. Kennedy of the Weather Bureau's Key West office said the disturbance was about 500 miles southeast of the city.

It didn't matter to Hemingway that the disturbance hadn't been classified as a hurricane or that it was hundreds of miles from his home. He pulled out his barometer and storm chart and started making calculations and plans.

He figured that, at its current speed and direction of travel, the storm could strike Key West around noon on Labor Day. He wasn't willing to gamble that the storm would not strengthen, or that it would not affect Key West even if it didn't make a direct hit on the city. He decided to get up early Sunday morning to start getting his house and boat ready for a blow.

Many miles up the Florida coast, Fred Ghent also was reading about the storm in one of Jacksonville's afternoon newspapers.

At about the same time that news of the storm was ruining Hemingway's good mood, the S.S. *Dixie* was leaving its berth in the New Orleans harbor and gliding down the Mississippi River toward the Gulf of Mexico. The *Dixie* had been scheduled to sail from New Orleans at 11 a.m., but Captain Einar Sundstrom decided to postpone the departure by seven hours to wait for some passengers who were delayed when their eastbound train derailed in Texas.

Sundstrom had only recently been given command of the *Dixie*. When he was appointed master of the ship on July 5, 1935, he was, at the age of 50, the youngest ship's captain in the Morgan Line. Despite his relative youth, however, he was a seasoned sailor who'd been breathing salty air all his life.

"You've always got to be on guard against the oceans," he said upon taking command of the *Dixie*. "They may look peaceful for a long time. That's your good luck. But you know the time is coming when the sea is going to rise and hand you all it's got in the way of trouble—and that's plenty."

Sundstrom grew up in the small seaport of Brunswick, Georgia, and got his first job on a ship in 1901 when he was 16 years old. He went to work for the Morgan Line soon afterward. When the United States entered World War I, Sundstrom became a lieutenant commander in the U.S. Navy and commanded the U.S.S. *Connelly*, a fuel and supply ship, through waters infested with German submarines.

Sundstrom returned to the Morgan Line after the war and in 1921 was given command of the *Tamaihu*, at the time the world's largest tanker. His excellent record at the helm of the Morgan Line's freighters prompted company officials to promote him to the command of passenger vessels.

The *Dixie* was the flagship of the Morgan Line's passenger ships. The 426-foot, 8,100-ton ship had been launched in Kearny, New Jersey, in January 1928. The *Dixie* was a state-of-the-art ship with luxurious accommodations.

First-class passengers traveled comfortably in staterooms decorated in American colonial style. They could stroll around the ship on a promenade deck that was partially enclosed in sliding glass windows. The ship also had such luxuries as lounges and music rooms with fireplaces, dance floors, game decks, and a sun parlor. More than 120 crew members worked aboard the *Dixie*.

Two massive steam turbine engines provided more than 7,000 horsepower to the ship's single propeller, and the ship had a top speed of 16 knots, or about 18 mph. The *Dixie* also was equipped with the most advanced directional technology that was available at the time—a radiotelegraph, a radio direction finder, and a gyrocompass.

On Saturday, August 31, Sundstrom hastily penned a letter to his wife, Marie, at their home in the Long Island village of Little Neck, New York. The captain told his wife and grown daughters Florence and Lillian that he'd delayed the *Dixie*'s departure from New Orleans by seven hours. Still, he said he expected to make New York on schedule by Thursday "if we have decent weather."

Sundstrom knew about the U.S. Weather Bureau's storm advisories and knew the danger of running into a bad storm in the Straits of Florida, where there's very little room to maneuver away from a blow. But storms at sea were nothing new to him. In 1932, while commanding the passenger liner S.S. *Momus*, he'd safely weathered a hurricane off the Florida coast. He thought he could avoid the worst of this disturbance as well. Besides, if he was going to meet his schedule, he didn't have time to wait and see what the storm would do. He'd have to push the *Dixie* hard enough as it was to make New York on time.

Rough weather was the last thing in passengers' minds as the *Dixie* sailed into the Gulf of Mexico. Florence Steiler, a passenger from San Francisco, joined the carefree crowd on deck to take in the Gulf Coast sunset and enjoy the first caress of the salty sea breezes. There was a holiday mood among those leaning on the deck rails and pointing to the sliver of a new moon that was just becoming visible in the darkening sky.

"Little did anyone realize when we sailed down the placid Mississippi, with the new moon just showing, what lay in store for us," Steiler said.

Almost half the passengers were from New York City and its surrounding suburbs. There were two newlywed couples on their honeymoons, and teachers returning from last-minute vacations before the start of the school year. Among the teachers was Grace Nichols of Philadelphia, who was returning from a visit with her sister in San Francisco. Nichols had flown out to California. But her sister fretted so much about the safety of those newfangled passenger airplanes that Nichols decided to make her return trip to Philadelphia by taking the train to New Orleans and boarding the *Dixie* there.

There also was a smattering of passengers whose home addresses on Manhattan's Upper East Side and in suburban Westchester County were badges of their prosperity and social prominence.

A few were traveling with small but precious personal items. Musician Cal Calman had his eighteenth-century Storioni violin. Anna Belcher brought along a friend she couldn't bear to travel without—a little Boston terrier named Skippy. Her husband, Frank, a former opera singer who ran a tobacco shop tucked amid the theaters on Broadway, was just as attached to Skippy as his wife and had tried to talk her out of taking the dog on the trip, but Anna won out. Skippy, however, would have to make the trip deep in the hold of the *Dixie* in the ship's kennel.

Ed Sheeran had planned to spend the Labor Day weekend with his wife in their comfortable home in Coral Gables. He left his job site at Lower Matecumbe Key late Saturday afternoon but decided to stop for a haircut. Around 8:30 p.m. Saturday he climbed into a barber's chair in Tavernier. When the barber finished, Sheeran went next door to McKenzie's Drugstore to see if he had any phone messages.

There were two. Fred Ghent had tried to reach him from Jacksonville, and B. M. Duncan, the state highway department engineer in Key West, had called to tell him that a tropical storm had formed near The Bahamas.

Sheeran had weathered many hurricanes since the terrible 1906 blow, and he'd learned not to play guessing games with them. He immediately forgot about spending the holiday weekend at home. He had a lot of expensive equipment that could be destroyed by rough weather, and he wasn't willing to wait to start securing it and see if the storm was going to come his way. He rounded up as many of his work crew as he could find in Tavernier and told them to be back at the job site at Lower Matecumbe Key at six o'clock the following morning. Then he got into his car and headed back down the islands. He knew he had a busy couple of days ahead of him.

At 9:30 p.m. Saturday, the U.S. Weather Bureau bulletin ordered Coast Guard stations, lighthouses, and weather stations from Miami to Fort Pierce to display northeast storm warnings. Along the coast, lighthouse keepers and stationmasters lit two red lanterns and hung them one above the other. Sailors and coastal residents who saw these lights knew instantly that this meant a violent storm was approaching, and its winds would begin from the northeast.

The Weather Bureau also issued an advisory. The storm had reached the northern end of Long Island in the southeastern Bahamas and was moving west-northwest very slowly, "attended by strong shifting winds and squalls over a considerable area and probably gale force near center." The advisory said the center of the storm would reach Andros Island—another island in The Bahamas chain, about 170 miles southeast of Miami—sometime late Saturday night or early Sunday morning.

Gayle and Ray Sheldon arrived in Key West around 7 p.m. Saturday. They had a late dinner and decided to go for a stroll around 10:30 p.m. Gayle stopped to buy some postcards.

As Sheldon waited for his wife to pay for her purchases, he happened to notice the same storm warning on the front page of the *Key West Citizen* that had jolted Ernest Hemingway out of his self-satisfaction.

The couple returned immediately to their hotel, and Sheldon called the Weather Bureau's Key West office.

At the bureau's two-story, concrete-and-stucco office on Front Street, meteorologist Gerald Kennedy answered the ringing telephone around 11 p.m. Sheldon told Kennedy that he was in charge of the veterans work camps on the Upper Keys and asked the meteorologist to update him on the storm.

Kennedy told Sheldon that conditions on the Upper Keys "did not appear very alarming" at the moment. The weatherman said he'd call Sheldon if anything changed during the night.

At that moment there didn't seem to be much to worry about. The disturbance was little more than a windy rainstorm when it crossed The Bahamas Saturday night. The highest winds that were reported reached only 46 mph.

Sheldon climbed into bed around 1 a.m. He intended to stay awake just in case Kennedy should call, but he soon fell asleep.

As Sheldon dozed in the wee hours of Sunday, September 1, Kennedy received barometric pressure readings from observers stationed in Miami and along the Keys. Something was happening with the storm, and the meteorologist didn't like what he saw. The storm had reached the warm, energy-laden saltwater of the Straits of Florida. When Kennedy compared his own barometric pressure reading in Key West with those reported from Miami, he discovered the Key West reading was considerably lower than the one in Miami. That meant the storm was closer to the Keys than it was to the peninsula.

"After our immediate observations at 2 a.m. conditions looked as though the storm might prove dangerous on the Florida Keys," Kennedy said.

Around five o'clock Sunday morning, the weatherman picked up his phone and called Sheldon's hotel to advise the camps' administrator to return to Islamorada on the next ferry.

"I intended to convey there was danger in that section," Kennedy said. "It was impossible to say just where the storm would strike and just how hard it would strike, but being familiar with hurricanes I thought it would be advisable to take every precaution in advance and thought he should be on the ground [at the work camps] as early as possible."

As Kennedy hung up the phone after talking with Sheldon, a few blocks away from the Weather Bureau office Ernest Hemingway was already out of bed to start preparing his boat and property for a blow. The author wanted to pull the *Pilar* from the water, but when he went down to the dock he found a long line of boat owners waiting to do the same thing. He had too much to do to wait. He went to a hardware store, bought heavy marine rope, and tied the *Pilar* securely to her moorings at the navy yard. Then he started boarding up the windows of his house.

The rest of Key West wasn't taking any chances either. Throughout the day the sound of banging hammers could be heard all around town as residents nailed boards over windows or closed and secured hurricane shutters.

"When we got to Key West on Saturday, all of the people were talking about the storm," said Tony Lapinski, a veteran from Detroit who'd gone to Key West for the long holiday weekend. "They had their windows nailed up.

Big apartment houses, big stores and the 10-cent stores had their windows nailed up. The natives at Key West had prepared for the storm on Saturday."

M. E. Gilfond, who was now in charge of Florida ERA operations in Key West, had never been in a hurricane, but since arriving in Florida he'd talked to lots of people who had, and what he heard made him very cautious. He boarded up all the buildings that were the responsibility of his agency and sent some of his workers to scour the city's streets and remove anything that could become a deadly missile if it was picked up by a hurricane's winds. As a final safety measure, he moved all his men into barracks at the U.S. Navy base, where they'd be safer in the substantial buildings.

In Miami, store owner Roland Craig rolled out of bed before daylight. He picked up a younger friend named Jack Crow, and by 5 a.m. the two men were en route to the Keys. Craig also had a lot of work to do in the next few days.

Around 5:30 a.m. Ray Sheldon called Fred Ghent in Jacksonville to discuss the storm. Ghent told him to catch the next ferry back to the camps. Shortly before 8 a.m. Sheldon drove his car aboard the northbound ferry at No Name Key for the trip back to Lower Matecumbe Key. His brief honeymoon hadn't even lasted 24 hours. As the ferry chugged away from its slip and into Florida Bay, Sheldon and his wife settled back for the four-hour trip.

Meanwhile, Ghent called the FEC dispatcher in New Smyrna, 125 miles south of Jacksonville. Ghent wanted the railroad to add four or five passenger cars to its regularly scheduled southbound and northbound trains to allow veterans to leave the camps—provided that the Florida ERA wouldn't have to pay for them. The dispatcher told Ghent that the extra cars would be added without charge.

Ghent hung up the phone thinking that he'd given the railroad notice that the evacuation train might be needed. He assumed that the train was already assembled and waiting to be dispatched.

As the sun climbed out of the Atlantic and bathed the Keys in its sunrise, Roland Craig and Jack Crow pulled into the ferry landing at Lower Matecumbe Key, where Ed Sheeran and his crew were hard at work securing their construction equipment. Craig parked his car and the two men started walking down the railroad tracks and bridges to Craig Key. When Craig reached his store, he called a friend who had access to the Weather Bureau's latest advisories. The friend promised to keep Craig updated on the forecasts.

Meanwhile, Sheeran moved his big dredge, the *Sarasota*, into the 1,000-foot-long canal he'd dug months earlier. The little man-made creek would provide the expensive dredge with some protection from winds and high seas.

Sheeran was keeping his eye on the weather, and he was seeing some ominous signs of impending trouble.

One sign of the approach of a hurricane is the long, rhythmic swells that start rolling in several days before the storm's arrival. The hurricane's winds create huge waves around its spinning eye. The waves are pushed out in all directions and become smaller as they move away from the storm center. Although the waves lose some of their size, they retain their energy and become swells, and they can travel for more than a thousand miles ahead of the hurricane when the storm is over open water. They also move much faster than the storm's eye.

When the swells arrive at a coastline, the normal pattern of breaking waves is altered. Under normal conditions as many as 12 to 15 breakers per minute roll onto a beach. But hurricane swells slow that rhythm dramatically so that only three to five waves per minute will be breaking on the beach. And the breakers caused by the swells will be much larger than the normal waves.

If the direction from which the swells approach the beach does not change, it's an indication that the center of the hurricane is approaching that stretch of the coastline.

The reefs that lie off the Florida Keys usually prevent breakers from rolling onto the beaches there, and so the swells produced by this hurricane may not have been visible from the islands. But local fishermen noticed the swells and talked about them when they returned to their homes.

Barometers also usually indicate the approach of a hurricane well in advance of the storm's arrival. When the weather is calm in and near the tropics, a barometer's needle fluctuates very little from its normal reading of 29.92 inches, and its slight changes are predictable according to the time of day. An approaching hurricane stirs a barometer in an unusual manner. When the storm center is roughly 500 miles from the coast, the needle can become restless, constantly rising and falling by a few hundredths of an inch. The pressure readings may even climb a little higher than usual for brief periods.

When the hurricane's center is 300 to 500 miles away—24 to 36 hours travel time for a storm moving at 12 mph—bands of wispy, snow-white cirrus clouds, known among sailors as "mare's tails," often appear. These clouds often indicate the direction of the center of the hurricane.

On the day before a hurricane's arrival, the weather is often unusually good, with exceptional visibility. Distant objects stand out distinctly even though the air is thick with humidity. Those inexperienced with hurricanes often comment later that the weather seemed so calm and beautiful that it was impossible to believe that a violent storm was almost upon them.

Around the same time the cirrus clouds appear, the barometer begins to drop slowly but steadily—an even more ominous indication that a hurricane is drawing near.

When the FEC's southbound passenger train made its regular stop at the Islamorada station Sunday morning, the weather in the Upper Keys was squally—gusty winds and intermittent showers. Word of the developing storm was spreading through the work camps, and the train, as promised by the FEC dispatcher who had talked to Ghent a few hours earlier, was pulling five extra passenger cars to take the veterans out of the Keys. Few, if any, vets got aboard, however. No one had notified them that the regular passenger train had been expanded so they could leave the islands. Fred Bomer Jr., a veteran from New York who'd been assigned to Camp 1, summed up the vets' attitude about the developing storm. "We all hoped it would blow the mosquitoes away and cool things off," he said.

The worshipers who gathered Sunday morning at Matecumbe Methodist Church had something on their minds besides the Reverend Carlson's sermon. After the service they chatted briefly about the bad weather that might be coming their way and discussed their barometer readings, but they cut short their usual socializing. They knew there was a lot of work to do, and hurried to their homes to begin the familiar ritual of preparing for a hurricane.

At Lower Matecumbe Key, Cardy Bradford, who ran a small cafe at the ferry landing, talked about the storm with his father, Carson Bradford Sr. The elder Bradford had made his usual Sunday trip down from Miami Beach. The men decided that Cardy's wife, Elizabeth, and their children should ride out the storm in Miami Beach. Carson Sr. cut short his visit, loaded the group into his son's car, and left.

The Weather Bureau issued another advisory at 9:30 a.m. Sunday. The warm waters off Florida were stoking the storm. The Weather Bureau said it had reached hurricane intensity and was moving westward at about eight mph. The storm was expected to pass through the Straits of Florida and into the Gulf of Mexico late Sunday night or early Monday morning. The northeast storm warnings had been extended to Florida's west coast, and the lanterns had been replaced by the signal that is hoisted during the day—a solid red pennant over a square red flag with a square black center. The warning was now displayed from Fort Pierce to Fort Myers.

The storm was moving faster than the Weather Bureau forecasters realized, however. Its speed was closer to 11 mph. The difference was important. It meant that the storm would travel almost 75 miles farther in a 24-hour period than forecasters realized. And unknown to the forecasters, its eye had started to drift a few degrees north of due west.

As soon as Upper Keys residents got home from church, they started getting ready for rough weather. The telephone lines hummed with conversation as the few dozen or so people who had telephones talked about their preparations and updated each other on the latest information.

At the Hotel Matecumbe the news about the developing storm was making Sam Cutler uneasy. He recalled the conversation he'd had in Miami two months earlier, when meteorologist Ernest Carson told him that a hurricane in the Straits of Florida meant dangerous conditions on the Keys. Now the Weather Bureau said that a hurricane had formed in the straits.

Cutler continued making phone calls to gather more information, and he pushed more thumbtacks into the map charting the hurricane's track. "I had never been through a hurricane, and never knew what they were," he said. "I didn't feel that I was in a position to judge on a matter of that sort, but I was fearful for the safety of the men."

Ed Butters, the owner of the Hotel Matecumbe, said he could tell the storm was making Cutler edgy. "I knew that Sam was very concerned, but he was very concerned when the first weather report came out that there was a storm over in Havana, so I didn't put much stress on that," Butters said. "You know, some storms strike some people one way and some another way."

Despite his concerns, Cutler wanted to know more before making a decision about a potential threat to the safety of the veterans. Around 10 a.m. Sunday he went down to Camp 3 to talk to Ed Sheeran.

The fact that the Weather Bureau wasn't predicting that the storm would strike the Keys didn't impress Sheeran in the slightest. "To hell with what they say," Sheeran said to Cutler. "Our barometer shows we are in a low area."

Sheeran told Cutler to get the vets off the Keys.

"It was squally and the barometer kept dropping," Sheeran said. "I asked Mr. Cutler if he'd ordered a train [to evacuate the veterans] but he said 'No,' as he could get one on three hours' notice. I told them they had a bad storm coming and they better have the men out of there because it was a bad place for them."

Cutler returned to the headquarters office in Islamorada feeling compelled to prepare for an evacuation. He sent a driver to Miami to pick up Eugene Pattison, another Florida ERA engineer on the camps' administrative staff. Around 10:30 a.m. he tried to call the FEC's assistant general passenger agent in Miami. He wanted to ask if two trains could be assembled to move the veterans out of the Keys. But Cutler didn't reach the agent. Instead, he talked to a clerk, who said he would pass along Cutler's message to his boss.

Cutler also ordered the camp canteens to stop selling beer. The last thing he wanted if the order came to evacuate was to have to round up a bunch of drunken, unruly veterans and herd them aboard a train, and he wanted to give the men plenty of time to sober up.

⌐⌐

At about the same time that the canteens were cutting off beer sales, Roland Craig's phone rang. It was his friend, who told him that the Weather Bureau reported the storm to be about 200 miles east of Havana.

Craig pulled out his map and studied it. He decided that the storm was about 150 miles south of his island. "I knew it was closer to the Keys than it was probably thought," he said.

Paul Jeans, editor of Miami Beach's audacious penny tabloid, the *Daily Tribune*, was also studying maps and trying to guess where the hurricane would go. The maps showed high-pressure areas that Jeans thought might steer the storm in Miami's direction. Or so he hoped.

The *Daily Tribune* was engaged in a circulation war with the *Miami Herald* and the *Miami Daily News*. Jeans—short, bespectacled, daring, and deeply cynical—was driving his staff mercilessly to dig up spectacular, scandal-mongering stories that he published beneath giant, shrieking headlines. He justified his anything-goes approach to newsgathering by presenting the *Trib* and himself as noble defenders of the First Amendment, friends and protectors of the common man, and tireless crusaders fighting crime and corruption in Dade County.

Jeans, a Chicago native, could trace his journalistic roots back to William Randolph Hearst. After graduating from the University of Chicago,

Jeans volunteered for the army when the United States entered World War I, but he was turned down because of poor eyesight. He got his start in the brutal world of Chicago journalism as a correspondent for the Hearst-owned *Chicago American*.

During the last decade of the nineteenth century and the first decades of the twentieth, Hearst newspapers masterfully exploited the prejudices, ignorance, fears, sentiments, and fascinations of the masses. The news became a breathtaking, gaudy melodrama. "A Hearst newspaper is like a screaming woman running down the street with her throat cut," said Arthur James Pegler, who also wrote for Hearst and was the father of Hearst columnist Westbrook Pegler.

In Miami, Jeans worked for publisher Moe Annenberg, a wily Chicago newspaper veteran who had jumped back and forth as circulation director for the *Chicago Daily Tribune* and its archrival, the *American*. There was nothing subtle about Annenberg's methods of selling newspapers. He had regularly relied on mobsters such as Dion O'Bannion, Hymie Weiss, and Bugs Moran to "encourage" news dealers to carry his newspapers.

Annenberg amassed his own fortune as the publisher of *Racing Form*, a nationwide newspaper specializing in inside information about horse racing. He moved to Miami Beach and started the *Daily Tribune* in 1934 with Jeans as editor. Under their direction the *Trib* became a throwback to the classic turn-of-the-century yellow journalism tabloids—right down to its one-cent price tag. The *Tribune's* stories sought immediate emotional involvement among its readers—fear, shock, disgust, anger, indignation, pity, and confusion. Sometimes it demanded all of these simultaneously.

For all the *Trib's* self-congratulatory posturing as a noble defender of justice and truth, however, Jeans used some decidedly ignoble methods, shaping the truth to his liking and narrowly avoiding convictions for libel thanks to a skillful attorney named Victor Miller. Jeans, the self-proclaimed champion of the people's right to know, also had a well-known fondness for sleaze, and once quipped that his idea of the perfect newspaper headline was "Sex Fiend Slays Six in Penthouse Orgy."

The *Trib*—like its turn-of-the-century ancestors—delighted in exposing the misdeeds of the rich and powerful, and if there wasn't a banana peel for the big shots to slip on or a stairway for them to fall down, the *Tribune* would happily provide both and then give them a shove.

By late 1935 the *Tribune* was providing readers a steady diet of stories about corruption in city government and questionable behavior by some of

Miami's leading citizens, as well as gory tales of crime and passion. Many of the stories the *Trib* published were quite true; others contained just enough truth to keep the newspaper a few steps ahead of a lawsuit. The newspaper's rapidly growing audience enjoyed the *Tribune*'s colorful reporting, but Miami's city officials and business leaders detested the tabloid, and some people on the receiving end of the *Trib*'s crusades started extracting harsh revenge. Police supervisors looked the other way as cops punched out *Tribune* reporters and smashed photographers' cameras.

As the Labor Day weekend arrived, the *Tribune* was offering readers its usual front-page stories of crime and corruption—the arrest of city officials for a scam involving property tax certificates and a deranged father who'd brutally murdered his daughters. Then the U.S. Weather Bureau's advisory that a hurricane had formed near The Bahamas rattled across the *Trib*'s Teletype machine.

Jeans studied the advisory and weather maps. Other newspapers were publishing the Weather Bureau's prediction that the center of the storm would stay offshore as it moved westward through the Straits of Florida. But Jeans decided to play a hunch that would prompt Miamians to snap up copies of the *Trib*. What better way to get readers' attention than to tell them a hurricane was heading for the city? The newspaper's Sunday edition included a brief front-page story saying the storm would strike Miami and a map on page two showing the path it would take from The Bahamas straight to Biscayne Bay.

Once again Jeans had embellished the truth, and once again he would get away with it, not because it was exactly accurate but because it was close enough.

The Weather Bureau's Sunday morning advisory ignited a flurry of activity at the U.S. Coast Guard's air station on Dinner Key in Miami. Like Sheeran, Coast Guard commanders weren't going to try to outguess the developing storm. They'd decided that small craft should clear out of the Keys immediately.

Around 11 a.m. Lieutenant William L. Clemmer and his crew climbed aboard their big General Aviation PJ-2 seaplane. Clemmer, who had earned his wings the previous year at Pensacola's Naval Air Station, allowed the two engines to warm up for a few moments, then he turned the aircraft's nose into the wind and opened the throttle. The big seaplane lumbered across Biscayne Bay, slowly gaining speed until it lifted itself free of the water and became airborne.

Clemmer swung the plane toward the Keys. He was about to spoil a lot of weekend fishing expeditions—and save many lives in the process.

In a few minutes he was looking down at dozens of small boats scattered along the islands. The pilot headed toward a cluster of the small craft. When he was over them a crewman dropped a block of wood trailing a long, brightly colored streamer. The block splashed into the warm water near the boats. A hurricane warning printed on the streamer advised boaters to leave the area.

Clemmer dropped dozens of warnings, and soon the fishing boats were speeding back to their harbors. But the Coast Guard pilot had run out of warnings, and there were still more boats to be warned. He headed back to the air station for more.

Out on Florida Bay the ferry carrying Ray and Gayle Sheldon back to Lower Matecumbe Key suddenly slowed. Captain Charles Albury discovered that he had a problem. One of the propeller shafts had broken, drastically reducing the ship's speed. The ferry would have to limp along with only one propeller for the rest of the trip. It would be hours late arriving at Lower Matecumbe.

By noon, the driver Cutler had sent to Miami to fetch Eugene Pattison had returned with the engineer. Pattison joined Sam Cutler for another meeting with Ed Sheeran to discuss the hurricane. Sheeran repeated his assertion that the storm was a bad one and that it was headed in their general direction. Memories of the helpless workers killed in the 1906 storm were still haunting Sheeran's thoughts.

Sheeran's edgy demeanor bothered Cutler.

"He was much perturbed," Cutler said. "He is a man of few words, but from his looks I knew he was very much worried."

Sheeran made a chilling prediction to Cutler and Pattison. Because so many of the veterans had no realistic idea of what a hurricane was like, he told the two men, a lot of them would be killed if they were not evacuated.

Lieutenant Clemmer was back in the skies over the Keys early Sunday afternoon. Coast Guard crewmen in Miami had hastily prepared more hurricane warnings, stuffing them into round cardboard ice-cream boxes and then waterproofing the boxes with a coating of paraffin. Clemmer dropped the improvised warnings all along the Keys to boats as far as five miles offshore. He thought about dropping warnings in the veterans work camps and then decided against it. The warnings might panic the vets, and besides, camp administrators had to be aware of the warnings and were taking appropriate precautions, Clemmer thought.

But the sight of the big Coast Guard seaplane overhead made some of the vets uneasy.

"I didn't feel right when I seen that plane come over and come down to just above the treetops and make three or four circles right down near the top of the trees," said Melton Jarrell, a veteran from Farney, Texas, who was assigned to Camp 5.

Satisfied that he'd warned everybody he could possibly find, Clemmer turned the nose of his PJ-2 northward and headed back to Dinner Key, where Coast Guard crewmen were already getting the station ready for a blow.

In the lukewarm waters between The Bahamas and the tip of the Florida peninsula, the storm began gradually slowing, almost as though it wanted to take full advantage of the opportunity to stoke itself from the warm waters. By 1 p.m., as the holiday fishing boats were scurrying away from the Keys, the hurricane's winds had increased to 86 mph. It had also turned slightly more to the north and was roughly 200 miles from Islamorada.

Up in Jacksonville, Fred Ghent was playing a round of golf at the city's municipal golf course when he was called to the clubhouse telephone at about 2:45 p.m. Sam Cutler—nervous, edgy, overreacting Sam Cutler—was on the other end of the line urging him to send an evacuation train to the Keys.

John Good, purchasing supervisor for the veterans work camps, was in the office with Cutler and listened as Cutler explained the situation to Ghent.

Cutler told Ghent that there were indications that "very nasty weather" was headed for the Keys, and that he thought "we would shortly have an exceptionally high wind," Good said. "He told Mr. Ghent . . . the veterans should be moved out of the camps area and asked him what arrangements had been made . . . for their removal."

Ghent sidestepped Cutler's concerns, however. He told Cutler that Sheldon was on his way back from Key West, and any decision about sending a train would be based on Sheldon's assessment of the situation. Cutler asked what he should do if something forced the ferry to turn back to Key West. Ghent dismissed Cutler's concerns, telling him that Sheldon would get back to Islamorada that afternoon. At that moment Sheldon's ferry was already almost two hours overdue.

In Islamorada Postmaster John Russell had reached his own conclusion about the deepening threat to the Upper Keys. Around 3 p.m. Sunday he moved his family into the citrus packinghouse that doubled as the family's hurricane shelter. The 12-by-20-foot building was typical of many of the Conchs' hurricane shelters, which were reinforced with strong timbers and held together with huge bolts. Russell had even screwed his shelter to the coral island beneath it.

Other families were going to their own similar shelters near the middle of the island.

Around 4 p.m. the ferry carrying Ray and Gayle Sheldon pulled into its berth at the foot of Lower Matecumbe Key, a full three hours late. A long line of cars snaked back up the road, waiting to board the ferry.

But those drivers were going to be disappointed. Soon after the ferry docked, Captain Charles Albury spoke with his boss on the telephone. Albury was ordered to tie up the ferry at Lower Matecumbe Key and stay there until the hurricane threat was over. After the captain hung up, a veteran from nearby Camp 3 asked him if the ferry would make its return trip to No Name Key that afternoon. Albury said the boat would stay docked until the storm had passed.

The veteran was fascinated by the prospect of experiencing a hurricane. "I want to see one of those tropical disturbances," he said.

Albury, a Conch who understood the power of hurricanes, was astonished at this naïve wish. He turned and looked at the veteran. "I hope you are the only one that sees it," he replied.

As Albury was speaking to the inexperienced veteran, another advisory was released from the Weather Bureau. The hurricane was 275 miles east of Havana, moving slowly to the west or west-southwest, the bulletin said.

In the Gulf of Mexico, however, Captain Sundstrom on the *Dixie* had no way of knowing that the Weather Bureau's calculations were still off the mark. He was studying every weather bulletin as it came in on the *Dixie*'s radio. As the *Dixie* steamed across the Gulf of Mexico toward Key West, Sundstrom believed the hurricane's eye was well south of him, and that soon the *Dixie* would be traveling in the opposite direction from the storm.

Most of the passengers were still in a festive mood and happily enjoying their cruise. "It was a gay crowd that cavorted under the deck showers and played in the water and at other sports," said Florence Steiler, the passenger from San Francisco.

Ray Sheldon reached his office in Islamorada 15 or 20 minutes after the ferry docked at Lower Matecumbe. He met briefly with Cutler, Good, and auditor D. A. Malcolm. Cutler briefed Sheldon on his earlier conversations with Ed Sheeran, telling Sheldon that Sheeran thought the storm was a bad one and heading their way, and that the veterans should be evacuated immediately. Good and Malcolm seconded Cutler's opinion.

"The majority of us thought they would go ahead and order out the train so we could get the men out," Malcolm said.

But Sheldon wasn't impressed. "He gave us to understand that he was in charge and would take care of the situation," Malcolm said.

A few minutes after the brief meeting, Sheldon telephoned Fred Ghent in Jacksonville. Sheldon, apparently thinking that if he couldn't see the threat it didn't exist, dismissed the concerns of Cutler and Malcolm, as well as Sheeran's warning relayed through Cutler. Sheldon told his boss that conditions in Islamorada did not look dangerous. Ghent told Sheldon to call him if conditions did get bad.

Unknown to Sheldon and Ghent, however, the conditions were indeed getting very bad. By 7 p.m. the hurricane had slowed to only 5 mph, and the warm water had increased the storm's strongest winds to 104 mph. The eye continued to turn northward, and it was now about 160 miles from Islamorada.

Something strange and terrible was happening to the hurricane. It was about to undergo "rapid deepening," a process that would quickly transform this storm from a minimal hurricane into a once-in-a-lifetime monster.

Scientists do not fully understand what makes this phenomenon happen to a few storms. It's a process that seems to defy some of the known principles of hurricane development. When a hurricane slows and its eye starts to turn to the north, there's usually a fair chance that the storm will weaken, because its winds will have more time to churn up deeper, cooler water. When the cooler water reaches the surface, the hurricane's primary source of fuel is dampened, and the storm can rapidly lose strength.

But once in a while, a hurricane's strength mushrooms when it slows and starts turning. Researchers think this could be caused by large, deep pockets of very warm water that occasionally form during the late summer. Instead of churning up cooler water as it slows and turns, the hurricane brings still more warm water to the surface, and its slower speed gives it plenty of time to stoke itself.

These warm-water pockets usually form in the Gulf of Mexico, and sometimes they pass from the Gulf into the Straits of Florida.

Scientists are still trying to figure out what happened to this hurricane between the afternoon of Sunday, September 1, 1935, and the afternoon of Monday, September 2. As it churned across the Straits of Florida, something turned it into a force of incalculable power. For this to happen, the storm had to have an unlimited supply of very warm seawater. It's possible that the hurricane crossed paths with a pocket of deep, warm water that had drifted from the Gulf of Mexico into the straits at exactly the right moment. Now there was nothing to weaken or tear it apart—no cooler water, no upper-level winds. As many veterans on the Keys were stumbling to their shacks to sleep off a holiday bender, this storm was becoming the most powerful hurricane that would ever touch land in the United States.

The approach of a hurricane often causes unusually spectacular sunsets featuring fiery-red clouds the color of copper. At sunset John Dombrauski, a Huntington, West Virginia, veteran, looked at the sky. "There were copper clouds," he said.

Later Sunday night, Sheldon called FEC district superintendent P. I. Gaddis in Miami to discuss possibly sending a train to the Keys to evacuate the veterans. Gaddis told Sheldon that the FEC's regular northbound evening train from Key West had just arrived in Miami. That train could be turned around and sent back to the Keys, arriving in Islamorada in about four hours, Gaddis said.

Gaddis said Sheldon told him that he did not want to order the train then, and that Fred Ghent's office in Jacksonville would take care of ordering the train when it was needed. Sheldon asked Gaddis again if a train could be in Islamorada four hours after it was ordered.

"Yes, now, if you order the train now," Gaddis said.

But Sheldon misunderstood what Gaddis had said to him. He hung up thinking that regardless of when the order was placed, a train could be in Islamorada four hours later. What Gaddis had actually said was that the train that was presently standing at the Miami station with steam up and ready to travel could be back in Islamorada in four hours. If the FEC had to put together another train later that would be pulled by another locomotive, it would take longer for the train to reach Islamorada.

It was a critical misunderstanding that would infect Ray Sheldon's thinking from that point forward. Every decision he made later about evacuating the veterans would be flawed because of it.

At 9:30 p.m. the U.S. Weather Bureau issued another advisory. The agency said the center of the storm was now about 260 miles east of Havana and moving slowly westward. The advisory noted that the storm probably had hurricane-force winds near its center and advised caution for vessels—such as the *Dixie*—that would enter the Straits of Florida during the next 36 hours.

Officials in Cuba were keeping a wary eye on the Weather Bureau reports, especially since the American agency said that the hurricane was heading straight for them. But barometers in Havana were still rising—not what you'd expect if a hurricane was headed your way.

Still, officials in Isabela des Augua, a small coastal town east of Havana, were taking no chances. Residents there were herded aboard a special evacuation train Sunday night that took them inland to higher ground and out of harm's way.

At Lower Matecumbe Key, Ed Sheeran's crew finished securing their construction equipment. He told his men to get out of the islands because things would start getting dangerous the following day.

Sheeran's prediction was uncannily accurate. The hurricane was less than 200 miles from Islamorada. Its winds were increasing by the hour, and its forward movement had slowed even more as it started turning more toward the north. By late Sunday night its peak winds had reached 120 mph. It was creeping west-northwest at about 4 mph, and its slow forward movement allowed it to continue feasting on the warm waters.

At the Hotel Matecumbe, Sheldon, his wife, and some staff members sat down Sunday night to play gin rummy while they waited for updates from the Weather Bureau. A few minutes after 10 p.m., the phone rang. William Hardaker, superintendent of Camp 1, put down his cards and picked up the receiver.

It was Ernest Carson, chief meteorologist at the U.S. Weather Bureau's office in Miami. Thinking that he was speaking to Sheldon, Carson read the Weather Bureau's latest advisory to Hardaker. The Weather Bureau said the center of the storm was about 260 miles east of Havana and advised caution for ships in the Straits of Florida. A northeast storm warning had been issued for the coast of southern Florida from Miami on the state's east coast around to Fort Myers on the west coast. Carson added that there would be enough time to get the men out of the camps by Monday morning. The weatherman said he'd call again if anything changed during the night.

Hardaker hung up the phone feeling relieved. We're off the hook, he thought. He repeated Carson's statement to the others. The rummy game broke up soon afterward. Hardaker had been uneasy about the hurricane, but now he was convinced the Keys were no longer threatened by the storm. "When I went to bed [I] told my wife it would miss us altogether and would probably hit up around Tampa or up in that section," Hardaker said.

As Sheldon was about to retire for the night, he told Pattison and clerk Robert Ayer Jr. to sleep on cots in the office in case the Weather Bureau tried to call during the night. "Should the report be serious, notify me at once," Sheldon told Pattison and Ayer. "But if not, wait until in the morning." Sheldon didn't bother to explain what he meant by "serious," however.

At 3:30 a.m. on Monday, the phone rang again in Sheldon's office. A sleepy Ayer rolled out of his cot. It was Carson again.

The meteorologist told Ayer that the Weather Bureau had issued another advisory, and he read the bulletin to the sleepy clerk. "Tropical disturbance still of small diameter but considerable intensity moving slowly westward off coast of north-central Cuba, shifting gales and hurricane-force winds at center," Carson said. "Probably pass through Florida Straits Monday. Caution high tides and gales on Florida Keys."

The last sentence in the advisory should have been an eyebrow-raiser for anyone on the Keys: "Caution high tides and gales on Florida Keys." Ayer repeated the advisory to the drowsy Pattison. They decided it wasn't worth awakening the boss. Ayer went back to bed without bothering to write down anything that Carson had told him.

The Labor Day sunrise a few hours later didn't throw much light on the camps. Intermittent drizzle fell from an unusually dark sky.

Albert Buck, the foreman at Camp 5, got out of bed around 5:30 a.m. and immediately grabbed his barometer. Buck's coastal hometown of Kinston, North Carolina, is on the Neuse River. He'd seen what a hurricane could do to a large body of water. And he knew how to interpret a falling barometer. He'd scarcely taken his eyes off the instrument since hearing about the storm Saturday. He watched it for an hour after he got up Monday morning. The needle fell steadily the entire time.

"The barometer showed that the storm was not going around us, but was advancing on us all the time, gradually," he said.

Around 7 a.m. Buck stepped outside and looked up at the threatening sky. Dark, sinister clouds seemed to be so low that they were almost within his reach.

"Monday morning, the clouds looked so muddy and so close until it looked like you could reach out and get hold of them," he said.

Others also were noticing ominous signs of trouble over the horizon. Seventeen-year-old Laurette Pinder looked out at the Atlantic. Unusually large waves were crossing the offshore reef, rolling onto Upper Matecumbe Key and breaking noisily onto the beach. And the water looked eerie. Instead of its usual clear, turquoise color, the breaking waves were laden with air bubbles and debris, giving it a cloudy, milky appearance.

Buck decided to go to the Hotel Matecumbe to see what his bosses had decided to do about the situation.

The dreary beginning to Monday, September 2, 1935, was, in a sense, the last time that the sun rose on the old Florida Keys. When the sun came up again 24 hours later, the islands would be forever changed.

At sea the hurricane had taken full advantage of its leisurely weekend stroll across the warm waters between The Bahamas and the Keys. As Buck stood on the beach looking out toward the menacing clouds, the winds around the hurricane's center were howling at almost 140 mph. The storm was now unquestionably a killer—and it was continuing to strengthen.

Buck had correctly interpreted his barometer's ominous message. The hurricane had turned to the northwest. It was now heading directly for the Keys, and its small but ferocious eye was only a little more than 100 miles away. The hurricane also had roused itself from its leisurely pace and was moving at 12 mph.

Ray Sheldon awoke around 7:30 a.m. Ayer filled him in on the latest advisories from the Weather Bureau—including the telephone call of four hours earlier warning of high tides and gales on the Keys. "I gave him the exact telephone message that came to me," Ayer said.

A few minutes later Buck, the Camp 5 foreman, and supply officer Junius T. Wigginton walked into the administrative office. As the men discussed the latest Weather Bureau advisories, someone pulled out a deck of cards. Soon a poker game was under way as men drifted in and out of the office.

"Anything to pass the time," Wigginton said. "We were all just waiting on those damn weather reports."

As more and more people crowded into the offices, clerks gave up trying to get any work done. "It was impossible to do any office work because of the conglomeration of people," Ayer said. "Therefore, we were waiting for instructions. We were playing bridge on a desk in the office, next to Mr. Sheldon's office, waiting for instructions."

Sheldon played cards sporadically when he wasn't on the phone or pushing more thumbtacks into the map on the wall. He also rescinded Cutler's order from the previous day stopping the sale of beer at the camp canteens. And he ordered O. D. King, who was in charge of the motor pool, to fill the gasoline tanks of the camps' trucks and have them ready in case he decided to use the vehicles to move the men.

But Sheldon wasn't ready to order an evacuation. He wanted to wait.

If the weather reports and predictions failed to impress Sheldon, they got the attention of a federal official far from the Keys. Perry Fellows, an administrative assistant for the WPA in Washington, was sipping his breakfast coffee Monday morning as he browsed the Labor Day edition of the *Washington Post*. He noticed a small but prominently displayed story directly beneath the masthead, in the center of the front page. The headline read "Hurricane Heads Toward Florida."

The lead paragraph was an attention-grabber: "Destruction, perhaps death, was feared in at least two sections of the Nation last night as summer began to give way to the season of autumnal equinox."

The story noted that the hurricane was moving through the Straits of Florida, and that big, storm-driven waves were rolling onto beaches as far north as Daytona Beach.

In Tavernier young Bascom Grooms Jr. waited for the regular southbound passenger train, which was due at 9:16 a.m. The teenager was feeling glum. He had to go back to school the next day.

But the Labor Day passenger load was unusually heavy, and the train was running far behind schedule as it waited for the crush of passengers to board at each station. It would be late morning before it arrived in Tavernier.

At 9:30 a.m. the U.S. Weather Bureau issued another advisory giving the hurricane's location about 200 miles due east of Havana, or just off Cuba's long northern coastline. The storm was moving slowly westward, the advisory said.

At the same time as the advisory was issued, *Miami Daily News* reporter William Johns picked up his phone in Homestead and called Ray Sheldon.

"I said, 'Well, how is your weather?'" Johns said. "He said, 'It's raining and blowing like hell down here right now.'"

Johns asked Sheldon what he was going to do about evacuating the veterans in case the storm struck the Keys. "I have two trains waiting in Miami that can get down here on about three or four hours' notice, and in case it gets too bad, why, we will send for them," Sheldon told the reporter.

Johns hung up, called the newsroom of the *Daily News*, and reported what Sheldon had said to him. He told his editor that he'd be aboard the train if the evacuation was ordered. He fully expected to be taking a train ride down to the islands soon. "I knew they were going to get an awful blow," he said.

Meanwhile in Washington, Perry Fellows decided to go to his office even though he had the day off. The story about the hurricane approaching Florida bothered him and he wanted to make a few phone calls to get more information. When he arrived, he discovered that Aubrey Williams, an assistant to WPA director Harry Hopkins, also had come in despite the holiday.

Fellows briefed Williams about the story he'd seen in the *Post*. Williams said that he didn't want to wait to see if the storm got closer to the Keys. He told Fellows to call Florida ERA administrators to make sure that the vets were moved off the islands.

Fellows got on the phone. Around 10 a.m. he reached Florida ERA administrator Conrad Van Hyning in Tallahassee and suggested that he contact the camps in the Keys to make sure the veterans were being evacuated. Fellows told Van Hyning that Williams wanted the men moved even if the storm didn't appear to be heading their way. Van Hyning replied that he'd talk to the administrators in the Keys.

But the telephone at camp headquarters was busy. Van Hyning decided to call M. E. Gilfond in Key West and ask him to relay Fellows's message to Ray Sheldon.

In the Straits of Florida, the *Dixie* had rounded Key West and was now steaming a course that was roughly parallel to the islands. The ship was running into the same rain that was pelting the Keys, and passengers were scurrying for cover.

Pan American Airways officials had been closely following the hurricane reports. By early Monday morning they'd decided to take no chances with the storm. The regularly scheduled flight from Havana to Miami that normally left the Cuban capital at 3 p.m. would instead depart at 11 a.m. to make sure the plane didn't run into dangerous weather.

Meanwhile, Cuban meteorologists told the Associated Press Monday morning that the storm would pose "more danger to Key West than Havana."

At the makeshift veterans hospital near Snake Creek, Elmer Darty, from Charleston, South Carolina, lay in a bed near the window of his second-floor room overlooking the porch. All morning he'd been glancing out to watch a vine that clung to the building. The wind first stirred the vine early that morning, causing it to tap ceaselessly against the window screen. Now wind-driven rain was splattering against his window, and the vine was flailing furiously against the screen.

Darty became uneasy.

Around 10:30 a.m. Sheldon spoke with Ernest Carson in the U.S. Weather Bureau's Miami office. Carson told Sheldon that hurricane warnings had been hoisted in Key West.

"That's it," Sheldon said to Carson. "We're getting out."

Carson thought Sheldon meant that a train had already reached Islamorada and the men would be leaving immediately. Sheldon was still under the mistaken impression that two special trains were ready and could be in Islamorada in a few hours.

Even though Sheldon had decided to evacuate the veterans, he wanted to run his decision past Fred Ghent before the train was called.

In Jacksonville, Ghent took advantage of the holiday and snoozed until around 11 a.m. in his room in the Mayflower Hotel. About 30 minutes later he checked in briefly at his office, then went to lunch. He didn't bother telling anyone where he was going, when he would be back, or how to reach him while he was away.

A few minutes after Ghent disappeared for his lunch break, M. E. Gilfond finally got a telephone line through to Islamorada to pass along Van Hyning's message. Gilfond told Sheldon that Van Hyning wanted the vets moved off the islands.

But instead of agreeing to order the train as Van Hyning wanted him to do, Sheldon told Gilfond that he had been through "three or four" hurricanes and that Van Hyning had nothing to worry about. "I told Mr. Gilfond we were watching the barometer and the course of the storm, according to the Weather Bureau reports, and that, at the first sign of danger, we would order the train out," Sheldon said.

After hanging up with Gilfond, Sheldon tried to reach Ghent in Jacksonville. It was about 15 minutes before noon. Ghent was nowhere to be found.

Still, there seemed to be no reason to be overly concerned. Sheldon figured that he had at least 12 hours to get the men off the islands before the storm posed any threat to them.

In the work camps the veterans weren't too concerned about the storm. Jacob Herbert, who was from Los Angeles and stationed at Camp 1, said the men had been told they'd be taken care of.

"We were sitting around talking, and I was playing my mandolin," Herbert said. "I thought there would be nothing to it, probably flooding of shacks, but not floating away."

Down at Lower Matecumbe Key, an FEC freight train backed a tanker car containing 10,000 gallons of water onto a sidetrack near Camp 3. Normally,

Ed Sheeran would have ordered that the water be pumped into the camp's storage tanks, but he decided not to follow the usual procedure. He decided that the tanks probably would be destroyed by the coming storm. If he left the water in the railroad tanker car, at least they'd have water afterward.

Sheeran's decision would save dozens of lives.

As the tanker car was being uncoupled on the sidetrack, Pan American's big seaplane glided across the water and slowly climbed above Havana. The pilots turned northeast toward Miami. Soon they were running into squalls, but they expected rough weather with a hurricane in the neighborhood. Still, they were puzzled.

When the flying boat landed in Miami, the pilot reported seeing heavy, dark clouds that probably were part of the hurricane. But if the clouds were an indication of where the storm's center was, the pilot said, the hurricane was much farther north than the U.S. Weather Bureau was reporting.

Out in the Gulf of Mexico, Einar Sundstrom also was puzzled.

"It was about 11 a.m. Monday when the weather appeared squally," said John Laycock, a passenger from Baton Rouge, Louisiana. "We were still in the Gulf. I spoke to the captain about it."

Sundstrom told Laycock there was "some rough weather ahead." Still, Sundstrom said that the center of the storm was behind them, off the coast of Cuba. "The captain said he could pass safely through the strait," Laycock said.

But Sundstrom wasn't sharing his weather observations with the U.S. Weather Bureau, and in Miami, meteorologist Ernest Carson was frustrated. There were about a dozen ships at sea from New Orleans to north of The Bahamas, but only a couple of vessels—including the *Dixie*—were anywhere near the hurricane. Around 11:30 a.m. Carson tore a sheet of paper off his Teletype machine with information from a ship at Sagua la Grande, just east of Havana. Carson studied the data, then looked up at George N. MacDonnell, director of public health services for Miami. "I hope more information comes in with the one o'clock report," Carson said to his friend.

Carson and MacDonnell also wondered why the *Dixie* wasn't sending any data to the Weather Bureau.

A few minutes before noon, Sam Cutler left his office on the second floor of the Hotel Matecumbe and went down to the lobby, where he bumped into Paul Vander Schouw, the assistant director of the Florida Transient Division. Vander Schouw's agency would be taking over supervision of the veterans work camps in the state, and he had come down to the Keys to take a look at the camps. With him was Leila Baggs, the supervisor for the Transient Division's caseworkers.

Vander Schouw and Cutler had met a few months earlier when Cutler was a safety inspector. Vander Schouw had a lot of respect for Cutler.

Despite the wind and blowing rain, Cutler offered to take Vander Schouw and Baggs on a quick tour. The group left the hotel and drove down to Camp 3. Cutler and Vander Schouw got out and walked around the camp, but the veterans' well-established reputation for crudeness prompted Cutler to advise Baggs to stay in the car.

Meanwhile, Lawrence Bow, the former assistant camp administrator and engineer working on the bridge at Lower Matecumbe Key, sat down at his desk to make some calculations about the hurricane.

The readings from Bow's barometer at Lower Matecumbe Key were lower than those reported from Key West to the south and Miami to the north. The engineer did some figuring and calculated that the eye of the hurricane was about 90 miles due east of the work camps. Bow put down his pencil and called his wife in Miami to tell her that the storm would be worse at Lower Matecumbe than it would be in the city. He had no way of knowing it, but his calculations about the position of the hurricane's eye were on the money. At 1 p.m. Monday the eye of the storm was about 80 miles southeast of Islamorada.

As Bow talked to his wife, Alligator Reef lighthouse keeper Jones Pervis was talking by phone to the U.S. Weather Bureau in Key West. Jones hung up his phone and went to the flagpole. He removed the red pennant and replaced it with a second square red flag with the black square at the center. The brisk, rapidly rising wind quickly unfurled the banners. It was a signal that grabbed the attention of anyone who had lived near the ocean for any length of time. The two identical red-and-black flags indicated hurricane-force winds were expected in the area within 24 hours.

Cutler, Vander Schouw, and Baggs returned to the Hotel Matecumbe shortly after 1 p.m. for lunch. Cutler disappeared briefly and returned with Sheldon. The director sat down at the table and chatted for a few moments, but he was called away for a phone call around 1:30 p.m.

When Sheldon was out of earshot, Cutler turned to Vander Schouw and Baggs. He was deeply worried and wanted to tell them something in confidence. "This thing looks bad to me and I want to go on record with you," Cutler said. "If I don't see you again or if anything happens, [I wanted] to get these men out of here."

Vander Schouw studied Cutler closely as he spoke. He was calm and collected, and Vander Schouw did not detect any nervousness or excitement in his friend that might indicate he was making a hasty or ill-considered statement.

Upstairs, Sheldon was finally talking to Fred Ghent, who had returned from his nearly two-hour lunch break. Sheldon told his boss that hurricane warnings were up in Key West and he thought the evacuation train should be ordered.

Ghent said he'd take care of it. Sheldon hung up and returned to the dining room. He apologized to Vander Schouw and Baggs and said he had to leave them to arrange for the evacuation of the veterans. Sheldon disappeared back into his office, and Baggs and Vander Schouw left a few minutes later to return to Miami.

As the pair left the hotel, the weather was becoming frightening. The ocean was creeping onto Upper Matecumbe Key. Vander Schouw began to understand why Cutler was so concerned about the veterans.

"I was glad to get out of there," Vander Schouw said. "As it turned out at one point—I think Whale Harbor, where the road is quite low—the waves were already splashing across the road, so they splashed, the spray from them splashed clear across the windshield of the car, and I thought it was a very good idea to get out of there."

William Thompson, a veteran at Camp 5 from Brooklyn, New York, was beginning to get the same idea.

"I had a little puppy dog I had ever since I was there, brought it from Clearwater," Thompson said. "It was restless, would not stay in the hut. We had two pups, six or seven months old. Usually they would run and play. They would not play or anything."

By Monday afternoon, Thompson was getting uneasy. "I had a feeling about the storm myself," he said. "It began to rain and the wind [started blowing], and by two o'clock Monday I really began to be scared. I began to think of getting away very seriously. I didn't want to wait for no train or anything after that . . . I started up to the road and the water was up to my knees and I went back to the railroad track."

In the Straits of Florida, *Dixie* passenger Florence Steiler was becoming concerned about the worsening weather. The wind was blowing the rain so hard that she gave up the idea of staying on deck and finally decided to return to her stateroom.

In Jacksonville, Fred Ghent placed a call to the FEC's train dispatcher. It was approaching 2 p.m. More than three hours had passed since Sheldon told meteorologist Carson that he was moving the veterans off the islands, and almost two hours had passed since Sheldon had been told that his bosses wanted the veterans moved off the islands regardless of where the hurricane went.

Still, Sheldon and Ghent thought they had time to evacuate the men.

The Weather Bureau's 1:30 p.m. advisory said the storm's center was at latitude 23 degrees, 20 minutes north and longitude 80 degrees, 15 minutes west and moving slowly westward. This position would have placed the hurricane's eye about 120 miles south-southeast of Islamorada, or 135 miles due east of Havana and only about 10 miles offshore from the northern coast of Cuba. The advisory predicted hurricane-force winds in the Straits of Florida and gale-force winds on the Keys through Monday night.

But the hurricane wasn't following the schedule that Ghent and Sheldon had laid out for it. It was actually almost 100 miles northeast of where the Weather Bureau plotted it. Even worse for the veterans, the storm was quickly gaining strength as it continued its rapid deepening in the tepid waters off the Keys. In 12 hours the storm's top winds had exploded from 121 mph to 150 mph, and its forward motion had speeded up a little. The eye of the storm would be just offshore of the islands at about sundown, although the sun's normally spectacular descent into Florida Bay would be invisible behind the hurricane's dark, malicious clouds and dense, driving rain.

A terrible evening was in store for the Upper Keys.

Chapter Four

It's Blowing Like Hell Down Here

F. L. Aitcheson was taking a bath at his home in St. Augustine when his phone rang just after 2 p.m. Monday. It was Fred Ghent in nearby Jacksonville. Ghent told the dripping FEC assistant superintendent that he wanted to send a special train down to the Keys to get the veterans off the islands because of the approaching hurricane.

Aitcheson told Ghent he'd go to his office immediately to order the train assembled. He hung up, dried himself, hastily pulled on some clothes, and dashed to his car.

As Aitcheson hurried to his office, Ghent called camps administrator Ray Sheldon in Islamorada to tell him the evacuation train had been ordered. Ghent detected some edginess in Sheldon's voice, but Ghent was confident the situation was under control. Using the U.S. Weather Bureau's latest advisory, he calculated it would be at least 10 hours before the hurricane posed a serious threat to the Keys. Ghent told his assistant he'd meet the rescue train in Hollywood, a small town between Fort Lauderdale and Miami.

Ghent then returned to the Mayflower Hotel and packed a suitcase. He stopped at a service station to fuel up his car and, thinking of the 350-mile drive from Jacksonville to Hollywood, decided to have the oil changed, too. He saw no reason to be in any hurry. It never occurred to him that the Weather Bureau might be wrong, or that he might have misinterpreted the agency's advisories, or that he may have misunderstood the availability of the evacuation train. But as he waited for his car to be serviced in Jacksonville, the eye of the hurricane was within 100 miles of Islamorada, and its outer winds already were tugging and tearing at buildings on the Upper Keys.

"The winds started about one or two o'clock in the afternoon," said Etta Parker Sweeting, whose husband owned a store in Islamorada. "Eddie and I went to the post office to see if there was any mail for the business, for the grocery store. When we came back, we slowed down in front of the store and the paper was being peeled off of the roof. That's how hard it was blowing already."

The winds made it difficult to move as well.

"You could not walk around," said Joseph Fecteau, a veteran from Massachusetts who was timekeeper for the veterans at Camp 5. "You were just tossed about by the wind."

Some of the flimsiest buildings in the veterans camps were already coming apart.

"At two o'clock the timber was starting to fly around," Fecteau said. "Some of the small buildings were starting to go."

Wind can become a deadly weapon during a hurricane. In winds blowing at hurricane force—74 mph—a person can lean forward into the wind at a 45-degree angle without falling. When the wind reaches 80 mph, it is impossible to walk without the support of a railing or other structure. Boards, tree limbs, and other flying debris can kill when wind speeds reach 120 mph. A 130 mph wind can lift people off the ground.

Down at the southern tip of Lower Matecumbe Key, First Mate Fritz Maggesen was securing the lines that held the privately owned houseboat *Rowena* to the docks. Maggesen had tied up next to the ferryboat *Monroe County*. As he worked on the lines, Maggesen called to some veterans and invited them to get out of the rising winds by coming aboard the *Rowena*. But the always cocky vets with their blustering bravado scoffed at Maggesen's offer. "They laughed at me and said if I would come up to Long Island Sound sometime they'd show me what a real wind was," Maggesen said.

At Craig Key, Roland Craig decided he didn't want to try to ride out this storm in the islands. Around 2 p.m. Craig told Jack Crow to go back to the ferry landing to get the car started and then wait for him. Crow started walking the railroad track to Lower Matecumbe.

But Crow soon realized he couldn't possibly reach Lower Matecumbe Key. When he started across the railroad bridge, a gust of wind blowing across the open water shoved him so ferociously that he almost tumbled into Florida Bay. Shaken, he returned to Craig Key.

"We knew then that we were sunk," Craig said.

As the veterans dodged flying debris, Aitcheson, the FEC assistant superintendent, called A. I. Pooser, an FEC dispatcher, starting a series of relay telephone calls to the railroad's offices and dispatchers along Florida's east coast to ready the evacuation train. Pooser called dispatcher J. L. Byrum in New Smyrna Beach and told him to contact George Branch, yardmaster in Miami, and tell him to assemble the train. In Miami, Branch ordered a crew to get locomotive number 447 ready. The 160-ton locomotive needed to get up steam before the train could leave, but because number 447's boiler was fired by fuel oil instead of coal, it would take only about two hours to generate the steam needed to pull the train.

The rest of the train—six passenger cars, three baggage cars, and a pair of boxcars—had to be hooked up. But the yard's switch engine—which would be used to assemble the cars—wouldn't go on duty until 3 p.m. Still, the FEC workers in Miami swung into action, dropping other tasks to work on the evacuation train. While workmen finished repairs on one of the cars, another dispatcher started calling in crewmen from their holidays to operate the train.

Down at Camp 3 the horrible memories of the 1906 hurricane wouldn't leave Ed Sheeran's mind. It all seemed to be happening again. "The first storm—it happened the same way," Sheeran said. "Lack of judgment and lack of knowledge of the storm."

For two days he'd been saying that the men should be removed from the islands, but he hadn't said anything directly to Ray Sheldon nor had he heard whether the evacuation train had been called. Now his barometer was falling rapidly, and he was getting ominous news from Key West where his boss, B. M. Duncan, had installed himself in the U.S. Weather Bureau office on Front Street. Duncan was calling Sheeran every 30 minutes to update him on barometric pressure readings from Key West, Miami, and elsewhere. Sheeran's barometer was reading lower than those in Key West and Miami, and he knew that meant the hurricane was headed toward them.

"I didn't know if we were getting the center or the edge or what, but I knew it was so close," Sheeran said.

Around 2 p.m. Sheeran decided he wanted some answers. With the rising winds whipping around Camp 3, he drove to the Hotel Matecumbe to see what was being done to evacuate the veterans.

When Sheeran walked into Sheldon's office, the administrator was talking on the phone. He ended his call and turned to face Sheeran. Sheldon's demeanor had changed as the winds rose and his barometer fell. Sheeran could tell instantly that Sheldon was scared.

Sheeran got right to the point. "I told him I thought it was close to us," he said.

Sheldon placed a call and talked for a few moments. Then he hung up and turned back to Sheeran. The train would arrive at 5:30 p.m., he said. Sheeran nodded, told Sheldon he couldn't stay any longer, and left.

Sheeran knew the arrival of the storm's eye would be preceded by steadily increasing gusts of wind that would come closer together as it neared. When the wind began rising Monday morning, the gusts were about 30 minutes apart. When Sheeran left Sheldon's office, he noticed the gusts were less than 10 minutes apart.

As Sheeran pulled into the camp, a screaming siren was audible above the wind. Superintendent Ben Davis sounded the alarm to call the men to an assembly. Davis told them the evacuation train was on its way and they should get ready to board it. Some of the veterans spotted Sheeran and asked him what was happening.

"All the boys gathered around and asked me about the storm, and I told them to be ready to jump the train as it could not wait for them," Sheeran said.

He also called B. M. Duncan to again compare his barometer reading with those in Key West. "I talked to Mr. Duncan and said the barometer was going down fast and the telephone wires were giving way and I wouldn't be able to talk to him anymore," Sheeran said. "We were getting about a 60-mile-per-hour wind."

Sheeran had already ordered his work crew to get out of the Keys. But the aging combat veteran who wouldn't run from German gunfire wasn't going to desert in the face of this threat. He would take his chances with yet another hurricane.

"I just didn't have the heart to leave while there was anybody on the Keys," he said. "I asked my men if they wanted to go, and we had everything tied up as far as our work was concerned. I refused to leave. I preferred to go down with the ship. If they went down, I was going with them. I preferred to stay with them."

At Tavernier young Bascom Grooms Jr. reluctantly boarded the southbound passenger train that would take him away from summer vacation and back to Key West for the start of school. The train was running late because of the holiday traffic. Grooms found a seat in a crowded coach and stared glumly out the window as the train made its stops at Plantation Key and Islamorada.

Just down the tracks from the Islamorada station at the Hotel Matecumbe, Rosalind Grooms Palmer knew her kid brother was on the southbound passenger train and unaware that she was nearby. She thought about getting him off the train to join her at the hotel but decided against it.

The train continued, making stops at the ferry landing at Lower Matecumbe, Craig, and the Long Key Fishing Camp. Things brightened up a bit for Bascom Grooms when the train stopped at Marathon. A girl he'd met a few times at birthday parties got aboard and sat down with him. The two youngsters chatted happily during the rest of the trip to Key West, unconcerned that the train was running hours late and oblivious to the worsening weather outside their passenger car.

At the Long Key Fishing Camp, caretaker and Weather Bureau observer James E. Duane Jr. clutched his barometer as he warily watched the ocean, which became angrier by the hour. With him were 19 other people, including railroad maintenance workers and fishing camp employees who lived on Long Key. Also in the group was a new railroad section foreman who had arrived at the fishing camp with his wife and four small children only that morning. The group would ride out the storm where they were. The only way off the island was by boat or train. It was suicide to take a fishing boat out into the giant waves, and no one boarded the train when it stopped at the small depot at Long Key.

Duane was as alarmed about the falling barometer as Ed Sheeran. For most hurricanes the lowest barometric pressure reading doesn't fall too far below 29.00 inches. When it does drop well below that, it indicates a serious hurricane that causes extensive damage if it makes landfall. Hurricane Fran, which struck North Carolina in 1996, had a low reading of 28.17 inches. Hurricane Andrew, which devastated South Florida in 1992, had a reading of 27.13 inches, making it the third most powerful landfalling storm in U.S. history. Camille, the second most powerful hurricane to hit the United States, had a reading of 26.84 inches when it struck Mississippi in 1969.

At 2 p.m. Duane's barometer read 28.90 inches, and the winds were steadily increasing. An hour later his barometer had fallen to 28.52, and the winds were blowing still harder.

At the Hotel Matecumbe, Fern and Ed Butters hadn't been too concerned about the weather advisories Monday morning. They'd been in the middle of the horrible 1926 hurricane that nearly wiped out Miami Beach, and it was hard for them to believe a hurricane could be more powerful than that one. They'd already put up the heavy hurricane shutters over the hotel's windows, but Ed decided there was no reason to postpone a trip he'd planned to Miami, about 80 miles away, to paint a boat he'd just bought and pick up supplies from wholesalers. He left with his son, Jack, Monday morning.

But when Ed learned of the U.S. Weather Bureau's 1:30 p.m. advisory, he decided he'd better check about conditions in the Keys even though the bulletin said the hurricane was well south of the islands. At 2:30 p.m. he ducked into a telephone booth in the lobby of a Flagler Street hotel and called his wife.

Ed asked Fern if he should cut short his trip and return.

The wind was beginning to unnerve Fern, but she didn't want to let her husband know she was frightened. "I tried to be nonchalant and say I didn't think it was necessary," she said.

But at that moment the wind pried a shutter away from a window and slammed it against the building with a loud bang. The sudden noise, coupled with her mounting anxiety, destroyed Fern's forced composure, and she jumped involuntarily as she clutched the telephone.

"Well, if you want to know the truth," she blurted to her husband, "it's blowing like hell here."

Hearing his pious wife use even mild profanity surprised Ed Butters as much as the banging shutter had startled Fern. He decided his wife's uncharacteristically strong language was an indication the weather was getting bad. "I'm on my way," he said. He ran back to his Plymouth and dashed away to secure the boat he'd been painting so he could return to the Keys.

Regaining her composure, Fern went downstairs to the hotel kitchen at 2:40 p.m. Hurricane or no hurricane, supper had to be prepared for the Florida ERA officials. She told her cook to have it ready by 4:30 p.m. Then she asked her father-in-law, Charles Butters, and her son-in-law Olin Perdue to double-check the preparations they'd made for the bad weather.

As Fern Butters tried to maintain order in the mounting chaos, FEC engineer J. J. Haycraft answered his ringing telephone in Miami. A dispatcher told him to report for work to take a special train to the Keys to pick up the veterans. As the engineer hung up his phone, he checked the time. It was 3:10 p.m.

In the roiling seas off the Florida coast, the hurricane began to lash the passenger liner *Dixie* with increasing ferocity. Around 3 p.m. the storm ripped away the ship's radio antenna. As the ship tried to push its way northward through gigantic waves, Captain Sundstrom gave an order that sent a chill down his passengers' spines—he told them to put on life jackets.

While the passengers struggled into the bulky life jackets, Henry Treger prepared to put his life on the line. Treger, a radio engineer for station WJZ in New York, had volunteered to climb the *Dixie's* smokestack to rig an emergency antenna.

The winds were hurling rain and seawater against the *Dixie* with so much force that Florence Steiler was convinced the porthole in her stateroom wasn't properly closed. As the ship rolled and pitched in the storm, three inches or so of saltwater sloshed back and forth across her floor. Steiler called for a ship's steward and asked him to close the porthole. She was astonished when he told her it was, in fact, tightly closed.

Steiler decided that she might be able to escape the pool of water on her stateroom floor by climbing into her bunk and lying down. But the *Dixie's* violent tossing pitched her out, and she landed on the floor with a splash. She climbed back into her bunk and managed to escape the water again. But once again she was tossed out. So she scrambled back into the bunk. And she was thrown out again.

Up on the bridge of the *Dixie*, Captain Sundstrom knew his ship was in great danger.

"We rounded the southern tip of Florida and were going up through the shoals, but all the time the wind kept blowing harder," said John Laycock, the passenger from Baton Rouge, Louisiana. "Throughout Monday afternoon we were fighting our way slowly ahead, pulling for deep water to get away from the shoals. The captain evidently thought he could make it."

Using the Weather Bureau advisories, Sundstrom and his crew had plotted the storm to be well south of the *Dixie*, and the captain had been assuming he was heading in the opposite direction from the hurricane. But the ocean was becoming increasingly ferocious, and his barometer was steadily dropping. That could only mean that the *Dixie* was much closer to the hurricane's eye than he wanted to be. Without knowing where the hurricane was or which way it was moving, Sundstrom couldn't steer the *Dixie* to the storm's weaker side.

The passengers tried to forget about their growing fear by singing. George Outland, who was heading east from California to start a teaching job at Yale, sat down at a piano in the passengers' lounge and started playing "California, Here I Come" and other familiar standards. A crowd gradually gathered around him and started singing along. Outland would stay at his post for hours, banging away on the piano as the storm relentlessly battered the ship.

In Jacksonville the mechanics finished servicing Fred Ghent's car. He got behind the wheel and started the long drive down the coast to Hollywood.

At the makeshift veterans hospital on Windley Key near Snake Creek, Elmer Darty, the veteran from Charleston, South Carolina, had been uneasily watching the rising storm all day from his bed next to a second-floor window. The wind rattled the window screens, and fierce gusts shook the entire building.

Darty expected the storm to shove the screen through the window and into his room at any moment. "When that building started to shake, then I started to shake," he said.

The three doctors for the veterans camps decided they would take no chances with their patients' safety. They would be sent to a hospital in Miami. At 3:15 p.m. Darty and three other patients were loaded into the back of an ambulance. But as the vehicle pulled away, Darty still wondered if he'd escape the storm alive. The fierce winds slammed against the ambulance, causing it to rock alarmingly.

"Our ambulance like to have turned over two or three times before we got to Snake Creek and across, which is about a quarter of a mile [from the hospital]," Darty said.

At Morro Castle, the ancient fort that had guarded the entrance to Havana Harbor for centuries, the brisk wind made the red-and-black hurricane warning flags stand out stiff as boards. One report circulating through the city said the storm would strike Havana around 6 p.m., and a day earlier police had knocked on doors throughout the capital warning residents of the approaching hurricane.

But barometers there had risen since late Saturday, an indication that the storm was either weakening or no longer moving toward the city.

Newspaper offices were swamped with calls from edgy residents who wanted to know if the hurricane was heading their way. At an army base near Havana, Cuban military officers huddled with meteorologists to discuss a bold plan to get a fix on the hurricane's position. At the center of the group was Batista's "El Phenomena," the American daredevil flyer Len Povey.

Back at the Hotel Matecumbe, Ray Sheldon decided not to wait for the arrival of the evacuation train to get his wife and the wives of several veterans out of the Keys. Around 3:15 p.m. Gayle Sheldon climbed into a pickup truck with another woman and her infant child. Sheldon told the driver to take them to Hollywood and wait there.

A few minutes later, Sheldon told Sam Cutler to go to Hollywood and arrange with city officials for the veterans' arrival.

Down in Havana a decision had been made. Cuban meteorologists were determined to find this hurricane, and they couldn't do it by guesswork. They'd devised a daring, dangerous, and unprecedented plan.

Captain Leonard J. Povey walked out onto the windswept tarmac and climbed into an American-made Curtiss P-6S "Hawk," one of the three biplane fighters that Cuba had recently bought from the U.S. government. Povey had done some crazy things in airplanes, but none of them seemed as crazy as what he was about to do.

He was going to fly out over the Straits of Florida and find the hurricane.

There's no way of knowing what went through Povey's mind as he went through his preflight checklist to prepare for takeoff. Nor is there any way of knowing whether the idea to use an airplane to find a hurricane was the brainchild of the *muy loco* American flyer or the Cuban meteorologists. But there's no doubt that there weren't many other people on the planet who possessed the combination of exceptional flying skills and plain old chutzpah that would be needed to take on such a mission.

Povey turned the airplane into the wind and opened the throttle of the 450-horsepower engine. The little open-cockpit fighter raced down the runway, tucked the wind under its wings, and lifted off.

Over the Straits of Florida, not far from where the *Dixie* was wallowing almost helpless in the monstrous waves, Povey sighted the storm.

"It appeared to be a cone-shaped body of clouds, inverted, rising to an altitude of 12,000 feet," Povey later told the Associated Press.

One of the first things the flyer noticed was a condition reported by sailors in the middle of a hurricane—a "confused sea." Normally, waves follow the direction of the winds that create them. But in the center of a swirling hurricane, waves come from different directions and collide.

"The waves in the sea below broke against each other like [they were] striking a seawall," Povey said.

Povey discovered that his altimeter—the instrument that recorded his altitude—was affected by the storm's low barometric pressure. The altimeter was essentially a barometer. As a plane climbed higher, the atmospheric pressure dropped. The altimeter was calibrated to record the plane's altitude according to the barometric pressure, so it indicated that Povey's plane was climbing even though he maintained a constant altitude.

Povey also made a chilling discovery—the storm was well north of the position given in weather reports. Havana was off the hook, but the Keys were undoubtedly going to be hit.

That fact was becoming increasingly clear to James Duane at Long Key Fishing Camp. Duane took another barometric pressure reading at 4 p.m. The needle read 28.42 inches and seemed in a free fall, dropping one one-hundredth of an inch every five minutes. The wind still blew from the north at well over 100 mph.

As Duane jotted down his 4 p.m. readings, Ed Butters finished securing his boat in Miami and, with his son Jack beside him, began a mad dash back to the Keys. He buzzed through South Miami in his big Plymouth, ignoring speed limit signs.

Soon Butters had cleared the city and hit the long, straight stretches of road that would take him back to the islands. He floored the accelerator, and the Plymouth's speedometer needle climbed to 80 mph and stayed there.

At Key Largo, Butters turned onto another segment of road that was unbroken by curves. Now Butters was traveling southwest and, with the hurricane's rising wind at his back, his big car fairly flew down the road. The tailwind whisked the Plymouth along as though a giant hand was shoving the car from behind. "I hardly had to touch the accelerator," Butters said. "I got it right in the stern of my car."

In the work camps the veterans were fed an early supper and told to go to their quarters to await the train. The men exchanged nervous glances as they ate their sandwiches.

"Along about supper time the wind and rain increased," said Jacob Herbert. "We noticed it was darker than usual. There was no lights, and with the increase of rain, it kept getting darker and darker. There was three of us that started kidding about riding tidal waves."

But as the vets tried to maintain their composure by kidding about the worsening conditions, their camps were beginning to disintegrate.

"We got uneasy about four o'clock," said John Dombrauski, the veteran from Huntington, West Virginia. "Roofs began coming out. It began taking the place down."

Dombrauski and Adam Rambowski, a veteran from Alexandria, Virginia, decided they weren't waiting for a train to get them out of the Keys. They hot-wired a pickup truck and headed north.

Camp 3 superintendent Ben Davis was beginning to wonder about the evacuation train. He got into his Dodge and drove through the storm to the

Hotel Matecumbe to see Sheldon, who told him the train was on its way. Davis started to leave, then turned back to Sheldon. Davis said he'd put his top assistant in charge of the veterans on the train and follow in his car.

But Sheldon said he'd rather have Davis aboard the train to help control the men, and added that he didn't think it would be a good idea to have women riding with several hundred boisterous, drunken vets. Sheldon asked Davis if he'd allow George Pepper to drive his car out of the Keys to evacuate four or five veterans' wives.

Davis agreed. He pulled a trunk of personal belongings from the car to make room for passengers. Pepper and his fiancée, Rosalind Grooms Palmer, got into the Dodge with him, and the three drove back to Camp 3 so Davis could rejoin his men. Meanwhile, the women gathered at the hotel to await the return of Pepper and Palmer.

In Miami, engineer Haycraft grasped the handle on the big throttle of locomotive number 447 and gave it a pull, setting nearly a thousand tons of equipment into motion. The evacuation train slowly rolled out of the FEC rail yard. It was 4:25 p.m. It had taken a little more than two hours to assemble the train, call in a crew, and get under way—not bad for a holiday. With Haycraft were trainmaster Branch, conductor J. E. Gamble, and fireman Will Walker. The FEC's daily passenger train run from Miami to the Upper Keys usually took about two hours.

The train had scarcely left the yard when Haycraft had to bring it to a halt. A drawbridge had been raised to let holiday boat traffic pass. The train idled on the track for about 10 minutes.

As the train crew watched the passing boats, the U.S. Weather Bureau issued a new advisory at 4:30 p.m. After the report from the Pan American flight and Povey's daring flight to find the storm, the Weather Bureau meteorologists had finally acknowledged that this small, elusive hurricane was well north of the position they'd been giving. The new advisory said the hurricane was "apparently" moving toward the Florida Keys.

At Camp 3, Ben Davis handed his car keys to George Pepper sometime around 5 p.m.

"I instructed Mr. Pepper to make haste, wished him luck and bid him good-bye," Davis said.

Pepper turned the big Dodge around and started back up Lower Matecumbe Key. He was only six miles from the Hotel Matecumbe, where the veterans' wives waited anxiously for him.

But the weather conditions were about to take a dramatic turn for the worse. At about the same time that Pepper and Rosalind Grooms Palmer pulled out of Camp 3, the winds suddenly increased in intensity. The hurricane's eye was now within 30 miles of the islands, and the storm's fiercest winds were beginning to claw at the Keys.

O. D. King, the motor pool supervisor who also owned a small service station in Islamorada, left the Hotel Matecumbe in his car around the same time that Pepper and Palmer left Camp 3. King was only a few minutes' drive from his home. Suddenly his car veered off the road as though a giant paw had swatted it. King realized that a gust of wind had swept him off the highway. Shaken but unhurt, he steered his car back onto the road and resumed his trip.

The winds were becoming more furious by the minute. The hurricane began tearing at larger buildings. And it started killing people.

At Camp 1 many veterans had gathered in the mess hall to await evacuation. Around 5 p.m., camp superintendent William Hardaker told the men that the train was due any minute.

"It was already blowing hard and we piled out as fast as we could," said Lloyd Fichett, a veteran at Camp 1 from Terra Alta, West Virginia, a small coal-mining town near the Maryland border. "As we came out the door the corners of the mess hall had started breaking off and it began blowing harder each minute. By the time we got to the railroad tracks, it hit us with all its force. The canteen blew down and wood started flying in all directions. It was terrible."

At about 5:15 p.m. the evacuation train stopped at Homestead, 26 miles south of Miami, to load telephone wire and allow a repair crew to board. Engineer Haycraft and Branch, who was in charge of the train, decided to turn the locomotive around during the stop. While that was being done, *Miami Daily News* reporter William Johns and several veterans boarded the train. The vets told conductor Gamble they wanted to go back to the camps to get their personal belongings, so Gamble reluctantly allowed them aboard as well.

The train resumed its journey at 5:30 p.m. The locomotive's nose was now coupled to the front of the train so the locomotive was traveling backward as it pulled the cars southward. Branch's plan was to run this configuration until the train reached Camp 3, the southernmost of the three camps. There, he planned to uncouple the locomotive and use a sidetrack to move it to the other end of the train. It would then be re-coupled so its nose pointed northward. That way the locomotive's powerful headlight would shine on the tracks during its return trip out of the Keys.

Soon the train had left the peninsula and was on a stretch of tracks that followed a narrow strip of land known as Cross Key, which separated Blackwater Sound from Barnes Sound. Waves were already breaking across the tracks on Cross Key.

"The old Atlantic was kissing our feet—or wheels, so to speak," Branch said.

Water across the tracks meant that Haycraft, the engineer, had to slow the train dramatically, and at times it appeared that the train was floating across the whitecaps as it plowed through the storm.

At Key Largo the train tracks turned sharply to the right. Conditions improved a little as the train chugged southward down the island. The dense mangroves and other vegetation served as a windbreak, and for 15 miles or so the ride was a little smoother.

In Islamorada, Ray Sheldon sat down to supper at the Hotel Matecumbe with several of his staff and Deputy Sheriff Louis Maloney. Sheldon told Maloney to make sure his deputies understood the veterans had to be loaded onto the train as quickly as possible.

The men were finishing their meal when Ed Butters and his son burst into the lobby. He'd made the 80-mile drive from Miami in just over an hour. He made another check of the shutters while Sheldon and his staff dashed from the hotel to Sheldon's Chevrolet and piled in for the short drive up the island to the Islamorada train station, where they intended to board the train to supervise the loading of the veterans. The downpour was so heavy they had to creep along slowly in second gear so the water would not drown out the automobile's engine.

As Sheldon left the hotel, the women waiting for George Pepper and Rosalind Grooms Palmer looked at each other with growing uneasiness. The storm was clearly worsening, and they wanted to get off the islands. But Pepper and Palmer hadn't arrived.

Down at Camp 3, Ed Sheeran was astonished. He had been in the middle of six hurricanes, and he'd never seen winds strengthen the way they did between 5 p.m. and 5:30 p.m.

"The wind was blowing 125 mph by five o'clock," Sheeran said. He went aboard the dredge *Sarasota*—which he'd tucked into the relative safety of the canal he'd dug months ago—to ride out the storm. With him were about 30 people, including some veterans and a few fishermen with their families.

Offshore, the *Dixie* struggled against the huge waves being shoved at it by the hurricane. The passenger liner climbed slowly up each mountain of water, balanced for a moment on its peak, then raced down the other side. The waves were so big and steep that the *Dixie*'s propeller broke free of the water and raced wildly for a few moments as the ship's bow tilted to plunge down into the trough. Too much racing could damage the engines, and Sundstrom was forced to cut his speed to five knots—just under 6 mph— to reduce the risk.

"The ship was hammered by such waves as I never saw in my life," said passenger Anna R. Chambers from New Orleans. "Great, towering, racing mountains of water that hurled themselves on us out of the dark and the murk."

The passengers clung to anything stable. "The deck never seemed to get level," Chambers said. "It was tilting always, forward or aft, to starboard or to port. If you moved around at all, you were climbing a hill or sliding down one."

The screaming winds were equally terrifying.

"That wind was like something solid hitting us," she said. "When that wind struck the ship, the *Dixie* staggered as if a charging locomotive had hit the steel sides."

Captain Sundstrom and his crew were blinded by the wind-driven rain and giant waves that smashed against the *Dixie*'s bridge 55 feet above the ship's normal waterline. They had only a vague idea of where they were. They tried to get a rough estimate of the distance they'd traveled by counting the number of propeller revolutions. Sundstrom knew his ship was being pushed toward the treacherous reefs that lie a few miles off the Florida coast.

To make matters worse, the rudder had been damaged and the ship was almost unmanageable. "Then it seemed all hell broke loose," said Laycock, the passenger from Baton Rouge. "The ship began to toss and rock helplessly, great waves breaking all around and over the superstructure."

The *Dixie* was exactly where Sundstrom did not want it—caught in the hurricane's dangerous semicircle, out of control, being pushed toward some of the most treacherous reefs in the world and sailing straight for the eye of the storm. But there wasn't much he could do about it.

Around 5 p.m. the ferocious winds suddenly stopped hammering the *Dixie*, and the sun and blue sky appeared overhead. Sundstrom had sailed his ship smack into the eye of the hurricane. Huge waves converged on the Dixie from all directions, but at least the winds were gone—for a while. Sundstrom decided to take advantage of the lull by sailing the *Dixie* away from the reefs.

He knew that when the backside winds reached the *Dixie*, he would again be fighting for control of his ship.

At 5:30 p.m. the dark clouds, fierce winds, and driving rain again enveloped the *Dixie*. The liner was back in the teeth of the hurricane.

In Islamorada about a dozen men, including Sheldon and Deputy Sheriff Maloney, waited for the train at the station. They became uneasy as the storm thrashed the structure.

"At six o'clock the wind was blowing so hard and the station building was shaking so violently that I did not see how it could stand much longer," said Robert B. Lee, the FEC ticket agent and telegrapher in Islamorada.

The Butterses were reaching the same conclusion about their hotel.

"I never knew a howling, raging wind to come so fast," Fern Butters said. "At six o'clock, we were forced to leave the hotel."

Ed Butters ordered his family into the Plymouth. He backed the automobile against a tour bus that had been parked behind the hotel beneath the gumbo-limbo tree. Eight people were packed into the car. Ed and Fern were joined by his father; their sons, Jack and Chester; their daughter, Loretta Perdue, and her son, Pete; and Sheldon's secretary, Mrs. L. A. Fritchmann.

They could hear the hurricane tearing at the hotel and outbuildings.

"We heard crashing and noise from the hotel, and a building blew down and landed beside the left front wheel of the car," Fern Butters said. "We watched it anxiously, fearing it might blow into the car."

Out at Alligator Reef, four miles offshore from Upper Matecumbe Key, lighthouse keeper Jones A. Pervis and his two assistants prepared the lighthouse for the blow. As they worked, assistant keeper James Duncan looked out at the fearsome ocean and saw a monstrous wave bearing down on the 136-foot-tall lighthouse. Duncan shouted a warning. The men dashed into the tower and scrambled up the ladder as the huge wave submerged the lighthouse's lower platform and then rolled on toward the islands.

The lighthouse keepers were soaked and frightened, but alive. "How I held on and why I wasn't drowned, I can't say," Duncan said.

The mountain of water—a freak "rogue wave" piled up by the hurricane's winds—barreled on toward the Upper Keys, where Joseph M. Lydon, a veteran from New York City, was eating supper with friends in a cabin at Camp 1.

"We heard the wind, and there were things flying through the air, but we thought we'd be all right till the train got there," Lydon said. "Suddenly the wind tipped the whole cabin over—carried everything out to sea. I got washed away from the cabin somehow. The waves were terrible big things."

As the hurricane approached, the veterans had tried to bolster their courage by reminding themselves again that they were the same men who'd stood face-to-face with death in France, and they weren't going to be frightened by a little bad weather. But when their camps began to disintegrate around them and they saw their buddies sent sprawling, their sad bravado evaporated. They realized they faced an enemy far deadlier than the German soldiers they'd confronted when they were younger men.

"We'd been telling ourselves how much better this was than France," said Leroy J. McMullen, a veteran from Akron, Ohio, who was discussing the storm with ex-boxer Jimmy Conway and three other veterans in another Camp 1 cabin. "I guess we shouldn't have been bragging. The next minute we were underwater. I guess a mountain wave hit us."

The men were washed across the railroad embankment. When the water receded, three of them had vanished. But the danger wasn't over for the two survivors.

"I saw a big beam swish through the air and hit Jimmy Conway in the back of the head," McMullen said. "He dropped as if a shell had hit him."

Conway—who had taken so many powerful punches to the head in the boxing ring and come back battling—was no match for this blow. He was one of the hurricane's first fatalities.

In Camp 3 at Lower Matecumbe Key, 75 veterans gathered in the mess hall to wait for the train. They looked at each other nervously as the hurricane shoved and tugged at the building as though it were testing the strength of the structure. Suddenly the howling wind found the grip it sought and ripped the roof off the building.

"Nearly everybody ran just like a bunch of rabbits," said James B. Lindley. "And when we ran out, we ran right into that wind, and after that I don't remember much what happened to the boys because the wind knocked me right on the banister of the mess hall, and I hit the ground, and I got up, and it knocked me down three times before I stayed down."

The vicious wind did Lindley a favor. The air was filled with flying timbers and other deadly debris. As Lindley clung to the ground he watched a board torn from the building whiz past him and impale Elmer Kreitzburg, a veteran from Baltimore. Other veterans helped the horribly injured Kreitzburg to a nearby automobile and tried to make him comfortable.

G. C. Sain, the timekeeper at Camp 3, was blown through two rooms and an outer wall when the mess hall collapsed. He grabbed the floor sill of the mess hall and held on for dear life. Timbers, stoves, iceboxes, and tables flew past his head. Sain felt safe for a while—until the water started rising. Eventually it reached his chin, and then it kept rising until it reached the floor of what had been the mess hall. The water lifted the floor from the sill and washed away the underpinnings. The sill dropped onto Sain's right foot. He was trapped.

"I finally succeeded in getting off my right shoe, and by this time I was entirely underwater," Sain said.

Sain grabbed a piece of two-by-four and worked it beneath the floor sill. With all his strength he tried to use the wood as a lever to lift the sill off his foot. He couldn't budge it. Then he had another idea.

He timed his lifting to correspond with the waves pushing against the sill. The force of the waves, combined with his makeshift lever, provided just enough lift to get the sill off his foot.

The pounding rain annoyed George Senison, a 39-year-old veteran from Bridgeport, Connecticut, because he'd planned to go fishing. Somehow, he'd managed to avoid hearing warnings that a hurricane was just offshore.

"I never even thought of a hurricane and had not heard any talk about one and I did not think there was any danger in staying there—until our shack began to shake," Senison said. "We four were in our shack waiting for the storm to blow over. I was going to go fishing and was monkeying around the shack getting things ready. I generally fished about two hours after supper most every night. On that evening it was raining. . . . It kept raining more and more and the wind was blowing. The wind kept blowing harder and harder and began shaking the shack, and things like toilet articles and mirrors began falling. I got nervous."

Then Senison could feel his cabin moving. He looked across the street and saw the roof leave the Camp 3 mess hall.

"We were all together leaning against the shack and holding on to each other," Senison said. "I heard William Clark holler that the roof was coming down. We all started away in the same direction and the roof came down on us. It must have hit every one of us. After the roof fell all I could hear was the grunting and groaning of the boys. I never saw any of them after that."

Senison clung to the roof of his shack as it sailed through the air and into the mangroves.

Not far away dozens of vets were sipping beers at Cardy Bradford's store when two men rushed in with news that the roof had been blown off the mess hall. The building shuddered under the wind's ceaseless pummeling as the newcomers breathlessly told their tale.

As the veterans described the destruction of the mess hall, store owner Cardy Bradford was talking on the phone with his father in Miami Beach. The elder Bradford urged his son to get off the islands.

"You'd better come up," Carson Bradford said. "Get out of there."

Cardy Bradford could hear debris from the mounting destruction slamming against his store. All hell had broken loose outside, and he realized it was too late for him to make a run for the safety of his father's home. "Well, Dad, I don't think I can make it now," he said.

Suddenly the loud crackling of splintering wood interrupted their conversation. Everyone in the store looked up in horror as one end of the ceiling sagged and the opposite end opened like the lid of a box. Then the entire roof was lifted from the building and carried away.

In Miami Beach, Carson Bradford slowly lowered the telephone receiver from his ear. The line was dead. He had no idea what had just happened to his son.

The veterans scrambled frantically for cover as the store flew to pieces around them. Some made it to safety, but the flying debris cut down many of them.

"Just as I got outside the door, I was struck in the back of the head with what I think was a filling station pump," said Gay M. Postell, a veteran from the tiny mountain hamlet of Ducktown, Tennessee. "I went out."

John Dombrauski and Adam Rambowski made a couple of stops to see if anyone wanted to make a run for safety with them in their stolen pickup truck, but they had no takers. They reached the bridge across Snake Creek at about the same time the mess hall at Camp 3 collapsed. The bridge was already starting to break up, but they decided to take a chance. "We heard the bridge kind of wiggling as we drove over," Dombrauski said.

On Alligator Reef, Jones Pervis climbed the lighthouse tower at 6:30 p.m., as he did every evening. His duties as keeper required that he light the beacon regardless of weather conditions. But as he tried to ignite the lamp, the half-inch-thick glass protecting it shattered with a terrible crash and the lens was lifted off the tower and carried away. Pervis scrambled for his life as deadly shards of glass flew all around him.

At about the same time Pervis was dodging flying glass, Fred Ghent reached Melbourne, roughly halfway between Jacksonville and Miami. He stopped at the FEC office, hoping for a message from Ray Sheldon about the evacuation train. But nothing had been heard from it since it left Homestead an hour earlier.

Aboard the train, George Branch and his crew were getting worried. They were plunging blindly into a raging storm that was becoming more furious with each passing mile.

"It had gotten so dark and the wind was whipping the raindrops in our faces with such fury that we could not see one another in the cab of the locomotive and could not tell just where we were or whether the track was covered with water," Branch said.

Some of the train crew were losing their nerve and wanted to turn back.

"I insisted that we go on," Branch said.

Down at Long Key, James Duane's barometer read 27.90 inches at 6:45 p.m. as he and the 19 others riding out the storm with him took refuge in his residence. The wind, which had backed around to the northwest, performed astonishing feats of strength. A giant beam—6 by 8 inches and 18 feet long—pulled loose from one of the destroyed buildings. The wind lifted the beam as though it were only a twig. The massive timber sailed 300 feet across the island until it slammed against Duane's house. The building was virtually destroyed, and Duane and the others scrambled through the storm to the hotel.

It was the start of a nerve-racking game of hide-and-seek that the terrified people on Long Key would play with the hurricane for the rest of the night.

At the quarry near Camp 1, a crane near the railroad track swayed violently in the vicious winds. Finally the boom gave way, lurching upward and buckling and pulling loose a thick steel cable that had anchored it. As the boom fell, the cable was hurled across the railroad tracks, taking down telephone lines and setting a trap for the approaching train.

Nearby, Mallie K. Pitman, a veteran from Gastonia, North Carolina, wondered how much longer his cabin could withstand the storm. Pitman was convinced the fearsome winds would send his trembling shack tumbling at any moment. Then, above the roar and shriek of the hurricane, he heard a single, wheezing blast of a locomotive's steam whistle. The evacuation train had reached Camp 1.

Pitman asked two other men in his shack to come with him to board the train, but they blearily refused. "I think both of those boys had been drinking some," he said.

Pitman set out alone. The downpour was so heavy he couldn't see the train, but he pushed his way through the storm in the general direction of the railroad track.

The train was moving at about 40 mph through the raging ink-black darkness. Branch and his crew had only a vague idea of where they were.

Suddenly the air was filled with "sheets of fire," Branch said. He shouted to the engineer to engage the train's emergency brake, and with a rattling shudder the train lurched to a sudden stop.

Branch leaped from the locomotive and pushed through the wind and rain trying to find out what had happened. It was 6:50 p.m.

CHAPTER FIVE

In the Heft of the Hurricane

George Branch kept the train between himself and the howling wind as he pushed through the storm.

"Finally I came to some refugees who had heard the train and were trying to make it to the protection of the steel equipment," Branch said. "They told me we had run into a big cable and parts of a huge derrick which had blown across the track."

Branch went back to the locomotive and told engineer J. J. Haycraft to resume. But the train's emergency brakes wouldn't release.

Branch again struggled through the storm to find the problem. A crew member had set the brakes to allow some storm refugees to get aboard. The trainmaster asked if there were any others. A man asked Branch to hold the train until he could get his daughters aboard.

Minutes passed, and the man did not return. Branch and another man fought through the storm to the man's house. The girls were terrified and refused to leave. Branch tried to persuade them, but they wouldn't budge.

"Finally I had to tell the father that I could hold the train no longer," Branch said. "He said that was alright, to go ahead and he would stay with them. He guessed they would be alright there."

Branch went back to the locomotive and told Haycraft to proceed. But again, the emergency brakes held. The crane's steel cable, three-fourths of an inch thick, had tangled itself among the cars. The train was held fast.

As Mallie Pitman neared the railroad track, he saw, through the driving rain and howling wind, men moving frantically between two of the train cars. A crewman spotted Pitman and asked him to give them a hand. He could see they needed all the help they could get.

Pitman scrambled atop one of the cars with Edgar Boatmen, a veteran from Knoxville, Tennessee. The men seized the cable and started pulling. As they loosened the cable it fell between the train cars.

"It was tangled pretty badly; it was wrapped around and everything," Pitman said. "They kept pulling it after I finished. Myself, the conductor, and a veteran got on the opposite side and straightened it, and the rest of them pulled it. It was a pretty bad mess."

While the men worked to untangle the cable, a few more veterans and some Windley Key residents struggled through the hurricane hoping to board the train. *Miami Daily News* reporter William Johns and the veterans who'd boarded in Homestead formed a human chain and dragged the others aboard.

Branch returned to the locomotive and told Haycraft to get going. The train had been delayed for an hour and 20 minutes.

At Long Key the old hotel trembled as the rising winds relentlessly hurled timbers from the disintegrating fishing camp against the building. When James Duane Jr. recorded his 7 p.m. barometer reading, he saw the needle had tumbled to a chilling 27.78. The wind, which by now had reached about 130 mph, was blowing from the northwest and pushing water out of shallow Florida Bay, piling it up against the railroad embankment near the hotel.

On the Atlantic side, the powerful winds were sweeping the ocean away from the islands.

Duane had been in half a dozen hurricanes, including a typhoon that smashed into Japan in 1923. He'd never seen anything like this.

Neither Duane nor anyone else had any way of knowing that this storm had become so powerful so quickly. Only a day earlier the storm's strongest winds were blowing at 104 mph. But for 24 hours the hurricane had greedily gorged itself on energy as it drifted slowly across the unusually warm waters between The Bahamas and Florida, moving at 4 mph. There was nothing to stop its strengthening—no upper-level winds to shear off its cloud tops and halt its development, and no cooler waters to deprive it of its fuel.

By 7 p.m. Monday the hurricane had quickened its pace so that its eye was less than 30 miles offshore from the Keys. The winds around its center were screaming at better than 160 mph. And this nightmare of a hurricane was still getting stronger as it approached the low-lying islands.

A hurricane's deadliest weapon is its storm surge, a mound of water that is piled up by its winds and pushed along just ahead of the eye. The size of the surge is directly related to the strength of the winds. A hurricane with 160 mph winds can create a storm surge of more than 18 feet—enough to easily bury the Keys, where the highest elevation is 18 feet above sea level. Like the most powerful winds in a hurricane, the worst part of the storm surge is to the right of the eye in what meteorologists call the front right quadrant of the storm.

Keys natives have their own word for this part of the storm that packs the deadly one-two punch of peak winds and maximum storm surge. They call it the "heft" of the hurricane. And the heft of this storm would strike Islamorada at exactly the right moment to make sure that no one would escape aboard the rescue train.

By 7 p.m. the hurricane had destroyed the flimsiest buildings in the work camps and was beginning to weaken the more substantial structures. In Islamorada the train station could no longer withstand the furious onslaught and began breaking up. As the wind tore away chunks of the station, Ray Sheldon and the others waiting for the evacuation train realized they'd have to find shelter somewhere else.

The men left the disintegrating building, struggled through the storm, and climbed into a boxcar that was parked on a nearby siding.

With buildings being blown to pieces around him, Sheldon knew the men under his supervision were in serious trouble. As the hurricane raged outside, he prowled uneasily around the boxcar, saying repeatedly that he'd done all he could to get the veterans off the Keys. Some of the men agreed with him. Others looked away in grim silence.

A few Islamorada residents had gathered at the home of Reverend Robert Carlson and his wife, Maude. As the storm intensified, Carlson, clutching a Bible, led the group in prayer.

A little farther down Upper Matecumbe Key, Ed Butters was flicking on his flashlight every few minutes to check his barometer. What he saw was unnerving him.

The needle kept plunging, and by 7:45 p.m. it had fallen to the lowest reading his barometer could register—26.00 inches. Butters was terrified by the astonishingly low reading—but he was strangely fascinated as well. He couldn't stop the needle's relentless nosedive any more than he could stop himself from staring at the instrument. He realized that watching it fall was only adding to his terror. He decided he no longer needed the barometer to tell him what was plainly obvious—this was one hell of a hurricane.

Butters held the barometer aloft and shouted above the roar of the storm for the attention of the others in his Plymouth.

"I called five witnesses, and I threw the light of my flashlight on it," Butters said. "And I said, 'I don't want to read that thing anymore.'"

With that, Butters rolled down the window of his car and flung the barometer into the storm.

Up at Windley Key the train crew finally freed the locomotive after working for 80 minutes in the driving wind and rain, and the rescue train continued its journey southward a few minutes after 8 p.m.

Seawater now covered the tracks, and engineer J. J. Haycraft could only creep along at a few miles per hour as the malevolent winds rocked the heavy train coaches.

As the rescue train crawled along the tracks, the northern edge of the hurricane's eye reached Alligator Reef. When the winds subsided, keeper Jones Pervis ventured out to check his lighthouse. About 50 feet above the normal sea level, the pounding of the hurricane had pushed a pair of heavy steel doors inward. Lighthouse windows were broken 136 feet above the water, allowing the vicious wind to rip interior wooden doors off their hinges. The light atop the spire was gone, but otherwise the structure was withstanding the blow.

A few minutes later the edge of the eye passed. Pervis and his assistants returned to their perch about halfway up the lighthouse ladder as the wind and rain resumed with renewed fury.

Lost somewhere amid the mountainous seas off Key Largo, Captain Sundstrom and his crew still wrestled with the storm for control of the *Dixie*. Meanwhile, George Outland had tired of playing the piano and organized a poker game. The players dealt the cards and placed their bets as the storm tossed and rocked the ship.

A few minutes past 8 p.m., Outland looked at his hand. It was not unbeatable, but close to it. He raised the betting until there was $10 in the pot—far more than a day's pay for many jobs in 1935. Other players folded their hands, but one player matched Outland's bet and called the hand. It was time to settle up.

But as Outland and his opponent were about to lay their cards on the table, there was a screeching, lurching crash. The hurricane's winds and waves had slammed the *Dixie* onto French Reef like a wrestler pinning his opponent. The ship was now helpless in the teeth of the roaring hurricane.

"The sound was horrible, even above the roar of the wind and the thunder of the waves," said passenger Anna R. Chambers. "A crunching, grinding sound, and the *Dixie* shuddered like a live thing that had received a death wound."

The poker players resettled themselves at their table. Outland and his opponent showed their cards. The other man had a king-high full house—cards that would win most poker hands. But Outland laid down an aces-high full house and raked his winnings across the table.

Still, his satisfaction was tempered by the frightening reality of the moment. "I wondered whether I'd ever be able to spend the money," Outland said later.

A frightened Florence Steiler dashed from her stateroom and into a nearby lounge. There she found other passengers clinging to chairs with expressions of terror frozen on their faces. One young man—who'd perhaps had too much to drink—had grabbed a soggy pillow, lain down on the floor, and fallen fast asleep.

A crew member stepped into the room. His voice was calm, but what he said sent a shiver through the crowd. "Get up, and everybody on with their life belts," he said.

Steiler looked around at the other passengers. "The crowd was immediately electrified," she said.

As the seas smashed against the helpless *Dixie*, Ray Sheldon peeked through a crack in the boxcar and saw a flashing red light. The rescue train had at last reached Islamorada.

Sheldon and Olin Perdue climbed down out of the boxcar. As they pushed through the storm toward the train, seawater suddenly began to rise around their ankles, and by the time they reached the locomotive less than 100 feet away, they were waist deep in saltwater. They didn't know it, but the hurricane's storm surge was coming ashore. The raging, flailing beast had finally set its watery foot on land.

Less than a mile away, the people packed into Ed Butters's Plymouth could hear the hurricane dismantling the Hotel Matecumbe.

"The hotel sounded like it was going to fall apart," Fern Butters said. "The kitchen had exploded."

Suddenly the back of the second story collapsed, and the debris tumbled onto the new fire engine the Florida ERA had parked behind the hotel. The rubble crushed the roof of the truck's cab, and Fern Butters heard a new scream. Somehow the falling wreckage turned on the fire engine's siren. The eerie, mournful wail joined the storm's cacophony of chaos.

Then, still more screams, but Fern realized these were human. Charles Butters snapped on his flashlight and pointed it into the storm.

The light revealed three hotel employees struggling against knee-deep seawater. At the same moment Fern Butters felt dampness around her feet and instinctively looked down. The rising water was seeping into the car. As she felt it swirling around her ankles, Fern was almost overwhelmed with fear. She slumped limply against the back of the car seat. "Oh, God!" she murmured.

Ed Butters pushed open the car door, slogged through the water, and helped each of the employees to the Plymouth. There was no room for them in the car, however, and with the water creeping above his knees, Butters decided the automobile was no longer a safe refuge. He decided to move everybody to the railroad embankment—the highest ground they could possibly reach.

Butters put his younger son on his shoulders, and the others formed a human chain behind him. But as the group started toward the railroad track, Ed stepped into a deep hole and lost his balance. He felt a sharp, stabbing pain in his foot and realized that he'd stepped on a long nail that penetrated his shoe. He struggled back to his feet.

Fern Butters saw her husband go down and decided that making the railroad was impossible. "Ed!" she shouted above the hurricane. "Let's stay together and get into that old bus!"

A friend from Chicago had driven the bus to Florida two years earlier and asked Ed to let him park it at the hotel. It hadn't been moved since then. Now it offered emergency shelter from the raging hurricane.

The group climbed into the bus. Soon the seawater joined them.

In the Russell family's storm shelter, the winds were pounding at the door, causing it to vibrate so furiously that John Russell feared it was about to be torn from its hinges. Several men, including Bernard Russell, leaned against the door to brace it and stop the vibrations.

Bernard Russell noticed that muddy water was seeping beneath it and into the shelter. He knew the building was about three feet off the ground, and the fact that the water was muddy indicated it wasn't rainwater being blown under the door by the storm.

Bernard Russell dipped a finger into the water and touched his finger to his lips. The water was salty. His family's worst fears were realized. Upper Matecumbe Key was underwater.

John Russell had an awful decision to make. The shelter shielded his family from the killer winds outside. But if his family stayed there, they risked being drowned. The postmaster pondered a choice that probably would mean life or death for him and those he loved.

Back at what had been the train station, Ray Sheldon and Olin Perdue climbed into the cab of locomotive number 447. Sheldon was very glad to see the train and tried to put a cheerful face on his fears. "You're the man we've been looking for," he said to engineer Haycraft.

Sheldon checked his watch by the lights that illuminated the locomotive's pressure gauges and other instruments. It was 8:20 p.m. He asked Branch if they could take the train down to Camp 3. Branch said he thought they could continue southward. But the trainmaster also had a problem—a steam-powered locomotive could travel only about 150 miles before it needed more water for its boiler. The locomotive's water tank would have to be filled before the return trip to Miami, and trying to do that in winds that were now blowing at better than 150 mph would be a nearly impossible task. But they had to try.

Haycraft gave the locomotive's big throttle a tug to move the train to a nearby railroad water tower, but the train wouldn't budge. Something had gone wrong. The brakes on the coaches had locked.

"I guess those damn boxcars have blown over," Branch grumbled. "I'll go back and see."

But Haycraft begged the trainmaster to stay in the locomotive. "Mr. Branch, when you put your foot on the ground in this storm, you are stepping into eternity," Haycraft said.

Sheldon and the conductor also pleaded with Branch. "I said we could not just sit there and do nothing and I was going," Branch said.

"Well, by God, brother, you don't have to go alone," Perdue said. "I'm going with you."

Branch and Perdue left the locomotive, climbed into the first passenger car, and worked their way through the train.

"You should have seen those coaches and us scurrying through them, the windowpanes blowing out and crashing around our feet; the poor, cold, frightened, water-soaked wretches cowering in the corners, closets, and toilets to avoid the crashing glass," Branch said.

The men entered a baggage car. As Branch suspected, the boxcars—weighing about 75 tons each—had been blown off the track. The water was rising. Still, Branch thought he could uncouple the boxcars so the train could continue. But before he could try, a car coupled to the baggage car turned over. Branch, Perdue, and another crew member already in the car were trapped.

And still the seawater rose. Finally it reached the level of the locomotive's firebox and extinguished the flames that heated the boiler. Branch's worries about taking on water for the boiler and detaching a derailed boxcar didn't matter anymore. Without the fire the boiler couldn't produce steam, and without steam the locomotive was dead.

At the Russells' storm shelter, John Russell had made his difficult decision. He would move his family to higher ground. They tried to brace themselves for the hurricane's fierce onslaught. Bernard Russell put his arms protectively around his sister, Marjorie Spitz, and her toddler son, Raymond Spitz Jr., as one of the men opened the door.

The hurricane roared into the shelter like a wet, savage beast pouncing on its prey. Bernard Russell tried to steady himself and hold on to his sister and nephew as the furious winds and blowing water engulfed them. But the teenager was no match for the storm's ferocity. Suddenly the woman and child were gone, ripped away from him and sucked into the howling blackness as though the storm had simply swallowed them whole in a single greedy bite. Stunned, he stepped backward into the shelter. But something else was terribly wrong. The door frame was tilting, and the floor was rising. Russell realized the hurricane was pulling the shelter away from the thick steel screws that held it to the coral island. The building was slowly turning over.

The peak of the storm surge had arrived. In the next few minutes, dozens of lives would be snuffed out as easily as the flames in the locomotive's firebox.

When a storm surge makes landfall, giant breaking waves riding atop the mound of water usually accompany it. A storm surge of 18 to 22 feet such as the one created by the Labor Day hurricane can have breaking waves 30 feet high. It is these breaking waves that cause much of the carnage when the storm surge comes ashore, smashing everything in front of them and sweeping away the wreckage like a giant wet broom.

While the waves riding the storm surge were ripping the Russells' shelter from its anchors, they were also slamming into the rescue train with an unearthly force. The cars, each weighing from 75 to 100 tons, were shoved off the tracks. Only the locomotive, weighing more than 160 tons, remained upright.

In the train's smoking car, reporter William Johns thought he was about to die. "We had been stopped but 10 or 15 minutes when a wall of water from 15 to 20 feet high picked up our coaches and swirled them about like straws," Johns said. "We felt them going and I imagine everyone thought it was the end. I know I did."

The storm had no difficulty pushing the train off the tracks. "It went over so easy that we thought that something was just lifting up and possibly something had blown under it," Johns said. "We didn't know exactly what it was."

As Johns felt the coach lifting off the ground, he screamed in terror to the others, "She's gone, boys!"

When the coaches came to rest, they stretched in an arc along the west side of the railroad tracks. A couple of the cars at the apex of the arc were carried about 150 feet.

"We came out of the swirl of water with a thump that tossed the inmates of the coaches across seats, against windows, and in crazy heaps on side walls that had suddenly become floors," Johns said. "Miraculously, none was hurt severely."

It took a few moments for the occupants to realize they were no longer moving. The foamy seawater swirling through the car gave them the impression it was still being carried along by the storm.

The worst of the storm surge sped quickly across the islands. "The wall of water passed as quickly as it came, else we would all have been drowned like rats in a trap," Johns said.

Johns and the others had no idea what had happened to them or where they were. The car leaned crazily, and for all the occupants knew, it was dangling over a ledge and could topple into the ocean at any moment. Rain and seawater blew through the smashed windows. "You couldn't see six inches to either side," Johns said.

In the baggage car the wind carried away one of the car's heavy steel doors. Branch, Perdue, and the crewman helped four other crewmen into the car.

The surging water also pushed over the boxcar where Deputy Sheriff Maloney, Ray Sheldon, Wilbur Jones, and others had sought shelter after the train station was destroyed. "All of a sudden, bang, [the boxcar] went over," Jones said. "It was dark as hell."

The peak of the storm surge had passed, but the water didn't completely leave the island. The Conchs' fears about the railroad embankments and the causeways between the islands were coming true. They were preventing the surge from flowing around the islands, and the water piled up and spread out across Upper Matecumbe Key instead of flowing into Florida Bay. It was still deep enough on the island to submerge the huge drive wheels of the locomotive.

Back at what had been the Russell family's storm shelter, Bernard Russell plunged into the watery, howling darkness as the structure disintegrated. The dozen other relatives who'd been in the shelter had simply vanished.

Russell struggled to keep his head above the water. The noise of the hurricane was deafening—a raspy, wailing, ear-splitting screech unlike anything he'd ever heard.

Something slammed viciously into Russell's back and began relentlessly pushing him downward until his head disappeared beneath the waves. The teenager involuntarily gulped a mouthful of saltwater and figured he was about to die.

But just as suddenly he was released, and his head popped back above the water like a cork. Still, he couldn't move. Something held his left foot, and he couldn't pull it loose. The waves continued to roll in, and Russell's head disappeared briefly beneath the water as each crest passed him. He had to time his breathing, cupping his hands around his mouth and hastily gulping air during the troughs of the waves before being dunked again by the next crest. He knew each breath might be his last.

Aboard the *Dixie*, Captain Sundstrom ordered that lifeboats be partially lowered on the side of the ship that was protected from the wind. Sundstrom had no intention of putting people into lifeboats unless the ship started to sink or break up, but he wanted them ready for immediate use if necessary.

But after standing near the lifeboats for about an hour, many passengers became bored. They drifted into one of the lounges, sat down, and started talking.

"The chief topic was death and whether one minded it," said Florence Steiler. Reverend F. A. Wakeman, a Catholic priest from San Diego, started praying. Occasionally a passenger would interrupt the priest's prayers to ask for absolution.

Others, however, started singing "That Daring Young Man on the Flying Trapeze."

"All the while, the ship was rolling badly and those on the down side would be in water up to their knees, and then as the ship rolled back, the other side was drenched," Steiler said. "Suitcases, shoes, and personal belongings were washed from one stateroom across the alleyway into another stateroom. But no one seemed to care."

One passenger spotted a friend's expensive new shoes floating across the deck and called to her friend. "Who the heck cares about shoes now?" her friend answered.

On the Keys the hurricane continued its relentless slaughter.

Islamorada resident Jimmy Woods took shelter at his parents' house with his brother and three sisters. When the storm surge came ashore, the house was lifted off the ground. The family tried to flee, but Woods's mother couldn't move quickly enough to avoid the refrigerator that slid down the tilting floor toward her. The appliance slammed into her, breaking her back and paralyzing her from the waist down.

Amid the swirling chaos, Woods heard his 11-year-old sister, Ruth, pleading for help. "Lord!" she screamed above the hurricane's roar. "Save me!" Then she disappeared into the blackness.

Woods held his baby sister in his arms, trying to protect her from the storm, but too many missiles filled the air. A chunk of flying debris struck the child's head. "It crushed her right against the side of my head," Woods said. "And she was dead. She was just killed instantly."

Before Woods could react to the tragedy, he was knocked unconscious by another piece of flying debris.

At the Hotel Matecumbe a thick tangle of mangroves lay between the old touring bus and the beach. The mangroves absorbed and dispersed the terrific force of the storm surge and kept the bus from being carried away.

Still, the water kept rising inside the bus.

"We had constant flashes of sheet lightning, and all this with the wind howling like a banshee, the siren moaning, and the water rising everywhere," Fern Butters said. "You would have thought there would have been mass hysteria. Yet with everyone looking into the face of death, there were no hysterics. Everyone was quiet."

Outside the bus the brilliant flashes of lightning briefly illuminated corpses floating past in the swirling seawater.

Nearby, Bertram Pinder decided that his house was about to go to pieces. He told his family they had to get out or be killed in the wreckage.

The Pinders gathered near the back door and steeled themselves for the dangerous dash through the storm. But before they could move, the house suddenly shattered as though a bomb had hit it. "It was like the house just blew up," said Evanette Pinder.

The family was suddenly thrown into the swirling, merciless night. The wind and flood carried away Evanette Pinder, her husband, and their four-year-old daughter, but miraculously they all landed together in a lime grove, where they clung to the top of a tree. Hanging on to the prickly tree was like "trying to hold on to a cactus," she said. But it saved their lives.

Back at the ruins of the Pinder house, Dolores Pinder and her mother, Elizabeth, clung to the wreckage trying to keep their heads above water.

Russell Pinder was knocked senseless when a small water tank slammed into his head.

At the Hotel Matecumbe, Ed Butters stationed himself at the door of the bus to keep debris away and help anyone trying to struggle through the storm. He spotted the dazed, semiconscious Russell Pinder and helped him into the makeshift shelter.

Farther up the island, Reverend Robert Carlson and his wife Maude were locked in a life-and-death struggle with the hurricane. The surging water lifted the Methodist parsonage off its foundation and shoved it across the island. With water rapidly rising around him, Carlson grabbed an ax and started hacking away at the ceiling of his home. If he could open a hole, he and his wife could climb up into the rafters and perhaps escape the water.

The veterans suffered horribly as their flimsy camps disintegrated around them. In Camp 1 the winds picked up one veteran, hurled him through the air, and slammed him against a post with a sickening thud. He died instantly.

John Conway, another Camp 1 veteran from the eastern Iowa prairie town of Marion, watched three men clinging desperately to a telephone pole, but by now there wasn't much that was big enough or tied down tightly enough to withstand the hurricane. "The pole went into the air with the men hanging on," Conway said. "It blew far out to sea. Those men [were] goners."

Many vets were killed as they fled the wreckage of their camps.

"When the buildings began to crack, men ran out like scurrying rabbits, only to be picked up and blown in the air in every direction," said veteran Jack Clifford, who was from the seaside town of Hampton, Virginia.

Many who had somehow survived the storm surge were being beaten to death by windblown debris. Some were killed by flying coconuts or chunks of coral. Others were speared by boards or tree limbs. One man was killed when a steel spike buried itself in his skull.

Some men never knew what hit them. One moment they were alive and alert, thinking about their families, praying they'd survive, and trying to hold on to their courage by reminding themselves they'd been terrified before when they were clinging to the mud in France as exploding German shells shook the ground beneath them. Then the next moment they were gone, their lives snuffed out as suddenly and easily as the flame of a candle.

Death came more slowly to others, who watched helplessly as seawater swirled around them. When the water started rising around their chins and filling their mouths, they knew they were going to die.

A few clung to life during a wild and terrifying ride across gigantic waves, carried along by the hurricane for miles until they were tossed, exhausted and half-dead, onto one of the many small, soggy islands that dot Florida Bay. A few were pitched onto Cape Sable at the tip of the Florida peninsula after riding the hurricane for 40 miles or more.

Some died quickly; others lingered horribly after the hurricane had passed, dying slowly from thirst and untended injuries.

Some simply disappeared from the face of the earth forever.

At Camp 5 John Ambrose, the talented artist from Louisiana who'd fretted that the veterans might not get to see a hurricane, clung to Lower Matecumbe Key with a hundred or so other men. But they were in the worst situated of the three camps on a narrow, low-lying section of the island that was only a foot or two above sea level, and they were taking a deadly pounding from the storm.

There were small acts of courage and compassion amid the chaos. At Camp 1 veteran George Sherman of Little Falls, New York, spotted a puppy struggling for its life in the water. Sherman dashed into the surf, grabbed the animal, and hauled it out to safety.

At Camp 3 the veterans who had scoffed at Fritz Maggesen's offer to ride out the storm aboard the *Rowena* had realized that Long Island Sound had never been stirred by a wind like this, and by 8:45 p.m. two or three dozen of them had piled aboard. The *Rowena* was standing up to the fierce blow, but Maggesen discovered that ceaseless tugging on the mooring lines was loosening the boat's steel ringbolts.

It was only a matter of time before the ringbolts were pulled out of the boat, and when that happened the *Rowena* would be swept away to God only knew where. Maggesen told the veterans they'd better figure out a way to get aboard the *Monroe County*, then he and several volunteers ventured out into the watery chaos and started rigging new lines to hold the *Rowena* to the dock. Suddenly, above the roar, Maggesen heard a sickening crash. The lines securing the *Monroe County* had broken, and the ferry careened wildly away from the dock. The wind and waves hauled the helpless craft onto Lower

Matecumbe Key and slammed it against the railroad embankment, where it began breaking up.

Then the raging winds and drenching downpour suddenly ceased. The hurricane's tiny eye had arrived at Camp 3. James Lindley, who had escaped the wreckage of the mess hall, poked his head above the railroad embankment during the calm.

"It quieted down just like that, just stopped," Lindley said. "The stars come up and the wind seemed to get warm, and it was just as still, a piece of paper wouldn't flutter in the air."

Arthur Mewshaw half waded and half swam through the seawater until he was within shouting distance of the *Sarasota*, where Ed Sheeran and others had taken shelter. He called for Sheeran and asked him what the men should do.

Sheeran warned Mewshaw that the worst of the hurricane was still to come and told Mewshaw to take the veterans to higher ground. About 100 men, including Mewshaw and camp superintendent Ben Davis, walked up the island to the tanker car that was parked on a sidetrack. They'd ride out the rest of the storm there.

Roland Craig, Jack Crow, and several others had ridden out the first part of the storm by moving from building to building on nearby Craig Key. When the eye arrived, Craig left his bungalow to look around.

"All my buildings on the east side [of the railroad tracks] were as flat as a pancake and all torn up and gone," he said.

As the veterans huddled behind the tanker car near Camp 3, they heard a strange, distant rustling. A few minutes later they discovered the source of the noise.

"We could hear this wave out there just rustling like somebody brushing leaves," Davis said.

What they were actually hearing was the Atlantic Ocean rushing to reclaim the seabed that the hurricane had forced it to abandon. During the first part of the storm, the fierce winds had piled up water on the bay side of the Keys, but pushed water away from the islands on the ocean side. Now, with the backside winds blowing in the opposite direction, the water that had been swept far offshore was charging back toward the Keys, piled high and moving with terrific force.

Soon the surge of water reached the reef, and the faint rustling became a deafening roar. It was a terrifying moment for the veterans, who could only watch helplessly as the saltwater—whipped into snowy white foam and illuminated by the feeble light of the new moon—hurled itself at them.

"It started coming in over the reef, and then we watched it coming in, and it looked like white foam," Davis said.

The men tightened their grips on the tanker car and tried to brace themselves for the inevitable. As the roiling water drew closer, they could feel the ground trembling from its massive weight. Then it was upon them, slamming into the tanker with a murderous impact.

The tanker disappeared briefly beneath the water, and the force of the wave ripped the main track from its bed and slammed the strands of steel against the railroad car sitting on the sidetrack. But the heavy tanker, loaded with 10,000 gallons of water, didn't budge. Then the wave was gone—and so were more than 25 of the 100 or so men who'd tried to cling to the tanker. Some of the men screamed in terror as the rushing seawater carried them away. Others silently rode the wave to their deaths.

The killer wave seemed to be towing the backside of the hurricane's eye. Immediately after the water was gone the winds resumed. They were even fiercer than before.

Aboard the *Rowena*, Fritz Maggesen looked around at the three dozen or so veterans now aboard the boat. Their fear was clearly evident on their faces. Maggesen had an idea. He pulled out his accordion and started playing an old sea chanty. A few veterans recognized the song and started singing along. Others joined in, and for a few moments the terror of the storm abated.

But the roar of the wind steadily increased, eventually drowning out Maggesen and his accordion. He suggested they start praying. Nearly all agreed, but one veteran refused—not because he was an atheist, but because he didn't think it would be right. "I've been an old son of a gun all my life, and I'll go out the same way I've lived," the man said. "It wouldn't be fair to the Lord to ask for mercy on my carcass at this late date. I'll just have to take the consequences."

Down at Long Key, James Duane Jr. continued to take his hourly readings even though it was impossible for him to report his information to the Weather Bureau with the telephone line gone. At 9 p.m. his barometer had fallen to 27.29 inches—well below the levels of three earlier terrible storms that had devastated parts of Florida. The 1919 storm that left Key West in ruins and then barreled across the Gulf of Mexico to strike Texas had a low reading of 27.37 inches, and the barometric pressure during the horrific hurricane of 1928 that killed roughly 3,000 around Lake Okeechobee had fallen to 27.43. Even the 1926 hurricane that had nearly wiped out Miami Beach wasn't this intense. That storm's lowest reading was 27.61 inches.

At 9:10 p.m. the torrential rains and raging winds suddenly stopped at Long Key as though an unseen hand had flipped a switch. The hurricane's eye was crossing the fishing camp. It was a bizarre contrast to the fierce winds of only a few moments earlier.

Stars were clearly visible—another indication of the hurricane's intensity. In many hurricanes the sky remains obscured by clouds in the eye. Very intense hurricanes, however, often have small, cloudless eyes. The clear eye of Hurricane Andrew in 1992, for example, was only about 14 miles wide.

The eye of this nameless hurricane was only about 10 miles across.

Duane and a few others cautiously ventured out to look at the ruins. Most of the camp's buildings had been reduced to piles of tangled lumber and debris. Amazingly, no one in the group was seriously injured, but Duane knew the backside of the hurricane would soon arrive, and with it would come winds as strong or perhaps stronger. He ordered the others into the only remaining building he thought might withstand the awful blast that was sure to come—the cottage of Britain's Countess of Suffolk.

At Craig Key, Roland Craig ventured down the railroad trestle to the home of R. G. Jackson, who operated the railroad drawbridge. Jackson, a veteran of many hurricanes, advised Craig to ride out the rest of the hurricane on the lee side of the railroad embankment. Craig hurried back up the tracks to prepare for the backside of the storm.

While Craig was looking for a safe place, Fred Ghent was running into rain from the hurricane's outermost fringes. Around 9:30 p.m. he stopped at the Florida East Coast Railway office in West Palm Beach to check on the progress of the train. But there was still no word.

Ghent walked back out into the wind-driven rain to his car wondering if the rescue train had encountered problems down in the Keys.

As the first pangs of uncertainty about the fate of the veterans stabbed at Ghent, Fern Butters stood in chest-deep seawater and thought about biblical references to water and flooding.

"I had great faith in what God could do," she said. "I was thinking of how He rolled back the Red Sea, parted the rivers of Jordan, and how Jesus spoke to the waves and they were still."

She started to pray aloud. "I mentioned all these things I had been thinking about and asked God, for Jesus' sake, to make the water go down," she said. She ended her prayer by lifting her arms out of the water and crossing them above her head.

Minutes passed. Nothing happened.

The heft of the hurricane continued to lash Upper Matecumbe Key, and the boisterous sea kept pounding relentlessly against the railroad causeways between the islands.

Then, suddenly, the water began dropping as though someone had pulled the plug of a bathtub. The railroad causeways had finally given way. The pent-up storm tide rushed into Florida Bay.

In the bus the refugees realized that the water was going down.

As the water receded, Bernard Russell discovered he was atop a pile of debris. He worked his foot free and scrambled off the pile. He was certain he was the only living thing on the island. Then, above the tearing winds and slashing rain, he heard someone calling for help. He shouted a response and started feeling his way through the raging darkness toward the voice.

Elizabeth Pinder and her daughter Dolores kept their heads above water by clambering atop the wreckage of their home. But the sudden drop in the water created suction so strong that Elizabeth was suddenly yanked down into the wreckage, pulled through small openings deep into the pile of debris that had been her home. Moments later she was hopelessly entangled, alive but badly injured with many cuts and broken bones. Her daughter could only hold a coat over her mother's head to keep the pounding rain off her face.

Ed Butters heard calls for help above the roar of the winds. He and his father plunged into the storm. Moments later they brought three more refugees—a woman and her two children—into the bus.

Butters left the bus again to go into the ruins of the hotel to get blankets. He found Ruth Woods in the lobby. The storm had torn the clothing from her body, and the girl was shivering with cold, but the prayer she'd screamed at the moment her house was destroyed had been answered. She was unhurt. Butters carried her to the Plymouth and went back to the ruined hotel to find something to cover her.

A few minutes past 10:30 p.m., the sea suddenly started rising at Long Key. James Duane pointed the beam of his flashlight toward the ocean. He saw a terrifying sight. The calm continued, but out toward the reefs Duane could see a "wall of water, many feet high" racing toward the island.

It was the displaced ocean returning.

Duane and a companion sprinted for the cottage where the others waited, about 60 feet away. Before they could reach the door they were waist deep in water. Then the cottage floated off its foundation.

At Craig Key, Roland Craig and Jack Crow had just reached the railroad embankment when the wind suddenly resumed and the sea quickly rose around them.

"The wave come clean over the track, bringing all kinds of debris . . . and throwing it on our heads, and knocked us into the water," Craig said. He and Crow scrambled atop the embankment and grabbed hold of the railroad tracks.

"I really, in fact, dug under the crossties and held onto the rail," Craig said. "I prayed a lot all night, and we stayed there until three o'clock and I never heard such a roar of wind in my life."

Not far away, Iver Olson had pulled his small, sturdy boat out of the water and secured it at the southern end of Craig Key to ride out the storm. His boat had held together, and those who were with him were unhurt.

Olson had a barometer that bottomed out at 28 inches. The needle had dropped far below that mark long ago. Still, Olsen kept an eye on the instrument, which also had a thermometer. During the lull he noted the barometer's needle dropped to the point on the thermometer that read 10 degrees above zero Celsius. Olson marked the needle's position even though he had no idea whether his barometer was still responding properly to the astonishingly low atmospheric pressure.

Down in Key West the fringe of the storm dumped torrential rainfall on the city. Bascom Grooms Jr. ignored the deluge, however, and escaped his gloom about the end of summer vacation by going to an early showing of *West Point of the Air*. He removed his soaking shoes, settled himself into his seat in the darkened theater, and became absorbed in the drama starring Wallace Beery, Maureen O'Sullivan, and Robert Young.

The youngster had no way of knowing that his sister Rosalind and her boyfriend, George Pepper, had never arrived at the Hotel Matecumbe to pick up the veterans' wives waiting to get off the island.

Around 10 p.m. Ernest Hemingway lay down for a couple hours of sleep. His home, like the rest of the city, was boarded up tightly. The winds hadn't reached hurricane force in Key West, but the rain hadn't let up all night. Hemingway expected the worst part of the storm to reach there in a couple of hours. The author put a flashlight and a barometer next to his bedside.

He intended to get up at midnight to go down to the docks to check on his beloved *Pilar*.

Up at Camp 1 on Windley Key about 40 people, including mothers and their children, had crowded into the makeshift veterans hospital. The storm-driven sea had flooded the first floor of the two-story building, and the refugees were crowded into the second floor.

Around 10 p.m. the unrelenting pounding of the storm and the fear it inflicted were taking a toll on the mental stability of some refugees. Leo Moran, a veteran from Philadelphia, watched as the strain worked on Stanley Warman, one of his buddies, who also was from Philadelphia. The terrified man was sitting, dazed, on the floor.

"He was like a madman, eyes staring out of his head," Moran said.

Monroe County deputy sheriff T. F. Russell was among the refugees in the hospital. He'd watched the rescue train crawl past earlier in the night and assumed it would soon be returning from Islamorada to pick them up.

Russell announced he would lead a group from the hospital to the lee side of the railroad embankment, where they would wait for the train.

The deputy led a group downstairs and opened the door. Some of the refugees shrank back at the sight of waist-deep water swirling outside the building.

"Who wants to go with me?" he called above the hurricane's roar.

"I'll go!" Elva Loper shouted, and she took Russell's hand. Her husband, Dave Loper, also a deputy sheriff, took her other hand, and the three of them pushed into the storm.

A few others ventured after them, but most refused to leave.

As the vicious winds hammered the building, Elva Loper saw an astonishing sight.

"As we were leaving I looked back, and it seemed to me the hospital jumped about a foot off the ground," she said.

The building shattered, collapsing into a heap of rubble. A dozen people managed to escape the ruins. The rest were trapped inside.

Harry Gaskins, a veteran from New Bern, North Carolina, was clinging to a telephone pole when the hotel disintegrated. "For a moment it seemed that I was only dreaming to see that big building lifted like a little paper bag in a breeze," Gaskins said. "I could hear the crunch of buildings as they were being smashed to shivers. Above the thunder of the waves and through the roar of the storm I heard screams. Many were killed by flying boards and planks. I was almost hit several times."

Albert Christie, a veteran from Detroit, was trying to protect a little girl when the hospital disintegrated. The air suddenly was filled with wreckage, and Christie was battered from all sides. Something smashed against his head, and he lost consciousness.

"I don't really know [what hit me]," he said. "It was so dark you couldn't see. It was flying timbers that hit me, I guess."

When Christie came to, the child he'd been trying to protect was gone. Somehow, though, in his stupor he'd managed to grab another child and keep her from being carried away.

"I was hanging on to a little girl," Christie said. "Mr. Van Ness came down with a little girl about six years old and I was trying to help her. He was outside trying to get her. That was the last I saw of her. When I came to, I was hanging on to another girl. Frances, I think her name was."

Lassiter Alexander, a physician who worked at the hospital, was one of those who pushed his way out of the ruins. With only the feeble light of a flashlight to guide him, Alexander struggled through the water toward the railroad embankment. He was repeatedly knocked off his feet by the wind and flying debris. An awful mélange flew past his head.

"Timbers and trees and the bodies of children were whirled through the air," Alexander said.

Alexander reached the small rock wall that had been built by Jimmy Conway, the ex-boxer, shortly after the camp was established. Conway's handiwork was withstanding the storm. Alexander scrambled over the four-foot-high wall and crouched behind it. He found about two dozen people huddled there.

In Islamorada, George Branch and the others expected to die at any moment. "I can tell you just how a fellow feels who knows it is the night of his execution and is waiting for the warden to come for him," Branch said.

He took stock of his situation. He had about $125 in cash that he'd intended to send to his wife, a watch worth about $100, and his wedding ring.

Branch had missed the last deadline for a life insurance payment. "I worried and wondered whether it was still carrying itself and thought how someone would get the ring and money if my body was ever found," he said.

He felt "the surge of resentment that I had to die trapped like a rat to be drowned when the bottle was filled with water and that I had to simply wait for it like a condemned criminal."

Someone suggested that they should pray. Pete Carlisle, one of the crew members, said Branch could probably do a better job of praying than the others.

"We knelt," Branch said. "I began, 'Oh Lord, this is Pete Carlisle and George Branch . . .'"

Hearing his name, Carlisle leaped to his feet. "Oh hell, it ain't no use," he shouted furiously. "You've gone and told him who we are."

The men sat in silence for about 30 minutes listening to the storm. Then one of the crewmen sidled up to Branch. "Captain," he said, "don't you think it is slacking up a bit?"

Before Branch could answer, the ferocious winds and surging water suddenly shoved a telephone pole through the opening where the car's side door had been. The pole disappeared through the door on the other side of the car.

The man who'd asked whether the storm was slackening watched the pole vanish into the blackness, then answered his own question with a perfectly timed quip that could've come from a W. C. Fields comedy skit. "No, sir, it isn't," he said.

⁓

At Long Key the sudden rush of water that had covered the island during the last part of the lull was only a hint of what was coming. At 10:10 p.m., Duane, standing in waist-deep water with the other refugees, checked his barometer. The needle had dropped yet again, to 27.02 inches. The wind was stirring again, this time from the southwest—the opposite direction from the earlier winds.

Five minutes later the backside winds were upon them. Duane glanced at his barometer. The dial read 26.98 inches. Then the hurricane—almost as though it had had enough of Duane's constant monitoring—snatched the instrument from his hands. The barometer disappeared beneath the wind-whipped saltwater.

The countess's cottage, where Duane and his party had taken refuge, started to break up. Duane was suddenly sucked out of the building and thrust into a life-and-death struggle against the wind and water. He grabbed at something to keep from being pulled out to sea. It was the top of a coconut palm tree. Duane seized an armful of palm fronds and hung on. He watched the cottage begin to float away. His companions were still inside. Then something slammed into the back of his head, knocking him unconscious.

Up at the remains of Camp 1, the refugees who had taken shelter behind the small stone wall decided to try to reach the railroad embankment—the highest spot on the island. Once there they scrambled to the lee side of the embankment and started clawing holes into the marl that supported the tracks, burrowing into makeshift bunkers to protect themselves from the deadly debris that still filled the air.

Elsewhere, those who were still alive clung to anything that wasn't moving. At Camp 1, Lloyd Fichett crawled from the wreckage and struggled to higher ground, where he found a telephone pole that had withstood the onslaught. Fichett unbuckled his belt and used it to tie himself to the pole.

"A barrage of stones kept hitting me all over the body and then I partly lost consciousness," Fichett said. "I hung on through the night in a semi-dazed condition."

Charles Van Vecten, who had been visiting friends at Camp 1, clung to the railroad embankment with the veterans. The scene around him resembled a battlefield.

"I saw bodies with tree stumps smashed through their chests—heads blown off—twisted arms and legs torn off by flying timber that cut like big knives," Van Vecten said.

In Islamorada, Bernard Russell followed the voice in the blackness until he found his father. John Russell had a chunk of flesh torn from his buttocks, but he was alive. The teenager also found his uncle Clifton Russell wandering in a daze through the windy, watery chaos. The three men huddled together in the darkness to wait for daybreak.

At Camp 5, Melton Jarrell, from the Dallas suburb of Forney, Texas, spent the night clinging to the railroad track. "A heavy sea came along and washed [the track] up and as it settled back down it pinioned my left leg under it," Jarrell said. "After lying there for what seemed countless ages, suffering horrible agony, I decided to try to cut my foot off but I couldn't get to my penknife. After that I passed out."

When Jarrell regained consciousness, he found himself being washed away from the railroad track. "I was thrown upon a tree," he said. "It was a mangrove."

Jarrell seized the stubborn mangrove and hung on.

Elsewhere in Islamorada, fisherman J. R. Beckham rode out the storm in his new home with his wife and grandchildren and 13 other people who sought shelter there. Beckham had survived three earlier hurricanes and was confident his new house would withstand this storm.

"All of a sudden, it was like some great hand picked up the whole house and dropped it in the ocean," Beckham said. "When I came out of the daze, I was clinging to bushes. There was no sign of any of the 16 other persons we'd been talking with only a few minutes before. I crept from bush to bush and from stump to stump trying to find my wife and grandchildren. It didn't seem this could happen to me."

The winds and rains still raged at 11 p.m., but as the final hour of the awful day began, those who could still read their barometers saw a long-awaited sight—the needles were finally starting to climb. The worst part of the hurricane had passed and was moving away from the Keys. The storm's eye continued its northward turn and was now on a course that would brush Cape Sable at the tip of the Florida peninsula.

Around midnight Ernest Hemingway got out of bed and, flashlight in hand, went out to his car to drive down to the docks. The rain was still falling in torrents in Key West, and the downpour drowned out the engine in Hemingway's car. He got out of the useless automobile and slogged through the storm to the naval base to check on the *Pilar*. With the winds and rain still lashing Key West, he decided to wait out the storm by his boat.

Around 12:30 a.m. Tuesday, Fred Ghent reached Hollywood, where he hoped to find the rescue train waiting for him. Instead he found only Sam Cutler. Ghent learned that FEC officials hadn't heard from the train since it pulled out of Homestead seven hours earlier.

Ghent and Cutler climbed back into Ghent's car and drove on to Miami. FEC officials there knew nothing about the train either, but said they intended to send a wrecker after it if they hadn't heard anything by 3:30 a.m.

Ghent and Cutler continued south.

As the winds and waves continued to thrash and rock the *Dixie*, many passengers tried to find a dry spot to catch a little sleep.

At about 12:15 a.m. Tuesday, Captain Sundstrom got his first bit of good news in a long time. The *Dixie*'s weak SOS broadcast over the antenna rigged by Henry Treger had finally been picked up by Tropical Radio in Hialeah, Florida, and relayed to the U.S. Coast Guard in Jacksonville. Tropical Radio was broadcasting the SOS to all ships at sea. Then the Coast Guard station in Key West picked up the SOS. The Coast Guard radioed a message to the *Dixie* that a cutter was on its way. Other ships in the area changed course for the *Dixie*'s position, which was mistakenly being given as aground on Carysfort Reef.

Around 2:30 a.m. Tuesday, James Duane shook the cobwebs from his head and discovered that he was still in the coconut palm tree. He looked around at a scene that was illuminated by terrific flashes of lightning. The floodwaters had receded, and Duane was about 20 feet above the wreckage of Long Key Fishing Camp.

The cottage where his companions had taken refuge had been blown back to the island, and their incredible luck had held. They had all gone through the storm with no serious injuries.

At about the same time Duane was climbing down from the palm tree on Long Key, Fred Ghent and Sam Cutler pulled into Homestead. A drenching, windblown rain was falling when they arrived at the FEC station.

Ghent ran into a section foreman who had just returned from Florida City, only a few miles to the south at the tip of the peninsula. The foreman told Ghent that the road linking the peninsula with Key Largo was underwater. Ghent decided to stay the rest of the night in Homestead.

On the Upper Keys many grim, battered, soaking-wet survivors huddled in the darkness behind whatever meager shelter they could find as the departing storm continued to batter them. The veterans at Camp 3 who'd survived the storm wave by hanging on to the tanker now crouched behind the car that saved their lives.

Near the ruins of the Islamorada train station, someone managed to shove an ax between the slats of the overturned boxcar that had protected Deputy Sheriff Louis Maloney, Wilbur Jones, and others from the fury of the storm. The men used the ax to chop an escape hole.

George Branch estimated that the winds were blowing at about 100 mph by 2 a.m. He climbed out of the baggage car to check on his train. All the cars had been blown off the track, and the two boxcars had been carried about 600 feet from the track. But Branch found no serious injuries among the people aboard the train.

Ray Sheldon spent the night in the locomotive cab with the engineer, fireman, and conductor. Back in the coaches the passengers settled down in the overturned cars to wait out the rest of the storm.

Around 2 a.m. the winds peaked at 45 mph in Key West. Ernest Hemingway watched his boat until about 5 a.m., when the needle on his barometer stabilized. The weary author decided to call it a night and trudged home through the debris-strewn streets as a dreary, windy, rain-soaked dawn gradually materialized.

Hemingway discovered that a few trees had been blown down on his property, but otherwise his home had gone through the storm unharmed. He went back to bed.

As the first light appeared on the Upper Keys Tuesday morning, Ray Sheldon climbed down from locomotive number 447 to look around. What he saw was almost beyond comprehension.

CHAPTER SIX

A Terrible Sunrise

The feeble, storm-shrouded sunrise Tuesday morning gradually revealed the horrible night's work done by the hurricane. As each layer of darkness peeled away, the awful landscape came more clearly into focus.

The eye of the hurricane was now in the Gulf of Mexico as the storm spun its way northward, heading for a second landfall on the Florida Panhandle. Although the hurricane was weakening, the winds around its center were still blowing at a furious 130 mph Tuesday morning, and the backside of the storm was lashing the Upper Keys with torrential rain and winds exceeding 60 mph.

John Russell had been badly injured, and somehow lost his shoes. Bernard Russell searched through the gloomy dawn until he found two sponges and some twine. He and his uncle Clifton Russell tied the sponges to John Russell's feet. The trio started looking for shelter.

They found the derailed evacuation train with only the locomotive and its tender still upright. The coaches tilted crazily against the denuded brush and rubble left behind by the storm. Pieces of buildings, automobiles, seaweed, and human bodies had been swept beneath the leaning train cars.

But the steel coaches were intact, and they offered shelter from the pouring rain and fierce wind. Bernard Russell and his uncle helped John Russell into one of the baggage cars, and then they climbed in after him.

"We curled back in that for protection, because there was stuff blowing and raining like mad, and that's where we stayed until we could get some help," Bernard Russell said.

While they waited for the storm to subside, they wondered if any of their relatives were still alive.

William Johns, the *Miami Daily News* reporter who'd boarded the train in Homestead, tried to get out of the overturned passenger car where he'd spent the night. But the wind was still blowing so hard he could barely walk. He gave up and climbed back into the wrecked train.

Edney Parker was trying to figure out where he was. He and his family had taken shelter in his brother's house. The storm swept the structure off its foundation and carried it away, and they'd spent the night wondering where the hurricane had taken them. For all they knew, they'd been washed to another island.

"Then it was not very light, but we knew it was day," Parker said. "I crawled out and located a road that ran from the ocean to the bay, and being so familiar with the place, I knew where I was at."

Still, it took a few moments for Parker to get his bearings. The storm had obliterated most of the landmarks. Finally he discovered that the hurricane had torn his house from its foundation and deposited it almost a mile away.

"I went back and told [my] wife we were still on Matecumbe," he said. "We were south of the hotel, about three-quarters of a mile, and I didn't know who was left. I didn't see a sign of a house anywhere, and no trees."

Parker and his wife discussed what they should do. As they talked, the wind-driven rain continued to soak them in the ruined, roofless remains of the house. They decided to look for shelter.

Parker gathered his family and walked to the highway. "I realized it was the highway because it was a tar and asphalt road. There was a little piece of Mr. King's filling station left, and Mr. King was in it. We went there and got under shelter, standing in water to our ankles all day."

Parker and his family joined a small group of refugees who'd also taken shelter at King's filling station. Among the group were the veterans' wives who'd been waiting at the Hotel Matecumbe for George Pepper and Rosalind Grooms Palmer to pick them up. No one had seen Pepper and Palmer since they'd left the hotel with Ben Davis around 4:30 p.m. Monday.

The departing hurricane blew over a scene of stark and total devastation. Buildings had been swept away or reduced to piles of lumber. The normally lush vegetation was gone; only bare, broken branches remained. Instead of leaves, the branches were covered with shreds of clothing. The tattered rags whipped in the wind like pathetic flags of surrender.

The Matecumbe Methodist Church was gone, and so was the Matecumbe Graded School. Only 10 of the school's 65 students were still alive.

Just offshore, about a quarter mile from the beach, was an astonishing sight—a 3,000-ton Danish freighter hopelessly aground. The ship, the *Leise Maersk*, had been picked up by a giant wave, carried over the reef, and deposited almost on Upper Matecumbe Key. The dazed crew members could see the overturned train from their ship.

The concrete foundation was the only reminder of the small hospital at Camp 1. Soon after daylight, Lassiter Alexander, who had clung to the railroad embankment after the hospital was destroyed, struggled to his feet. His back had been painfully injured when the building collapsed. To his surprise, he saw his car. He managed to walk the 100 feet or so to it, then opened the door, eased himself into the vehicle, and lay down on the backseat.

Corpses were scattered everywhere. They were dangling from palm trees, floating in the surf, entangled in the mangroves. High overhead a corpse clung tenaciously to a telephone pole. The lifeless body of a toddler lay curled on the ground, his head resting on his hands as though he'd lain down to take a nap. An elderly man who died during the storm sat in a chair amid the roofless ruins of his house.

A piano had been slammed into the railroad embankment. The body of a young woman sat next to the piano.

Arms and legs protruded from mounds of debris. A puppy crouched next to one of the piles, gratefully licking a motionless hand. The hand belonged to George Sherman, the veteran who'd dashed into the deadly brine to rescue the struggling animal. Sherman had been killed later when a large, jagged splinter of wood, propelled by winds far in excess of 160 mph, was driven through his skull.

From some of the piles of rubble came the weak, pitiful calls of helpless survivors hoping to hang on to life until someone found them and dug them out.

Not far from the derailed train stood a battered but intact remnant of the home of Leo Johnson. The storm had deposited a large rowboat between two cypress trees near Johnson's house. The oars were still in their locks, both pushed forward as though the boat was about to land. On the seat next to the oars was a child's teddy bear, looking exactly as though it had rowed the boat through the storm to safety and then, too exhausted to move, slumped against the railing to rest.

The raging winds and water had killed the ex-servicemen in droves. In one place the storm swept the bodies of 39 veterans into a windrow like so much windblown sand.

The flimsy work camps—the veterans' end-of-the-line, edge-of-the-cliff refuge from the economic chaos of the Depression and the emotional turmoil of their own confused lives—were simply gone, blasted to splinters and blown into oblivion. Dozens of veterans had died at each of the camps, but Camp 5—only a couple of feet above sea level, so close to the ocean that normal high tides had sometimes invaded the kitchen—had been turned into a slaughterhouse. Fewer than a dozen men of the 125 or so who'd been in the camp when the storm began were still alive Tuesday morning.

The vets' pathetic boasting that no hurricane could be worse than their horrible experience in the Great War was gone. "I would rather face machine-gun fire than go through an experience like that again," said veteran George Senison of Bridgeport, Connecticut, who was at Camp 1.

Long-standing landmarks were obliterated or smashed almost beyond recognition. The post office, which had been a daily gathering place for Islamorada residents, was reduced to only the three porch columns, part of the front wall, and the foundation. The roof and much of the second floor of the Hotel Matecumbe had been sliced off and carried away.

Behind the ruins of the hotel, Fern and Ed Butters and the others who'd taken shelter in the bus looked around them in disbelief.

"The wind shrieked and howled all through the night, and as it abated and daylight came, devastation was all around us," said Fern Butters. "We could hear the screams of neighbors as they searched for loved ones, and they could not find them or they were so badly injured when they did find them."

Ed Butters and some of the other men left the bus to look for survivors. Soon they returned with a dozen and helped them into the vehicle. Some were injured. Butters and the others went into the ruins of the hotel, found a couple of rooms that were still dry and relatively intact, and put the injured there.

Charles Butters tried to provide something for the group to eat. He found an oil stove still in working condition and dragged it into the lobby of the hotel, out of the rain. He set out drinking glasses, pots, bowls, and other containers to catch rainwater and scrounged through the ruins of the hotel for canned food. He lit the stove and soon had a pot of coffee and hot boiled tomatoes for the survivors.

The men brought more survivors, some of them gravely injured. Bertram Pinder appeared and asked Ed Butters if he could borrow a saw. His wife, Elizabeth, who had been sucked into the ruins of their house when the floodwaters suddenly drained off the island, was still alive and would have to be cut out of the wreckage.

Someone took a sheet from the hotel and stuffed one end down into the gasoline tank of Ed Butters's Plymouth, withdrew it, and used the gasoline-soaked sheet to start a fire near the bus.

All that remained of the Caribee Colony was a bathtub—a single plumbing fixture—surrounded by the splintered stumps of palm trees. Nearby was a storm-mangled automobile belonging to Caribee manager Wade Dumas. The car's roof had been torn off and the windshield frame flattened. Both doors were wide open.

There was no trace of Dumas and his wife, Marie.

Other wrecked automobiles were strewn along the road. Some had been pushed into piles of debris or overturned in ditches. One car had been left resting on its rear bumper, its radiator pointing skyward.

The railroad track was impassable. About 40 miles of track between Tavernier and Marathon had been destroyed. In some places the wind and storm surge had lifted one side of the crossties and tracks upright so that they looked like a big picket fence. The concrete railroad bridges and viaducts had easily withstood the hurricane, but tracks that were 30 feet above normal high tide had been ripped off the bridges and carried away.

Even the ground beneath the survivors' feet was unrecognizable. In some places the scouring force of the storm surge had scrubbed off the thin layer of topsoil, exposing the islands' coral foundation.

Survivors desperately clawed and tugged at piles of rubble searching for missing family members, or wandered aimlessly through the ruins, too stunned to comprehend what had happened to them. Some of the wanderers were so dazed they didn't realize that the hurricane had torn every stitch of clothing from their bodies.

Nearly everyone who was still alive had injuries of some type. Most had had their ears and the backs of their necks scrubbed raw by windblown sand. Others who spent the night climbing up and down telephone poles to stay above the flood or clinging to lumber floating on the raucous seas had splinters painfully imbedded in their arms, legs, and torsos.

A veteran too seriously injured to walk sat helplessly in the driving rain, leaning against the foundation of a ruined house and pleading for help.

Near Snake Creek a group of veterans huddled behind a railroad tanker car. Somehow they got a fire going and made coffee.

At Lower Matecumbe Key, Fritz Maggesen surveyed the damage to the *Rowena*. The roof had been torn from the houseboat's cabin, and a timber ripped from the wreckage of Camp 3 had been driven through the Rowena's hull and into the engine room. And there wasn't a square inch of paint left on the vessel. The hurricane's winds had sandblasted the boat clean. But with the timber removed from the hull and the hole patched, the *Rowena* would be seaworthy enough to make it to Miami for major repairs—as soon as the seas quieted down. Maggesen checked his lines again and settled down to wait.

Aboard the *Sarasota*, Ed Sheeran was sizing up the situation. He knew that dozens of veterans had been killed, and many more injured. He took no satisfaction from the fact that he'd tried to warn the people in charge that this would happen if those men were left on the islands.

But the men under his care were safe. Most of them had left the Keys when he told them to. Those who stayed had taken shelter and survived. Some of his construction equipment had been damaged, but thanks to his preparations the damage was repairable, and for the most part the $400,000 worth of equipment he was responsible for was OK. Once again, Ed Sheeran had outfoxed the raging elements.

In Islamorada a dazed Ray Sheldon and six other survivors began walking north. They trudged through a bizarre landscape of destruction that held no resemblance to what had been there before the storm. As they neared Snake Creek, they heard the roar of rushing water. They saw that both the railroad and highway bridges were gone. The massive storm surge that the hurricane had pushed into Florida Bay was returning to the Atlantic. The noisy rush of water nearly drowned out conversation.

There was nothing for them to do but go back to the ruins of the Hotel Matecumbe to wait for help.

The outside world had no idea of what had happened in the Keys. Tuesday's newspapers published front-page stories about the plight of the *Dixie* and fretted about whether the ship would be pounded to pieces before its passengers and crew could be rescued.

"Fate of 800 Veterans on Matecumbe [Is] Mystery; Train Is Trapped" read the *Miami Daily News* headlines of Tuesday afternoon.

Aboard the *Dixie*, passengers were seeing daylight for the first time in what seemed like ages. Florence Steiler, the passenger from San Francisco, ventured onto the ship's main deck early Tuesday afternoon. She was amazed at the damage.

"Furniture was broken and piled up in heaps," she said. "Windows smashed, three lifeboats torn off, the galley and dining rooms complete wrecks."

With the galley wrecked, the ship's cooks couldn't prepare hot meals. But the crew still tried to reassure the passengers as best they could, and plenty of food—even if it was sandwiches, soda crackers, and fruit—was one way to do it. Everyone got all they wanted to eat. With the deck furniture swept away or smashed to bits, a few passengers simply sat down on the deck, leaned against the ship's superstructure, and sipped soft drinks as they watched the heaving ocean.

No one outside the Keys—not even the U.S. Weather Bureau—had the foggiest idea how powerful this hurricane had been. Weather Bureau officials told the Associated Press that the storm "can not be compared with the great hurricanes of 1926 and 1928. The hurricane area is much smaller and the winds are of far less velocity."

The Weather Bureau's description of the hurricane was comically inaccurate. The two earlier storms were indeed very bad—the 1926 hurricane nearly wiped out Miami Beach, and the 1928 storm pushed Lake Okeechobee out of its banks and probably killed around 3,000. But meteorologists would soon determine that the storm that had just swept through the Keys was the most powerful hurricane ever to strike the United States.

Even the Conchs, who had weathered many violent storms, were astonished by the unearthly intensity of this hurricane.

"Nobody expected what we had," said Edney Parker. "Nobody seemed to have any expectation of what we were going to have. We were prepared only for gales."

The murderous storm surge and the railroad causeways that piled up the water on the islands were responsible for the death toll, he said.

"I think the railroad officials, the weatherman, the camp officials, and all the natives were fooled, and fooled bad," Parker said. "I don't think they knew what was going to happen. We never dreamed anything was going to happen such as that."

It would be a full day before the rest of the world learned what had happened to a 40-mile stretch along the remote Keys.

At Long Key, James Duane Jr. and his band of storm survivors crawled out of the wreckage of the fishing camp and looked around at the chaos. A couple of the buildings had stayed more or less intact, but the hurricane had shoved them around like toys in a child's sandbox. The rest of the cottages, the hotel, and the boardwalks had been chewed up and tossed into a wild tangle of lumber, coconut palm trees, and seaweed. The railroad track had been ripped from its bed and haphazardly woven into the jumble of wreckage.

But, unbelievably, no one at Long Key had been killed or even seriously injured. The group took shelter in the surviving cottages to rest and wait for the rains and winds to subside.

Out near French Reef off Key Largo, ships were braving the still-ferocious ocean to come to the aid of the *Dixie*. The passenger-carrying freighter S.S. *Platano* was among the first to reach the grounded passenger liner. The *Platano* had been en route from Cortez, Honduras, to New York when the ship picked up the *Dixie*'s SOS signal. Without hesitation Captain C. D. McRea had sent his vessel charging through the storm-tossed seas at full speed when he picked up the distress call.

The *Platano* reached the Dixie's reported position on Carysfort Reef Tuesday afternoon, but the liner was nowhere in sight. Had the ship been pounded to pieces by the storm? McRea hoped *Dixie* captain Einar Sundstrom had been wrong about where his ship had grounded. He ordered his freighter to come in dangerously close to the reef-lined shore and search for the passenger ship. His hunch paid off. He spotted the *Dixie* on French Reef.

W. H. Depperman, a passenger aboard the *Platano*, could make out the stranded ship "through squalls of rain and mist from mountainous waves." The *Dixie* was visible "intermittently . . . about three miles off our starboard bow."

Three other vessels eventually arrived to aid the *Dixie*—the *Limon*, the *Gatun*, and the *El Occidente*. They dropped anchor to wait for the seas to subside so they could begin taking passengers off the *Dixie*.

Aboard the stranded passenger liner, there was nothing for the weary, relieved passengers to do but try to find a quiet, dry spot to settle down and wait to be rescued. Their fears of being dumped into a raging ocean were gone, but they'd still have to endure discomforts until they could get off the ship.

On the Keys the survivors scrounged for food, clothing, anything they could find to make themselves even a little more comfortable. A group of survivors talked about their experiences during the awful evening as they stood around a fire next to the FEC locomotive at Islamorada.

Down at Camp 3, Elmer Kreitzburg, who'd been impaled by a board when the mess hall was destroyed, had clung to life for almost 24 hours with the two-by-four still protruding from his body. But he became steadily weaker. Around 6 p.m. Tuesday he died.

As darkness fell Tuesday, some of the survivors gathered at the ruins of the Hotel Matecumbe. Ray Sheldon, tired and dazed, was among them. He spent the night at the bedside of 18-year-old William Baker, who had been seriously injured in the storm.

At Lower Matecumbe Key, Ed Sheeran's decision not to unload the railroad tanker containing 10,000 gallons of fresh water had proved to be a lifesaver. The heavy car had withstood the backwash of the Atlantic Ocean as it swept over the island and saved the lives of dozens of men who managed to hang on to it. Later it provided a source of drinking water when everything else had been destroyed.

Sheeran was exhausted. He had been wearing the same clothes for three days. "I was about whipped," he said. "I didn't have a thing left."

The following day, Sheeran's boss, B. M. Duncan, ordered him to go home to Coral Gables. "I had to borrow a shirt to come home in," Sheeran said.

Early Wednesday morning, William Johns climbed out of the wrecked train and walked down to the Hotel Matecumbe. The *Miami Daily News* reporter found Sheldon, and the two talked as they walked along the highway. Johns asked Sheldon why the veterans hadn't been evacuated from the Keys before the hurricane struck.

"He told me that he had been in touch with Washington, trying to get permission from Washington to move those veterans, and he was instructed to stay there to await further developments," Johns said. "Now, the man had gone through an awful lot. Maybe he was excited, and maybe it [wasn't] the truth."

Later that day, Johns's story about his experience aboard the ill-fated rescue train was the lead story for the afternoon *Miami Daily News*. Johns did something very unusual for a newspaper reporter—he didn't include Sheldon's quote in the story.

"I'll tell you the reason I never wrote that in my story," Johns said. "I believed at the time when Sheldon told me that, that he was possibly mistaken. He was worried, and scared, and trying to do the best he could down there. But he actually did say that to me."

In the coming months, Ray Sheldon would be repeatedly answering the same question that Johns had just asked him.

CHAPTER SEVEN

Just a Catastrophe

At daybreak on Tuesday, September 3, Fred Ghent left Homestead with a small crew of Florida ERA workers and headed south into the Keys. He still had heard nothing about the train sent to evacuate the veterans.

The road into the islands was a battered pathway across a vast lake. Mangled tufts of palm trees, mangroves, and other vegetation protruded from the water, their tops looking as though a grazing sea monster had chewed them off.

Ghent had to stop a few miles south of Tavernier, where downed trees blocked the way. He left his work crew to clear the road and drove back to Homestead, where he dispatched a quick report to his superiors giving his impressions of what he'd seen. Then he started rounding up help to send to the Keys.

Ghent also talked briefly to a reporter for the *Miami Daily News*. The afternoon newspaper was preparing stories about the hurricane for that day's edition. Ghent sidestepped the reporter's question about what had happened to the veterans waiting to be evacuated, saying he "would rather not express an opinion."

Others were realizing, however, that something was very wrong in the Florida Keys.

A few minutes past 7 a.m., Roy Hurley, a veteran from the Lake Erie harbor town of Sandusky, Ohio, boarded the FEC train in Miami to return to Camp 1. As he entered the passenger coach, he spotted two women he'd met a few days earlier—a nurse and a hairdresser, both from Key West.

Hurley sat down and immediately struck up a conversation with them. They'd chatted for a few minutes when the conductor stepped into the coach and called for the passengers' attention. As heads turned his way, the conductor announced that the morning train to Key West was suspended indefinitely because several sections of track in the islands had been washed out by the hurricane.

"That was the first actual news that told me that there was something wrong down there," Hurley said.

The hurricane had lost some of its punch after inflicting the savage beating to the Keys, but it was still a very powerful and dangerous storm. By Tuesday morning the eye had crossed Florida Bay, brushed Cape Sable at the tip of the Florida peninsula, and was moving northwest. The storm's circulation had expanded some—an indication that it was weakening—but its strongest winds around the eye were still blowing at better than 130 mph.

Although the eye was well offshore in the Gulf of Mexico, the fringes of the hurricane were raking Florida's west coast with strong winds and heavy rainfall. And even though it was weakening, it managed to take the life of one more veteran. Edward Kettner, a 58-year-old bus driver who'd served in the U.S. Navy during the Spanish-American War and World War I, was driving across the state from West Palm Beach to Fort Myers. Near the small town of LaBelle, Kettner lost control of his empty bus in the blinding rainfall. The bus veered off the road and overturned, throwing Kettner from the vehicle. A passing motorist found his body lying by the roadside.

Coast Guard commanders wanted very badly to get search-and-rescue planes aloft to assess the damage to the Keys and help survivors, but winds were still gusting at 50 mph or better at the air station on Dinner Key, and all planes were grounded. High seas prevented cutters from coming to the aid of the *Dixie*.

Roy Hurley and the women from Key West left the train depot and walked to a nearby filling station, where they met a young man who was filling up his car with gasoline to drive down to the Keys. He agreed to give them a lift, and the four headed south.

The evidence of the hurricane's handiwork became steadily more dramatic as they drove deeper into the islands.

"It seemed as though every house in Tavernier was blown in one spot," Hurley said. "They weren't smashed up so much, they were lifted bodily."

There was more gruesome evidence of the storm's savagery.

"I saw three bodies up alongside of the railroad tracks, and one on the railroad track," he said.

Hurley realized that he recognized the people who'd been killed. Two of the victims were a married couple who ran a saloon, and another was a man he knew as Harry who worked at the hospital at Camp 1. The bodies were already starting to decompose.

In Miami, Elizabeth Bradford had been worried sick about her husband since the phone line went dead Monday night. After spending an awful night of uncertainty, she was determined to get back to Lower Matecumbe Key and find Cardy Bradford.

She called Pan American and other airlines trying to charter a plane to fly down to the islands. They all refused. No one was willing to challenge the powerful and freakish winds of the departing hurricane.

Finally someone told her a pilot named Charles Collar might be willing to make a flight to the Keys. Bradford dashed to the Miami airport, catching Collar as he was about to leave after checking to see how his amphibious airplane had weathered the storm.

Bradford begged Collar to fly her to Lower Matecumbe, but he refused. She didn't give up, however, and finally the pilot relented.

Collar had second thoughts as he tried to get airborne, however. The winds whipping across the airport shoved his airplane around and nearly caused him to crash. Collar coaxed his plane higher until he'd gained enough altitude for the flight. He turned the nose of the amphibian toward the Keys.

By mid-afternoon Roy Hurley and his three companions had reached the north bank of Snake Creek. That was as far as they could go. The highway and railroad bridges linking Plantation Key to Windley Key were gone. Hurley walked to the edge of the creek, which was now a racing torrent well out of its normal channel. He joined a group of people gazing helplessly toward the opposite shore, where two men were trying to communicate to them with shouts and gestures.

"I tried to talk to two men across the gap, but the wind was blowing pretty hard and you couldn't hear what they were saying," Hurley said. "So by signs they told us they had counted 78 dead, and 30 that had broken legs and arms."

Among those who stood on the north side of Snake Creek was Fred Ghent, who had driven back down from Homestead after preparing his report and talking to the *Miami Daily News*. Eugene Lowkis, a veteran from Brooklyn who had been in Miami during the holiday weekend, happened to be standing next to Ghent when someone asked him if many of the veterans in Camp 1 had been killed.

Lowkis heard Ghent respond, "I don't think so."

Ghent shouted and waved to the two men on the opposite bank, then returned to his car and headed back toward Homestead.

At about the same time Ghent was leaving the Keys, a rescue party led by Homestead mayor Preston Bird rolled out of the town. But it was slow going over the debris-strewn road, and it would be dusk before the group reached Snake Creek.

When the Homestead group arrived, 25-year-old Henry Day, a strong swimmer, tied a rope to his waist and plunged into the water. He got about halfway across the racing creek and paused to rest on one of the abutments that had supported a bridge. Before he could continue, two men sculled past him in a small rowboat they'd found and fished out of the creek. More Homestead rescuers arrived with small boats and outboard motors, and soon the little craft were chugging back and forth across Snake Creek.

The first rescue boat brought six-year-old Dorothy Van Ness across. She and her family had sought shelter in the ill-fated hospital at Camp 1. The storm had torn the child from the protective arms of Albert Christie when the hospital at Snake Creek had collapsed. But she had somehow survived. The child's face and legs were cut and scratched from her ordeal. Someone asked her where her father was.

"Papa is gone," she answered. "My big brother is gone, too. So is Katherine, and so is Gene. All are gone except me and Mama."

Laura Van Ness arrived in another boat a few moments later. The child ran to her mother, who burst into tears as she embraced her daughter.

The girl's simple, sad tale was a story that would be repeated many times in the coming days. Entire families had been wiped out. A few, however, were lucky.

J. R. Beckham, the fisherman who spent Monday night crawling from tree stump to tree stump searching for his wife and grandchildren, crossed Snake Creek in a small rescue boat and climbed aboard a truckload of refugees bound for Homestead. When he arrived, he saw another truck with more refugees. He waved for it to stop, ran up to it, and peered inside anxiously. He was delighted by what he saw.

"There were my wife and two grandchildren," he said. "My wife was unhurt, and the two children only slightly injured. God was certainly good to us."

Miami Daily News reporter William Johns was among the survivors ferried across Snake Creek late Tuesday. Johns then caught a ride back to

Homestead, where he wrote a dramatic first-person story about his experience aboard the ill-fated evacuation train.

Reporters and photographers from Miami's other two dailies, the *Herald* and the *Daily Tribune*, were pushing through the wreckage of the Keys for stories and photos.

Above the islands, Elizabeth Bradford and Charles Collar were peering intently down at the Keys looking for something familiar. But the winds had ripped away landmarks, and the floodwater distorted and concealed so much of the islands that they had no idea which one was Lower Matecumbe.

As the sunlight faded, Collar told Bradford that he'd have to land somewhere for the night. They finally recognized Snake Creek, and Collar put his amphibian down there.

At Dinner Key the Coast Guard was preparing for an all-out rescue effort as soon as weather conditions permitted. Ground crews cleared storm debris away from hangars and got two seaplanes ready to take off at daybreak Wednesday. A crew also loaded radio truck number 1455 with equipment—spare parts, medical supplies, a small boat, an outboard motor, and rifles and sidearms. By 10 p.m. Tuesday the seas had calmed enough to allow three Coast Guard boats loaded with food and supplies to cast off from Fort Lauderdale and head for the Keys.

In Key West, Monroe County sheriff Karl Thompson met with Major William Albury, commander of the 2nd Battalion, 265th Coastal Artillery of the Florida National Guard. Thompson asked Albury to assemble his troops and take them to the hurricane-devastated Upper Keys as quickly as possible.

By Tuesday night Homestead was swamped with hurricane survivors. The Sunday school building of the First Baptist Church was converted into an emergency hospital and refugee shelter. Residents took more hurricane refugees into their homes.

As the survivors found refuge in Homestead, Fred Ghent talked by telephone with an Associated Press reporter. His description and interpretation of what he'd seen and heard earlier on the northern bank of Snake Creek was quite different from the impressions of Roy Hurley and others who'd witnessed the same thing. Ghent told the reporter that the two veterans standing on the southern bank of the creek "did not appear to be greatly perturbed and gave no signals that he interpreted as meaning any men had been killed."

Ghent also told the AP that he didn't think there had been "any great loss of life" at Camp 1.

The Coast Guard truck and its crew of six reached the northern bank of Snake Creek about 2:30 a.m. Wednesday. An hour later National Guard troops from Key West landed at Lower Matecumbe Key. The rescuers had their work cut out for them.

As the sun came up Wednesday, Coast Guard lieutenants Carl Olsen and William Clemmer were at the controls of their big amphibious airplanes. Olsen took off first. As soon as his Douglas Dolphin was airborne, Clemmer gunned his engines and the PJ-2 glided across Biscayne Bay and lifted off.

Olsen swung his plane southward to search around the Keys. Clemmer turned westward to have a look around Cape Sable.

At 5:55 a.m. the radio crackled at the Coast Guard air station at Dinner Key. It was Olsen, who was looking down at the devastation between Tavernier and Grassy Key. The pilot reported that he saw "a scene of utter desolation, not more than three houses remaining upright."

The veterans camps simply didn't exist anymore. The only way Olsen could even tell where the camps had been was from "a few pieces of lumber hanging in the mangrove trees."

And at last the fate of the evacuation train was revealed. Olsen told an astonished radio operator at the air base that something had shoved the train off the tracks at Islamorada, leaving only the locomotive upright.

As Olsen reported his grim findings, Bernard and Clifton Russell climbed out of the overturned train car where they'd spent Tuesday night and looked around in disbelief. The Keys were bathed in a typically gorgeous sunrise, but the day's beautiful beginning was a cruel contrast to the scene illuminated by the rising sun.

Daybreak brought with it the steamy, stifling heat that always follows a hurricane. Hundreds of corpses were strewn for miles along the islands. The humid heat was already accelerating the decomposition process, and the breezes off the ocean now carried the pungent and unmistakable odor of death.

The stench summoned blowflies—big, green, buzzing insects—that start the next stage of decomposition. The wind fanned the fumes of death up and down the Keys.

As the sun sparkled on the perfectly calm turquoise waters of the Atlantic Ocean, Bernard and Clifton Russell joined other survivors shuffling numbly through the nightmarish landscape of storm wreckage, swelling corpses, and buzzing flies, searching for friends and family members. They found a relative who'd been pinned in the top of a palm tree by a heavy timber, injured but alive.

But Bernard Russell also discovered two small legs protruding from a pile of debris. He pulled away some of the rubble and discovered the body of a three-year-old cousin. He marked the spot and walked away.

On Monday morning 53 members of his extended family lived in and around Islamorada. Two days later 38 members of the Russell family were dead, and Bernard's home had been swept away in the blink of an eye. It was too much to comprehend.

Bernard and his uncle helped the injured John Russell out of the overturned train. They tied him to a board for stability and laid the board across the bed of a pickup truck. The truck wouldn't start, so, with the help of other survivors, they began pushing it northward, joining a stream of storm survivors walking toward Snake Creek.

More people continued to arrive to search for friends and relatives, clear the wreckage, or simply gawk at the carnage. Members of a CCC company from Miami started building a temporary footbridge across Snake Creek while National Guard troops from Miami and West Palm Beach set up a roadblock at Tavernier to keep out sightseers who were already clogging the road between Florida City and Key Largo.

Two people who got through the roadblock were Herbert Harper—who was Elizabeth Bradford's brother-in-law—and Gifford Bunnell, a friend of the Bradfords. When they met Elizabeth Bradford and Charles Collar at Snake Creek, the four climbed into Collar's plane to resume their search for Cardy Bradford.

They found him, alive and unhurt, amid the ruins of Camp 3. When the roof came off their cafe, Bradford and a veteran had taken shelter in an automobile parked nearby. The hurricane had picked up a corrugated tin garage and dropped it over the car, where it stayed for the rest of the storm and shielded Bradford and the veteran.

On the morning of Wednesday, September 4, the rest of the world was getting its first look at the horror on the Upper Keys. Miami newspapers published stories of the death and destruction, accompanied by full-page photo spreads.

One of the most haunting pictures was a *Miami Herald* portrait of eight-year-old Robert Adams of Plantation Key, who spent Monday night clinging to the railroad track near his home. Friends who found the terrified boy Tuesday had to pry his hands loose from the track. They took him to their damaged home and began massaging his hands. In the *Herald* photo, the boy's sunken eyes are still wide with terror as he stares intently into the distance.

The news of the tragedy also sent the nation's major newsreel producers rushing to Florida. Newsreel cameramen descended on the Coast Guard air station demanding to be flown to the Keys to shoot footage.

Lieutenant Olsen said he could take only one photographer and told the others to choose one from among their group. A cameraman was chosen, and he agreed to share his footage with the companies who'd also sent cameramen to the air station.

Down at Long Key, James Duane and the other survivors started walking south along the ruined tracks of the Florida East Coast Railway. Duane hoped to meet a repair train dispatched from Key West to check the condition of the tracks—unless the tracks had been destroyed for the entire length of the line. He had no way of knowing how far down the Keys the hurricane damage extended.

In Washington, Roosevelt Administration officials were getting the first inkling of what had happened in the work camps. By nightfall Wednesday in a soggy Washington, where a steady rain had been falling for two days, they would be scrambling to head off what could easily become a public relations fiasco for the president and his men.

Wednesday began with wildly varying estimates in newspapers about the death toll in the Keys.

The *Miami Herald* cautiously reported that 25 to 100 were dead, but added that the newspaper had received "widely conflicting reports" about the death toll. The *Miami Daily News* published a list of about 30 people thought to be dead or missing. The *Miami Beach Daily Tribune* saw no reason to be cautious about estimating the number of victims, however. The emerging picture of what had happened in the Keys was so awful that even *Trib* editor Paul Jeans would have difficulty exaggerating it.

Still, he would try.

"Death Toll on Keys Over 700," the *Tribune* headline screamed to its readers Wednesday morning.

The *Tribune* also eagerly—almost gleefully—pointed an editorial finger at a scapegoat to blame for the exaggerated death toll it was reporting. The *Trib*'s lead editorial said the U.S. Weather Bureau was responsible for the loss of "nearly a thousand lives" because it hadn't accurately reported the hurricane's position or correctly predicted its track in the Straits of Florida.

An editorial cartoon showing a blindfolded weatherman pointing to a map of Florida and chanting "Eeny-meeny-miney-moe" accompanied the opinion piece. The cartoon was titled "Where, oh, where, has my hurricane gone?"

Citing the American Red Cross as its source, the *Washington Post*'s lead story said 100 were dead, but did not distinguish between veterans and residents. But Coast Guard reports—including Lieutenant Carl Olsen's description of dozens of bodies floating in the surf and entangled in the mangroves at Camp 5—were beginning to reach officials in Jacksonville and Washington, and it was becoming clear that conditions in the Keys were far grimmer than the newspapers were reporting.

Soon after copies of Wednesday morning's *Post* landed on doorsteps in the District of Columbia, George Andrews, a Federal Emergency Relief Administration engineer in Washington, took a phone call from R. G. Unkrich, assistant administrator of the Florida Emergency Relief Administration in Jacksonville.

"We have possibly 300 men lost," Unkrich told Andrews.

Unkrich's grim report started the telephone lines buzzing between Florida and the District of Columbia. That afternoon Marvin Porter, a Florida ERA engineer who'd rushed to Miami to supervise rescue operations in the Keys, talked briefly with George Andrews.

"It looks bad," Porter warned Andrews.

Andrews told Porter that Charles Forbes, a public relations specialist, had been dispatched to Florida and would arrive there the following afternoon. He then transferred Porter's call to Colonel Lawrence Westbrook, assistant director of FERA.

"What is the number of the known or estimated dead?" Westbrook asked.

"There are 300 estimated dead," Porter answered tersely. "That's the best we can do on that."

"Our people alone?" Westbrook asked incredulously.

"Our people," Porter said.

Meanwhile, Stephen Early, one of FDR's secretaries who'd made the trip to Hyde Park, New York, with the president after Congress adjourned, was talking with Marvin McIntyre, another Roosevelt secretary, and General Frank Hines, director of the Veterans Administration. Knowing that the hurricane had hit the Keys, they assumed some of the men in the work camps had been injured and perhaps even a few had been killed. After the three laid out plans to care for the injured and bury the dead, McIntyre called Westbrook.

"I've been talking to Mr. Early and General Hines," McIntyre said. "The general has instructions from the President with regard to the veterans in the camps down there, about taking care of the injured and arranging about funeral services and all that. You don't mind, do you?"

"No, not at all," Westbrook said, adding that he'd just gotten an estimate of the death toll from Marvin Porter in Florida. "He said he believed 300, at least, were lost. Another hundred were injured, the remainder surviving. They are evacuating those people rapidly."

McIntyre was stunned.

"My God!" he exclaimed. Regaining his composure, he asked the question that would echo for months through the halls of power in Washington.

"Between us, Colonel," McIntyre said. "There is no blame that can be attached to the administration or to your office, is there?"

"No," Westbrook said. "It is just a catastrophe."

"Nobody suggested that there was any undue risk, or anything?" McIntyre asked anxiously.

"No," Westbrook said.

But Westbrook was about as wrong as he could possibly be. A furious flurry of accusations was already erupting, and some of the accusers were pointing at Roosevelt and his aides. At about the same time that Westbrook and McIntyre were concluding that federal officials couldn't be blamed for the veterans' deaths, U.S. Representative J. Hardin Peterson, a Democrat from Florida, was demanding some answers.

Peterson had returned to his home in Lakeland after the long session of Congress ended. He was in Lakeland when rescuers learned of the huge death toll in the work camps.

Peterson discussed the aftermath of the hurricane with Arthur Boring, who lived in nearby Plant City and was commander of Florida's American Legion posts. Both men were incensed that the veterans had been left in the path of the storm. Peterson fired off an angry telegram to WPA director Harry Hopkins demanding to know why the veterans were not evacuated from the Keys before the storm struck. "They had plenty of notice, and I want to fix the responsibility," he said.

Meanwhile, U.S. Coast Guard Lieutenant William Clemmer was following the hurricane's path of devastation across Florida Bay and Cape Sable searching for people who needed help.

The cape, at the tip of the Florida peninsula, had been scrubbed bare of buildings and vegetation. Near the tiny bayside settlement of Flamingo,

Clemmer spotted about two dozen survivors clinging to the wreckage of a houseboat. The Coast Guard pilot carefully set his seaplane down in the shallow, debris-strewn water.

Three were badly hurt and needed medical attention as quickly as possible. Promising to return, Clemmer and his crew loaded the three injured survivors aboard the PJ-2 and flew them to Snake Creek, which had become the staging area for rescue operations.

Clemmer took off again, but he'd scarcely gotten airborne before he was setting the amphibian back down on Florida Bay, this time in about a foot and a half of water. He'd spotted more survivors at Upper Matecumbe Key.

Clemmer and a crewman waded ashore to size up the situation. Sixteen people needed help immediately. One was barely alive, and others undoubtedly would die soon if they didn't get medical aid. Clemmer knew his PJ-2 was designed to carry a maximum of 12 passengers, but he realized that making two trips wasn't an option because some of these people wouldn't be alive when he returned. He decided he had no choice but to cram all 16 survivors into his plane and get it into the air somehow.

The seaplane sank lower and lower into the water as the injured were helped aboard. Then the crewmen closed the hatches. Clemmer gunned the engines, and the PJ-2 began slogging heavily through the water, struggling to pull itself into the air. Clemmer winced as he felt the overloaded plane's hull sliding along on the muddy bottom of Florida Bay. If the amphibian struck a piece of coral or submerged debris, it would rip the bottom out of the hull. But finally, to his relief, he felt the seaplane lift itself free of the grasping mud and water. He was airborne.

Clemmer decided his passengers' injuries were too serious to be handled by first-aid workers at Snake Creek. He turned the amphibian northeast toward the Coast Guard air station at Dinner Key.

Although the eye of the hurricane was now many miles away, the storm's backside winds were still kicking up choppy seas in Biscayne Bay. Clemmer carefully settled the PJ-2 and its bulging cargo of humanity into the bouncing water and glided to a stop. The water was too rough for him to taxi the airplane up the seaplane ramp and into the Coast Guard hangar. The hurricane victims were loaded onto a small motor launch, taken ashore, and transported to hospitals.

But Clemmer wasn't finished. He'd promised to return to the wrecked houseboat near Flamingo. As soon as his airplane was refueled, he was in the air headed back to Cape Sable. This time he loaded 10 more injured survivors aboard the PJ-2. In the fading light Clemmer brought the amphibian in for one more landing on Biscayne Bay. It had been a busy day for the Coast Guard pilot and his crew. They had plucked 29 lives from the ruins of the hurricane.

Clemmer and Olsen weren't alone in the skies over the Keys Wednesday. A Pan American chartered plane carrying a correspondent for the *Chicago Daily Tribune* flew low over the islands. Colonel Robert McCormick, the *Tribune* publisher and President Roosevelt's old nemesis, was sharpening his sword for an attack on FDR and his New Deal programs.

While *Tribune* correspondent Spearman Lewis peered down at the devastation on the Keys, Ernest Hemingway and two friends, Bra Saunders and Sully Sullivan, loaded food and other supplies onto the *Pilar* in Key West and headed the boat northward to pitch in with the relief effort for the Upper Keys.

Hemingway was astonished by what he found as he approached Lower Matecumbe Key. "The foliage absolutely stripped as though by fire for forty miles and the land looking like the abandoned bed of a river," he later wrote. "Not a building of any sort standing."

Hemingway and his companions counted 69 corpses in the waters around Lower Matecumbe. The appalling body count reminded him of his days as an ambulance driver in France during the war.

When the author arrived at what had been the ferry slip at Lower Matecumbe, he saw two corpses that he recognized—the bodies of two women who ran a filling station and sold sandwiches near the ferry landing. But it took him a few moments to realize who they were. Their bodies had already become swollen and grotesque and covered with blowflies.

Hemingway was amazed at the power of the hurricane. "Indian Key absolutely swept clean, not a blade of grass, and over the high center of it were scattered live conchs that came in with the sea, craw fish, and dead morays," he wrote. "The whole bottom of the sea blew over it."

The author was infuriated by the deaths of the veterans. "The veterans in those camps were practically murdered," he said.

George Branch was among the survivors who reached Snake Creek late Wednesday morning. He could go no farther on foot and had to wait for a boat. As he waited he overheard two men talking about finding the bodies of a young woman and small child.

"I don't know what prompted me to do it, but I walked a hundred yards or so to see if possibly I might identify them," Branch said. "They were the girls we had tried to get to leave their little home and board the train and who were so afraid of the storm."

By Wednesday afternoon word reached Fern and Ed Butters that help had arrived at Snake Creek.

"We were all in a state of shock, I think, and we started the five-mile trek to Snake Creek where a boat was waiting to take us across," Fern said.

Her husband limped along, his foot sore and swollen from the nail he'd stepped on during the storm, and Fern Butters struggled to walk on a badly sprained ankle.

"When we reached the place where the boat was waiting, we had walked by the bodies of the dead and had recognized many," she said. "At the embankment there was a pile of bodies stacked up with a piece of canvas over them, but all of their feet were exposed, and so many were children's feet that finally it was just too much for me. The last thing I remembered was falling toward the embankment. Someone must have caught me, for when I came to, we were in the boat being taken across [Snake Creek]."

Ed and Fern were treated at a first-aid station in Tavernier, and then taken by ambulance to Miami.

"A wilder ride I have never taken," Fern said. "I guess we all looked in such terrible shape that they thought we should be gotten there in a hurry. I was not aware of it, but my face looked like a minute steak after it had been run through one of those mincers."

The ambulance took them to a Red Cross station at the Everglades Hotel. As they sat in the lobby, a woman who knew Fern walked through calling her name.

"She failed to recognize me when I rose from my chair," Fern said. "She looked astonished. I was still not aware of the way I looked—face beaten by the wind and sand for two days and a night, a speckled tweed skirt and maroon turtleneck sweater, my whole body raw and sore from the wet clothes, wind, and rain. I neither laughed nor cried when I saw myself in the mirror. I guess I was still in a state of shock."

Miami hospitals were filling up with other hurricane victims. Red Cross physician William DeKlein reported that 57 survivors were being treated for "major" injuries that included serious wounds, fractures, and illnesses caused by prolonged submersion in water. At least two of the survivors had been paralyzed by broken backs.

Others were suffering from simple shock and exhaustion. At Jackson Memorial Hospital a young woman sat in a wheelchair trying to pull her skirt down far enough to conceal her muddy ankles. She'd been visiting in Islamorada when the hurricane struck. A reporter from the *Miami Daily News* asked her to talk about what had happened to her during the storm.

"I thought it was the most beautiful place I ever saw—Islamorada," she said. "I came down from Brooklyn, and the sea was so pretty and blue. And then suddenly Monday night it was sort of a hell turned inside out. The sea was gray and muddy and the wind was like something solid that moved over the land and knocked things down."

Around 3 p.m. Wednesday, rescue workers from Homestead reached Lower Matecumbe Key. Among those who arrived at the ruins of Camp 3 was Father Alfred McDonald, the Catholic priest who had once pleaded with the veterans to attend his masses. The first thing the priest did was administer the sacrament of Last Rites to seven dying veterans.

Not long after that, officials in Miami received orders for 240 plain pine boxes in which to bury the storm victims.

By 2 p.m. Wednesday the seas had finally settled enough to allow passengers to be taken off the *Dixie*. Only one passenger—Dora Spira of New York City—suffered significant injuries when she fell down a passageway during the *Dixie*'s struggle with the hurricane.

Although the seas had settled some, getting off the ship was a hair-raising experience. Sizable swells were still rolling across the Straits of Florida.

The passengers put on life jackets, and *Dixie* crew members carefully helped them climb down a rope ladder and into a waiting lifeboat. The crewmen called encouragement as the lifeboats were filled. "Don't drop this sweetheart!" a crewman called as he helped a child down the ladder. A nimble young man impressed the crew as he quickly descended. "Hey, here comes an athlete," someone said.

When Florence Steiler's turn came, she carefully picked her way down the ladder and gratefully sat down on a lifeboat seat. Her ordeal was almost over.

A small motorboat took Steiler's lifeboat in tow. "The ride over was like having a continuous trip on a roller coaster," Steiler said.

The motorboat towed Steiler's lifeboat to the S.S. *Atenas*, one of the ships waiting to take on passengers from the *Dixie*. Steiler faced the difficult task of climbing up a rope ladder while wearing the bulky life jacket. When she reached the top, *Atenas* crewmen pulled her aboard.

Steiler was greeted by a ship's stewardess, who hugged her and asked, "What can I do for you?"

"Honey," Steiler answered, "just give me a bath."

In the Gulf of Mexico the hurricane continued churning northward. The winds ahead of the storm's eye pushed much of the water out of Tampa Bay, then the winds to the south of the eye shoved the water back with such force that Tampa's seawall along Bayshore Boulevard was six feet underwater Wednesday and neighborhoods near the bay were flooded. The relentless battering of storm-driven waves finally caused the seawall to collapse.

Added to the seawater flowing in the streets near the bay was more than five inches of rain that fell on Tampa and St. Petersburg between Tuesday afternoon and Wednesday afternoon. The winds also peeled the roof off the U.S. post office in Tampa's Ybor City neighborhood.

At Cedar Key, a small island hamlet north of Tampa Bay, most of the town's 1,200 residents took shelter in schools and other larger buildings as the storm approached Wednesday afternoon. As the hurricane came ashore for the second time in less than 48 hours, W. M. Pepper Jr., editor of the *Gainesville Daily Sun*, parked his car in the center of the little town's business district.

The heft of the storm was still strong enough to land a punishing blow. At 3 p.m. Pepper watched the rising, windblown waters of the Gulf of Mexico invade the streets of Cedar Key. "Up, up, that water is coming, the top layer vanishing into salt spray," he wrote. "What will go next? There, to the left, goes a roof. The car is swaying badly now. . . . The car feels like it is going to fly."

Knee-deep saltwater soon rushed through Cedar Key. "Main Street . . . looks like a turbulent river now," Pepper wrote at 4:45 p.m.

Farther inland, winds toppled trees in Gainesville, throwing a huge pine into the building that housed the Engineering Department on the University of Florida campus. The hurricane dealt a savage blow to poor, sparsely populated Taylor County, where it demolished the homes of 350 families and heavily damaged another 175 homes.

As evening approached, a dazed and exhausted Ray Sheldon reached Miami. But there would be no rest for the camps' supervisor. Fred Ghent, thinking, no doubt, of the intense scrutiny he would undergo in the wake of the tragedy, was waiting for Sheldon with a court stenographer to take his statement about what had happened. Sheldon, still numb and disoriented from his awful experience, sat down and started talking. His first words were an explanation of why he had waited until Monday afternoon to call for an evacuation train.

It was only partly factual, and it left out many details about the information that had been available to him.

Sheldon told Ghent that he had been "in constant communication with every available source of information regarding the storm" and added he'd called the U.S. Weather Bureau at noon Monday to check on the status of the hurricane.

That much was true. But his next statement simply was not.

"The Weather Bureau stated there was absolutely no danger, from the reports they had received, to the Florida Keys," Sheldon said.

In fact, Sheldon had been repeatedly warned by the Weather Bureau that the Keys would be hit with at least gale-force winds and dangerously high tides regardless of the path of the hurricane's eye. He didn't mention that the Weather Bureau's Key West office had advised him early Sunday morning, September 1, that conditions probably would become dangerous on the Florida Keys even if the hurricane followed the Weather Bureau's predicted course and passed through the Straits of Florida into the Gulf of Mexico.

Sheldon also didn't mention the Weather Bureau's advisory of 3:30 a.m. Monday, September 2, warning of "high tides and gales" on the Keys, nor did he say that the Weather Bureau called the work camps' headquarters at the Matecumbe Hotel minutes later to inform camp officials of that advisory and its implications for the islands.

The statement laid the foundation for an alibi that would absolve Ghent and Sheldon from any responsibility for the vets' deaths. The alibi—blaming the U.S. Weather Bureau for not providing adequate warning about the danger that the hurricane posed to the work camps—would persist throughout the investigations that would follow.

By Wednesday, Roosevelt Administration officials were scurrying to respond to the catastrophe. Roosevelt's secretary Stephen Early told General Hines, the VA director, that the president was very upset and wanted an immediate investigation to determine whether anyone in his administration was responsible for the veterans' deaths.

Early may have been keeping tabs on events in Florida, but the secretary was carefully avoiding making any record of his thoughts on the disaster or what was going on behind the scenes. It was a marked departure from his usual habits.

Throughout his years as Roosevelt's personal secretary, Early kept an unofficial White House diary in which he made brief notations of daily events, FDR's appointments, and his own thoughts. When natural disasters struck—such as an earthquake in Montana or spring flooding on the East Coast that drove thousands from their homes—Early usually made note of the events in the diary and discussed in a few words the administration's response to help victims.

But Early's entries for September 1 through September 8 make no mention of the hurricane in Florida or the deaths of the veterans.

Around 6:30 p.m. on Wednesday, September 4, General Hines summoned his assistant, Colonel George E. Ijams, and told him to get down to Florida immediately.

Ijams would be the personal representative of President Roosevelt, and he would be responsible for making sure the injured veterans were properly cared for and the bodies of those killed were either sent home or to Arlington National Cemetery, whichever the family preferred. Captain Harry Farmer, also attached to the Veterans Administration, accompanied Ijams.

General Hines had one more important meeting Wednesday. The administration had had a thorny relationship with the American Legion, one of the most vocal veterans' groups, almost from the moment FDR took office, and the president hadn't helped his standing with the veterans group a few months earlier by vetoing a bill that would have allowed early payment of the bonus.

With another election year approaching, Roosevelt could not afford a repeat of the outrage that followed the deaths of two vets during the 1932 eviction of the Bonus Marchers from Washington. It wasn't unreasonable to assume that the voters' fury would be multiplied beyond measure if they believed hundreds of veterans had been killed in a hurricane because of governmental carelessness. That anger could linger for months and cause disastrous results for FDR and the Democrats in November 1936—especially if the American Legion and Republican political operatives had a full year to fan the flames of voter outrage.

Hines sought to head off some of that potential backlash.

Around 11:30 p.m. Wednesday the general went to Washington's Union Station to meet a train from Huntington, West Virginia, carrying Frank Belgrano Jr., the national commander of the American Legion. Hines spent about 90 minutes with Belgrano, discussing the tragedy on the Keys and, as he later phrased it, "Roosevelt's wishes in the matter." Belgrano—who hadn't yet talked to his Legion colleagues in Florida—told Hines that he would cooperate.

As soon as conditions permitted Wednesday, the Florida East Coast Railway had crews inspecting the damage to its roadbed and property in the Keys. By Wednesday night they'd seen enough. Around 40 miles of track had been "obliterated," including structures that were thought to be stormproof.

"It is still undecided what will be done," George Branch noted later, "but the consensus of opinion is that it will never be restored."

Meanwhile, the hurricane lost more strength as it moved farther inland, but it was still packing a punch. By nightfall the storm had crossed into south Georgia and was heading northeast toward Macon. In Valdosta the barometer dropped to 28.90 inches—the lowest reading ever recorded there. More than five inches of rain fell in Thomasville, and Quitman was drenched with almost six inches. The winds also tore down a power line that fell on a store in Quitman and set the building ablaze.

As the storm created an unusually windy and rainy night in Georgia, George Ijams and Harry Farmer were trying to find a flight out of Washington to Florida, but the relentless rainstorm soaking the District of Columbia had grounded all planes. Ijams and Farmer finally gave up and boarded a train for Miami at 3 a.m. Thursday.

CHAPTER EIGHT

An Act of God

Editor Paul Jeans undoubtedly was pleased with the edition of the *Miami Beach Daily Tribune* that hit the streets Thursday, September 5, 1935.

The *Tribune*'s front page had all a tabloid editor could hope for—tales of bravery, a whiff of scandal in high places, and a gruesome photo. And it was all related to the same story—the hurricane that had blasted the Keys three days earlier, exactly as the *Trib* had predicted. The headlines told of the daring rescue at sea of the passengers aboard the wrecked S.S. *Dixie* and hinted that a cover-up scandal was developing in the deaths of the veterans in the hurricane. The tabloid's front page also included a photo of dead veterans lying amid the wreckage of Camp 3, and on page two was a photo of a stack of coffins and a headline saying the death toll from the hurricane was more than 800. *Tribune* stories repeatedly described nude, disfigured corpses and declared the "rotting bodies" to be "mute evidence of government indifference."

In an editorial the *Daily Tribune* claimed that two rescue trains had been assembled Sunday in Miami and were waiting to evacuate the veterans, but that U.S. Weather Bureau meteorologist Ernest Carson had told federal officials in Washington that the veterans were not in danger and the camps didn't need to be evacuated. The anonymous writer crowed that the *Trib* had accomplished "the greatest scoop ever scored by a Florida newspaper" by correctly predicting that the hurricane would strike the Keys.

As usual, the reporting was a blend of lurid facts and cynical fantasy, and the outrageous claim that Carson had told officials in Washington not to remove the veterans from the Keys bordered on libel. But by Thursday morning it was becoming clear that a stunning catastrophe had occurred in Florida. The *Washington Post* of September 5, 1935, reported that as many as 500 people may have died in the Keys. A *Post* editorial said the veterans' deaths were a "tragedy," but offered only backhanded sympathy for the victims, referring to them as "drifters, psychopathic cases or habitual troublemakers."

Reporters risked their necks to get the story from the hurricane-blasted Keys. Associated Press photographer Willard K. Brown persuaded a pilot to fly him over French Reef Tuesday—before the Coast Guard was allowing its pilots to fly—to get a shot of the stranded *Dixie*. When rescuers stopped a newsman from landing on a pier at Snake Creek, *Miami Daily News* reporter Cecil Warren and *Daily News* staffer Frank Malone devised a daring and ingenious way for Malone to get Warren's notes and supply him with more film. They rigged a clothesline between a moving tugboat and a speedboat to make the exchange.

Editor & Publisher magazine praised the efforts of Miami reporters to get the story under nearly impossible conditions. But the magazine did not mention the *Daily Tribune*'s coverage.

As Thursday, September 5, dawned in the Keys, conditions were becoming more horrifying by the hour. Blowflies rose in thick, noisy clouds when rescue workers approached a corpse. The pungent stench of decomposition carried for miles up and down the Keys. The men who'd come to the islands to try to help were struggling to overcome their own revulsion at the awful task confronting them.

Around 8 a.m. Thursday a Coast Guard patrol boat cast off from Lower Matecumbe Key with a gruesome cargo—the bodies of 38 veterans that had been recovered by their surviving comrades before the National Guard took control of rescue operations. About 90 minutes later the patrol boat reached the rescue staging area at Snake Creek, where the corpses were to be unloaded, placed into pine boxes, and hauled to Woodlawn Cemetery in Miami. But the shallow water prevented the boat from getting close enough to unload the bodies directly onto the shore. The Coast Guard officer in charge of the vessel cut its engines, dropped anchor, and waited for help from the men standing on shore.

Minutes passed and no one moved. The rescue workers on shore grimly studied the patrol boat. "The stench was something that made men turn and leave the vicinity," said John Teets, a Red Cross field representative helping with the rescue work.

Finally Dade County sheriff Dave Coleman got fed up. "Either you come down here and help get these bodies off," he roared at the men standing motionless on the shore, "or get the hell out of the country! One or the other!"

Teets, a physician, and a few other men waded tentatively into the shallow water and waited for someone to start unloading the corpses. But the men aboard the cutter were no more eager to handle the bodies than the workers onshore. An argument erupted over how to get the corpses off the ship. Finally a large man wearing a VFW cap offered a solution. "We'll throw 'em overboard into the water, you grab 'em down there," he said. "Anyhow, they need washing off."

The men aboard the cutter dropped the first body into the water. Teets and the physician reached for it. The victim's scalp came off in Teets's hand. The decomposition was now so advanced that it was almost impossible to handle the bodies.

The rescue workers had more to contend with than the horrible task of recovering bodies.

The workers were composed of military personnel, state and federal government workers, Red Cross workers, and volunteers. The lines of authority were hopelessly tangled. Confusion reigned and tempers were short.

The main conflict was between a colonel representing Florida governor David Sholtz and Sheriff Coleman, who was out of his district but had been sent as a Red Cross representative. "The colonel was taking charge, countermanding here, making new orders there," Teets said.

But the others decided to make Sheriff Coleman the director of rescue operations, and the indignant colonel immediately sent a telegram to Sholtz. Then National Guard troops arrived at Snake Creek, and their officers started giving orders as well.

At the same time, a Red Cross representative in Tallahassee told reporters that his agency was in charge of rescue work in the Keys.

David Sholtz had had enough. The governor boarded an airplane and headed for Miami to take charge of rescue operations.

"Behind it all was politics," Teets said. "Veterans had been killed, President's representatives were coming, governor's retinue already on the ground, Colonel Ijams arriving. There were political aspects. Investigations. And the press criticizing unto high heaven."

The press also was squabbling. A nasty dispute had erupted among five newsreel companies over the rights to copies of the film shot by the Universal cameraman whom Coast Guard lieutenant Carl Olsen had flown down to the Keys the day before. Angry telegrams and phone calls bounced from New York to Miami to Los Angeles and back. Charles Ford of Universal Newsreel—who'd been allowed aboard a Coast Guard plane on the condition that he share his footage—refused to turn over the film to the other news agencies.

In Washington the telephone lines were humming again at the offices of the Federal Emergency Relief Administration as administrators there sought more information about the catastrophe in the Keys—and began laying plans for political damage control.

Lawrence Westbrook, an assistant director of FERA, had a long conversation with Fred Ghent in Florida. Westbrook was especially interested in the hurricane warnings issued by the U.S. Weather Bureau. He wanted to know when Ghent had learned the hurricane was heading toward the Keys. Ghent said he'd had a report around 1 p.m. or 1:30 p.m. Monday that the storm was still about 200 miles away.

Westbrook was intrigued. "The storm actually hit on Monday afternoon, didn't it, and you had a report between 1 and 1:30 that it was 200 miles from the Keys?" he asked.

"Yes," Ghent answered.

"And you got that report from the Weather Bureau?" Westbrook continued.

"Yes," Ghent said.

"Is there a published report on that?" Westbrook asked.

"That the storm was 200 miles away? Yes. I'm sure there is," Ghent said.

Ghent explained to Westbrook how he and Sheldon had decided to order the evacuation train for the veterans. Westbrook wanted more information about the Weather Bureau's advisories.

"Did you say that between one and two you had a warning that the storm would hit the Keys?" Westbrook asked.

"No," Ghent said.

"Then you acted on your own initiative on the assumption that if the storm did come your direction it would take about 20 hours to get there?" Westbrook said.

"We had no information that the storm would hit the Keys at all," Ghent said.

Ghent's evasive response was technically accurate. As of 1 p.m. on September 2, the Weather Bureau hadn't said specifically that the eye of the storm would cross the Keys. But Ghent's answer was still misleading. At least 36 hours before the hurricane's landfall—beginning with meteorologist Gerald Kennedy's warning to Sheldon at 5 a.m. on Sunday, September 1—the Weather Bureau had repeatedly warned that dangerous conditions were likely in the Keys even though the center of the storm was not near the islands.

Westbrook was left with the impression that the Weather Bureau had given no hint of danger to the Keys, and that the Florida East Coast Railway had promised to have a special train waiting to be dispatched on a moment's notice.

Both impressions were wrong.

Westbrook also took a call from Marvin McIntyre at the White House. The secretary got right to the point. McIntyre told Westbrook that Roosevelt wanted "a complete report as to whether there was any unnecessary delay in getting the train off, or with the Weather Bureau." McIntyre said FDR wanted assistant WPA director Aubrey Williams to send "an outstanding man" to Florida to work with Ijams.

McIntyre said he thought Harry Hopkins should dispatch Williams to Florida immediately. He added that he expected veterans' groups to react angrily to the death toll in the work camps.

"The Veterans of Foreign Wars will start something," McIntyre warned. "They will want to know why something wasn't done to warn those people or to take care of them."

"The Weather Bureau reported the storm at 1:30 p.m. Monday afternoon to be 200 miles away," Westbrook responded helpfully. "I think it will be pretty hard on them."

McIntyre's ears pricked up. "What about the Weather Bureau?"

"I wasn't the least bit concerned because it only travels 10 mph and it was reported 200 miles away," Westbrook answered.

Westbrook found his most useful—and imaginative—informant in Julius Stone, the former Florida ERA director who had boasted in the *New York Times* about his New Deal transformation of Key West.

The two men discussed the Weather Bureau advisories suggesting the hurricane could make landfall near Havana. Because the Weather Bureau's erroneous information caused Florida ERA officials to delay evacuating the veterans, Stone thought there could be only one possible reason for the disaster on the Keys. "I think you will have to call it an act of God," he said.

Westbrook leaped at Stone's suggestion. "That's right," he said eagerly. "That's about the conclusion we had made."

Stone tried to reassure Westbrook that the Federal Emergency Relief Administration hadn't taken an unnecessary risk by putting the work camps in the Keys. "No hurricanes have hit there within the last 25 years, and there was no reason to expect one," he said.

That was an absurdly ignorant statement. Stone had somehow forgotten or ignored or didn't know that four powerful hurricanes struck the Keys between 1906 and 1919, killing hundreds, as well as the hurricane in 1929 that destroyed railroad tracks near Key Largo and kept trains from running for 10 days.

Westbrook added his own delusional notion that the vets had been safer during the hurricane in the isolated camps than they would have been in a city. In a city there would be more danger from flying debris, he reasoned.

The men were apparently unaware that dozens of vets had been beaten to death and impaled by flying lumber when the camps disintegrated.

But Westbrook was now satisfied that nothing could have been done to protect the veterans from the storm. "That thing blew a train 50 feet off a track," he said.

"In the face of such violence no building that we could reasonably have constructed would have stood," Stone said. "It is just one of those things."

Westbrook told Stone that WPA director Harry Hopkins had been on the verge of going to Florida to investigate the veterans' deaths but had decided instead to send his assistant, Aubrey Williams.

Stone said there was no reason to go to so much trouble—especially since the veterans hadn't done much to ingratiate themselves with the administrators who supervised their work program.

"There isn't anything more that [Hopkins] could or should do," Stone said. "The fact of the matter is those fellows had a very bad name."

"Who had a bad name?" Westbrook asked.

"The veterans," Stone answered. "There will be some remarks made at headquarters that we would not want to repeat over the telephone."

"What are they?" Westbrook asked.

"If the thing had to happen, it might just as well take them."

"Who would say that?" Westbrook asked.

"Everyone I have heard talk about the accident," Stone said, and suggested that Hopkins should simply order Florida ERA director Conrad Van Hyning to prepare a report about the disaster and be done with it. "That's what I'd do, but I don't think this thing merits too much attention."

"I think that is right," Westbrook said. "I think Harry thinks Aubrey ought to go, but I hope he will not."

"I do not think it would do a bit of good," Stone concluded.

Meanwhile, Federal Emergency Relief Administration engineer George Andrews was seeking information about the Weather Bureau's hurricane advisories from a reluctant R. G. Unkrich, who was Conrad Van Hyning's assistant in Florida.

Andrews wanted to know when Florida ERA officials received their first warning about the hurricane. Unkrich sidestepped the question, adding that his agency was trying to learn more about what had happened. He added that the Florida ERA didn't have time to answer a lot of questions and that he had been asked not to make any statements about the disaster.

Andrews pressed. "What time did you receive the first warnings of the storm?"

Unkrich dodged again, saying he had been spending the Labor Day weekend at a lake and had heard Sunday, September 1, that a hurricane warning had been issued for Fort Pierce—about 200 miles up the coast from Islamorada. Florida ERA officials were told Monday that the hurricane was headed toward Havana.

"By eleven o'clock we decided that even though there was only a remote possibility that the storm would hit the Keys, it was planned to take them up to Hollywood and run them back the next day," Unkrich said.

Andrews wanted to know who had ordered the train, but again Unkrich avoided the question, saying only that he thought it had left Miami around 4:30 p.m. Monday.

Andrews asked Unkrich if he had copies of the Weather Bureau's advisories. Unkrich told him he was only aware of what had been published in newspapers and passed along by telephone.

"Can you get the official Weather Bureau reports down there, showing just what time they were sent out and just what they stated?" Andrews asked.

"It will take quite a little time to get them," Unkrich said evasively. "We have not much communication left, and it will take some little time."

"If you have anybody you can put on that, put them on that job and get all the reports together," Andrews ordered, and hung up.

Florida ERA engineer Marvin Porter was no more enthusiastic about talking. Again, Andrews asked when Florida ERA administrators had received the first warning from the Weather Bureau.

"I am checking up on it," Porter said. "I am not in a position to say right now. I am checking up on what time the train left and when the requisition was made for the train."

"How soon will you have that?" Andrews demanded. "Can't you put somebody on it now and let them call the Weather Bureau and read off the time their warning went out?"

"I am having somebody do that right now," Porter said.

Andrews kept pushing. "Hopkins is hot on that right now," he said.

The task of getting copies of the advisories was handed off to J. P. Hallihan, a WPA engineer who went straight to the Weather Bureau's acting director, Charles C. Clark. Hallihan also submitted a list of questions to Clark about the Weather Bureau's performance during the storm.

With the advisories finally in hand, Lawrence Westbrook drafted a statement exonerating Florida ERA officials from any blame in the veterans' deaths—even though the investigators sent to look into the tragedy hadn't even reached Florida.

His statement was a work of fantasy.

"There is every indication that the officials of the Florida State Emergency Relief Administration took every precaution in the light of the information at their disposal," Westbrook wrote. "Nothing in the weather reports up to this time could have given officials in charge of the camps any cause for serious alarm, but in order to be on the safe side, a train was ordered at 1:30 p.m. to evacuate the veterans' camps, but of course it arrived too late."

Later that day, WPA director Harry Hopkins met with reporters and criticized the U.S. Weather Bureau's advisories. Hopkins's comments were based on Westbrook's written statement, and Hopkins also included one of Julius Stone's remarks to Westbrook from their earlier telephone conversation.

"Our information from the weather reports showed that the storm was jumping all around there and nobody could tell where it would hit," Hopkins told reporters "Wherever we had a camp, at Key West or anywhere else, had the storm hit it, it would have been wrecked."

Hopkins added that the Weather Bureau's advisories hadn't been alarming enough to prompt anyone to move the vets off the islands. "I don't think anyone reading the weather reports—and I have been reading them—would necessarily have evacuated those people," he said.

Clark, the acting director of the U.S. Weather Bureau, was furious about Hopkins's statement and angrily denied that his agency was responsible for the deaths. Alexander J. Mitchell, the retired director of the Florida Weather Service, was also enraged by the insinuation that the Weather Bureau had somehow been at fault. Mitchell sent a telegram to President Roosevelt call-ing Hopkins's comments a "discreditable libel."

In Hyde Park, President Roosevelt announced that veterans killed in the hurricane would be eligible for burial at Arlington National Cemetery. But when Colonel Ijams's train arrived in Jacksonville Thursday night, he learned that public health officials in Florida were going to order that the bodies be cremated. Ijams protested. He had "specific orders from the President to col-lect and identify those bodies," he insisted.

Meanwhile, the storm continued to cause havoc on the East Coast Thursday. In Gastonia, North Carolina, Maggie Gamble was killed when the storm's blinding rainfall prevented her from seeing an oncoming train at a railroad crossing.

Virginia had been primed for disaster by steady rain that had been falling for days, soaking the Old Dominion—as well as Maryland's Eastern Shore—until the ground just couldn't absorb any more moisture. When the rains reached Virginia, the James River leaped out of its banks and put downtown Richmond underwater.

Tornadoes spawned by the storm touched down across Virginia and the Carolinas Thursday morning. E. F. Arrington, a farmer near Danville, Vir-ginia, had to battle a twister for the lives of his wife and daughter. The winds tried to carry away his child, but Arrington seized her in midair, pulled her back to the ground, and held her there with one hand. With his other hand he tried to keep his wife from being carried away, but the storm twice yanked her from his grasp. Each time Arrington caught her in midair.

The farmer finally threw his wife and daughter to the ground, lay down on top of them, and grabbed a fencepost.

In Farmville, Virginia, a tornado killed Mrs. Preston Simanski and her daughter-in-law, and in Courtland a twister destroyed the home of Nathaniel Turner, killed his six-month-old son, and seriously injured his wife, who was carried about 200 yards by the wind.

The same tornado also damaged venerable Hampden-Sydney College, tearing the roof off the administration building, uprooting six ancient oak trees, and plucking about 20 tombstones from a campus cemetery. The winds swept the stones into piles and hurled one high into a cedar tree.

The storm was still battering the East Coast when an angry Governor David Sholtz arrived in Miami late Thursday night. He was in no mood to wait until he'd cooled off to call a meeting of representatives of the agencies doing rescue work in the Keys. Sholtz immediately summoned them to the

McAllister Hotel. Around midnight Thursday the governor called the meeting to order. He looked around at the 15 people in the room. Dade County sheriff Dave Coleman was there, and so were Marvin Porter and Conrad Van Hyning of the Florida ERA. Field representative John Teets attended for the Red Cross.

Finally Sholtz spoke.

"The governor announced that he was the boss, and asked if there were objections," John Teets said. "There were none."

When the meeting broke up, the men attending the conference had sorted out their differences, devised a clear plan, and assigned responsibilities for cleaning up the awful mess in the Keys.

As the meeting ended in Miami, the storm continued its destruction in New Bern, North Carolina, where it set a lethal trap for residents of Contentnea Street. The storm blew into the city shortly after midnight and began taking down electrical poles and strewing live wires through the neighborhood, setting several of the modest houses ablaze.

Seeing that one of the downed power lines was about to set fire to his daughter's house, David W. Thompson, 55, ventured into the storm to try to move it. He was electrocuted, as was his 48-year-old wife when she tried to pull him away from the wire.

A few houses away, Carlton Smith wrestled with his wife to prevent her from running out into the storm—and certain death—to go to the aid of her dead parents. Then Smith smelled smoke.

He dashed into the bedroom where his two children slept and discovered that the fallen wires had started a fire.

As Smith extinguished the small blaze and hustled his children from the room, W. C. Hurley fought through the storm hoping to find someone to help him extinguish the fire in his home. But Hurley received a near-lethal jolt of electricity when he stepped into a pool of water charged by a fallen power line. His life was saved when Sam Smith—no relation to Carlton Smith—pulled him out of the water.

The storm continued pounding Virginia. Around 5 a.m. Friday, attorney Thomas A. Williams looked out the window of his townhouse on South Colonial Avenue in Richmond and saw a brilliant flash of lightning. Then he heard a loud buzzing noise. A red ball of fire rolled up the alley behind his house. But the only damage done by the phenomenon before it dissipated was to stop all the electric clocks in the neighborhood.

By Friday morning floodwaters were running through the streets of towns in Delaware, and on Maryland's Eastern Shore flooding forced about 1,000 people to leave their homes.

In Federalsburg, Maryland, the water steadily rose around a telephone office building. But operators Reba Pusey and Mollie Wheatley realized rescue workers were dependent on them for communications. So the women stayed at their switchboard.

"We are dead tired," Pusey told local reporters. "We had to wade up to our waists to get in here yesterday, and both Miss Wheatley and I knew we would be trapped by the flood."

Telephone linesman Charlie Marine swam through the floodwater to check on the women, then returned with linesman Edgar Ireland to bring them coffee and sandwiches.

Three crewmen aboard a Pennsylvania Railroad freight train in Delaware died early Friday morning when a flood-weakened culvert gave way beneath the locomotive, sending it plunging into a rain-swollen creek.

But the storm finally ended its deadly rampage that same day.

"With surprising suddenness, the tropical hurricane swept away from the Maryland coastal section today and swirling storm clouds broke to let the sun peep through," the Associated Press reported from Ocean City on September 6. "The Coast Guard station here announced the cheering news to the apprehensive city that 'the danger is all over.' The wind, which had dashed towering seas against breakwaters and over the jetties, shifted suddenly to the northwest. The abnormally high tide reacted by beginning to recede."

The U.S. Weather Bureau monitored the storm for several more days as it barreled northeastward past Long Island and Canada's Maritime Provinces. Incredibly, it began intensifying again as it rolled across the Atlantic. By Saturday, September 7, it had regained hurricane strength with winds of better than 90 mph. Then, at last, it began to weaken and die as it made a sharp turn to the northwest toward Greenland. On September 10, the Weather Bureau made its last notation of the storm, noting that it still had winds of about 40 mph.

It would be months before rescue workers and government officials could come up with a realistic determination of how many people had been killed. The official death toll is 408, but so many victims were literally blown into oblivion that the actual number of deaths could easily be higher.

The best estimate of veterans killed is somewhere between 250 and 260—almost two-thirds of the men who stayed in the work camps during the Labor Day weekend. With so many vets coming and going from the camps during the holiday, it was difficult for officials to know exactly how many men were blown off the Keys never to be seen again and how many of those who'd taken holiday leave simply decided not to return to the islands after the hurricane.

As the storm headed back into the wilds of the Atlantic Ocean that had spawned it, the political tempest it left in its wake was beginning to intensify. And Colonel McCormick's *Chicago Daily Tribune* was stoking it.

"Lay Vets' Deaths to Neglect," blared the *Tribune* headlines on Friday morning, September 6, 1935. The *Tribune's* lead story reported that Roosevelt Administration officials were bracing themselves for "a scandal of shocking proportions."

Filing his story from Hyde Park, *Tribune* reporter Willard Edwards wrote that unnamed sources close to the president were saying FDR thought someone in the Federal Emergency Relief Administration was, at the very least, "guilty of extremely bad judgment."

An accompanying story from the *Tribune's* Washington correspondent warned that "a congressional inquiry and far reaching political repercussions appeared inevitable" and reminded readers of an incident that was no doubt troubling the Roosevelt Administration. "Republican senators here believe it will be even more serious in its consequences [than] Mr. Hoover's ousting of the bonus army with machine guns and tear gas," the *Tribune* said.

The story hinted that Republicans would make sure voters had every gory detail of the tragedy explained to them before the elections of November 1936.

As Chicago readers read the *Tribune's* prediction of scandal, President Roosevelt and Stephen Early met with reporters for a news conference at FDR's home in Hyde Park Friday morning, September 6. The president entered the room with a chipper, earthy quip about the pale complexion of one of the reporters and suggested that another reporter take him outside for a sunbath. "They have a good nudist colony across the river," Roosevelt joked.

Roosevelt mentioned his appointment of Stewart McDonald to the post of federal housing administrator and answered a question about a recent meeting with New York mayor Fiorello La Guardia. Then a reporter asked FDR about the hurricane.

"The papers were interested in the Florida hurricane deaths—why no precautions were taken," the reporter said. "Anything you can tell us along that line?"

BILL: "HEY POP, DO YOU THINK WE'LL EVER GET THIS BRIDGE BUILT?"
POP: "I DUNNO, BUT IF I DONT LIVE THAT LONG, I GOT A GRANDSON TO TAKE MY PLACE"

John Ambrose was a talented artist from Baton Rouge, Louisiana, who drew finely detailed cartoons for the *Key Veteran News,* a newspaper published by the World War I vets who were working on a highway construction project in the Florida Keys in the summer of 1935. This cartoon shows two vets working on a bridge that would have linked Lower Matecumbe Key with what is now Fiesta Key. FROM THE AUTHOR'S COLLECTION

Eight partially completed piers that would have supported the bridge in Florida Bay are an enduring reminder of the vets' presence in the Florida Keys. In the foreground is one of the piers that was completed. The piers in the background were still under construction when the hurricane struck on September 2, 1935.
PHOTO BY WILLIE DRYE

The Labor Day Hurricane of 1935 decimated Bernard Russell's family and destroyed his home and his father's place of business in Islamorada, Florida. Russell was thrown into the worst of the storm when it made landfall but somehow survived. In this 1997 photo he sits on the foundation of the building that housed the Islamorada post office, where his father, John Russell, was postmaster. The building also housed a small store and cafe operated by his family. Russell died of complications from Parkinson's disease in 2004.
PHOTO BY WILLIE DRYE

Captain Einar Sundstrom, master of the passenger liner S.S. *Dixie*, brought his ship safely through the Labor Day Hurricane of 1935. The *Dixie* was caught in the storm while sailing through the Straits of Florida on September 2, 1935. The hurricane threw the ship onto a reef off Key Largo. But the *Dixie* held together and no one was seriously injured. In this photo, Sundstrom is greeted after his ordeal by his wife, Marie, seated far left, and his daughters Florence, seated far right, and Lillian, standing. PHOTO FROM THE AUTHOR'S COLLECTION

In the summer of 1932, thousands of World War I veterans assembled in Washington, DC, hoping to persuade Congress and President Herbert Hoover to pay them a bonus they'd been promised for their wartime service. The bonus wasn't due to be paid until 1945, but marchers were out of work because of the Great Depression and desperate for cash. In this photo, some of the so-called Bonus Marchers are parading down Pennsylvania Avenue to the U.S. Capitol.

Dozens of wooden coffins were shipped to the Florida Keys after the Labor Day Hurricane of 1935 killed about 250 veterans working on a highway construction project. Some of the bodies were placed into the coffins and sent to Miami for burial in Woodlawn Cemetery. But the bodies decayed so quickly that health officials stopped the shipment of coffins. Instead, the remaining coffins were stacked and lighted, and the bodies were cremated. PHOTO FROM THE JERRY WILKINSON COLLECTION, FLORIDA KEYS HISTORY AND DISCOVERY CENTER

The bodies of the 250 veterans killed when the Labor Day Hurricane of 1935 struck the Keys decomposed quickly in the heat, and rescue workers collecting them wore gas masks because of the odor of the decaying corpses. PHOTO FROM THE JERRY WILKINSON COLLECTION, FLORIDA KEYS HISTORY AND DISCOVERY CENTER

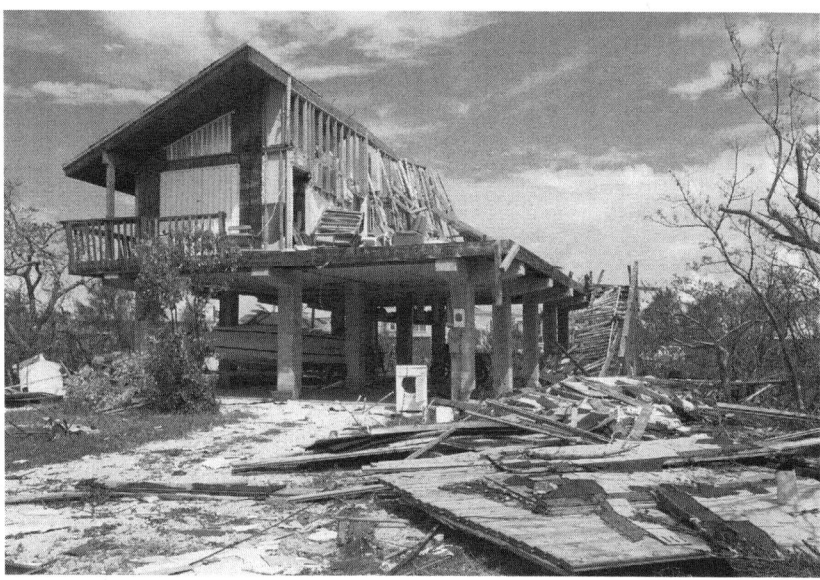

The fierce winds of the powerful Labor Day Hurricane of 1935 sliced off the second floor of the Hotel Matecumbe in Islamorada, Florida. PHOTO FROM THE JERRY WILKINSON COLLECTION, FLORIDA KEYS HISTORY AND DISCOVERY CENTER

Hurricane Irma's peak winds were at least 135 miles an hour when its eye came ashore at Big Pine Key, Florida, on September 10, 2017. Although Irma was not as powerful when it made landfall as the Labor Day Hurricane of 1935, the storm did catastrophic damage to Big Pine Key. This elevated home was destroyed by the hurricane. PHOTO BY CAROL TEDESCO

The U.S. Weather Bureau's plotting of the eye of the Labor Day Hurricane of 1935 was off by many miles on the day the storm struck the Florida Keys. In this illustration the Weather Bureau's calculation of the eye's position is shown by the gray diamond. The actual position of the storm's center is shown by the black diamond. Cuban meteorologists did not think the Weather Bureau's calculation was accurate. So on the afternoon of September 2, 1935, Leonard Povey, an American aviator serving with the Cuban army air force, was sent on a mission over the Straits of Florida to try to find the actual location of the hurricane. He found the storm's eye well to the northeast of the Weather Bureau's plot. Shortly after Povey's historic but now forgotten flight, the U.S. Weather Bureau issued a hurricane warning for the Florida Keys. GRAPHIC BY WILLIE DRYE

The Key West Extension of the Florida East Coast Railway—known informally as the Overseas Railway—spanned the Florida Keys between Miami and Key West and was considered one of the world's greatest engineering achievements when it was completed in 1912. Viaducts such as the one shown in this postcard photo connected the chain of islands. But the railroad operated only 23 years before it was destroyed by the Labor Day Hurricane of 1935.

PHOTO FROM THE AUTHOR'S COLLECTION

Rosalind Grooms Palmer and George Pepper were very much in love in the summer of 1935. They planned to get married as soon as Rosalind's divorce was final, but were killed when the fierce Labor Day hurricane swept their car into Florida Bay on September 2, 1935. PHOTO FROM THE AUTHOR'S COLLECTION

Rescue workers who came into the Florida Keys after the Labor Day Hurricane of 1935 found the grotesque handiwork of the fierce storm in the rubble of the beachfront work camps that had housed the veterans working on the highway construction project. PHOTO FROM THE JERRY WILKINSON COLLECTION, FLORIDA KEYS HISTORY AND DISCOVERY CENTER

Two members of a veterans' group drape the coffin of a veteran who was killed on the Florida Keys during the Labor Day Hurricane of 1935. The flag-draping was in preparation for services at Woodlawn Cemetery in Miami for 116 of the vets who died in the storm, which struck the Keys on September 2, 1935. About 20,000 people would gather for the somber funeral service a few hours later. PHOTO FROM THE JERRY WILKINSON COLLECTION, FLORIDA KEYS HISTORY AND DISCOVERY CENTER

Leonard Povey, far left, was an American stunt pilot who was brought to Cuba by political strongman Fulgencio Batista to train pilots for the Cuban army air force. Batista is third from left. To Batista's right is Cuban president Carlos Mendieta. On September 2, 1935, Povey flew the first known hurricane hunter mission when he piloted a small biplane fighter from Havana over Florida Bay seeking the eye of the fierce Labor Day Hurricane of 1935. LEONARD POVEY COLLECTION, HISTORY OF AVIATION COLLECTION, SPECIAL COLLECTIONS AND ARCHIVES DIVISION, EUGENE MCDERMOTT LIBRARY, THE UNIVERSITY OF TEXAS AT DALLAS

"Nothing more," Roosevelt said. "No more news than we have."

The president was startled when another reporter told him that rescue workers in the Keys would begin cremating bodies instead of following his instructions to ship them to families or Arlington National Cemetery for burial.

"I do not think so," Roosevelt said. "Certainly they are doing everything by order."

Stephen Early also was surprised. "I didn't . . . ," he began, and then stopped. "Actually burning?" he asked incredulously.

A reporter held up a copy of that day's edition of the *New York Daily News* and read aloud the story's headline: "Florida Burning Dead." The story reported that rescue workers had started cremating bodies in the Keys against the wishes of federal officials.

When reporters from the *Daily News* and Associated Press got into a half-serious debate about how the story had been written, Roosevelt saw an opportunity to steer conversation away from the hurricane.

"I will have you both up here before an investigating committee," FDR joshed, prompting an outburst of laughter from the gathering. "We will get Colonel Ijams to subpoena you both and we will get the truth."

Soon after the president's press conference, Colonel George Ijams, Governor David Sholtz, and Captain Harry Farmer climbed into Lieutenant Olsen's Douglas Dolphin seaplane for a look at the carnage in the Keys. Olsen flew as low as he dared over the islands—low enough for the odor of decomposing bodies to waft up to them. Sholtz told Olsen he wanted to go ashore to get a closer look at what the rescue workers were dealing with.

Coast Guard lieutenant William Clemmer also was airborne Friday heading for Cape Sable with J. C. Stoddard, who owned a waterfront vacation cottage at the tip of the Florida peninsula. Stoddard's daughter and son-in-law had gone to the isolated cottage for the Labor Day weekend, and Stoddard hadn't heard from them since.

Stoddard made the sad discovery that his cottage—and his daughter and son-in-law—were simply gone. The hurricane had passed Cape Sable during the early morning of Tuesday, September 3. The spot where Stoddard's cottage had stood was now clean, bare sand.

"The cape had been swept so bare that not one piece of wreckage from his home could be found," Clemmer reported.

Around 4:45 p.m. Friday, Lieutenant Olsen eased his seaplane down onto the waters of Biscayne Bay. His VIP passengers had been shaken by what they'd seen.

Sholtz met with reporters soon after he landed. He had seen the horrible aftermath of a killer hurricane when he'd gone into the shattered towns around Lake Okeechobee after the devastating hurricane there killed around 3,000 in 1928. Still, he said he was "shocked beyond words" by conditions in the Keys.

Sholtz also told reporters that rescue workers would begin cremating the badly decomposed bodies in the Keys instead of trying to ship them out for burial.

In Washington, WPA director Harry Hopkins and Federal Emergency Relief Administration officials were trying to smooth over the furor caused by Hopkins's earlier disparaging comments about the U.S. Weather Bureau.

Hopkins tried to put some distance between Washington officials and Florida ERA administrators, telling reporters the veterans were "technically" under the supervision of the state administrators, with the obvious implication that federal officials in Washington therefore were not responsible for the death toll.

After talking with reporters, Hopkins left Washington for Hyde Park to talk with his boss about the situation.

That same day the Federal Emergency Relief Administration issued a statement saying Hopkins's earlier comment that he would not have evacuated the veterans based on the wording of the hurricane advisories was not intended as a criticism of the Weather Bureau's competency. FERA "regrets the misunderstanding caused in some quarters by Mr. Hopkins' statement clearing Florida ERA camp officials of negligence in not evacuating the camps before the storm struck," the statement added.

In Florida, Hopkins's assistant Aubrey Williams was about to begin his probe into the conduct of the administrators who'd been hired by his agency. Williams talked briefly with reporters Friday.

"Everybody seems to have done what they thought was the right thing at the right time," Williams said. "But we mean to follow this thing relentlessly and let the chips fall where they may. If any of our men are to blame we want to know it."

By Friday afternoon news editors had had almost four days to sift through accounts of the hurricane. As the week ended, stories began appearing in newspapers across the country about local veterans who'd been killed in the storm.

"Grady C. Lewis, Concord Mechanic, Listed Among Dead in Florida," read a small headline in North Carolina's *Charlotte Observer*, while the

Virginian-Pilot of Norfolk reported, "Portsmouth Man Probable Victim of Florida Storm."

The Bee of Danville, Virginia, noted that Nan Morris of Bristol had received a telegram telling her that her husband, Owen Hughes Morris, had been killed by the hurricane.

President Roosevelt, at his home in Hyde Park, New York, probably saw the *Poughkeepsie Eagle-News*'s brief stories about veterans from Schenectady and Saugerties dying in the hurricane. The *Eagle-News*, published only a few miles from FDR's home, noted that the dead veteran from Schenectady, Lawrence Broderick, was among the first to enlist in the U.S. Navy when the United States entered World War I. Broderick had been killed at Camp 3, the newspaper reported.

Editorial writers also had had time to ponder the news of the hurricane's death toll and the comments from officials in Washington.

The *Washington Post* questioned the competency of the administration that had hired the men in charge of the veterans' work program. "Plans that make no allowance for these unforeseen and often inexplicable actions of nature are obviously too shallow to make much impress upon the growth of a nation," the editorial concluded.

On the Gulf Coast—where hurricanes are a routine fact of life—newspapers weren't buying the notion that the Weather Bureau was responsible for the tragedy.

"We do not hesitate to say . . . that it is simply nonsensical to impute the blame for the disaster to the Weather Bureau," the *New Orleans Item* said on its editorial page of Saturday, September 7. Hopkins's comments indicated he was "entirely ignorant" about hurricanes. "All of us in the hurricane belt know that nobody can tell exactly where a hurricane center is going to strike the coast until half a day or less before it gets there," the *Item* editorial said. "But everybody knows a day or two before that the blast may center anywhere on a line 100 or more miles long."

The *Tampa Daily Times* called Hopkins's statements about the Weather Bureau "ridiculous" and said work camp administrators were to blame for the veterans' deaths.

The *Pensacola News* unequivocally supported the Weather Bureau. "When the Weather Bureau gives warning of a hurricane to a community in plenty of time for the people of that community to prepare for a blow, its work is finished," said the *News*. "It cannot be expected to hunt up the individuals in that community and personally warn them to get out or suffer the consequences."

Other newspapers speculated about possible long-range consequences from the investigations being launched. Even papers less inclined to blatant Roosevelt-bashing than the *Chicago Daily Tribune* were commenting on the possibility of dire political consequences for the Roosevelt Administration.

"The tragedies [the hurricane] wrought [in Florida] are numerous; and in the still unsettled question of why the evacuation of the veterans was delayed, there is the possibility of a national scandal," said an editorial in the *Virginian-Pilot* in its edition of Sunday, September 8.

The Sunday edition of the *Miami Beach Daily Tribune* again shrieked that 1,000 had died in the hurricane and published another front-page photo of a dead body from its seemingly inexhaustible supply of gruesome pictures. Again, the paper blamed the Weather Bureau for the veterans' deaths.

On Sunday, September 8, *Chicago Sunday Tribune* reporter Spearman Lewis proclaimed that Roosevelt Administration officials were trying to recover from a "colossal blunder" that could threaten Roosevelt's political survival.

"The heat is on and a national scandal that might well imperil the New Deal's next political campaign must be smothered," Lewis wrote. "The administration seems willing to forego for the time being any serious effort to fix responsibility for the delayed evacuation train."

Lewis's story included a quote from Colonel Ijams hinting that tension might be building between the WPA and Federal Emergency Relief Administration on one side and the Veterans Administration on the other.

"I was sent here to bury the dead and serve the living," Ijams said. "But I find an increasing public tendency to pin the responsibility for the delayed relief train on the Veterans Administration. We merely rounded the men up in Washington and turned them over to the FERA and WPA, Florida division. Any responsibility is theirs and I shall look into that phase of the catastrophe when I have completed my original assignments."

The colonel was working diligently Saturday to accomplish those tasks. The bodies of the men who'd been sent to Miami before the decision was made to cremate the remaining vets in the Keys had to be buried. While workmen used jackhammers and a steam shovel to dig a large trench grave in Miami's Woodlawn Cemetery big enough for the veterans' coffins, Ijams worked his way through a long list of preparations for a memorial service planned for Sunday evening at the city's Bayfront Park. If his boss in Hyde Park was going to be deprived of the opportunity of laying the hapless veterans to rest amid military pomp and splendor at Arlington National Cemetery, then he was going to make sure they got a proper send-off in Miami. Ijams, with the backing of President Roosevelt, rounded up an army general and a navy admiral to attend the service.

At the cemetery the bodies in the pine boxes were so far gone there was little morticians could do. Rescue workers—including police officers from Miami and Miami Beach—had made an extraordinary effort to identify as many of the bodies as they could. The Veterans Administration had even sent fingerprint records to Florida to help identify the victims. It may have been the first time that fingerprints were used to identify victims of a catastrophe.

But by the time the bodies reached the makeshift morgue at Woodlawn, there wasn't much more that could be done with those who hadn't already been identified.

"The bodies were considerably swollen, all of the faces looked absolutely alike and not recognizable," said Arthur Bilsbrough, a Florida ERA engineer. "They were in a bad state of decomposition and it was impossible to identify [them] other than by physical defects or by marks such as tattoos, missing teeth, bridgework, gold, and so forth."

Morticians filled the pine boxes with a special preserving compound to reduce the odor. Each wooden box then was placed inside a metal casket and soldered shut.

Meanwhile, Ijams set about finding enough American flags to cover the coffins. Many of the flags in the Keys had been blown away by the storm, but the resourceful colonel had been sending telegrams seeking flags since before he arrived in Miami, "and within two days I had enough flags to bury the whole state of Florida," he said.

He also came up with a replica of the Tomb of the Unknown Soldier, and roses—hundreds and hundreds of roses.

Down in the Keys a sad and simple ritual was being performed on the banks of Snake Creek. Heeding the orders of Governor Sholtz and state health officials, National Guardsmen and other rescue workers had built a funeral pyre of 36 pine coffins interlaced with driftwood, lumber from the nearby wreckage of Camp 1, and railroad ties. Clergymen from all faiths conducted services, and a small detachment of National Guard troops fired a salute. Then a man, dressed in bib overalls and a jacket despite the heat and wearing a Salvation Army cap, raised a bugle to his lips.

The brief, mournful strains of "Taps" floated across the ruined island. As the notes faded away, a soldier stepped forward with a blazing torch, touched it to the pile of coffins and stepped back quickly as flames greedily enveloped the gasoline-soaked pyre.

~

In New York City, chartered trains carrying passengers from the *Dixie* were arriving.

The mood had been lighthearted as the trains chugged northward from Miami. During stops along the way, some got off long enough to buy local newspapers, then re-boarded the train and eagerly read stories of their hurricane experience as their journey resumed. Some of them happily shouted the lyrics to "Dixie" to the accompaniment of an accordion played by Harry Burk of New Orleans.

The train stopped in Washington for a few minutes, and 11-year-old Eleanor Shields of Philadelphia stepped off to stretch her legs. She was wearing a life jacket emblazoned with "SS Dixie" in large letters. The life jacket had been signed by members of the *Dixie*'s crew. A waiting newspaper photographer spotted her and snapped her picture.

When the trains reached the Pennsylvania Station passenger platforms beneath the streets of Manhattan, however, all the pent-up emotions—excitement, fear, awe, despair, hope, overwhelming relief—came pouring out.

As passengers stepped off the train, Ben Grill searched the crowd for his sister, Goldie, a teacher who lived in Brooklyn. They spotted each other and rushed into an embrace. Goldie threw her arms around him as he pressed her face to his and kissed her on the cheek.

Ida Flatow and Ann Cinder, also teachers from Brooklyn, were so overwhelmed with relief at the sight of their families that they collapsed and had to be helped to a nearby hotel to recover.

Eight-year-old Herbert Shprentz of Brooklyn, who rode out the storm with his mother, Freda, told his father, Isidore, that the wreck of the *Dixie* had been "swell." Frank Belcher, the opera-singer-turned-Broadway tobacconist, was happily reunited with Skippy, his Boston terrier, and his wife, Anna.

As Sunday morning, September 8, dawned in Miami, workers at Woodlawn Cemetery were making final preparations to lay the hurricane victims to rest. The flags that Colonel Ijams had hustled to round up were draped over the coffins, and a veteran stood guard beside each of the flags.

Many Miamians were in church seeking explanations about the tragedy on the Keys. During an evening service at Little River Baptist Church, Reverend Carl Moberg tried to offer a few answers with his sermon, "God's Relationship to Hurricanes."

Services for the burial of the hurricane victims at Woodlawn Cemetery were brief and simple. Representatives from the armed forces and veterans groups made up most of the crowd.

The memorial service that evening, however, was quite a different affair.

At 6:15 p.m. ranks of soldiers, sailors, Coast Guardsmen, and veterans began forming near the entrances to Bayfront Park. Twenty minutes later they marched somberly into the park and stood at attention around a band shell near the center of the park. A few minutes before 7 p.m. three U.S. Navy fighter planes droned overhead and released their payloads—hundreds of roses.

Massed bands from the military groups played "America." As the last notes of the music faded, R. V. Waters stepped to the podium and looked out at the faces of about 20,000 people. Waters tried to make some sense of the veterans' tragic deaths.

"Fellow veterans and citizens," he began. "We are gathered here in solemn assemblage this evening to do honor to a group of American veterans who but a few days ago gave up their lives in the line of duty. We do not believe—we do not say—that this is our last tribute to these departed comrades, for we know that in the heart of every patriotic citizen of these United States there will ever dwell a proper sense of appreciation and of gratitude for the sacrifice and heroic deeds of those veterans and their comrades who a few years ago offered their all upon the altar of civilization.

"Nor do we believe that these men have died in vain. It is rare indeed that such sacrifice is made but some great truth is established—and some noble principle maintained—or some remedy discovered; some agency developed to insure the future welfare of others. Time will surely prove that these veterans did not give up their lives in vain."

A Catholic priest, a Protestant minister, and a rabbi offered prayers, soloists sang "There Is No Death" and "The Vacant Chair," and Colonel Ijams delivered a brief message from President Roosevelt.

"I wish I might be present to express my profound grief and deep sense of loss because of the tragic death of these defenders of the nation," the message read. "Will you be good enough to convey my condolences to the families of these gallant men."

It was an impressive ceremony with lots of military flourishes for the earthy, boozy, ragtag veterans who were so disdainful of formality and authority. But an anonymous and very perceptive editorial writer for the weekend edition of Washington's afternoon newspaper the *Sunday Star*, gave them an eloquent eulogy suffused with a much clearer understanding of the sad irony surrounding their deaths.

"On the hurricane-swept Florida keys has been enacted the final episode of the tragedy of The Bonus Marchers," said the September 8 editorial. "The men died as they lived, helpless orphans of the storms. The lightning-lit madness of war tore them loose from the relative simplicity and security of the slow-moving age into which they had been born. When the cannon ball storm had passed over the desolated fields of the earth they were blown into a fast, strange post-war world by the inflating breezes of hero worship. These subsided and they found the calm uncomfortable. After a brief lull they were torn loose from whatever security they had been able to find by the blasts of the great depression."

The *Sunday Star* predicted that investigations probably would determine who was responsible for the veterans' deaths but noted that the real cause of the tragedy "lies beyond the reach of any investigator. They were the victims of a hurricane sweeping the earth whose path no meteorologist can forecast nor understand. It was the tragedy of these men—and perhaps the tragedy of all of us—to be born into an age of hurricanelike transition such as history has not known. Life demanded of them a rapid series of readjustments which they were not equipped by nature to make. Consequently they made them clumsily and with infinite pain."

The "Great War" had been responsible for the vets' inadequacy in dealing with modern life, wrote the anonymous editor. It left some with physical disabilities, but many who'd come back physically intact had been hampered by "spiritual wounds and disabilities" caused by wartime service that were even more difficult for them to overcome.

Some who'd served in the war had learned skills and self-reliance they hadn't had before going overseas, and "some came back far less adequate than before for any self-directed coping with the multiplying complexities of living," the *Sunday Star* said. "Among the latter were many of these poor victims of the hurricane."

As the veterans received a formal send-off in Miami, President Roosevelt was reading Aubrey Williams's report on the circumstances surrounding their deaths.

Williams had arrived in Florida Friday morning. He'd made a flight down to the Keys to see the hurricane's aftermath, interviewed a dozen witnesses, and read transcripts of the testimony of six other witnesses who had been interviewed for an investigation being conducted by Dade County State's Attorney George Worley. A fair amount of his time also had been taken up writing the report for FDR. Barely 48 hours after Williams had set foot in Florida, his report was in the hands of the president.

"It is impossible for us to reach the conclusion that there has been negligence or mistaken judgment on the part of those charged with the responsibility for the safety of the men engaged on the Keys projects," he wrote.

Williams's report contained the phrase suggested by Julius Stone that had been circulating among FERA officials before Williams even left for Florida. "To our mind the catastrophe must be characterized as 'an act of God' and was by its very nature beyond the power of man or instruments at his disposal to foresee sufficiently far enough in advance to permit the taking of adequate precautions capable of preventing the death and desolation which occurred."

Williams listed Colonel Ijams as a contributor to the report, but Ijams had been far too busy organizing the funeral to contribute anything. Still, Williams put the colonel's name on the report, implying he had helped write it.

Williams's hasty report to FDR exonerating officials of the Federal Emergency Relief Administration and Florida ERA undoubtedly eased the minds of some of his inner circle who were concerned that the veterans' deaths could cause serious political problems for the president. That same night another event was unfolding that would also improve Roosevelt's chances for reelection.

While the president was looking over the hurricane report, Louisiana senator Huey Long—who had become a legitimate threat to FDR's hopes for a second term—was in Baton Rouge supervising a session of the state legislature, which he controlled with an iron fist. As the legislators went through a pantomime of democracy under the dictatorial Kingfish's watchful eye, Carl Weiss, a young physician whose father's career as a judge had been ruined by Long, slipped behind a column in the capitol's rotunda.

Around 8 p.m. Long, surrounded by his ever-present heavily armed bodyguards, left the assembly. Suddenly Weiss stepped from behind the column and fired a single bullet into Long's stomach.

Weiss died in a hail of gunfire from Long's protectors, but the senator would linger for two days before dying.

The attack on Long was splashed across the front pages of the nation's newspapers, stealing some of the attention from the news of Williams's "act of God" findings in his report to President Roosevelt.

Still, the hurricane report was noticed.

The Greater Miami Ministerial Association was among the first to howl in protest at Williams's conclusions. As soon as the news appeared in the morning newspapers of Monday, September 9, the indignant clergymen drafted a letter to President Roosevelt telling him that Williams had pointed the finger at the wrong culprit. The clergymen accused Williams of trying to steer responsibility away from Florida ERA administrators by blaming an entity that couldn't be questioned about the part it played in the tragedy.

While the ministers in Miami raised a holy ruckus about Williams's conclusions, Charles Clark, acting director of the U.S. Weather Bureau, was defending his agency's hurricane advisories in a private meeting with his bosses, Secretary of Agriculture Henry Wallace and Undersecretary of Agriculture Rexford Tugwell.

Wallace and Tugwell didn't think the scathing criticism being leveled at the Weather Bureau was justified, Clark wrote in a memo after the meeting. They believed the Weather Bureau "had given sufficient and ample warning to influence those proceeding with caution to evacuate the camps, and it was not just or fair that we should take the blame for the destruction of these camps," Clark wrote.

They did have some criticism for the advisories, however. "They, as laymen, did feel that the warnings and advisories were worded in a too stereotyped and technical way to be entirely and clearly understood by the public," Clark noted. Clark, Wallace, and Tugwell had no intention of publicizing this opinion, however.

As the Weather Bureau administrators critiqued their agency's performance in the hurricane, General Frank Hines, director of the Veterans Administration, was pondering Aubrey Williams's report on the tragedy.

It was becoming clear to Hines that the catastrophe in the Keys and the "act of God" conclusion were creating a serious public image problem for the VA. Clarence Barringer, a veteran in Newark, Ohio, who was furious that the vets in the Keys had been left in harm's way, poured his anger into a letter and mailed it to the "Veterans Extermination Bureau, Washington, D.C." The U.S. Post Office delivered it, as addressed, to Hines.

Letters and telegrams expressing outrage and heartbreak had been pouring in to the VA from across the United States for days. Most of the people who sent them didn't seem to realize that the VA had had nothing to do with the decision to put the veterans in the Keys. That perception had to be changed.

Hines decided it was time to get some answers about what had really happened. He knew the man to provide those answers, but unfortunately, that man was out of town. On September 11, Hines told his staff to find VA investigator David Kennamer right away.

CHAPTER NINE

Regret to Inform You

It wasn't hard to figure out why the public was heaping so much blame for the tragedy in the Florida Keys on the Veterans Administration. The VA had the difficult and unpleasant task of notifying the families of the men who'd died in the hurricane, and it was only human nature to blame the messenger for the bad news. Every day, telegrams beginning with the phrase "Regret to inform you" were being dispatched from Washington to all parts of the Unites States.

One of those telegrams was delivered to Theresa Kreitzburg in care of the Eckhart Mines in Allegheny County in western Maryland. "Regret to inform you that Elmer Kreitzburg is reported among those dead in the Florida hurricane," it read.

A telegram also was sent to Betty Neel in tiny Brandon, Texas, just south of Dallas. It read: "Regret to inform you that John T. Neel is reported among those dead in the Florida hurricane stop Body was cremated at Snake Creek, Florida stop."

The telegrams went to the big cities—Chicago and Cleveland, Milwaukee and Memphis, Pittsburgh and Philadelphia; they went to Denver, Los Angeles, New York, and Baltimore. But Western Union delivery boys also found their way to front doors in Tucson, Arizona, and tiny Prague, Nebraska. They delivered telegrams to Irvington and Elizabeth in New Jersey and to Greensburg and Altoona and Wilkes-Barre in Pennsylvania. The sad tidings went out to Everett, Newtonville, and Roxbury in Massachusetts and to Russell and Covington in Kentucky. The telegrams were delivered to St. Francisville, Louisiana; to Asheville, Concord, and Gastonia in North Carolina; to Danville and Richmond in Virginia; and to Pensacola and Winter Haven in Florida. They went to Clarksville, West Virginia. They went to Marietta, Georgia, and Frostburg, Maryland, and Peebles, Ohio. And they went to Knoxville and Nashville in Tennessee and to dozens of other large cities and small towns and isolated farms in 30 of the 48 states, and to the District of Columbia. Regret to inform you . . . regret to inform you . . . regret to inform you.

A delivery boy went to 440 Senator Street in Brooklyn with a telegram regretting to inform John Conway—father of Jimmy Conway, the ex-boxer who'd once been a contender for the heavyweight crown—that his son had been killed in a hurricane in Florida. Whoever answered the knock said he'd never heard of John Conway.

Hundreds of people were left to wonder. They knew their husbands, fathers, sons, brothers, and uncles had been in one of those New Deal work camps someplace in Florida. There had been something in the newspaper about a bad storm down there. They hadn't heard a word in weeks. What had happened?

Many would never know. The burial detail at Woodlawn Cemetery had tried to identify the bodies shipped to them for interment, but in some cases there just wasn't anything to indicate who the man was. Fingerprints were useless because there was no skin left on the fingers.

The workers made notes of whatever details they could. They wrote that one man had a tattoo of an American flag and the words "Sylvia 1906" on his left forearm. Another was missing the second and third fingers of his left hand. Still another had a tattoo on his left forearm of a red shield with "Co. L—28th Inf" in blue letters. They noted that one man was wearing a belt buckle with the initial "F."

It wasn't much, but it was the best they could do.

And then there were the families of veterans who had simply disappeared. There was no body to identify or even any remains to puzzle over. They were just simply gone.

Joseph Karpus of Brooklyn contacted the VA asking what had become of Andrew Beganske. The VA sent a telegram to Karpus that read: "Government and our records show body not recovered as yet stop Continuing search."

Grief and anger inevitably followed the visits from the Western Union delivery boys, and in Phillipsburg, New Jersey—on the Delaware River near the border with Pennsylvania—Andrew Koleser was furious.

Koleser, a member of the American Legion post in Phillipsburg, was trying to help a grief-stricken mother whose son, J. Rodney Thompson, had been killed in the hurricane. Thompson's mother wanted to bury her son in his hometown. Federal officials told her that his body would be sent to her, so she'd hired an undertaker in Phillipsburg and made arrangements for her son's funeral. Now some bureaucrat was telling her Thompson had already been buried in Miami.

Koleser went to the Western Union office and told the clerk he wanted to send a telegram to President Franklin Roosevelt in Hyde Park, New York. In the terse, abbreviated language used in telegrams, Koleser explained the situation and asked FDR if there wasn't something he could do to help. "Aged widowed mother heartbroken stop. . . . Won't you help us have this veteran sent home," Koleser said.

Lots of other people were just as angry and bewildered as Koleser about what had happened in Florida. They weren't buying Aubrey Williams's "act of God" conclusion, and they were pouring their anger and cynicism into letters to President Roosevelt, General Frank Hines, and anybody else they could think of.

"May our Great Savior forgive the ones who are guilty, who caused these poor sick and crippled men to be placed in a death trap," Joseph Hilbun of Eudora in eastern Kansas said in a letter to President Roosevelt.

A. M. Coffin of Cisco, Texas—about halfway between Abilene and Fort Worth—told FDR the tragedy reflected poorly on him because he was ultimately responsible for hiring the men who'd been so indifferent to the veterans' welfare. The men in charge of the work camps should have had the "ordinary common sense" to remove the vets at least 24 hours before the hurricane struck, he wrote.

Edward Felker, a veteran in Erie in northwestern Pennsylvania, told Roosevelt that a gruesome news photo showing veterans' bodies lashed to a crude sled tied to an automobile's rear bumper had affected him deeply and prompted him to write FDR. Felker said he'd campaigned for Roosevelt in 1932 but said he blamed officials in Florida for the vets' deaths and feared many other veterans would as well.

A few days later the photo that had shocked Felker was published in *Time* magazine with a story about the hurricane.

Roosevelt supporter Charles Pemburn, a veteran in Akron, Ohio, warned FDR's secretary Marvin McIntyre that Democrats hadn't been responsible for the storm but were responsible for putting the veterans on the Keys. Should people be convinced that FDR was responsible for the vets' deaths, public opinion would shift dramatically against him, and veterans would be working diligently to make sure that perception was maintained, he said.

"[A] veteran will fight and work hard against a candidate—yes, much harder against than for," Pemburn wrote.

Others were astonished that those in charge had waited to decide whether to move the men. Frank Hamilton, pastor of the First Methodist Episcopal Church in Daytona Beach, Florida, said the Keys were "a place of great danger" during the hurricane season. "The delay of that train in getting away from Miami and in getting down to the Keys is by this time a nation-wide fiasco," he wrote.

Anthony Morse of Jacksonville, Florida, predicted political repercussions if FDR didn't determine who'd left the veterans in harm's way. "There seems to be a disposition to whitewash everybody connected with the matter, but believe it or not, for your own political good you better not let it go that way," Morse said.

"I have had great respect for your motives, Mr. President, even though I have not always agreed with your methods," wrote L. Garland Biggers of West Palm Beach, Florida. "Your action in this matter will determine whether or not I shall continue to respect your motives."

Letters from veterans' groups across the United States underscored many veterans' intense dislike of FDR and revealed smoldering anger that could cost the president dearly in the upcoming campaign.

Albert Grosskopf and Thomas M. Daugherty of the National American Veterans in San Francisco told the president they were speaking for all members of their group when they said the deaths in the Keys were proof of the Roosevelt Administration's "undying enmity toward the veteran."

Veterans of Foreign Wars national commander James E. Van Zandt called Aubrey Williams's hasty report "a whitewash as wide as the breadth of the combined white crosses that cover America's heroic dead buried in France." He urged the president to disregard Williams's conclusion and order a new investigation. Just to be safe, the VFW decided to conduct its own investigation into the veterans' deaths.

"If these officials had heeded the storm warnings or been in the least familiar with seasonal climatic conditions, the tragedy could have been averted, all witnesses agree," Van Zandt said.

Ernest Hemingway had been deeply affected by what he saw when he and friends went to the Upper Keys to help with the rescue effort two days after the hurricane. Soon after he returned to Key West, Hemingway—who had no use for Franklin Roosevelt and the New Deal—vented his emotions in an essay that was published by *New Masses* magazine.

Hemingway wrote that the wealthy are fond of fishing in the Keys during the mild winters, but they avoid the area during the summer. "There is a known danger to property" during those months, he wrote. "But veterans, especially the bonus-marching variety of veterans, are not property. They are only human beings, unsuccessful human beings, and all they have to lose is their lives."

Hemingway didn't actually accuse the Roosevelt Administration of being responsible for the veterans' deaths, but the accusation was clearly implied. "Whom did they annoy, and to whom was their possible presence a political danger?" he wrote. "Who sent them down to the Florida Keys and left them there in hurricane months? Who is responsible for their deaths?"

The *Chicago Daily Tribune* also was taking aim at Williams's "act of God" verdict. In an editorial published September 12, the *Tribune* conceded that the hurricane may have been an act of God, but putting the veterans on the Keys during the hurricane season was "a piece of criminal folly committed by someone in Washington.

"The camps on the Florida Keys were established to avert another bonus march on Washington, with all the political embarrassments involved in such a demonstration of discontent," the editorial said. "Naturally, a site was selected as far from Washington as it conveniently could be while still providing free labor for a southern constituency which wanted public improvements at somebody else's expense."

Senators and representatives were getting into the act, and the White House was deflecting some of the demands to an overloaded General Hines. On September 10, Florida senator Duncan Fletcher sent a telegram to President Roosevelt telling him that his constituents demanded a thorough investigation. A copy of the message was forwarded to the VA director, and now the general had a memo awaiting his attention from Rudolph Forster, the executive clerk at the White House. Although the request was politely phrased in the form of a delicate understatement, Hines knew he had to respond immediately. "Will you not be good enough to let us have draft of appropriate reply to Senator Fletcher for the President's signature?" Forster wrote.

Hines met with WPA director Harry Hopkins to discuss the situation. They decided to launch a joint investigation in Florida, using investigators from the Veterans Administration and the Works Progress Administration, which had absorbed the Federal Emergency Relief Administration. The VA and WPA then would prepare a joint report for President Roosevelt.

Hines explained the plan to Stephen Early, who said he'd pass it on to Marvin McIntyre at the president's temporary offices in Poughkeepsie, New York.

If Early had any thoughts about the joint investigation or anything else about the hurricane in the Keys, he still wasn't bothering to jot them down in his White House diary.

At the U.S. Weather Bureau, acting director Charles Clark was wrapping up a "Special and Confidential" report on his agency's performance during the hurricane to Secretary of Agriculture Henry Wallace. In a September 12 letter to Wallace, Clark said he was keeping the report under wraps because the veterans' deaths had become a highly charged political issue, and he didn't want anything he said to be interpreted as criticizing other government agencies and thus adding to the controversy.

Clark gave a detailed accounting of the Weather Bureau's actions from August 27—when meteorologists first realized that a disturbance of some sort had formed somewhere northeast of Puerto Rico—until the remnants of the hurricane went back to sea near Norfolk, Virginia, on September 6.

In Clark's estimation the Weather Bureau had done a good job of tracking the hurricane and warning people in its path. To underscore his contention, he included letters from Pan American Airways, Barnett National Bank, the Superintendent of Lighthouses, the Collier County (Florida) Board of Commissioners, and others commending the Weather Bureau on the timeliness and accuracy of the advisories.

Without knowing it, Clark refuted Lawrence Westbrook's silly notion that the veterans were safer on the sparsely populated Keys because there was less danger of them being killed by flying debris than in a city. Clark pointed out that most of the deaths on the Keys were caused by the massive storm surge that inundated the narrow, low-lying islands. There simply was no place for the veterans to escape this deadly flood. If they'd been on the mainland, the veterans almost certainly would have escaped the storm surge, and the loss of life would have been minimal, Clark said.

As far as Clark was concerned, the catastrophe in the work camps was due to the inexperience of the men in charge.

"The warnings issued by the Weather Bureau were sufficiently accurate and timely to urge a person reasonably familiar with the dangers of seas due to gales washing over low-lying keys to leave the keys and go to a place of safety on the mainland," Clark said. "Many persons in the southern part of

Florida did act on the same advices of the Weather Bureau and took steps to protect lives and property."

Across town, Hines still hadn't heard from his ace investigator, David Kennamer. Where was he?

At last the VA director got a radiogram from a VA official in upstate New York. They'd found Kennamer in the small town of Canandaigua. He was leaving immediately and would be in Washington the following morning.

The general had Kennamer's orders waiting for him. Hines wanted him to determine whether the men in charge of the camps had received hurricane advisories and, if they had, what they'd done in response. Kennamer was instructed to work with John J. Abt, a lawyer who was handling the investigation for the WPA, which had taken over the Federal Emergency Relief Administration.

Hines told Kennamer to interview every survivor he could find.

David Wendall Kennamer had taken a winding route to his position as an investigator for the Veterans Administration. He had grown up in northeastern Alabama, which would soon benefit greatly from the electricity provided by the Tennessee Valley Authority that had been created by President Roosevelt's New Deal. But Kennamer and his family were not especially fond of President Franklin Roosevelt. They had been die-hard Republicans since before the Civil War. David Kennamer's brother Thomas had served in the Alabama state legislature and was the Republican National Committeeman for the state. President Calvin Coolidge—also a Republican—had a great deal of respect for the legal skills of the Kennamer family, appointing one of David Kennamer's brothers to a federal judge's position in Alabama and another brother to an identical post in Oklahoma.

David Kennamer had been a shy young man who hadn't been especially interested in legal matters when he was growing up in Alabama. After earning a degree in veterinary medicine, Kennamer entered the U.S. Marine Corps and saw combat in France during World War I. He joined the Veterans Administration in 1924. By the summer of 1935, Kennamer was 47 years old and one of the VA's most capable investigators.

Kennamer arrived in Miami Thursday morning, September 12. He checked into the McAllister Hotel and met briefly with Captain Harry Farmer, who'd come down to Florida with Colonel George Ijams and stayed on after the colonel went back to Washington.

Kennamer and Farmer then met with John Abt and asked the lawyer about the joint investigation they were supposed to conduct. Abt said he

knew nothing about it and didn't think it was a good idea to continue looking into the matter. Nor did he want Kennamer interviewing Florida ERA
employees. Abt reluctantly gave Kennamer copies of transcripts of some of
the testimony he'd taken with Aubrey Williams.

Kennamer was deeply concerned about Abt's belief that there was no
need to keep digging into the tragedy on the Keys.

He had quickly looked over some of the transcripts Abt had given him
and was already questioning Williams's "act of God" conclusion. Maybe the
Weather Bureau advisories hadn't been 100 percent accurate, but they had
warned that a bad storm was near the Keys. "I cannot agree with Mr. Abt that
no one was guilty of negligence," he wrote in a September 12 letter to Sam
Jared, director of the VA's investigative division.

Kennamer also mentioned some of his concerns to Abt after he'd looked
at the statements of Fred Ghent, Ray Sheldon, and meteorologist Gerald
Kennedy of Key West, who'd advised Sheldon to return to the work camps
at 5 a.m. Sunday morning, September 1. Abt said the meteorologist hadn't
advised Sheldon to go back to the camps because there was impending danger, but because of the uncertainty about whether the ferry service would
continue uninterrupted.

Kennamer saw it differently, especially since Kennedy said in a second
interview that he told Sheldon the Keys might be in danger.

The VA investigator was suspicious of Abt's influence on the no-fault
report that Aubrey Williams had submitted to President Roosevelt. And he
had deep misgivings about whether he should even be working with Abt on
this so-called joint investigation—so deep that he wanted Harry Hopkins to
designate someone else to handle the WPA's part of the inquiry.

General Hines sent a letter to Hopkins on Saturday, September 14, telling him that Abt hadn't been given any instructions about continuing a joint
investigation with the VA. Hines didn't mention Kennamer's concerns about
working with the WPA attorney.

Hopkins was surprised. That same day, Aubrey Williams had a telephone
chat with the reluctant Abt in Florida.

Williams scolded Abt and told the lawyer he didn't want him giving
anyone the impression that the WPA wasn't being cooperative. Abt warned
Williams that Kennamer thought the administrators of the work camps had
been at fault for the veterans' deaths. But Williams told Abt not to worry
about that because they could deal with that problem in Washington.

Abt was persistent. "It would be a terrible mistake to start going through those witnesses again," he said.

"We can't help that," Williams said. President Roosevelt had placed General Hines in charge of the investigation, and the WPA had to give the appearance that it was cooperating fully. Williams told Abt he didn't want Kennamer returning to Washington with doubts about the WPA's motives. "I want you to develop a very cordial relationship," Williams said.

Abt stuck to his guns. "I think it would be a mistake to go through the whole thing again," he protested.

"But we can't say anything about that," Williams said. He reminded Abt that they'd have a chance to shape the final report before it went to the president, and they could take care of any problems then.

Williams ordered Abt to make it clear to Kennamer that the WPA would do anything the VA wanted. Then, Williams said to Abt, when Kennamer's report arrived in Washington they would untangle any problems before it reached the president.

While Williams and Abt discussed their plans for dealing with Kennamer's investigation, Sam Jared, the director of the VA's investigations division, was making a few inquiries of his own in Washington, and he'd come across something he wanted to know more about—immediately. He sent a telegram to Kennamer telling him to find out if Ray Sheldon had received the Weather Bureau's advisory of 3:30 a.m. September 2 warning of high tides and gale-force winds on the Keys.

"Wire prompt report of all circumstances pertaining to this matter," Jared ordered.

Kennamer asked Abt where he could find Sheldon. The lawyer said he had no idea, and said he thought Sheldon had left the area to take another job.

On Saturday, September 14, Kennamer and Farmer went to Jackson Memorial Hospital in Miami, where John Russell was still recovering from his injuries. The postmaster was known up and down the Keys as a man of wisdom and honesty. The investigators wanted to know how he had prepared his family for the hurricane.

"We were afraid because it was in our area and because it is the custom of these storms to make a turn," Russell said. "We were afraid it would turn and we had not wanted to wait until the last moment."

Kennamer asked Russell if Ray Sheldon or anybody else from the Florida ERA asked him whether the hurricane would be dangerous to the Keys. "No, they did not," Russell answered. "They didn't ask me anything about it at all."

Kennamer asked when he thought the vets should have been evacuated from the Keys. "They should have been moved out on Sunday," Russell said. "The indications were there would be a storm. When there is a storm in the straits we always get a heavy wind from it."

Kennamer asked him if he thought a "prudent man" would have evacuated the veterans on Sunday, September 1.

"Yes," Russell said. "If I had been in charge of the camps, I would have moved out every man from the camps. You see, their situation was different from ours. Those in Camp 1 were in a very low piece of land, right open to the sea. Any sea at all would sweep it. There was nothing to shelter them in their little huts at all. No anchorage. They were just set up on piers, and I told them some time ago when they first built them that they wouldn't have the huts when the storm was over."

Kennamer asked Russell if he thought there had been "carelessness or negligence" on the part of administrators who hadn't evacuated the veterans in time.

"I do," he answered. "I think they should have been moved on Sunday, and they had plenty of time on Monday morning with continuous warnings. Even midday Monday they could have taken them."

Russell said the officials—"those in charge of the camps"—were responsible for the deaths of the veterans.

Farmer and Kennamer still had work to do after they finished interviewing John Russell. They had to track down Ray Sheldon to ask him about the Weather Bureau advisory of 3:30 a.m. September 2.

The investigators went to the Florida ERA offices in Miami to ask where they could find Sheldon. A worker there said Sheldon told them he was leaving Miami because he didn't want to be questioned about the hurricane. He might be in West Palm Beach, someone offered.

In West Palm Beach, Kennamer and Farmer learned that a Mr. Gordon might know where Sheldon was. Farmer got Gordon on the phone. Gordon was suspicious. He didn't know where Sheldon was. Why did they want to talk to him?

Farmer told Gordon they needed to talk to Sheldon about the tragedy in the Keys. Gordon said to call him in 10 minutes.

The investigators waited exactly 10 minutes, and then Farmer dialed Gordon's number. Sheldon was at the Flagler Apartments on Trinity Place, near historic Holy Trinity Episcopal Church a block or so from Lake Worth and near the bridge that goes over to Palm Beach.

Sheldon was edgy and didn't want to talk to Kennamer and Farmer unless Abt was present. Sheldon said he had already chewed out one snoop who had tried to talk to him about the hurricane.

A few days earlier, Edward O'Ryan, a WPA writer, had been sent to talk to Sheldon for a report on the hurricane he was doing for Florida ERA director Conrad Van Hyning. O'Ryan knocked on Sheldon's door, but there was no answer. The writer started to leave, but he could hear someone moving around inside the apartment. He wrote an explanation of who he was and what he wanted on a piece of paper and slid it under the door. Minutes passed. Nothing happened. Finally an angry Ray Sheldon snatched open the door. He was furious, he said, because O'Ryan was making it appear as though he was trying to hide.

Kennamer tried to ease Sheldon's concerns. He didn't want Sheldon to make any statements without Abt; he just wanted him to clear up one small detail. Sheldon asked what it was. Kennamer asked Sheldon if he'd received the 3:30 a.m. Weather Bureau advisory of September 2. Not exactly, Sheldon answered. He'd had one of his clerks sleeping next to the office phone in case the Weather Bureau called, he said, and when he went in to the office around 8:30 a.m. the clerk reported there had been "no change" in the advisories.

That didn't fit the version given by clerk Robert Ayer Jr. Ayer told Kennamer that he had repeated the advisory exactly as it was read to him over the phone.

Sheldon told the VA investigators that there had been so much "passing the buck" and so many investigators poking into what happened on the Keys that he was going to be careful what he said. And another thing—he wasn't happy at all with the way Kennamer and Farmer had tracked him down like he was hiding out or something.

The investigators told Sheldon that Abt said he didn't know where he was, and the employees at the Florida ERA office had said the same thing.

Not true, Sheldon said. Lots of people knew his telephone number and home address, and lots of people—including Aubrey Williams, Conrad Van Hyning, and Abt himself—had told him he needed to get away for a while, get some rest. They all knew where he was staying.

Immediately after meeting with Sheldon, Kennamer sent a letter to Sam Jared. He reported what Sheldon had said about the 3:30 a.m. warning, and added that he thought many of the statements taken by Abt and Williams were "incomplete and unsatisfactory" and he'd need to question the respondents again.

Kennamer then left for Camp Foster, a U.S. Army base in Jacksonville, where he was going to interview veterans who'd survived the storm and been sent to a VA hospital there. He was going to conduct the interviews with the suddenly cooperative Abt.

At the moment, however, the veterans were in no mood to talk.

Many of the survivors who'd come out of the Keys after the hurricane were still in shock. Those who weren't in shock were seething with anger. They'd been put on a special train in Miami and arrived at Camp Foster on September 9. Soon after their arrival, an army captain told them they'd be enrolled immediately in the Civilian Conservation Corps and shipped out to CCC camps.

But the weary vets would have none of that, and they made their feelings clear about the matter. They weren't joining the CCC, and they weren't leaving Camp Foster anytime soon. The men were "in a very bad frame of mind and in open rebellion," camp administrators reported.

Two VA officials—J. G. Wright and Gladstone Pitt—went to meet the surly veterans in their barracks. Henry Redkey, a Florida ERA official, and Colonel Thomas Lowe went with the VA officials.

They walked into a hornet's nest. "The men were in a very ugly mood," Wright said.

The four men tried to explain their plans for helping the survivors, but angry veterans interrupted and shouted insults. They'd been promised reimbursement for the personal items they'd lost in the storm. Where was their money? They'd been promised new clothing to replace the storm-torn rags they were still wearing. Where was that?

No one had any intention of helping them, they angrily accused. The only reason they'd been sent to Camp Foster was to keep them from talking to investigators and newspaper reporters and contradicting the whitewash that had been applied to the Keys catastrophe. They absolutely would not agree to anything until Ben Davis—the former superintendent of Camp 3— arrived from Miami. They would trust him, and nobody else.

The VA delegation gave up and trudged back to their headquarters to talk things over. Henry Redkey, the Florida ERA official, said he'd talk to clothiers about providing some clothes and see if he could hire a dentist and an optometrist to replace false teeth and eyeglasses the men had lost in the hurricane.

On Tuesday, September 10, J. G. Wright walked around Camp Foster chatting with the vets. If nothing else, the outbursts the previous night had provided an outlet for much of the simmering anger and frustration. Many of the vets seemed willing to cooperate. A few said they were interested in joining the Civilian Conservation Corps—just as quickly as the promises of Mr. Redkey had been carried out.

Still, many men at Camp Foster would never accept the official verdict that no one was to blame for their awful experience. Oscar D. Griffin, a veteran from Union City in northwestern Tennessee, told Wright that old-timers on the Keys had warned camp administrators to get the men off the islands. Griffin said Ray Sheldon and Fred Ghent were responsible for the tragedy, and neither of them would be truthful about what had really happened.

Monto French of Chicago, who'd been at Camp 3, was heartbroken that his brother John had been killed in the storm. It wouldn't take any investigators to figure out why his brother had died, French told Wright. The reason, he said, was simple—"pure damned carelessness."

At the other end of Florida's long coast, another survivor tried to make some sense of his own experience in the storm.

James Duane Jr. and the Long Key survivors had walked south from Long Key after the hurricane, crossing railroad bridges until they reached Marathon. There they were picked up by a repair train and arrived in Key West on the evening of Thursday, September 5. Duane's family was astonished, and then overjoyed. They had assumed he was dead.

Duane told the *Key West Citizen* that he thought the wind had reached 175 to 200 mph at times, and the ocean had been terrifying. He told the *Citizen* he thought he'd be ready to go back to work after a few hot meals and a little rest, but he didn't care to experience another storm like the hurricane of September 2.

Duane took it easy for a week, then sat down at a typewriter at his residence at 703 Eaton Street and wrote a report about the hurricane to the U.S. Weather Bureau. He penned a more personal report to Ernest Carson at the Miami office of the Weather Bureau. Despite his harrowing experience, the conscientious Duane asked Carson to critique his report on the hurricane that had nearly taken his life.

"I am writing you to find out if you found anything wrong or anything I failed to do in making these few observations during this last storm," Duane wrote. He apologized for not phoning or telegraphing his 6 p.m. report to Miami on the day of the hurricane, but explained that the lines had been torn down.

Duane described the eeriness of the hurricane's eye as it passed over Long Key. "During [the] lull there was always a very light breeze—somewhat shifting," he wrote. "Sky clear, stars shining brightly, water was a terrible sight to see on the ocean side. Never will I forget the water raising—no, not a wave but looked just like the vacuum drew it right up, then let go. Raining very, very fast, then it began to pound."

Still, he remained a detached observer in the midst of this deadly chaos. "Very interesting, these storms, and have learned that this last kind are ones to avoid in the future." And after his rest and hot meals, Duane's interest in hurricanes was returning. He told Carson he wished some type of weather station could be established on Long Key. "I'd like to have the job down here, as I'm very, very interested."

Duane had one final question for Carson: "What would your figures be on the velocity of wind with pressure at 26.98 inches?"

While James Duane pondered his personal questions about the hurricane—such as how he'd lived through it—David Kennamer and his staff, who had set up headquarters at Miami's McAllister Hotel, were working 16-hour days to collect and analyze information about the actions of Florida ERA officials before and after the hurricane.

The investigators were digging into every possible source of information. Captain Harry Farmer dug up evidence contradicting the rumors that Sheldon had prevented the veterans from leaving the camps before the evacuation train arrived. When Farmer asked Paul Pugh, a veteran who had been at Camp 3, whether the vets had been stopped from leaving, Pugh said he'd "never heard of such a thing."

Pugh denied that he'd repeatedly insisted that Sheldon order the train long before Monday afternoon. Pugh said he'd talked with Sheldon about the storm and possible plans to move the men out several times between Sunday afternoon and Monday afternoon, but had never demanded that the camps administrator order the train immediately.

Nor did he doubt Sheldon's abilities as an administrator.

"I had confidence in the man," Pugh said. "The man had a responsible job and I felt like he was capable of handling it."

But much of what Ray Sheldon said bothered Kennamer, starting with his conversation with Weather Bureau meteorologist Gerald Kennedy early Sunday morning, September 1.

In testimony taken on September 7 by Dade County State's Attorney George Worley in Miami, Sheldon had said Kennedy suggested he return to the Keys because seas might be too rough for the ferry to run Monday. Kennedy had a different version of the conversation, however. He said he told Sheldon that conditions on the Keys were likely to become dangerous and he might want to get back to the work camps as quickly as possible.

There were other inconsistencies. Sheldon denied telling anyone that two trains were waiting in Miami to be dispatched at a moment's notice. But two people—Florida ERA administrator M. E. Gilfond and *Miami Daily News* reporter William Johns—testified under oath to Aubrey Williams and John Abt, respectively, that Sheldon had told them exactly that.

When Kennamer questioned Sheldon about these inconsistencies, Sheldon said someone must have misunderstood him.

Kennamer also noticed Sheldon's habit of ignoring advice. "Mr. Sheldon ... said he had been through hurricanes, and from the testimony it seems that no one could tell him anything about a hurricane," the investigator observed.

Sheldon was blaming everyone but himself for the tragedy and considered himself a victim of everyone else's mistakes. Sheldon told Kennamer that if the train had arrived when the FEC had promised, he could have moved every man in the camps to safety. The fact that the train crew braved the hurricane, were delayed by the crane cable on Windley Key, and worked heroically in deadly conditions to free the train didn't penetrate Sheldon's thinking.

"He cannot conceive or imagine why it would take one hour and 20 minutes to remove a guyline cable," Kennamer noted.

Kennamer understood Fred Ghent's difficult position but was puzzled by his failure to evacuate the veterans from the Keys before the hurricane struck.

"No one was more sympathetic with the veterans or more interested in their welfare and problems," Kennamer said of Ghent. "His failure to act is not satisfactorily explained by the evidence."

Kennamer also was puzzled about why Ghent, Sheldon, and Conrad Van Hyning—who all had abilities as administrators—did not do more to protect the veterans from the hurricane. The answer, he decided, was because there had been friction and pettiness among Ghent, Sheldon, Sam Cutler, and Van Hyning.

"Mr. Cutler had been at the camps months and had a very high regard for Mr. Ghent," Kennamer said. "Mr. Sheldon had only been at the camps a month. Cutler has more ability than Sheldon and didn't have a very high personal regard for him or his ability. Possibly Sheldon didn't become alarmed [about the hurricane] when he returned to the camps to prove that Cutler's judgment wasn't so good."

The tension that lingered after Van Hyning told Ghent in August that he was going to be dismissed soon may have prompted the two administrators to avoid talking to each other at a critical time during the three days before the hurricane arrived, Kennamer said.

Kennamer didn't at all like it that other investigators had allowed Sheldon to be present when they were questioning survivors. Sheldon had even been allowed to ask leading questions of several witnesses and draw answers from them that supported his actions.

During Ed Butters's testimony to John Abt in Miami on September 9, Sheldon blurted out, "I would like to have you tell these fellows if, according to your opinion, there was anything more under the circumstances that could have been done to safeguard these men?"

"No, I do not," the obliging Butters responded. "I have said that all the time. No, sir."

Sheldon asked similar questions to Sam Cutler and other witnesses during their testimony the same day: Was there anything more that could have been done to protect the men?

"Sam, there has been quite a little talk been heard, and various ones have said this and that, and a lot of it we haven't paid any attention to," Sheldon said to his assistant. "I have asked each and every one in here if they thought that, with the information we received at headquarters, whether we did everything that was humanly possible for a person to do. What is your opinion?"

Cutler, unexpectedly on the spot, didn't mention that the weather reports and other information he'd received Sunday had prompted him and others to urge Sheldon to move the veterans off the island late Sunday afternoon, September 1.

"As I say, I never went through a hurricane," Cutler responded. "I knew nothing about it, and I never did know anything about that, but as far as what I have read, you did everything that you could, with the reports that you received."

"Thank you," Sheldon said.

When Camp 3 superintendent Ben Davis was questioned, he also supported Sheldon's leadership.

"Why, I think we did everything we could possibly do with the information we had," Davis said.

If a witness was reluctant to grant his endorsement of Sheldon's actions or didn't remember an event exactly as Sheldon wanted, he kept prompting and pushing until he got a response he wanted.

During the testimony of Junius Wigginton, supply officer for the veterans work camps, Sheldon asked him if he'd overheard one of his telephone conversations Monday.

"Did you hear me call anyone and repeat a conversation into the phone that I was getting," Sheldon asked Wigginton.

"If I remember right, you called Mr. Ghent," Wigginton said. "Yes, you told him something that somebody had told you, if I remember right."

This wasn't what Sheldon wanted to hear. "No, this was a little earlier than that," he prompted. "You remember we were playing cards there, and it was about time to go to lunch, and I went to the telephone, and called a Miami number, and asked them regarding the storm, and I repeated their story back to them on the phone. Do you remember what that was I said?"

"If I remember right, they said that the storm was still . . . ," Wigginton tried. "I . . . if I remember the report right, the storm was central near Santa Clara province, Cuba, about 160 or 200 miles—now I won't say which it was—miles east of Havana, moving slowly, and in a westerly direction, and that their opinion was that there was no immediate danger to the Florida Keys. Now, as near as I can remember, I heard Mr. Sheldon repeat that message. Now, I don't know whether he was talking to Mr. Ghent, but at the time that he repeated it, I thought he was. I don't know."

Sheldon pushed ahead. "Well, could it have been the Weather Bureau I was talking to?"

"It could have," Wigginton said.

"Well, that's who it was," Sheldon said. "That's all."

Sheldon's presence—and his questioning—during the testimony of other witnesses was "unusual and undoubtedly subjected them to intimidation," Kennamer said.

John Abt's refusal to hand over the transcript of Ghent's testimony of September 7 to Aubrey Williams puzzled and annoyed Kennamer. And he sparred with the WPA lawyer over how the Weather Bureau advisory of 3:30 a.m. September 2 should have been interpreted. The advisory predicted gale-force winds and high tides on the Keys, and Kennamer thought this warning clearly indicated that the veterans camps were endangered by the hurricane.

Abt disputed that interpretation of the warning.

While Kennamer sorted through testimony and documents, workers continued sifting through the wreckage on the Keys. A group of local African American men were recruited to help with the rescue effort. They worked as a crew in the blazing heat, hefting piles of timber and lumber, searching for victims.

They also continued finding bodies.

On September 18 rescue workers found 11 corpses that had been washed up onto a mud flat 25 miles north of Tavernier. The workers speculated that the victims' bodies had been carried along by the Gulf Stream and gradually pushed back to the shore by the tides.

That same day, workers discovered Ben Davis's 1934 Dodge, in which George Pepper and Rosalind Grooms Palmer had left Camp 3 with the intention of picking up a group of veterans' wives at the Hotel Matecumbe. Pepper and Palmer never showed up.

The car was submerged in Florida Bay, between Upper Matecumbe Key and Lower Matecumbe Key, about 100 feet from the shore.

A diver went down to take a look. There were no bodies in the Dodge. The car's doors were locked, and its oilcloth roof had been pushed out from the inside.

The diver found one other clue about the car's occupants—a pair of women's white high-heeled pumps.

The following day, rescuers found the owner of those shoes. A passing boater discovered Rosalind Grooms Palmer's body on Coon Key, one of the dozens of tiny islands that dot Florida Bay.

There's no way of knowing exactly what happened to Pepper and Palmer. The young couple left Camp 3 sometime around 5 p.m. on Monday, September 2—at the same time that the winds increased so much it astonished even Ed Sheeran, who had been in six other hurricanes and had never seen winds escalate so dramatically in such a brief time. Others also described the terrifying escalation of the storm's winds between 5 p.m. and 6 p.m. One of the storm's fierce gusts shoved O. D. King's car off the road as he drove from the Hotel Matecumbe to his home.

It's possible a vicious blast from the hurricane swept Davis's Dodge and its young occupants off the causeway and into Florida Bay, although the railroad embankment on the same causeway could have provided them some protection from the wind. It's possible that Pepper's well-known fondness for fast driving could have played a role. The combination of terrible weather conditions and high speed could have caused him to lose control of the car on the narrow causeway, sending it plunging into the bay, and the high winds and giant waves made it impossible for Rosalind and him to swim back to safety.

Pepper and Palmer fought their way out of the sinking car. Both were young, and Palmer was a strong swimmer and probably was still alive but perhaps injured when she landed on Coon Key.

George Pepper's body was found a few weeks later near Cape Sable. He'd been carried more than 20 miles across Florida Bay by the hurricane.

Slowly, the survivors of the decimated Russell family learned what had happened to dozens of their kinsmen who'd disappeared during the horrible evening of September 2.

The body of Emma Russell, Bernard Russell's mother, was found near the beach of Florida Bay, not far from her family's hurricane shelter. She was identified by the plain gold wedding band she wore, engraved with the initials "ELR" and "Feb. 1910."

Reverend Robert Carlson lost his struggle to escape the rising waters of the storm surge. The surge carried Carlson's home several hundred feet, and his body was found not far from the nearby Hotel Matecumbe. His wife's body was found beneath a big pile of seaweed.

On September 10 the crew of a Coast Guard cutter from Biloxi, Mississippi, found the body of a young woman and an infant boy near the beach at Cape Sable. The dead woman was wearing a school ring engraved "MGS 1932."

Playing a hunch, Coast Guard lieutenant commander L. H. Baker wrote a letter describing the ring and the woman to Charles Albury, principal of Matecumbe Graded School in Islamorada. Albury told Baker that the body was that of Ruth Booth.

Booth was Bernard Russell's first cousin. She'd clung to her son as the hurricane blew her across Florida Bay. Miraculously, she was still alive when the storm hurled her onto the beach at Cape Sable. She crawled a few hundred feet from the pounding surf, lay down, and curled her body around her son. That's how the Coast Guardsmen found the mother and child. They buried them both where they lay.

Key West residents mourned the death of a teacher at the Harris Elementary School. Mary Ingraham was visiting her brother Robert Ingraham and his family on Upper Matecumbe Key when the hurricane struck. They were all killed in the storm. The flag at Harris Elementary flew at half-mast for a month in remembrance of Ingraham and Ruby Roberts, a member of the school's PTA who also died in the hurricane.

The body of Sarah Hodge—who'd gone with her sister Myrtle to spend Labor Day with their friend Rita Berteau—was found September 17 on Pelican Key in Florida Bay. Her sister's body was found a few weeks later on a small island more than 30 miles from Islamorada. Rescue workers identified her by the comb and powder puff she'd stuffed into her sweater pocket before leaving Homestead.

The bodies were so badly decomposed that rescue workers didn't even bother trying to bury them. The black smoke from cremation fires became a common sight on the Keys.

On French Reef, salvagers had gotten the *Dixie* ready to refloat. On September 19 two tugs from the Merritt-Chapman & Scott Salvage Company pulled the passenger liner off the reef. The ship was towed into harbor for some temporary repairs, and then towed to New York.

On September 30 the Merritt-Chapman & Scott tug *Relief*, with the battered *Dixie* in tow, chugged into New York Harbor. The ships glided past the Statue of Liberty, and the *Dixie* was docked at Pier 51 at the foot of West 12th Street in lower Manhattan.

As soon as his ship was secured at the dock, Captain Einar Sundstrom left the bridge to greet his wife, Marie, and his two daughters. A photo of a happy Einar Sundstrom being welcomed home by his family was published in newspapers across the country.

But the captain had little time for celebrating. On October 1, Sundstrom walked into the offices of the Department of Commerce's Bureau of Marine Inspection and Navigation at 45 Broadway to testify before a board of inquiry. The six-member panel wanted Sundstrom to explain how the *Dixie* had ended up on French Reef.

Sundstrom told the board he knew there was a storm in the Straits of Florida, but he'd sailed from New Orleans on September 1 because he thought he could outmaneuver the bad weather.

When the *Dixie* ran into the hurricane, the huge seas and winds made the ship almost unmanageable, and he'd reduced the ship's speed to five knots, Sundstrom said.

"The hurricane was doing so much damage to the windows and we were shipping so much water that I just couldn't give her more speed," Sundstrom said.

The captain told the board the Labor Day hurricane was the fiercest storm he'd encountered in his three decades as a sailor. "I have never experienced such weather in all my life," he said.

Dennis Folds, the *Dixie*'s second officer, told the board that the gigantic waves almost lifted the ship out of the water at times.

After hearing the officers' story, the board decided the grounding was due to "extreme and unusual weather conditions," and the ship's officers and crew had not been negligent in any way.

The marine salvagers had pulled the *Dixie* out of Florida waters just in time to avoid another hurricane. As the *Relief* was towing the *Dixie* up the East Coast, a tropical storm formed in the Caribbean Sea. The storm became a hurricane as it approached Cuba, and its winds eventually peaked at about 120 mph as it crossed into the Straits of Florida.

This time Florida ERA supervisors were taking no chances. About 600 workers were moved from the Keys to Homestead and Miami. Many Miami residents crowded into hotels to escape the blow. Many of them brought cats and dogs. But the hurricane turned to the northeast and slid past the Keys and the peninsula with its eye offshore. The storm refugees, with the memory of the horrible Labor Day hurricane still fresh, turned the evacuation into a party when they learned the storm had turned.

As the hurricane spun northeast across the open waters of the Atlantic, the American Legion assembled for its annual convention in St. Louis. The legionnaires quickly decided they'd conduct their own investigation of the veterans' deaths in the Keys. Quimby Melton, editor of the *Griffin Daily News* in Griffin, Georgia, was appointed chairman of the three-member investigation committee. The Legion also appointed Vice Commander W. E. Whitlock of High Springs, Florida, and Catesby A. R. Jones of Selma, Alabama, to the panel.

Melton said his committee would first go to Key West to interview witnesses, then to Miami for more interviews. This would be at least the third investigation into the tragedy in the Keys.

Melton would have to board a steamship in Tampa to get to Key West. The hurricane had destroyed about 40 miles of track between Tavernier and Marathon. The Florida East Coast Railway was still operating under bankruptcy, and FEC officials hadn't announced when—or if—they'd repair the tracks. But rumors were rampant that the FEC was going to abandon its famed Key West Extension. Henry Flagler never would have let that happen, the old Conchs muttered, but bureaucrats were running the FEC now, and they would be too concerned with the cost to spend the money to repair the railroad.

On the morning of Saturday, October 12, the passenger ship carrying the American Legion's investigating committee sailed into Key West's harbor. Melton, Whitlock, and Jones went straight to the auditorium of Key West High School, where Melton called his investigating committee to order.

"We have come into Florida with perfectly open minds," he told participants. "We are not here to whitewash anybody. If there is blame to be fixed, we want to find on whose shoulders it properly rests."

Arthur Brown of Hastings-on-Hudson, New York, was the first to testify. Brown had been the timekeeper at Camp 3, where the motor pool for the work camps was located.

"There was sufficient time to get all veterans out from Camp 3, and the trucks could have picked up men at Camp 5, seven miles to the north, and prevented great loss of life there," Brown said.

The committee also heard testimony in public from U.S. Weather Bureau meteorologist Gerald Kennedy of Key West, Major William Albury of the National Guard, and Florida ERA supervisors M. E. Gilfond, and Conrad Van Hyning.

The committee then flew to Miami Sunday morning and interviewed engineer Lawrence Bow and construction supervisor Ed Sheeran in sessions that were closed to the public. From there the investigators went to Tallahassee to meet with Governor David Sholtz.

Sholtz gave the committee copies of the hurricane report by State's Attorney George Worley and said that he too wanted to know whether carelessness had caused the veterans to be killed. But the governor told the Legion board that the storm had been unusual in many ways.

"You must take into consideration in this matter that a modern steamer equipped with the best in radio facilities was in the path of this storm and was tossed upon a reef," Sholtz said. "You must also consider that a modern freighter was picked up by a wave and driven aground. Also, you must consider that there was a tidal wave along with the storm, and that civilian residents of the Keys as well as the veterans were the victims."

The American Legion committee disbanded after its visit to Tallahassee, and Melton went home to Georgia to write his report. He'd tried to set up an interview with or at least get a statement from Ray Sheldon but hadn't been able to contact him.

As Melton studied the testimony and organized his thoughts to write his report, Florida East Coast Railway workers arrived in Islamorada to start salvage work on the ill-fated evacuation train. They'd built temporary tracks to Upper Matecumbe Key and planned to use a crane to set the derailed passenger cars back on the tracks. Then they'd use another locomotive to pull number 447 and the 11 cars back to the Miami yards. It would be the last train ever to depart from Islamorada.

By late October David Kennamer and his staff were wrapping up the investigation into the deaths of the veterans. Kennamer was writing a massive, detailed report to VA director General Frank Hines that incorporated testimony from more than 400 people and information from hundreds of pages of supporting documents. It was a thorough and painstaking examination of the tragedy in the Florida Keys.

John Abt also was finishing up his report on the tragedy.

On October 30, Kennamer's report landed on Hines's desk. Six days later, on November 5, Abt sent a copy of his report to Kennamer.

In Kennamer's mind there was no doubt about why the veterans had died during the Labor Day hurricane. Ray Sheldon, Fred Ghent, and, to a lesser degree, Conrad Van Hyning had not done what they should have to protect the men who were their responsibility.

The men in charge of the Keys work camps knew hurricanes posed a threat to the veterans' safety and knew they had to devise a practical, effective way to protect them from this threat. Despite Ghent's and Sheldon's claims to the contrary, they never followed through with their plans for one of the most logical methods for getting the men out of harm's way—loading them on a train and hauling them out of the islands.

Kennamer noted that Jacksonville attorney Scott Loflin had sent a letter dated June 6, 1935, to Ghent explaining the FEC's limitations in providing an evacuation train.

"No definite agreement had been made with the railroad to furnish a train and the railroad had not been advised as to who would have authority to order a train in the event of an emergency," Kennamer wrote in his report. "Mr. Loflin's unanswered letter to Mr. Ghent appears to be about the last positive action taken relative to plans to evacuate the veterans in the event of a hurricane."

Ghent, Sheldon, and Van Hyning should have made sure that definite arrangements had been made weeks in advance to have a train ready if it was needed, Kennamer said.

Kennamer conceded that the advisories from the Weather Bureau "were not entirely accurate," but added that they clearly told "of danger lurking in the Atlantic east of the camps and was sufficient to alarm Mr. Cutler and others at the veterans camps." He also decided the advisories "were not as inaccurate as some have alleged."

"They told of danger and were sufficient to alarm several people employed at the camps and were sufficient to have caused any prudent man to have been ready to get the men out when the danger became imminent," Kennamer wrote. "With these facts well established, the Weather Bureau must be acquitted of any culpability."

Kennamer decided that Sheldon was less than convincing in much of his testimony about receiving warnings of the danger the hurricane posed to the Keys. In several interviews Sheldon said that he hadn't been told the situation was dangerous, but this was not true.

Sheldon also had fudged the truth in another way. "His statement that he left Mr. Cutler in charge of the camps and told him to call him if anything came up before leaving for Key West cannot be accepted as entirely true," Kennamer wrote. "He left without saying anything to Mr. Cutler and only told his stenographer where he could be found."

Sheldon had committed a serious error by delaying the evacuation, Kennamer said. "The poor judgment used by Mr. Sheldon was his failure to be ready to move when it became apparent this would be necessary," Kennamer wrote. "The evidence is . . . conclusive that no time should have been lost getting ready to move after the 10 a.m. advisory Sunday, September 1, and that part of the readiness to move should have included a definite agreement with the railroad to furnish a train."

Kennamer included a long list of actions Sheldon should have taken that would have prevented the tragedy. Among other things, he faulted the camps administrator for allowing beer sales to resume in the canteens; not contacting Ghent after he learned of the weather advisory of 3:30 a.m. September 2 predicting gales and high tides on the Keys; not assuming authority to order the train himself after the advisory of 10 a.m. September 2; and not visiting the camps the afternoon of September 2 to make sure everything was ready to move out.

Kennamer blamed Fred Ghent for not completing arrangements to have an evacuation train ready weeks before the worst part of the hurricane season arrived. Ghent also should have stayed in close contact with the camps during the Labor Day weekend after he'd learned that a hurricane had formed, and not have disappeared for two hours on Monday, September 2, when Sheldon was trying to reach him.

Conrad Van Hyning should have made certain that Ghent had arranged for an evacuation train with the FEC and kept in touch with Ghent after he knew a hurricane had formed near the Keys.

Kennamer praised the crew that took the evacuation train into the teeth of the hurricane on the night of September 2. He concluded that the FEC was not in any way responsible for the deaths.

He acknowledged that other investigations had concluded that no one was to blame for the tragedy. But he thought his investigation was far more thorough than the others because he'd assembled much more information.

Kennamer also acknowledged that "reasonable men may honestly differ about this matter regardless of the facts." But several inarguable facts led to his conclusion that Florida ERA officials had seriously blundered—Ghent and Sheldon didn't order a train after the crucial 3:30 a.m. advisory; Ghent and Sheldon didn't communicate with each other from 4:50 p.m. Sunday until 1:37 p.m. Monday; Ghent disappeared for almost two hours when he was needed; and Ghent and Van Hyning did not communicate with each other at all. Because of these omissions, Kennamer said he could not conclude "that they did all the things they should have done or all the things demanded of them by nature of the representative positions."

The conclusion, in David Kennamer's mind, was clear and simple—more than 250 veterans were dead because Ray Sheldon, Fred Ghent, and Conrad Van Hyning hadn't done their jobs. But in the minds of some influential insiders in Washington, DC, the well-reasoned and well-supported conclusions that Kennamer drew from his painstaking investigation would be undermined by his long Republican pedigree.

CHAPTER TEN

For the Record

On the morning of April 2, 1936, Ray Sheldon was talking about hurricanes with some very important people in Washington.

Sheldon, who had left the Keys and not worked since the September hurricane, sat before the House Committee on World War Veterans' Legislation, which was chaired by Representative John Rankin, a Democrat from Mississippi and a loyal ally of President Franklin Roosevelt. The committee was investigating the deaths of the veterans in the Florida Keys as part of its review of a bill that would compensate the families of the men who had been killed. The members of Rankin's committee—14 Democrats, six Republicans, and one member of the Progressive Party—were questioning Sheldon about his experience in the storm.

As far as Sheldon was concerned, no one in the Keys—or the state of Florida, for that matter—knew more about hurricanes than he did. He told the committee that he had lived in Florida since 1923 and that he had been through about half a dozen hurricanes before the Labor Day storm. He had been driving from his home in West Palm Beach to Miami when the infamous hurricane of September 17, 1926, nearly leveled Miami Beach and sent seawater surging through downtown Miami. Two years later he stayed in his home when the terrible hurricane of September 18, 1928, smashed ashore at West Palm Beach and roared inland to kill around 3,000 people around Lake Okeechobee. So, as far as Sheldon was concerned, he was a seasoned and knowledgeable observer of hurricanes whose judgment about the storms was as sound and reliable as anyone else's.

John Rankin had no intention of letting anyone seriously challenge the image that Sheldon was trying so hard to project to the committee. In fact, Rankin intended to set up as many opportunities as he could to allow Sheldon to polish that image.

People had been clamoring for months for a congressional investigation to answer once and for all the questions surrounding the deaths of the veterans in the hurricane of September 2, 1935. Republicans wanted the hearings because they hoped that powerful political ammunition might be uncovered that could be used against President Roosevelt in the election that was only a few months away. The American Legion, Veterans of Foreign Wars, and other veterans groups, which had been causing trouble for FDR for years, had been insisting that Congress conduct the hearings since the day after the hurricane tore through the flimsy work camps on the Keys and killed more than 250 of their buddies.

So John Rankin was going to give the Republicans and the veterans their investigation. On January 3, 1936—the first day of the new session of Congress—Rankin introduced a bill in the House of Representatives to compensate the victims' families. A few days later, A. D. Hiller, an assistant director of the Veterans Administration, estimated that it would cost the government about $30,000 per year—about $530,000 in twenty-first-century dollars—to compensate the victims' families. That would amount to about $217 per month—about $3,800 in twenty-first-century dollars—for each family. The total figure would, of course, go higher as more deaths were certified and more dependents became eligible, Hiller said.

Rankin knew that the bill would be referred to his committee for review and a recommendation on whether to pass it, and that would give him a reason to hold the hearings. He would make a big show of getting to the bottom of the questions surrounding the veterans' deaths, and he would parade a couple dozen witnesses before his committee and let them tell their stories. But as chairman of the committee, he would decide who testified. And he would make sure that no troublesome witnesses were called. Rankin would also make sure that the testimony that went into the permanent record of these hearings led to one conclusion: that no one, least of all the administrators hired by the Roosevelt Administration to supervise the work camps in the Keys, had been at fault for the deaths of those veterans.

As a lawyer, Rankin knew how to selectively present facts to steer a jury to the conclusion he desired. In an ideal situation a lawyer would allow only those facts supporting his argument to be submitted as evidence to a jury, and he would block anything that might diminish or detract from his argument. It didn't matter if the information he blocked was true. If it hurt his argument, he kept it out.

As chairman of the committee holding these hearings, Rankin had set up that ideal situation. He was not presenting a case to a jury, but he was presenting it to the American public and to posterity. His committee would collect facts about the disaster that would go into a permanent record of findings. Rankin would decide what facts were relevant and went into that permanent record, and what facts were excluded. Period. No one could challenge his decisions or appeal to a higher authority.

Rankin needed the record to show that Ray Sheldon was knowledgeable about hurricanes and would not have done anything foolish that would have caused the deaths of the veterans. So if Sheldon wanted to present himself as knowing a great deal about hurricanes, Rankin would do everything he could to help.

That included fending off questions from Representative Edith Nourse Rogers of Massachusetts, who was one of the Republicans on the House Committee on World War Veterans' Legislation. Rogers had been sniping at Rankin and Roosevelt Administration officials for weeks, insisting from the floor of the House of Representatives that the administration was trying to cover up the blundering that had killed the veterans and complaining that General Frank Hines, director of the Veterans Administration, was aiding in this cover-up by withholding information she was entitled to as a member of Congress.

After listening to Sheldon explain to the committee how to interpret a falling barometer, Rogers asked the camps administrator if he could have loaded the veterans aboard construction trucks and taken them out of the Keys before the hurricane hit. Yes, he answered, they could have done that. Wouldn't that have been quicker than waiting for a train to arrive? she pressed. But Sheldon would not bite.

"We had no reason to have the train," he replied. "We had no storm, from outward appearances, that was going to hit the Keys, at that time."

"But they do—storms sometimes change their courses?" Rogers asked, trying another approach.

"That is what the records show," Sheldon said.

"They often do that?" Rogers asked.

"Yes," Sheldon answered.

"And in your experience, they have changed their course often?"

"Of storms, there is no telling where they will go," Sheldon said.

"So," Rogers continued, closing in on her point, "you have to be ready to move at once?"

Rogers had backed Sheldon into a corner. Rankin jumped in before Sheldon could answer. Since the start of the hearings eight days earlier, Rankin and fellow Democrat Wright Patman, a committee member from Texas, had been hammering away at the fact that the work camp administrators had not been the only people in the Keys who hadn't evacuated the islands because of the hurricane. The Conchs—who undoubtedly knew more than anyone else about the threat hurricanes posed to the Keys—hadn't left either. As far as Rankin and Patman were concerned, that meant no one should blame Ray Sheldon or anybody else for not acting sooner to evacuate the veterans.

"Mr. Sheldon, right there," Rankin said, "what was the attitude of the people who lived on the Keys? Were they excited over the storm?"

"Some of them closed and got the boards together to nail up their houses, and some of them did not nail them, but that was done, because if there was a storm, it was a whole lot easier to nail them up during pleasant weather than to wait until the last minute and get out in the rain and struggle with the boards," he replied.

Rankin told Sheldon to continue, but instead of answering Rogers's barbed question, Sheldon started talking again about his experiences with other hurricanes in Florida.

Patman asked Sheldon whether the Russell family left the Keys because of the hurricane. Sheldon answered that they hadn't, and incorrectly told Patman that 73 of the 76 members of the Russell family had died in the hurricane.

"Did they have automobiles?" Patman asked.

"They all had cars," Sheldon said.

"They evidently had the same idea that you had about the storm?"

"Yes, sir."

Sheldon's preposterous inference would go unchallenged. In fact, John Russell hadn't had anything resembling the same idea about the hurricane as Sheldon. During his interview with David Kennamer on September 14, 1935, Russell went into great detail about his conviction that the veterans in the work camps were in great danger and should have been evacuated from the Keys long before the hurricane struck.

Russell wasn't asked to testify at the hearings, however, so the committee members never heard his thoughts about who was responsible for the tragedy of September 2, 1935. And, more important to Rankin and Patman, Sheldon's absurd assertion that John Russell had shared his opinion that the Keys weren't in danger and the veterans didn't need to be evacuated would remain untouched in the record.

Rankin would repeatedly use the fact that John Russell hadn't taken his family out of the Keys as an argument that there was no reason for Sheldon, Ghent, and Van Hyning to have been unduly alarmed. As the hearings progressed, he and Patman developed a standard line of questioning that they used to lead witnesses to the conclusions they sought. One of those witnesses Rankin walked through his routine was Joseph Fecteau, the veteran from Massachusetts who'd been the timekeeper at Camp 5. Rogers had insisted that Rankin call Fecteau, assuming that his statement would raise legitimate doubts about the judgment of camp administrators.

"Now, you were down there," Rankin said to Fecteau, "and I am just trying to put myself in your place, because I have no interest whatsoever in this hurricane, except as a member of Congress and an American citizen and an ex-serviceman, and my usual interest in humanity. Those people were down there—you knew Mr. Russell, did you not?"

"Yes, sir," Fecteau answered.

Rankin began the familiar call-and-response questioning that he'd used with other witnesses, establishing that Fecteau knew John Russell, that he knew the Russells had lived on Upper Matecumbe Key for many years, and that Russell hadn't moved his family off the island before the hurricane. He also established that the Methodist minister, the Reverend Robert E. Carlson, hadn't left before the storm, and that he and his wife had been killed.

Rankin went into a windy summary leading up to his clincher.

"I want to put myself in the condition of those people down there," he said. "They had been there all their lives. I have long since learned that when you are in Rome, do as Romans do as nearly as is possible. If I go into a strange territory and a cloud comes up, I look around to see how the neighbors feel about it, because I would feel uneasy running into a storm and have everybody laugh at me. But these people lived there, and they had, according to the testimony here, the usual reports on this storm, and the indications were that if it struck Florida at all it would strike Key West. They had no idea, and you say you had no idea, nobody else had an idea, that there was going to be a flood, because any man with any intelligence at all, whether he was a native or a veteran, would have gotten out of there the day before, every single human being who lived on the Keys, if they had an idea that a flood was coming, they would have gotten out, would they not?"

"I guess they would," Fecteau said. "I know that I would."

Rankin had once again protected the record from Rogers.

It would have been very difficult to find two people in the 1936 House of Representatives more dramatically different from each other than Edith Nourse Rogers and John Elliott Rankin. Rogers, a Republican representing Massachusetts's Fifth District, was the daughter of a wealthy textile mill manager from Lowell. She had been educated by a private tutor until she was 14, attended a private girls' school in Lowell, and completed her education in France at a private finishing school for young women.

She returned to Lowell and married John Jacob Rogers, a Harvard-educated lawyer, in 1907 and moved with him to Washington, DC, when he was elected as a Republican to the House of Representatives in 1912.

Her husband enlisted when the United States entered World War I, and Edith joined the American Red Cross. She toured the battlefields in France, saw the war's awful death and destruction, and developed a deep and enduring concern for the welfare of veterans.

When John Jacob Rogers died suddenly in 1925, she entered a special election to fill her husband's House seat and won by an overwhelming margin. After the election she said she hoped everyone would "forget that I'm a woman as soon as possible." But her finishing-school polish, tasteful wardrobe, aristocratic bearing, and the orchid or gardenia that was often pinned to her shoulder set her apart from her colleagues and guaranteed that her gender would not be overlooked.

Still, she established a reputation for two traits that weren't often associated with women in 1936—toughness and aggressiveness. She wouldn't back down from a fight, and she pursued her political goals with a gentle but unrelenting determination.

She was exactly the kind of woman likely to annoy Rankin—an articulate, sophisticated, uppity Yankee female from Massachusetts, who was a Republican to boot.

Rankin, a Democrat, represented Mississippi's First District. He'd grown up in rural Itawamba County in northeastern Mississippi.

Rankin graduated from the University of Mississippi's law school in 1910 and moved to nearby Tupelo in neighboring Lee County, where he was the county's prosecuting attorney. He served in the U.S. Army during World War I and was elected to his first term in the House of Representatives in 1920, polling 10,400 votes to a mere 480 for his opponent.

Rankin was bold, outspoken, and absolutely certain of the correctness of his convictions. He was well known for his long, uninterrupted, impromptu speeches on the floor of the House. During one of his especially lengthy monologues, the House clerks worked furiously to keep up with the ceaseless flow of Rankin's oration. One clerk turned to another clerk and asked him if he'd managed to copy everything the loquacious Mississippian had said.

"Yes," the clerk replied, "I got it copied down during a burst of silence by Mr. Rankin."

Rankin also had a dramatically different background from Franklin Delano Roosevelt, who'd grown up with the comforts and advantages of wealth in a part of the country where the opportunity to prosper was taken for granted. Rankin was a shrewd politician who recognized that Roosevelt could be a useful ally for accomplishing his own objectives, and so he established a political relationship with FDR even before the new president had taken the oath of office. Soon after the election of November 1932, which swept Roosevelt into the White House, Rankin wrote to the president-elect seeking help in his bid to become Speaker of the House of Representatives.

Roosevelt didn't have to do much to fulfill Rankin's request. Rankin asked FDR to stay neutral in the contest for Speaker rather than endorse anyone for the post. Roosevelt responded with a letter saying he'd comply, but Rankin's attempt at taking control of the House of Representatives failed anyway. Still, as chairman of the House Committee on World War Veterans' Legislation, the representative from Mississippi was a powerful figure in Congress.

The congressional district Rankin represented lay in the heart of an impoverished region that hadn't changed much since the nineteenth century. Many housewives still cooked meals on wood-burning stoves and lit kerosene lanterns at dusk. Industries that could have brought prosperity to the region ignored it because there was not enough cheap electricity to power their factories.

The region's greatest potential for energy—its rivers—went untapped. That would change, however, thanks to the efforts of an unlikely benefactor—a Republican senator from the Midwest.

Senator George Norris of Nebraska was an ardent supporter of making cheap electricity available for farming and industrial development, and his passion for this effort went well beyond his party loyalty. He campaigned for Roosevelt in 1932 because he thought FDR would do more to help bring this about than President Hoover.

FDR took up Norris's cause almost immediately after he was sworn in as president, and the first chance to advance it was the creation of the Tennessee

Valley Authority (TVA), a plan that would bring new opportunity to seven southern states.

"By controlling every river and creek and rivulet in this vast watershed, and by planning for a highly civilized use of the land by the population of the whole area, we believed that we could make a lasting contribution to American life," Roosevelt wrote in his 1934 book, *On Our Way*.

The TVA also would serve a political function identical to the economic revitalization of Key West—it would become another example of how the programs of the New Deal would pull the nation out of the Depression. If the TVA worked in the South, its principles could be applied nationwide.

There was a political hook as well to the plans for the TVA. The prospect of bringing financial investments and jobs to the South would inevitably pull southern Democrats into the New Deal's camp, and Roosevelt—no slouch as a politician himself—knew he had to have the Southerners aboard if he had any hope of pushing his ambitious programs through Congress. If some of his Deep South supporters such as Rankin had antebellum attitudes about race relations, that was regrettable, but it was a trade-off FDR felt he had to make.

As a representative from one of the poor rural states that would benefit greatly from the TVA, John Rankin was very interested in the project. He pushed the legislation establishing the authority through the House of Representatives, and in May 1933 President Roosevelt signed the bill establishing the Tennessee Valley Authority.

Eighteen months later—after a resounding Democratic victory in the 1934 off-year congressional elections—FDR made a campaign-style swing through five states that would be served by the TVA. The president visited sites where dams being built with federal money would provide cheap electricity that would, in effect, bring the area into the twentieth century. The *Washington Post* reporter accompanying FDR described the TVA as a "staggering blow to private interests," but thousands of people in Kentucky, Tennessee, Mississippi, Alabama, and Georgia felt otherwise, turning out to hear Roosevelt praise the TVA and promise them that it would improve their lives.

More than 40,000 people gathered in Harrodsburg, Kentucky, to hear the president speak on November 15, 1934. It was an impressive crowd, especially considering that only about 14,500 people lived in the surrounding county.

Roosevelt's rising political rival, Louisiana senator Huey Long, managed to divert some attention from FDR's visit to Mississippi the following day when he accompanied the Louisiana State University football team to Jackson for the game against the University of Mississippi. Long made himself the center of attention from the moment he and his entourage—which included the LSU marching band and a squad of eight Louisiana highway patrolmen mounted on motorcycles—got off the train in downtown Jackson. News reports estimated that 10,000 people greeted Long when he marched down Capitol Street at the head of the band, flanked by his imposing mounted bodyguard.

Long and the band paused at the governor's mansion for a brief concert, then continued down Capitol Street to the football stadium and onto the playing field. Long was delighted with the band's—and his own—performance.

But while Long's crowd was impressive, President Roosevelt's was overwhelming. At Corinth, Mississippi, about 250 miles north of Jackson, FDR was greeted by around 80,000—almost four times more people than lived in the county. John Rankin was at Roosevelt's side, introducing the president during some of his stops. In Tupelo, the first city to announce that it would buy electricity from the TVA, the president looked out at a crowd of more than 25,000 and told them he was "glad to come into the district of my friend, John Rankin."

Roosevelt noted that during his swing through the South, people welcomed him "literally by the acres." And the president undoubtedly understood that many of them had turned out thanks to John Rankin.

When the 74th Congress convened for its second session in January 1936, the Tennessee Valley Authority had become an accomplishment that the New Deal coalition could point to with pride as President Roosevelt prepared to begin his campaign for a second term. Rankin—who'd also gone to bat for FDR's tax plan by making a speech supporting it over national radio—had been named to Roosevelt's reelection campaign committee.

Although Roosevelt still had a powerful influence in the Democrat-controlled Congress, he undoubtedly knew he'd have a hard time preventing the early payment of the World War veterans' bonus. On January 9 the House of Representatives passed a bill approving early payment, and the Senate followed the next day. Roosevelt vetoed the bill, but both chambers of Congress easily overrode his veto, and the veterans had their hard-fought bonus.

But there was another New Deal project that many Roosevelt supporters feared contained the potential for disaster at the polls in November. Although the effort to revive Key West's economy with tourism seemed to be showing results, questions were still being raised about why government officials in Florida—who were part of the vast new bureaucracy created by the New Deal—hadn't moved quickly enough to get those veterans building a highway in the Keys out of the way before that hurricane struck in September 1935.

Adding to the Democrats' anxiety was a worrisome political poll conducted by *The Literary Digest* magazine in late January 1936. The magazine had mailed a poll to its 10 million subscribers seeking their opinions of President Roosevelt and his New Deal policies. When the results were published on January 25, 1936 there was ominous news for FDR—more than 62 percent of those who responded said they didn't like the New Deal. And there was more bad news. The magazine poll predicted that Kansas governor Alf Landon—considered the Republicans' most likely candidate—would win 57 percent of the popular vote and receive 370 electoral votes in the November election.

The Literary Digest had been conducting its polling in every presidential election since 1916, and it had never been wrong.

On the same day that Rankin introduced the bill to compensate the dependents of the veterans who'd been killed in the hurricane, the House approved a resolution offered by Representative J. Hardin Peterson, a Democrat from Florida, calling for an investigation of the tragedy. With *The Literary Digest* poll results casting a dark shadow over FDR's reelection hopes, Rankin's investigation of the veterans' deaths in the hurricane took on a new political urgency for the Democrats.

The following day, Representative Edith Nourse Rogers sent a letter to General Frank Hines, asking the director of the Veterans Administration for information about the "Florida Keys tragedy." It was the first step of her effort to bring to light more information about the hurricane of September 2, 1935. And although her well-established concern for the welfare of veterans undoubtedly was a motive for her interest in the catastrophe, there were political ramifications to her request as well.

Republicans were desperate to avoid a repeat of the 1934 midterm elections, when voters had nearly thrown them out of Washington by handing almost 70 percent of the seats in Congress to Democrats. It was the worst thrashing the Republicans had suffered since the party was formed in the mid-nineteenth century, and the GOP was searching for an issue—any issue—that it could hold up as an example of New Deal inefficiency or bumbling to halt the Democrats' political rout.

A hurricane that had killed more than 250 veterans because their New Deal–appointed bosses hadn't troubled themselves to get the men out of harm's way could be just the ticket. The nation was incensed when two veterans were killed during their 1932 march on Washington, and voters had taken it out a few months later on a Republican president. How would they react to the deaths of a couple hundred veterans under a Democratic chief executive?

It was logical that Rogers should play a pivotal role in any Republican effort to stop the surge of New Deal reform. She was the senior Republican member of the House Committee on World War Veterans' Legislation. But more important, her seat was safely in the hands of the GOP.

In the five elections in which she'd defended her seat, her Democratic opponents had never posed a serious challenge. Her percentage did slip from 66 percent of the vote in 1930 to 59 percent in 1932, but in 1934—when Republicans were being buried by the New Deal landslide—she increased her take of the balloting to 62 percent. If she could add to her vote total during the most disastrous election in the history of the Republican Party, there was little reason to worry about repercussions if she took on President Roosevelt—especially in the aftermath of *The Literary Digest* poll forecasting disaster for the Democrats in the upcoming 1936 election.

But if Rogers's seat in the House wasn't likely to be threatened, Rankin's was carved of stone. Rankin won his first term in the House in 1920 with a staggering 96 percent of the votes cast in the election. And he upped that percentage when he ran for reelection in 1922, receiving 99.7 percent of the vote.

Rankin ran unopposed from 1924 through 1930. Two opponents dared to challenge him in the 1932 election, and he steamrolled them with 97 percent of the vote. He ran unopposed again in 1934.

In late February Rogers received a response to her request for information about the hurricane that she'd sent to General Hines almost two months earlier. He refused to provide what she'd requested and suggested she ask Representative Rankin for the information she wanted.

Rogers was infuriated and immediately fired back a letter to Hines on February 24 telling him she was "astounded" by his response.

"Other departments always take the position that Members of Congress are entitled to the fullest and most complete information about any matter pertaining to the work of the departments," Rogers told Hines. "Yours is the only department in Washington that has not cooperated with me."

That same day on the floor of the House of Representatives, Rogers took an indirect jab at the administrators in charge of the veterans work camps when Representative Mark Wilcox, a Democrat from Florida, told the assembly that he wanted to provide more money to the U.S. Weather Bureau for tracking hurricanes. He noted that the tragedy in the veterans work camps had been caused in part by the fact that the U.S. Weather Bureau's tracking of the hurricane had been hindered by inadequate equipment.

But Rogers said there were more reasons why veterans had died.

"Does not the gentleman think that someone was very remiss in not removing the veterans earlier?" Rogers asked Wilcox. "I have the report released in September of the WPA," she said, referring to Aubrey Williams's report, "and it seems to me clear, after reading this report, that there was some mismanagement resulting in great tragedy."

Wilcox refused to be lured into a debate. "There is quite a conflict of opinion as to who, if anyone, was to blame," he said.

On February 25, VA director Hines sent another letter to Rogers about her request for information. He told the representative that the VA was preparing a report for Rankin and would send it to him "within the next few days."

"I am sure it will be made available to members of the Committee," Hines said.

Hines also hinted that Rogers could ask WPA director Harry Hopkins—who'd received copies of Kennamer's documents and report—to give her the information she sought.

"What that organization releases is, of course, a matter entirely in their hands," Hines wrote. "Nevertheless, I do not feel that with propriety I can release the report of the Veterans Administration in this regard until it has served its original purpose and is available for release."

Rogers was still angry a day later when Wilcox presented the appropriations amendment he'd discussed two days earlier. She saw an opportunity to get in a few more jabs at the Roosevelt Administration and House Democrats.

Rogers said she supported the increased funding for hurricane warning improvements, but instead of explaining why she thought the appropriation should be approved, she attacked the Roosevelt Administration's motives for sending the veterans to the Keys, hinting that the men had been sent there to prevent them from becoming a problem for the president. She charged Democrats with wrapping a veil of secrecy around the catastrophe.

"Why they were sent there no one seems to know," she said. "Were they sent in order that they might be as far away from Washington as possible?"

Rogers said Hines had refused to provide information she had requested. "Why is this veil of secrecy thrown around the veterans' tragedy on the Florida Keys?" she asked. "Why is it that the information from the Veterans Administration is available only through the chairman of the World War Veterans' Committee? Things have come to a pretty pass if members of Congress are obliged to seek information only through committee. It does not seem open and aboveboard to me."

Six weeks had passed since the House had approved Representative Peterson's motion to investigate the tragedy, and nothing had been done, Rogers said. It was time to end the secrecy surrounding the veterans' deaths.

Rogers's cutting criticism undoubtedly left Rankin seething. But in late March he was ready to give the Republicans and other critics of the Roosevelt Administration what they wanted.

On March 25, 1936, Rankin got permission from the House of Representatives to subpoena witnesses and put them under oath during hearings he planned to conduct on the bill to compensate the families of hurricane victims. Later that day Rankin talked to a reporter for the *New York Times* about his plans for his committee's hearings. "There has been much criticism of the administration policy in this matter, and I intend to build up a record on just what happened," he said.

On the surface, Rankin's promise to "build up a record" of the events surrounding the veterans' deaths seemed to be a promise to use the power of Congress to gather as much information as possible about what had happened in the Keys, and from that determine whether anyone was to blame for the tragedy. But Rankin had more important priorities than leading his committee through an open and unfettered inquiry into the sad events of September 2, 1935. That was the last thing he wanted.

Rankin had every reason to believe that the mutually beneficial relationship he'd established with the president would bear more political fruit during a second Roosevelt Administration, and as a member of the president's reelection campaign committee, Rankin had a responsibility to make sure FDR won that second term. And that meant stamping out any brushfire scandals before the Republicans could stoke them into an inferno that might incinerate Roosevelt's chances of reelection.

Rankin had had more than a month to study the information provided to him by the VA—plenty of time to decide what information could support the "no fault" finding and who could provide it, and what information could undermine the finding and who to avoid bringing before the committee. David Kennamer's VA report thus became a set of guidelines for Rankin to help him decide in advance what information he would allow into the record and what information to keep out.

At 10 a.m. on Thursday, March 26, 1936, Rankin gaveled his committee to order. Besides Rankin the panel's Democrats were Charles Buckley of New York, William Carpenter of Kansas, William Connery Jr. of Massachusetts, Joe Eagle of Texas, Joseph Gray of Pennsylvania, Glenn Griswold of Indiana, John Hoeppel of California, John Houston of Kansas, Joshua Lee of Oklahoma, Herron Pearson of Tennessee, Wright Patman of Texas, Jared Sanders Jr. of Louisiana, and Joe Starnes of Alabama.

In addition to Edith Nourse Rogers, the Republicans on the committee were Albert Joseph Engel of Michigan, Charles Halleck of Indiana, Charles Plumley of Vermont, Chauncey Reed of Illinois, and Charles Risk of Rhode Island.

Harry Sauthoff, a member of the Progressive Party from Wisconsin, was the committee's 21st member.

Rankin got straight to business, calling as the first witness Representative J. Hardin Peterson of Florida, who had just returned to his home in Lakeland after the marathon first session of Congress ended when the storm struck the Keys. Peterson was the first to angrily call for an investigation to determine why the veterans hadn't been evacuated.

"They had plenty of notice, and I want to fix the responsibility," Peterson said in a telegram to Harry Hopkins on September 4, 1935.

But when he took the stand before John Rankin's committee, it was clear that Peterson's anger had diminished.

As part of his testimony, Peterson read into the record an excerpt from the minutes of the American Legion's executive committee meetings of September 22 and September 26, 1935. The segment included part of a statement by Howard McFarlane, a Tampa lawyer who conducted a quick preliminary investigation into the veterans' deaths for the Legion soon after the hurricane.

McFarlane said he'd found "no culpable or criminal negligence chargeable to any person or groups of persons.

"On the contrary," McFarlane had said, "it is my opinion that so far as the human element and the men involved are concerned, they functioned as well as might reasonably be expected. After a disaster such as this, which shocked the nation, there is always a cry that the blame should be placed, the meaning being that it should be placed upon the shoulders of some one or more men—that a scapegoat should be had. Such is the case now. Such a feeling ordinarily does not involve the doing of justice. In making this investigation, I have attempted to put aside any such feeling, and to place myself as nearly as I could in the shoes of the men who had the decision to make. It appears to me that the loss of life is not fundamentally due to what occurred on the first and second of September, but goes considerably deeper than that."

McFarlane added that the "main cause of the disaster was the nature of the Weather Bureau reports," and said Sheldon's and Ghent's lack of experience with weather conditions in the Keys had been a contributing factor.

Peterson added that after American Legion officials heard McFarlane's comments, they appointed the committee composed of Quimby Melton, Catesby A. R. Jones, and W. E. Whitlock to do a more thorough investigation. "For the purpose of brevity and in view of the fact that representatives of the American Legion will also be here, I will not go into great detail with reference to the report of the special investigating committee on the Florida hurricane disaster," he said.

Peterson's move seemed reasonable and considerate. Why take up the time of Rankin's committee to discuss information that would be provided by other witnesses?

But Peterson also knew that the Melton-Jones-Whitlock report of November 2, 1935—the one he'd so considerately refrained from discussing—contained a blistering condemnation of Aubrey Williams's "act of God" conclusion.

In their report Melton, Jones, and Whitlock acknowledged that, without the authority to summon witnesses and put them under oath, their investigation had been hampered. "But we did gather enough information to satisfy ourselves, at least, that the disaster at Matecumbe was not 'An Act of God' and that the lives of the veterans could have and should have been saved," they wrote. Their report went on to blame the tragedy on the "inefficiency, indifference and ignorance" of the people in charge of the work camps and said the veterans' deaths in the Keys amounted to "murder at Matecumbe."

It was a far different take on the disaster than the one presented in McFarlane's statement. The Melton-Jones-Whitlock report was the justification upon which the American Legion's top officials had based their call for a congressional investigation.

By selectively mentioning one Legion report that exonerated FERA and Florida ERA officials from any blame and acknowledging but not discussing a second Legion report that harshly condemned them, Peterson had subtly supported and protected Rankin's all-important record. Also, by not going into details about the Melton-Jones-Whitlock report, Peterson had avoided putting Rankin—a fellow Democrat—in the awkward position of having to make a ruling about what evidence could be admitted to his record and what would be excluded.

It was a slick performance by the Florida congressman. But he was also fed questions from some Democrats on the committee that allowed him to start laying the foundation for the record of selected facts that Rankin wanted to build. Patman asked Peterson if there was any reason why anyone connected with the work camps in the Keys should have anticipated that this hurricane would be so powerful. Peterson said there wasn't.

Rankin or Patman would ask this question or variations of it to witnesses throughout the hearings. If they didn't get the response they sought, they kept asking until they'd led the witness into saying exactly what they wanted.

The two congressmen would establish a pattern of often interrupting Edith Nourse Rogers when she tried to ask a question or make a statement that challenged the "act of God" conclusion. Patman was the first to jump in when she tried to ask Peterson whether Florida residents are typically reluctant to leave their homes when they receive a hurricane warning.

"Is it not true that the inhabitants of the area that has been flooded, or has had a hurricane, or disaster of some sort, are always very unwilling to leave their homes?" Rogers said to Peterson. "I know, recently, in Lowell, where we are recovering from a flood, that although the water was in the first floor of people's houses, they had to be hauled out by policemen."

"Yes," Peterson said. "That has been my observation."

Rogers had a letter from Everett McComb, a veteran from Milwaukee who'd been at Camp 1, in which he described his experience in the hurricane. She wanted to make McComb's letter part of the record of the hearings.

"These veterans were not inhabitants of Florida and were very anxious to leave," Rogers said. "Mr. Peterson, did you receive a letter from . . ."

But Patman jumped in before Rogers could finish, saying he did not understand everything she'd just said. Rogers repeated that the veterans were anxious to leave the Keys before the hurricane struck.

"Is the lady testifying?" Patman asked.

"Here is a letter right here from Mr. McComb, and I ask unanimous consent, if Mr. Peterson is willing, to have this inserted in the record at this point," Rogers said.

But Rankin wouldn't hear of it. He insisted that if Rogers wanted McComb's comments to go into the record, she would have to have him come to Washington and testify. Rogers said she thought McComb would be willing to do that.

"That may be true, but we are not going to fill the record with unsworn testimony, because people who put their statements in this record are going to have to take the responsibility for them," Rankin said, ignoring the fact that he'd already allowed Peterson to read into the record the statement of Howard McFarlane despite the attorney's absence—and obvious inability to swear under oath that he was telling the truth.

Rogers tried to resume her questioning of Peterson, but Patman interrupted repeatedly until an exasperated Rogers started to take another swipe at Rankin.

"I do not believe it is the chairman's fault that we have not had hearings about this matter, and . . . ," Rogers began.

Rankin was incensed. "The truth of the business is, I did not know the lady was so anxious to have the hearings," he shot back.

Rankin also would accumulate testimony to the effect that the Keys were not a dangerous place to put the veterans and that the living conditions in the work camps were quite comfortable for them.

He would establish in his record that Florida ERA administrators had correctly interpreted the hurricane advisories issued by the U.S. Weather Bureau and had taken reasonable and prudent precautions based on their interpretations.

He would allow some witnesses with little knowledge of relevant facts to make statements that couldn't possibly be verified. Many of these statements would be presented as facts, but they would simply be wrong or misleading. Some of these incorrect or misleading statements were undoubtedly inadvertent. Others were just as undoubtedly deliberate. Regardless of the witnesses' motivation, the inaccuracies all became part of Rankin's permanent record.

Rankin intended to make Edith Nourse Rogers pay for the accusations she'd made on the House floor that the Roosevelt Administration had sent the veterans to the Keys to get them out of sight and that Rankin was being secretive about the Keys tragedy. Rankin and Wright Patman would disrupt or challenge Rogers's questioning at every opportunity.

Rogers was not the only committee member who attempted to ask penetrating questions that might prompt witnesses to make statements casting doubt on the "act of God" conclusion. Harry Sauthoff, the Progressive Party congressman from Wisconsin, frequently asked questions that cut through the no-fault contention, as did Republican Albert Joseph Engel of Michigan.

Engel, however, gave clear indications that he was going to side with the majority Democrats on the committee—perhaps because he felt there wasn't enough solid evidence to conclude that anyone had been at fault. Or perhaps because he was a first-term Republican who'd wrested Michigan's Ninth District seat from its Democrat incumbent in a close, hard-fought election. Engel's margin of victory was so narrow that the winner hadn't been determined until the day after the balloting. He knew he risked alienating the swing voters in his district who'd put him in office if he went against a popular Democratic president.

Sauthoff's and Engel's attempts to question the no-fault theory often drew defensive responses from Rankin and Patman, but Rogers's efforts to challenge the "act of God" conclusion were often met with open hostility, especially from Rankin.

When Rogers raised questions about the living conditions in the camps, Rankin interrupted with a barbed reference to President Hoover's 1932 fiasco with the Bonus Marchers, when General Douglas MacArthur exceeded Hoover's orders and used excessive force to rout the veterans from Washington, DC. The vets would have preferred living in the Keys, he accused sharply, to "being driven out of Washington at the point of a bayonet and having their tents burned down."

He continued his tirade. "I do know that a former administration drove these same men out of Washington at the point of a bayonet, when they were looking for work," Rankin said. "If you want facts in the records, those are facts."

Rankin and Patman used three witnesses—Representative Mark Wilcox, a Democrat from Florida; Julius Stone, the former director of the Florida Emergency Relief Administration; and Aubrey Williams—who'd written the now famous "act of God" report—to establish for the record that the Florida Keys were a safe and comfortable place to send the veterans.

"If you had been one of those soldiers and they left you the selection of the place, you would have gone right there [to the Keys]?" Patman asked Wilcox.

"I expect I would, knowing as much as I do about the climate and the surroundings," Wilcox said.

"You would have considered it one of the most likely places?" Patman continued.

"There is nothing wrong with the location," Wilcox said. "There is nothing wrong with the project."

"And you did not consider it a dangerous place to send them?" Patman asked.

"No," Wilcox said. "I did not consider it a dangerous place to send them."

Patman also asked Wilcox about the actions of Captain Einar Sundstrom, master of the S.S. *Dixie*, with the objective of establishing that Sundstrom—like Ghent and Sheldon—had been misled about the storm's position and had been driven aground as a result. "If a ship that was well equipped with the proper instruments could not tell which way the hurricane was coming, how would you expect anybody else to do it?" Patman asked Wilcox.

"I am not sure he could not have gotten out, if he had wanted to," Wilcox said. "He probably did not try to get out."

"You do not think he would purposely go into it, do you?" Patman asked.

"I do not know whether he did or not," Wilcox said.

"We will presume he did not," Patman said.

Julius Stone described the work camps by using his unusual talent for weaving fact and fantasy into appealing tales of deception.

Sending the men to remote islands many miles from a city and depriving them of any amusement except drinking was not subjecting them to hardships—it was exactly what the men needed, Stone said.

"The minute you put a group of detached men anywhere near a city, they have got two strikes on them before they start," Stone told the committee. "They are blamed for every crime that is committed in the city, and they do not have a chance at leading anything like a normal life because the environment will not permit it. . . . So we felt that, if the men were to have any chance to do something besides putting some brick and mortar into place, it was necessary to give them a social environment in which they could escape their nerves, calm their nerves, and so on."

Stone didn't mention the excessive drinking among the veterans, nor did he mention the serious sanitation problems that prompted the vets to go on strike in February 1935.

"What do you consider the standard of health conditions in the camp, and in the Keys?" Rankin asked Stone.

"Well, I would say they were excellent, and so did the Florida State Health Department, under whose auspices all of our operations were," Stone answered without flinching. Somehow, the comments from federal inspectors about the filthy living conditions that existed in the camps soon after they were established were left out, as was the fact that two veterans had died from a form of meningitis that is spread by crowded conditions.

Stone also glossed over the reasons why B. M. Duncan and Lawrence Bow were removed from supervising the veterans camps. Instead of telling the committee of the engineers' indifference to the veterans' living conditions, he attributed the change in administration simply to the growth of the camps.

Stone achieved his masterpiece of glibness, however, when he told the committee that the only discomfort the vets experienced in the camps was having to watch millionaires at play as they worked under the hot sun.

"The only feature of these camps that I can think of that was at all unsettling was the fact that whenever these fellows unbent their backs from sawing rocks, they looked out and saw a millionaire's yacht," Stone said. "The millionaires came down to fish in these waters and the weather was wonderful. So we saw no reason why we should not put these fellows in the same weather as where these millionaires went."

Aubrey Williams told the committee that Florida officials were "enthusiastic about having that road built and thought the Keys would be an excellent place for the veterans."

"They felt that this was an excellent type of project for men that were in need of rebuilding and conditioning, out of the way from the ills and troubles that had beset them," Williams said. "And, as a matter of fact, I know of no place I have ever been that I would rather go to and take my chances of rebuilding myself than there."

Williams added that many people had told him how well the camps had been administered, "and that anyone who attempted to make a goat of anybody in this thing was either vicious or ignorant, and that it was absurd" to attempt to make any agent of the government responsible for the freaks of nature, as this sort of thing obviously is."

Williams defended the no-fault conclusion he presented in his report without using the "act of God" phrasing that had upset so many people across the country.

"I was unable to do otherwise than come to the conclusion it was through no one's fault," he said. "It just happened, that is all. It was tragic and deplorable, but something that was beyond the power of anybody to have averted."

Edith Nourse Rogers told Williams his hastily completed report was "not a very complete description of what actually took place."

When she asked Williams for more information, Rankin hurried to Williams's defense, again attacking Republicans for the rout of the Bonus Marchers in 1932.

"Your administration had jurisdiction of these men in 1932," Rankin said. "And these same men, instead of being given jobs in Florida, as I have said, were driven out of Washington at the point of a bayonet. And to come at this late hour and criticize this setup down there and say they did not have enough assistants, when you had no information to that effect developed by the testimony here, under oath, I think is a belated cry."

Rankin allowed Williams's full report, which had been completed in 48 hours, to be made a part of the record.

General Frank Hines, whose top investigator had spent three weeks compiling a detailed report, could have seriously undermined the credibility of Williams's report during his testimony by discussing David Kennamer's investigation for the VA. But the VA director had scarcely been sworn in when he made it clear he wouldn't lift a finger to contradict the no-fault conclusion.

"Mr. Chairman, I would say that the procedure followed by the committee is undoubtedly producing the facts, and I congratulate you on the procedure," Hines said. "I would like, first, to say to the committee that I am sure you appreciate that, in my position, as head of the Veterans Administration, there is little that I can directly testify to regarding this matter; that I must rely upon reports that have come to me, and the official records of the Veterans Administration."

No one asked Hines about David Kennamer's investigation, and Hines didn't mention the detailed report his skillful but staunchly Republican investigator had assembled. Nor did Hines mention that he'd defended Kennamer's findings in a March 31, 1936, memo to Undersecretary of the Interior Charles West.

On March 27—the day after Rankin convened the first session of his hearings on the bill to compensate the families of the vets who'd been killed in the hurricane—Hines had received an 11-page memo from O. W. Clark, the VA's assistant administrator. Clark had carefully read the proposed bill and pointed out several objections, such as whether vets should be required to have a minimum period of military service and an honorable discharge to qualify for the compensation.

"I do not feel that the reaction of the Veterans Administration to the Bill should be a favorable one," Clark told his boss.

There's no record of whether Hines had private discussions with Rankin or other members of Congress after he read Clark's assessment. But it's possible that he was willing to cooperate with Rankin's "investigation" after a few revisions were made to the proposed bill.

Colonel George Ijams did mention Kennamer's report when he testified, but did not discuss any of the VA investigator's conclusions.

Rogers asked Ijams if he thought everything possible had been done to get vets out of way of the hurricane, and if he'd talked to survivors about this question when he was in Florida immediately after the storm. Ijams said he "did not go into that end of it." He didn't mention that on January 10, 1936, he'd written a memo to Hines in which he explained why he completely agreed with Kennamer's findings.

Fred Ghent, who had landed a new federal job in Washington, tried to explain how he had intended to protect the veterans from hurricanes. He told the committee that he had talked to Ray Sheldon in Key West around 5:30 a.m. on Sunday, September 1. Immediately after this conversation, Ghent said, he told a Florida East Coast Railway dispatcher that he would probably want a special train sent to the Keys on short notice the following day. Ghent said that since he had given the railroad 32 hours' notice that he would want a train, the FEC should have been able to assemble it and get it from Miami to Camp 3 at Lower Matecumbe Key—a distance of about 80 miles—within three hours after he gave them a definite order. That meant that because he had ordered the train at 2 p.m. Monday, it should have reached Camp 3 around 5 p.m., he said.

Ghent told the committee that his expectations weren't unreasonable. He was very familiar with how the FEC operated, he said. The train should have been able to travel at 60 mph, he said. But Ghent either didn't know or didn't tell the committee that the FEC trains seldom approached such a high speed in the Keys. And the hellacious conditions in the Keys during the storm—including flooded tracks and possibly storm-driven debris on the tracks—would have kept the train well below 60 mph.

Although Rankin had assured committee members that there was plenty of money to pay travel expenses for witnesses to come to Washington to testify, he refused a request from FEC officials to reimburse them for travel from Florida to the capital, and so they didn't testify. Had they come before Rankin's committee, it's likely that they would have told the members that no firm agreement had ever been reached with Ghent in the summer of 1935 to provide an evacuation train and that because Ghent hadn't given them a definite order for the train on Sunday, September 1, 1935, they hadn't assembled it then.

On May 1—after the hearings before Rankin's House Committee on World War Veterans' Legislation had been in session for more than a month—Edith Nourse Rogers discovered she'd been working at an even greater disadvantage than she'd thought. On that day she learned that copies of transcripts of the testimony taken by VA investigator David Kennamer had been filed in an office just down the hall from where the hearings were being held. Somehow, no one had bothered to tell her that these transcripts were available for her to examine so long as she didn't take them out of the office.

By early May 1936, Rankin was ready to wrap up his committee's hearings and bring the bill to compensate the hurricane victims' families to a vote on the floor of the House of Representatives. But there were a couple of details he still needed to take care of to protect his record from being tarnished by any testimony or statements that might contradict the "act of God" verdict.

On Saturday, May 9, representatives of the Veterans of Foreign Wars and the American Legion came before the House Committee on World War Veterans' Legislation. Rankin knew that both agencies had conducted their own investigations of the hurricane disaster, both had condemned Aubrey Williams's report, and both could and probably would offer testimony that would undermine the no-fault conclusion.

But he disposed of them quickly and harmlessly, beginning with Colonel John Thomas Taylor of the American Legion.

Taylor told Rankin that he'd brought copies of the American Legion's full report—the report compiled by Quimby Melton, Catesby A. R. Jones, and W. E. Whitlock that concluded that the veterans' deaths had been "murder at Matecumbe"—to give to the committee so that it could become part of the record of the hearings.

Rankin immediately decided that the committee could not accept the Legion's report because "we could not accept conclusions drawn from another investigation such as we have conducted here."

It was a bizarre ruling considering that he'd already allowed two other outside "investigations" to be made part of the record—the statement from Tampa lawyer Howard McFarlane and the hasty investigation of Aubrey Williams. Both of those investigations, of course, had supported the no-fault verdict that Rankin had so tenaciously defended throughout the hearings.

Patman suggested that Taylor leave his documents for the committee to review. "Of course, we are not saying that we will put them in the record," Rankin cautioned.

Edith Nourse Rogers tried to get Rankin to call witnesses from the American Legion who had gone into the Keys after the hurricane, but Rankin refused, and Patman hinted at possible repercussions if Rogers pushed to call more witnesses.

"I hope the lady will not insist upon prolonging this investigation," Patman said. "If she is opposed to the compensation bill . . ."

"The gentleman knows that is not true," Rogers retorted.

"That would be a good way of postponing action on the bill," Patman said. "Why not read the testimony here?" he suggested, referring to the documents Taylor had just turned over. "Perhaps that would pacify the lady?"

Rogers made a motion to call an American Legion witness, and Rankin refused to even put the motion to a vote. Nor did he make the Legion's "murder at Matecumbe" report part of the record.

Rankin dismissed Taylor and turned to Millard Rice, who represented the Veterans of Foreign Wars.

"Mr. Chairman, the VFW did have a special committee that made an investigation relative to this matter," Rice began.

"I know you are not going to say anything, unless you know it of your own knowledge," Patman interrupted patronizingly. "You are under oath, and any suggestion or statement made by someone else is not admissible."

"I was about to say the chairman of the commission is not available," Rice continued. "He is now in Japan. I am not able, under oath, of course, to report what he stated in regard to that investigation, nor, I assume, am I permitted to submit any of the affidavits gathered by the chairman of that committee. They are available if this committee wants them. But they are quite similar to the affidavits gathered by the WPA, although some of these were gathered very shortly after and may differ in some respects."

Rankin didn't ask Rice for his documents. He thanked Rice for offering to testify and declared that the committee was going into an off-the-record executive session.

And with that, Rankin's hearings on the Labor Day Hurricane of 1935 were over.

A few weeks later Rankin submitted a report recommending that the House of Representatives approve the bill to compensate the dependents of the veterans who'd died in the hurricane. Rankin's report included a few sentences saying that camp administrators were not to blame for the veterans' deaths.

Rogers submitted her own report explaining her take on the hearings conducted by Rankin. Not surprisingly, she lambasted Rankin's "no fault" conclusion.

"There is no doubt in our minds that while it would be impossible to place blame for the terrible loss of life, yet the evidence shows a surprising lack of judgment on the part of those responsible for the welfare of the men under their charge," Rogers wrote. "Many blunders were made. This hurricane has been called an act of God. God may be held responsible for this storm, but He cannot be blamed for leaving these men in the path of the storm, nor can He be blamed for depriving them of their only available method of leaving."

Besides Rogers, Rhode Island Republican Charles Risk and Harry Sauthoff, the Progressive Party member from Wisconsin, signed the report.

On June 1, 1936, Rankin's bill to compensate the dependents of the hurricane victims came up for a vote in the House. Rogers said she was in favor of the compensation bill, but she again attacked the no-fault conclusion and the Roosevelt Administration.

"I feel that there was gross negligence," Rogers said. "I blame no one person, but a number, and I hold this government directly responsible for the death and injury of those veterans. There has been no more horrible tragedy than the Florida hurricane, which killed so many of our veterans entirely unnecessarily, their wives and their children."

Rankin protested and pointed to his carefully constructed record as proof that no one had been at fault.

"I ask every member of the House to read this record," Rankin said. "I ask you to read these sworn statements. I ask you to consult the members of this committee who are unbiased and who heard all of this testimony. You will see that we reached the only conclusion that we could have reached."

"There have been some silly efforts made by some members of the committee to play politics with this matter," Rankin added, "but I am glad to say that the more responsible minority members of the committee have been sincere in their efforts to get the facts and to assist in arriving at a proper conclusion."

Rankin thanked Albert Joseph Engel, the Republican from Michigan, "for his able and diligent services."

Rogers came back for another attack.

"I am delighted to have the membership of the House read the hearings," Rogers said. "Whitewash is written all over them. If you will read these hearings, you will see the efforts made to ban testimony when certain questions were asked by the ranking minority member, myself, and by others."

Rogers also accused Rankin of refusing to call witnesses who could have cast doubt on the no-fault conclusion.

"I sat through those hearings and allowed my rights to go by because I feared if I did not the hearings would be closed and the testimony end," Rogers said. "They had the votes on the majority side to stop the hearings, and I wanted the facts to appear in the record."

Sauthoff supported Rogers's contentions.

"I have come to the conclusion that the government was negligent in the method in which it provided protection for the people on the Florida Keys," he said. "It must be remembered that the government put them there. The government had a responsibility and a duty. Having put them there, it was the government's duty to take care of them."

Risk criticized Rankin's shameless manipulation of rules of evidence against anyone who might offer testimony or evidence he didn't want to hear.

"I saw the technical rules of evidence which apply in a court of law applied time and time again against the gentlewoman from Massachusetts and other members of the committee," Risk said.

But the other Republicans on the House Committee on World War Veterans' Legislation were silent, offering no reasons why they had quietly sided with the Democratic majority. Perhaps they had decided it just wasn't worth the effort and they didn't want to become entangled in a squabble they couldn't possibly win.

The bill to compensate the veterans' dependents was passed, and the House moved on to its next item of business—a bill authorizing the U.S. Marine Corps Band to play at a reunion of Confederate veterans in Louisiana and centennial celebrations in Arkansas and Texas.

On June 4, 1936—after Rankin's hearings had ended and Congress had approved the bill to compensate hurricane victims' families—VA director Frank Hines sent a copy of Kennamer's report to Edith Nourse Rogers. But if Rogers and other Republicans found any of the political ammunition they were seeking, they didn't use it against President Roosevelt in the 1936 election. By the time John Rankin hit the campaign trail to stump for FDR's reelection, the Labor Day Hurricane of 1935 was officially on its way to obscurity.

Congress also approved Representative Wilcox's request for more funding to protect Florida residents from hurricanes, and in July 1936 the WPA sent a recently hired engineer from its Jacksonville office to Key West to determine what public buildings there might be converted to hurricane shelters.

The engineer who inspected the structures had learned a great deal about the power of hurricanes and what the storms could do to poorly constructed buildings. His name was Ray Sheldon.

Chapter Eleven

The Illusion of Remoteness

On September 7, 1936—Labor Day Monday—Bascom Grooms Sr. and his family were returning to Key West after a two-week trip to Georgia. One year had passed since his daughter Rosalind had been killed in the hurricane, and he and his wife were still grieving over their loss.

They'd learned the awful details of what had happened to her the previous Labor Day—the car carrying her and her fiancé, George Pepper, plunging into Florida Bay; their escape from the submerged vehicle, and Rosalind fighting to stay alive as the hurricane carried her across Florida Bay; her lonely, tortuous death on a tiny, isolated island. Those grim facts were in their thoughts as they drove down the islands to catch the ferry at Lower Matecumbe Key.

Reminders of the hurricane were strewn along the roadside. In Tavernier a storm-battered house still stood by the road where the hurricane had left it. Several wrecked cars also remained where they'd landed a year earlier. They were now rusting hulks being gradually overtaken by the returning vegetation. But there was talk of erecting a more appropriate reminder of the storm, a monument or memorial of some sort.

They drove through Islamorada, where the American Red Cross was building small houses for hurricane survivors whose homes had been destroyed by the storm. It would take a hurricane of unimaginable power to destroy these houses—their foot-thick walls were made of steel-reinforced concrete.

They passed the spot where the Hotel Matecumbe had stood. Soon after the hurricane, Fern Butters had salvaged the tablecloth stained by Thomas Edison and returned Rosalind's suitcase and the clothing she'd packed to the Grooms family, but the hotel—and Ed Butters's $80,000 uninsured investment—were gone. They'd left the Keys to look for work.

Grooms reached the southern end of Upper Matecumbe Key and started across Indian Key Fill. As they approached the spot where the car carrying

Rosalind had left the highway during the hurricane, they saw an eerie, unsettling sight—another battered, rusting automobile was sitting by the road. Only this one hadn't been there two weeks ago, and it looked exactly like the car Rosalind Grooms Palmer and George Pepper had been in when the storm had hurled them into Florida Bay a year earlier.

Surely it wasn't real. It had to be a mirage, a fleeting hallucination brought about by their grieving and the fact that it was the anniversary of their daughter's death.

But it wasn't a ghostly apparition. It was indeed the 1934 Dodge the young couple had been in.

The automobile had been submerged since the storm. It had been declared a menace to navigation, and the U.S. Coast Guard wanted it removed. But whoever hoisted it out of the bay had just dropped it beside the road and left it there to be hauled away.

Bascom Grooms Sr. pulled his car off the road and stopped. He and his son got out and walked over to the Dodge. Bascom Jr., prompted by motives only a 14-year-old boy can understand, broke off the chrome plate that covered the front of the Dodge's radiator and took it back to his father's car.

He kept the macabre souvenir for many years.

Bertram Pinder moved his family back to Islamorada in April 1936. Their home had been destroyed in the hurricane, but no one was living in the Methodist parsonage, so they made a temporary home there. The family cleared the storm debris out of the house, and Bertram repaired the damage as best he could. He replaced the windows that had been blown out by the hurricane, but the hole in the ceiling remained as a reminder of Reverend Robert Carlson's desperate but futile attempt to save himself and his wife from drowning in the storm surge.

They were glad to get back to Islamorada, but their lives would be different after the Labor Day Hurricane of 1935. The flooding had carried away much of the thin layer of topsoil on Upper Matecumbe Key, so there would be no more lime groves or tomato gardens. They'd have to find new ways to provide food and earn a living.

Every so often during the years after the hurricane, Alma, Dolores, and Laurette Pinder found odd personal reminders of the tragedy. Dolores found her grandfather's rusted pocket watch. Alma found dishes that had somehow been buried in sand beneath an overturned washtub that kept some of them from breaking, and Laurette found the plate that had held their mother's wedding cake.

Slowly they recovered from the shock and terror of their awful experience. There were no grief counselors to help them deal with that difficult task. Eventually they came to accept it simply as part of life.

≁

Amid the dozens of pleas federal officials received from distraught relatives seeking information about missing veterans was a note scrawled on the back of a penny postcard from Mrs. Amanda Ambrose of 2176 Cherokee Street in Baton Rouge, Louisiana. She was the mother of John Hanson Ambrose, the talented artist at Camp 5 who'd contributed finely drawn cartoons to the *Key Veteran News* and told readers on August 31, 1935, that perhaps they'd get to see a hurricane "next month."

Amanda Ambrose said she'd heard that her son had been seen at a first-aid station soon after the hurricane, but she hadn't heard from him. She theorized that he might be suffering from shock or amnesia and asked if anyone could tell her where he might be.

Nothing was ever heard from John Ambrose after September 2, 1935, however. VA officials created a carefully indexed file of three-by-five cards on which they jotted notes about veterans who were killed in the hurricane or missing afterward. That file and thousands of other pages of documents about the hurricane eventually were placed in the National Archives at College Park, Maryland. The card for John Ambrose has only a single brief notation: "Missing unaccounted for 9/28/35." Another card notes that the Red Cross received an inquiry from Amanda Ambrose asking about her son. The date is not given. But a small notation in the corner of the card indicates that on January 28, 1937, the government sent a check for $645.35 to Amanda Ambrose as the beneficiary of the so-called "Bonus" payment that was owed for her missing—and presumed dead—son.

≁

Despite the prediction by the previously infallible *Literary Digest* that Franklin Roosevelt would be soundly defeated in his bid for reelection in 1936, the Democrats' worries proved to be unfounded. The magazine had predicted that Alf Landon would smother FDR, winning 57 percent of the popular vote. Instead, Roosevelt took 62 percent of the popular vote and carried 46 of the 48 states.

The obvious question was how could a poll that had been on the money since 1916 be so badly off, especially since the magazine had sought the opinion of about 10 million potential voters—a large percentage of the voting population. The answer was because even though *The Literary Digest* sought responses from a huge group, only about 2.4 million responded. And those who did respond tended to be a little better off financially than the average voter during the Great Depression and thus less inclined to vote Democrat. So *The Literary Digest* had made its bold prediction even though three-fourths of its readers ignored the poll. Later studies of the 1936 election concluded that the magazine's flawed polling techniques had caused the badly inaccurate prediction.

In 1937 Julius Stone decided to leave government service and return to Harvard University to study law. When he graduated in 1940, he returned to Key West to set up as an investor and real estate broker. His Florida connections—and his trademark artistry as a word slinger—served him well. He bought a beautiful house overlooking the Gulf of Mexico and prospered—for a while.

But by 1960 Stone was deeply in debt and scheming to avoid the IRS. He had one more slick trick up his sleeve, however. He sold his house in a quick, furtive cash transaction and skipped town to Cuba. He left behind a horde of angry creditors—and a permanent legacy in Key West as the man who saved the city from possible abandonment by turning it into a tourist attraction.

In the summer of 1948, a federal grand jury in New York indicted a dozen Communists on charges of plotting to overthrow the government. A tremor of fear pulsated through the country, and there were more accusations that government officials who were secretly members of the Communist Party had been spying for the Soviet Union. Among those accused was John Abt, the former lawyer for the WPA.

Abt admitted that he'd been a Communist since 1933 but denied he was a spy.

Abt's name popped up again in 1963 when a man who was in a lot of trouble was trying desperately to get in touch with him. But the man died before he could speak to Abt.

The prospective client's name was Lee Harvey Oswald.

Abt died of a stroke in New York in 1991. His memoir, *Advocate and Activist: Memoirs of an American Communist Lawyer*, was published in 1993 and included some candid comments about his experience in the wake of the 1935 hurricane.

He was proud of the mark that the New Deal had left on American society. "Opponents of the New Deal called the WPA pay for raking leaves, but in fact the parks, public buildings, works of art, and theater produced under WPA have left a legacy that to this day continues to enrich the country," he wrote.

But he acknowledged that his work with Aubrey Williams and U.S. Representative John Rankin of Mississippi after the vets' deaths in the hurricane had been a cover-up.

Abt compared the hapless World War I vets who'd been sent to the Florida Keys to veterans of the Vietnam War 30 years later. Both groups had been "driven to the margins of society, without benefits, without attention."

The hasty report that he'd written for Williams during their weekend trip to Florida in September 1935 was not a thorough inquiry into the tragedy, Abt said.

"Obviously, with only a day of looking around, talking to Weather Bureau people, camp administrators, and a few veterans, we hadn't gathered much evidence and couldn't say we'd conducted a serious investigation," he wrote. But, he added, the Veterans Administration was "full of Republicans, who sought to discredit the report and thereby embarrass the administration" in the run-up to the 1936 elections.

Abt held no affection for Rankin, who'd chaired the House Committee on World War Veterans' Legislation and directed the hearings about the hurricane in 1936 that proved to be the final chapter in the sad saga. Abt wrote that Rankin's "antebellum mentality made him one of Congress's worst reactionaries."

"But he was a Democrat with a political stake in the administration, so he and I teamed up as allies to exonerate the government, in an episode of my life I look back on without pride," Abt wrote.

Abt completed his report on the disaster for WPA chief Harry Hopkins in late 1935. It was a lawyerly piece of work that included whatever might exonerate his clients and excluded any inconvenient facts to the contrary.

Abt concluded that Sheldon and his boss, Fred Ghent, handled the hurricane emergency exactly as they should have. They made no mistakes, nor were they guilty of even minor lapses of judgment. The camps' directors were victims of the unprecedented and unpredictable fury of nature and the human shortcomings of those around them.

If Ed Sheeran was concerned about the hurricane, he didn't bother telling Sheldon until the evacuation train had already been ordered, Abt wrote. He acknowledged that Sam Cutler was concerned about the storm from the moment he learned of it, but everyone knew Cutler was too nervous to be taken seriously. The Weather Bureau advisories were inaccurate and understated the danger the hurricane posed to the Keys, so no reasonable person would have been alarmed, he wrote. And Abt defended Sheldon's and Ghent's delay in ordering the evacuation train by saying, in effect, that as long as they couldn't see obvious indications of danger—such as the approach of a massive storm surge or winds approaching 200 mph—they weren't compelled to act.

Abt acknowledged that some witnesses gave testimony that blamed Sheldon and Ghent for the veterans' deaths. But he brushed these aside simply by concluding that the witnesses' recollections of events had been addled and distorted by their awful ordeal, and therefore their testimony wasn't reliable.

"The contradictions which appear in the evidence are readily explainable in the light of the fact that, almost without exception, the witnesses had been subjected to the most severe mental and physical strain, either in the hurricane itself or in the arduous task of rescuing the survivors and disposing of the dead," Abt wrote, concluding that "we cannot condemn the judgment which [Sheldon and Ghent] made."

David Kennamer, the staunch Alabama Republican, had no reluctance to blame Sheldon and Ghent for the tragedy.

"The poor judgment used by Mr. Sheldon was his failure to be ready to move when it became apparent this would be necessary," Kennamer wrote in the massive report he submitted to the Veterans Administration. Sheldon and Ghent should have begun preparations to move the vets after the Weather Bureau's 10 a.m. advisory on Sunday, September 1, 1935. That advisory warned that the storm probably would pass through the Straits of Florida with hurricane-force winds and prompted Coast Guard officials in Miami to urge holiday boaters to get out of the Keys.

And while Kennamer found fault up and down the administrative chain of command, he cited two particular reasons for the delay in calling for the evacuation train.

First, there was friction between Ghent and his immediate supervisor, Conrad Van Hyning, because Ghent would be out of a job on November 1. Because of this awkwardness, the two men were reluctant to talk to each another.

Kennamer also realized that, in many ways, the rowdy, troubled vets were their own worst enemy. Before the hurricane the Florida East Coast Railway had taken the extraordinary precaution of requiring vets boarding FEC trains in the Keys to ride in separate cars to protect other passengers from their often-obnoxious behavior.

Ghent knew that keeping several hundred vets—dozens of whom would be staggering drunk—confined to the train and under control during an evacuation would be a nightmare, and so he "naturally delayed their evacuation until he was certain it was absolutely necessary," Kennamer wrote.

Ghent also wanted to minimize the time the vets would be on the train. He'd planned "to get them out after dark and take them back early the next morning, which undoubtedly would have been very desirable if it hadn't been too late," Kennamer wrote.

In January 1936, Hopkins sent a copy of Abt's report to General Frank Hines, director of the Veterans Administration. Hines gave the report to his assistant, Colonel George Ijams, who'd accompanied Aubrey Williams to the Keys for the hasty investigation shortly after the hurricane. Ijams responded with a detailed memo that pointed out many fallacies in Abt's contentions—especially that no one was to blame for the tragedy on the Keys. Ijams reinforced his own support for Kennamer's conclusions that the vets died because Sheldon, Ghent, and Conrad Van Hyning had ignored obvious danger signals.

In February 1936, Hines sent a letter to Harry Hopkins that included Ijams's comments on Abt's conclusions. Hines said it was "practically impossible to agree entirely on all the points at issue" and suggested he and Hopkins send copies of both Kennamer's and Abt's reports to President Roosevelt so he "may have the views of all points at issue."

Decades later, however, VA investigators would discover that President Roosevelt never received either report.

Ray Sheldon didn't talk much about the Labor Day hurricane after the investigators, lawyers, and politicians finally left him alone. But he did not put the memories of that terrible holiday entirely out of his mind. For the rest of his life he kept a small collection of reminders of the storm. His keepsakes included a packet of postcards showing the gruesome aftermath of the hurricane and two memos from the U.S. Department of Commerce about the wrecks of the passenger liner *Dixie* and the Danish freighter *Leise Maersk*.

But the centerpiece of his souvenirs was an unsigned carbon copy of Abt's 56-page report absolving him of any blame for the veterans' deaths. The report somehow was not added to the National Archives files that contain thousands of pages of documents about the catastrophe. Nor could it be found in the files of the Franklin D. Roosevelt Library and Museum in Hyde Park, New York.

Ray Sheldon's only surviving child, Rae Sheldon Cummings of Vero Beach, Florida, took possession of her father's documents when her mother died in 1976. She had no idea how her father managed to obtain a copy of a sensitive, classified report that was intended for the president of the United States. Her father didn't discuss his experience in the hurricane with her.

Ray Sheldon got on with his life after U.S. Representative John Rankin's hearings exonerated him of any blame for the veterans' deaths. His daughter was born in 1936. He worked as an engineer for the WPA for a few years, and then started his own construction company in West Palm Beach. He moved his family into a modest house, built a small office behind his home, and became a loving, middle-aged, first-time father.

"He really doted on me, I think because of his age," said Rae Sheldon Cummings. "First child and all that. He couldn't do enough for me. He was a very loving father."

Cummings recalled only one oblique reference that her father made to the 1935 hurricane. It came during a brief vacation in the Keys sometime in the 1940s. "We took a trip down to the Keys, and stayed in Key West," Cummings said. "And I think at some point he was talking to my mother and they said things, but you know, I was so young I wasn't that interested. Now, of course, I wish I'd stayed right there and listened."

Cummings said her parents might have stopped in Islamorada, and this could've been where Sheldon made a few comments about the storm. She has one other memory of that long-ago trip to the Keys. "I remember being really struck at how close the water was on both sides of the road," she said, adding that her father used to say, "You could stand in the center of the road and spit in either direction and hit water."

Ray and Gayle Sheldon had a son in 1938. Sheldon did well in his contracting business. One of his first big jobs was building a blimp hangar for the U.S. Navy during World War II. He also did a lot of work in West Palm

Beach, including a theater, a hardware store, and other commercial buildings on Dixie Highway.

Eventually, Sheldon bought a big, expensive Packard—the era's status symbol of success—and built a dream house for his family on Monceaux Road in West Palm Beach. He made sure his home would stand up to almost anything nature could throw at it, building it about four feet off the ground with steel reinforcements for added strength.

Sheldon loved the handsome, two-story house. He sometimes relaxed by settling into a lawn chair in his backyard to smoke a Lucky Strike cigarette and sip a tall glass of iced coffee.

But his happiness was brief. In December 1951 he had a heart attack. He recovered enough to take a long summer vacation with his family in 1952 in the Berkshire Mountains in his home state of Massachusetts.

Not long after returning from his vacation, Sheldon was admitted to Good Samaritan Hospital in West Palm Beach, where he died of heart failure on January 31, 1953, at the age of 64.

—

By the spring of 1937, the *Daily Tribune* of Miami Beach had moved into a beautiful new Art Deco–style office building, and the newspaper's name had been changed to the *Miami Tribune*. But the ambitions of publisher Moe Annenberg hadn't changed. He still had dreams of making the *Tribune* the dominant newspaper in South Florida by either buying or bankrupting the *Miami Herald*.

It appeared that he had a chance of reaching his goal. Under the leadership of editor Paul Jeans, the *Trib*'s circulation had steadily increased. Jeans also had recently finished writing *Tropical Disturbance: The Story of the Making of the Miami Tribune*. The book, which was published as a special insert in the *Trib*, was both a history of the newspaper and Jeans's valentine to himself. He covered the *Trib*—and himself—with glory, describing the newspaper's brief existence as "unique in the annals of American journalism."

Jeans devoted an entire chapter of *Tropical Disturbance* to praising the newspaper's reporting of the Labor Day Hurricane of 1935. In his estimation only the *Tribune* had had the courage to fully and accurately report the tragedy. He gave the *Trib* credit for everything from being the only publication to publish the "real" death toll from the hurricane—he still insisted that 1,000 had died even though there were scarcely that many on the islands between Key Largo and Key West when the hurricane struck—to prompting state officials' decision to cremate victims' bodies—due, no doubt, to the *Tribune*'s fixation with publishing photos of decaying corpses.

Jeans boasted that the *Tribune*'s coverage of the Labor Day hurricane "impressed as perhaps nothing else could have upon the community the value and importance of honest, accurate reporting." He claimed that the *Trib*'s hurricane coverage had boosted the newspaper's prestige and increased its daily circulation by 10,000.

On April 18, 1937, Jeans was returning from a trip to Tallahassee with the newspaper's lawyer, Victor Miller, who had skillfully and successfully defended the *Tribune* against several libel suits.

Florida has long been one of the nation's leading producers of cattle, and in 1937 the state had no restrictions on where cattle could graze. Cattlemen weren't required to keep their livestock fenced in, and the animals could wander freely, grazing wherever they found grass—even beside busy highways.

About 20 miles south of St. Augustine, a cow ambled onto U.S. 1 right in front of Jeans's southbound car. The editor swerved to avoid the animal, but his automobile crossed the center line and collided head-on with a northbound car carrying Edward Morr and his wife, Bertha, of Cincinnati.

Miller was thrown through the windshield and killed instantly. Jeans was crushed against the steering wheel column and died soon afterward in a St. Augustine hospital.

Edward Morr also died at the scene of the accident. Bertha Morr died of her injuries 12 days later.

The *Miami Tribune* gave Jeans a hero's sendoff, filling its front page with photos of him and Miller and packing its stories of Jeans's death with condolences from local dignitaries. The *Trib* then began a crusade to change Florida law to prohibit unrestricted grazing.

Jeans's sudden death ended Moe Annenberg's dream of journalistic conquest in Miami. In December 1937 he sold the *Miami Tribune* to John Knight, who'd also purchased the *Miami Herald*. Knight closed the *Tribune*, and Annenberg bought the *Philadelphia Inquirer*.

On a clear, hot day in mid-November 1937, nine-year-old Faye Marie Parker, who survived the hurricane with her family, stood in front of a canvas-covered obelisk in Islamorada. She held a short length of rope and was flanked by two Boy Scouts. She looked out at a crowd of 4,000 from beneath an old-fashioned sunbonnet that gave her a nineteenth-century appearance.

The crowd—more than four times the population of the islands outside of Key West and the largest ever to gather for an event in the Keys—had come for the dedication of a WPA-built memorial to the victims of the Labor Day hurricane.

Although patches of green had returned to the islands that had been blasted by the storm two years earlier, those who made the trip into the Keys for the ceremony saw many lingering scars from the hurricane during their journey. The storm-damaged house in Tavernier was still there, and so were some of the wrecked cars along the roadside.

Parker tugged the rope and the canvas fell away, revealing an 18-foot-tall shaft of coral with an Art Deco–style bas-relief sculpture showing waves rolling past windblown palm trees. Beneath the sculpture was a plaque with the inscription: "Dedicated to the memory of the civilians and war veterans whose lives were lost in the hurricane of September second, 1935."

The 18-foot shaft was roughly the same height as the storm surge that had swept across parts of the Upper Keys in 1935.

Cameras clicked and the crowd applauded.

The memorial included a crypt in front of the coral shaft. The remains of Herman Sauter, a veteran from Philadelphia who was killed in the hurricane, were interred during the unveiling ceremonies, and the crypt's lid served as a frame for a ceramic tile map of the Keys.

O. A. Sanquist, district director of the WPA, presented the memorial "to the people of Monroe County. We leave it in their care and possession."

P. J. O'Shaughnessy, chairman of the committee that planned the dedication ceremonies, reminded the crowd of the 1935 hurricane's awful toll in the Keys. "Out of 270 who made their homes in the Keys, we know that 167 are missing," he said. "Out of 682 World War veterans who were camped on the Keys, 253 are missing."

Thomas Kelly, commander of American Legion Post Number 29 in Miami, made no attempt to mask the anger he and other veterans still felt about the deaths of their comrades. Government agencies in charge of the work program may have meant well in sending the vets to the islands, but they failed to protect the men in their care, he said.

"We admire their courage, but we question their judgment," Kelly said.

Florida had been lucky in 1936—no hurricanes had struck the state, he said. But he added that state and federal officials should take immediate action to prepare for the next disaster.

"We should not be lulled into a false sense of security," Kelly warned.

━

Although Cuban strongman Fulgencio Batista had a reputation for brutal political tactics, Len Povey insisted that he'd never felt uncomfortable around him nor been threatened in any way. Still, after a few years as head of Batista's air force, he gave up his commission in the Cuban army and returned to the United States.

He was briefly an inspector for the federal Air Commerce Bureau. In a 1938 interview he complained about "a few problem flyers" that every inspector had to deal with. "Crazy people who insist in flying unlicensed and unsafe crates and who can't be trusted out of sight."

Povey was still capable of surprises. He met and fell in love with Edith Thompson at an annual air show in St. Louis in 1936. At the 1937 show the couple hopped into Povey's plane and dashed off to Columbia, Missouri, to get married.

In 1939 Povey became a vice president with Embry-Riddle School of Aviation. The flying school formed a partnership with the University of Miami, and during World War II Povey supervised four schools under contract to train pilots.

After the war Povey helped found Mackey Airlines, which later merged with Eastern Airlines. Rumor had it that he was the inspiration for a popular comic strip character called "Smilin' Jack." The strip, which chronicled the adventures of a daredevil aviator, debuted in the early 1930s and became one of the nation's favorites for 40 years. "Smilin' Jack" creator Zack Mosley never confirmed that his popular character was based on Povey, but some of Povey's adventures found their way into the comic strip.

Povey's knack for escaping potentially deadly situations continued. In 1965 he made a left turn into the path of another car near an airport in Fort Lauderdale, Florida. His car was hit broadside on the passenger side, and the impact caused his car to roll over. Povey's car was totaled, but he was unhurt.

As he entered middle age, Len Povey's name regularly popped up in newspapers, and his exploits became a favorite topic of reporters looking for colorful, exciting stories. But his encounter with the Labor Day Hurricane of 1935 and his distinction as the first airplane pilot to go looking for a hurricane were all but forgotten.

Povey moved to Highlands, North Carolina, in 1972 with the intention of retiring. But he was soon persuaded to become director of public relations for Stevens Aviation in Greenville, South Carolina.

In the summer of 1984, he was interviewed by a reporter for the *Greenville* (South Carolina) *Sun*, and that became the lead feature story in the edition of Sunday, July 8. His delight in flying still sparkled. "If anyone had more fun in aviation than I had, I want to know who it is," he told the reporter. And his long-ago flight to find the hurricane in 1935 was briefly mentioned.

Povey died in Highlands on September 26, 1984. He was posthumously inducted into the South Carolina Aviation Hall of Fame in 1991, but the brief biography about his career on the hall of fame's website does not mention his history-making flight on the afternoon of September 2, 1935.

⌐

Lieutenant William Clemmer was awarded the U.S. Coast Guard Gold Lifesaving Medal for his remarkable search-and-rescue efforts in the days after the Labor Day Hurricane of 1935. He continued flying mercy missions for the Coast Guard, and his exploits were regularly chronicled in the *Miami Daily News*.

On July 15, 1939, Clemmer—now stationed at Floyd Bennett Field in Brooklyn—took off in a seaplane to pick up a seriously ill crewman aboard the research ship *Atlantis*, owned by the Woods Hole Oceanographic Institute. The *Atlantis* was about 150 miles southeast of New York City.

Conditions were treacherous—sporadic thunderstorms and high, choppy seas—when Clemmer and his crew reached the *Atlantis*.

But Clemmer had routinely put his seaplane down in risky conditions since his heroics following the 1935 hurricane. He'd performed a very risky night landing off Cuba in February 1936 to airlift a sailor who'd suffered a compound leg fracture. With the broken bone protruding from the sailor's leg, Clemmer took off in darkness to fly the man to a Miami hospital.

A month later he'd gone to the aid of a sick child on a steamship off Cuba. Again he'd landed in rough water—so rough that his plane was damaged and he couldn't take off. While waiting for parts to make repairs, Clemmer and his crew stayed aboard their plane, eventually taxiing it into the Cuban port of Nuevitas for repairs.

In July 1936 Clemmer had once again landed a seaplane in dangerous, choppy waters to pick up a sailor who'd been gravely injured in an accident aboard a tanker off Jacksonville. Clemmer and his crew took the unconscious sailor aboard the seaplane and flew him to a hospital while a doctor worked on his injuries during the flight.

Clemmer landed in the choppy seas near the *Atlantis*, and the sick man was taken to the plane by rowboat and loaded aboard. Clemmer turned his plane into the wind and began taxiing for takeoff. The big plane lifted free of the water for an instant, and then suddenly, at full throttle, something went terribly wrong. The nose of Clemmer's plane dropped, and it plunged into a swell. Clemmer and his copilot, probably stunned by the sudden impact, could not get out of the plane and drowned. The man they'd been sent to rescue also died.

Five crewmen were rescued from the wrecked plane by the crew of the *Atlantis*. It was a tragic end for a brave and selfless young man.

The bankrupt Florida East Coast Railway decided not to rebuild its roadbed to Key West, and once again the city was cut off from the rest of the United States. But the dream of linking Key West to the mainland with a highway didn't die. The FEC sold its right-of-way in the Keys to the Florida State Highway Department, and the state built a highway on the railroad's roadbed.

Steel outriggers were added to the old concrete viaducts and piers that had once carried trains and shrugged off the blasts of the Labor Day hurricane, and they were converted to highway bridges.

Engineers realized they couldn't widen the steel suspension railroad bridge at Bahia Honda, so they routed the highway across the top of the span and attached the outriggers there. On July 2, 1938, the Overseas Highway—the final segment of U.S. 1 stretching from Maine to Key West—was opened with a ceremony atop the Bahia Honda Bridge, 75 feet above the Atlantic Ocean.

A few months after the Overseas Highway opened, President Roosevelt briefly drew the nation's attention to the unusual road. On February 18, 1939, the president and his entourage drove the length of the highway to Key West, where Roosevelt boarded the U.S.S. *Houston* to watch naval training exercises in the Caribbean Sea. The presidential caravan stopped briefly on Summerland Key—well south of where the hurricane had done its worst damage four years earlier—to eat a picnic lunch. FDR's route to Key West took him within a few yards of the hurricane memorial erected two years earlier in Islamorada. If the president made any comments about the hurricane or the memorial, the reporters accompanying him either weren't listening or weren't interested.

The opening of the highway and the construction of a freshwater pipeline from Florida City to Key West in 1942 sparked rapid population growth on the islands. Almost 16,000 people moved into the Keys between 1940 and 1950.

A couple of those new residents weren't exactly newcomers. Fern and Ed Butters returned to Upper Matecumbe Key in the mid-1940s and built the Fern Inn on the site of the old Hotel Matecumbe. Fern became famous for her key lime pies, and they ran the small inn until Ed died in 1965.

Ed Sheeran became an engineer for the Florida State Highway Department and was assigned to the Keys. He was given an office at Pigeon Key, a small island beneath the Seven Mile Bridge near Marathon. His devotion to his work didn't diminish in the slightest with advancing age, nor did the thought of retirement even enter his mind. He continued his practice of staying in the Keys during the workweek and returning to his home on weekends.

On a Monday in 1946, Sheeran, as usual, arose around 4 a.m. to drive from Coral Gables to Pigeon Key. He got into his new 1946 Ford and headed south.

It was still dark when he reached the Keys—too dark for him to see the unlighted tractor-trailer truck that had broken down in the southbound lane of U.S. 1. Sheeran's car slammed into the rear of the truck.

Sheeran was seriously injured in the wreck and hospitalized for many weeks. He recovered from his injuries, but his working days were over. He returned to his comfortable, spacious home in Coral Gables, but he wasn't prepared for life without work.

"He was too involved with his job to be bothered with home-type things," said his grandson Edward H. Sheeran. "After the accident, he sat at home in front of the radio. He didn't do anything except sit there and wait for death, more or less."

Death arrived for Sheeran around 6:35 a.m. at the Veterans Administration Hospital in Coral Gables on December 28, 1951. He was buried on New Year's Eve with full military honors—including a 21-gun salute—in Miami's Woodlawn Cemetery.

~

Between 1950 and 1960 another 18,000 new residents moved to the islands, and by the end of the decade Monroe County's population had swelled to almost 48,000. Except for a few hundred Indians of the Seminole and Miccosukee tribes who still lived in the Everglades at the southern tip of the peninsula, the population was packed onto the narrow 130-mile stretch of islands.

Visitors became fascinated with the Keys. One visitor in particular attracted a great deal of attention to the islands. President Harry Truman started coming to Key West regularly in 1946 and loved it so much he once quipped that he had a notion to move the nation's capital there so he could stay.

By December 1951 Truman had visited Key West 10 times in five years. The president was drawn by the city's remoteness and relaxed environment. Here he could run the country by day while dressed in comfortable tropical attire, play poker and drink bourbon with his staff at night, and take brisk early morning walks.

The city that once had been too broke to pay its bills was becoming linked with celebrities. Authors Elizabeth Bishop and Tennessee Williams bought houses in Key West, and although Ernest Hemingway moved to Cuba after his marriage to Pauline Pfeiffer Hemingway ended in 1939, he still visited Key West occasionally. By the time President Truman became a regular visitor, the isolation that made the Keys and Key West so unusual and appealing as an escape from the rest of the world was endangered—the rest of the world had discovered the islands.

Frequent visitors such as *The New Yorker* magazine writer Richard Rovers were already fretting about the disappearance of Key West's unique ambiance in the early 1950s.

"The old town is too small for the present flow of visitors and the fear now, as more marl is pumped up daily from the sea to be used as fill for enlarging the island, is that the motels and drive-ins will eventually surround and overwhelm it," Rovers said in the December 15, 1951, edition of *The New Yorker*. "It is not resentment of outsiders that makes some people worry about this possibility but the fact that if Key West succumbs to the motels and drive-ins, there will be much less for the tourists to enjoy. Even the illusion of remoteness will be gone."

As more people moved into the Keys, public concern increased about getting people out of harm's way when the next big hurricane took aim at the islands.

In 1960, on the 25th anniversary of the Labor Day Hurricane of 1935, *St. Petersburg Times* writer Colin Jameson warned that a catastrophe could happen one day when thousands of Keys residents faced an approaching hurricane with only U.S. 1—the "narrow, vulnerable highway"—as their only way to escape.

"In many cases, too many cases, it will be every man for himself," Jameson wrote, noting that it had been years since a really bad hurricane had hit the Keys. "All we know is that it will (come)," he concluded. "Meanwhile thousands of people may be living on time borrowed from the wind."

Six days after Jameson's story was published, Hurricane Donna blasted across the Keys.

For a while there was serious talk of building a second highway into the Keys that would connect Florida's west coast with the islands. The plan called for 42 miles of bridges and causeways to be built across Florida Bay from Cape Sable at the tip of the Florida peninsula to Big Pine Key.

In 1959 the Monroe County Board of Commissioners paid for a survey for the new road. But the proposed project went no further.

The Keys provided much of the inspiration for singer-songwriter Jimmy Buffett's rise to the top of popular music in the 1970s and enticed more people to visit the islands.

Between 1978 and 1985 the former FEC bridges that had been converted for automobile traffic were replaced with modern, wider spans, and U.S. 1 was rerouted slightly in places to line up with the new bridges. But Henry Flagler's old railroad bridges, which have endured for more than a century, are still there as a monument to what can be accomplished by a wealthy, determined man when he's not hindered by government regulations.

By the 1990s, Key West had achieved a bizarre pinnacle of distinction as a tourist attraction. The city became the theme for a new amusement park in Orlando—Key West at SeaWorld. The five-acre park offers a manufactured, sanitized, family-safe fantasy of Key West, an illusion of the town's once remote charm without the inconveniences of homeless panhandlers, Duval Street drunks, traffic jams, and hurricane evacuations. Advertisements for Key West at SeaWorld described the park as "wacky," "exotic," "funky," "quirky," and "festive."

It's difficult to imagine the hard-up residents of Key West thinking of their destitute, dying city in those terms in 1934.

Three decades after the Labor Day Hurricane of 1935, federal officials were still unwilling to release details of the veterans' deaths to the public.

In January 1968 Mathias von Brauchitsch, a writer and television producer in Pittsburgh, asked Veterans Administration officials for permission to see David Kennamer's report on the tragedy. In a January 23, 1968, letter to John Radowich of the VA's Information Service, von Brauchitsch said he'd already read the testimony of witnesses interviewed by Kennamer that was at the National Archives. Von Brauchitsch said he might write a book about the tragedy.

Von Brauchitsch's request was passed on to Manuel Mota, a VA special investigator, who reviewed the documents at the National Archives. Mota passed along his findings to W. L. Retew Jr., the VA's assistant director for investigations. Retew dug into the VA's files on the hurricane and Kennamer's report and wrote a memo to his boss, the VA's director of investigation and security service, saying he didn't think it was a good idea to allow von Brauchitsch to see Kennamer's report and supporting documents.

In his memo of February 26, 1968, Retew said he'd found "documents, as well as a lack of documents, which indicate there could be problems in the release of Kennamer's report itself."

Retew noted that Aubrey Williams had submitted a report to President Roosevelt concluding that government administrators were not to blame for the veterans' deaths. After Williams had sent his report to FDR, Retew said, Kennamer conducted a joint investigation with John Abt, the attorney for the Federal Emergency Relief Administration and the WPA. Kennamer and Abt were supposedly going to submit separate reports on the disaster to President Roosevelt.

Retew had found several documents in the VA file clearly indicating that Abt had indeed written a report on the disaster. But neither Abt's report nor the one written by Kennamer ever reached FDR's desk, he wrote.

A copy of Kennamer's report and supporting documents were still in the VA's files, but if Abt's report had ever been included in the files, it had vanished by 2002.

Retew added that Kennamer's report was "highly critical" of federal officials.

"Kennamer's comments and conclusions appear quite harsh in relation to the facts developed," Retew said. The investigator "appears to have been 'hard-headed' about his report and any attempts to modify it. FERA disagreed with his conclusions of negligence and publicly took the position that there was no negligence. While the records do not establish the VA's final position with respect to negligence of FERA officials, there is much evidence to indicate that it was considerably milder than as expressed in Kennamer's report. The only known report to the President was the VA-FERA report prior to the Kennamer investigation which concluded there was no negligence."

Though he could find no legal basis for denying von Brauchitsch access to the files, Retew did just that, noting that allowing the writer access "would present a misleading picture of the VA position in this matter and do a grave injustice to the FERA officials the report criticizes."

In a March 26, 1968 letter to von Brauchitsch, Retew told the Pittsburgh writer his request was being denied.

Retew justified his decision by citing a provision of the Freedom of Information Act allowing federal agencies to refuse to make public the same internal memos or letters they could legally withhold if they were involved in a lawsuit. Although Kennamer's report had been intended for President Roosevelt, FDR had never actually seen it. So it was still technically an internal memo. Retew used that legal loophole to prohibit von Brauchitsch from seeing Kennamer's report.

When another author was prevented in 1978 from seeing the VA's documents about the 1935 hurricane, U.S. Senator Lawton Chiles of Florida broke through the barricade. Thanks to Chiles's intervention, the Veterans

Administration released its documents on the tragedy to Florida author Karl Meyer.

In July 1978 Meyer told the *Lakeland Ledger* and the *Tampa Tribune* that he was going to write a novel titled *Matecumbe: Place of Sorrow* about the tragic deaths of the vets in the Labor Day Hurricane of 1935. He'd received a $2,000 grant from the Florida Arts Council to help pay for his research, and said he planned to go to the Keys with an unnamed 70-year-old North Carolina man thought to be the last living veteran who had survived the hurricane.

Meyer said he'd been working on the project for about nine months and expected it would take at least another 15 months to complete it. But either he never finished the novel or was unable to find a publisher.

There's no way of knowing why the reports written by Kennamer and Abt never reached President Roosevelt's desk. They may have been deliberately withheld from him by one of his subordinates, who decided that there was no reason for FDR to see these reports—especially after the carefully orchestrated hearings conducted by Representative John Rankin put the final stamp of exoneration on FERA and Florida ERA officials.

Or it may have been accidental. Filing accidents happen, especially when office workers are trying to keep track of the thousands of pages of documents that are produced by the office of the President of the United States. But if it was accidental, no one bothered to check up on whether the chief had been sent the reports as promised, or to track down extra copies to replace the ones that had gone astray.

Regardless of how this little mystery unfolded, President Roosevelt never had to reconsider whatever impression of the tragedy he may have formed after reading the hasty, incomplete report that Aubrey Williams knocked together during a weekend trip to Florida. Being ignorant of the facts and conclusions developed by Kennamer—and presumably Abt—also means that FDR never had to make any decisions or take any action that might have gotten the attention of reporters and Republicans and kept the tragedy in the public spotlight longer than it was.

There's also no way of knowing how a scandal might have affected the 1936 election. It's hard to believe that anything—even a scandal over the deaths of more than 250 veterans—would have derailed FDR. Still, *The Literary Digest* poll had to have been unsettling to the president's campaign strategists.

Representative John Rankin apparently made sure the Republicans didn't get any help from his committee's "investigation" of the tragedy. A file at the National Archives intended to preserve documents from Rankin's hearings on the hurricane is empty. Archivist Kate Snodgrass said Rankin left very few documents from his committee's activities during the 74th Congress. The Rankin family also denied a request to allow their collection of the congressman's documents to be used for research for this book.

～

Representative Edith Nourse Rogers continued to represent Massachusetts's 5th district until her death in September 1960. She was a staunch supporter of veterans throughout her career and a driving force behind the so-called G.I. Bill of Rights for returning World War II vets.

Her image as a prim, proper and polished New England matron was tarnished, however, when she was named a co-respondent in a lawsuit that the unhappy wife of a U.S. Navy captain filed against her husband in 1949. The wife charged that Rogers, who was then 67, had been on "close and intimate terms" with her husband for 20 years, and that Rogers's relationship with her husband had broken up her marriage.

Rogers said the charges were "ridiculous," and a judge agreed, ordering all references to Rogers removed from the court records.

Representative John Rankin held on to his seat in the House of Representatives until 1953. His clashes with Rogers over Veterans Committee issues became so frequent that in 1947 political columnist Drew Pearson noted that their disputes "have been cloakroom gossip for years."

Rankin's "antebellum mentality" that John Abt described in his memoirs was frequently displayed during his 32 years in the House. In 1944 while making comments on the floor of the House, he referred to famed journalist Walter Winchell as a "little kike." When Adam Clayton Powell, an African American, was elected to Congress from New York that same year, Rankin vowed never to sit next to him, prompting Powell to make a diligent effort to sit next to Rankin whenever possible.

Rankin lost his seat when his district was combined with that of incumbent Tom Abernathy—another Democrat—after the 1950 Census. Abernathy defeated Rankin in a primary election in 1952 and faced no Republican opposition in the 1952 general election.

Rankin returned to Mississippi and practiced law until he died in November 1960 only a few weeks after his longtime colleague and antagonist, Edith Nourse Rogers.

The dramatic story of the SS *Dixie*'s grounding and subsequent rescue appeared in newspapers across the United States and abroad. Captain Einar Sundstrom gained international fame as the brave and resolute captain who'd brought his ship and 350 souls safely through a terrible storm, and he enjoyed—or perhaps endured is a better word—a few months of celebrity afterward.

On September 30, 1935, the *Dixie* arrived in New York under tow and went into drydock for repairs. Sundstrom was guest speaker at a New York Advertising Club luncheon, and his remarks were broadcast over radio station WOR. *New York Daily News* columnist Ben Gross noted that Sundstrom "lived up to the traditions of men of action by saying very little and saying that very modestly."

A few days later Sundstrom sat stiffly on a couch in his living room in Little Neck. He wore a sea captain's dark dress winter uniform and was flanked by his wife, Marie, and daughters Florence and Lillian. As a Pathé News cameraman framed his face in a tight close-up, Sundstrom glanced nervously to his left and right, then looked uneasily into the camera. Viewers easily could've gotten the impression that he'd rather have been facing another hurricane.

In five terse, halting sentences, Sundstrom told the story of the *Dixie*'s grounding on French Reef and concluded with a brief, tight smile.

On October 28, Sundstrom and Henry Treger, the radio engineer who'd risked his life to rig up an emergency antenna so the *Dixie* could broadcast an "SOS" signal, were the guests of honor at the Rotary-Lions-Kiwanis dinner in Metuchen, New Jersey. A reporter at the gathering said Sundstrom "confined his remarks to a summary of the causes of the accident and to its little humorous interludes."

After the hurricane publicity died down, Sundstrom got on with his life and kept his name out of the newspapers. When he retired, he bought a modest house in Pompano Beach, Florida.

But violent weather wasn't quite through with Einar Sundstrom. On December 11, 1969, a tornado ripped through Sundstrom's neighborhood. He was standing in his kitchen when the storm struck. His house was destroyed around him, but the kitchen was left intact and he was unhurt.

Sundstrom died in Pompano Beach on February 21, 1971, at the age of 86.

On a warm afternoon in mid-November 1997, almost 60 years to the day after the dedication of the hurricane memorial in Islamorada, Bernard Russell walked up to the foundation of the old Islamorada post office, picked up a chunk of coral about the size of a cantaloupe, and inspected it. "You know," he said, thinking of the time when he and his neighbors gathered tailings from the road grading to build the post office, "we probably picked this up by the side of the road in 1928." DeLeon Street is paved now, and there's a bank next to the old foundation.

Bank officials wanted to remove the foundation to expand the parking lot, but preservationists led by Jerry Wilkinson of Tavernier, president of the Historical Preservation Society of the Upper Keys, talked them out of it. Now there's a plaque explaining the significance of the site next to the foundation.

The road that once was Upper Matecumbe Key's only highway runs past the old post office site, and the house where Russell lived is about a mile and a half south of the foundation.

A few hundred feet up DeLeon Street from the old foundation, the new Islamorada post office sits where the FEC station stood until the hurricane blew it to pieces. Any trace of the old railroad is long gone. Every day hundreds of cars on U.S. 1 whiz past the spot where the train cars came to rest after the powerful storm surge swept them off the tracks.

Bernard Russell married Laurette Pinder in 1939. They shared a bond beyond their love for each other—they'd both somehow survived one of the most cataclysmic events in recorded history. The same year they were married, they moved into one of the steel-and-concrete houses built by the American Red Cross. They spent the rest of their lives there, a stone's throw from the hurricane memorial, a couple of blocks from Florida Bay and not much farther from the Atlantic Ocean.

Russell compared their sturdy little home to living in a bank vault. There are about two dozen of the concrete houses scattered in Islamorada and Tavernier. The locals call them Red Cross houses.

Near the end of his life, Russell's hands trembled from the debilitating effects of Parkinson's disease. More than 60 years after the Labor Day hurricane, he still found it difficult to talk about his experience. Tears came to his eyes as he tried to describe the moment his sister and nephew were torn away from him when the storm surge came ashore. Yet, he was almost apologetic for his sorrow.

"Those memories of what happened, you don't blot them out overnight," he said. "You lost everything but the shirt on your back. Some of us didn't even have a shirt on our back."

In some ways, he spent the rest of his life trying to understand what happened on that long-ago night after his father opened the door of the family's hurricane shelter for the ill-fated attempt to get them to higher ground. One moment his family was together, frightened by the storm but consoling each other that everything would be all right. The next moment they were snatched up and scattered, blown to kingdom come by the screaming, deadly winds.

"I can remember being so numb, all of it happened at once," he said. "A flash, and everything was gone, and everything had to be new."

Russell also remembered the terrifying sound the winds made on the night of September 2, 1935. He went through many hurricanes after the 1935 storm, but he never heard a noise like the deafening unearthly screech he heard that long-ago Labor Day.

The survivors of the most powerful hurricane in U.S. history didn't have much time for grieving. They had to get on with the grim but necessary business of burying their dead, clearing the wreckage, and rebuilding their lives.

"You didn't have time to dwell on it," Russell said. "It sounds silly, or crazy. You say, 'Didn't it bother you?' Sure, it bothered you, but that wasn't the answer. The answer was, we had to buckle down and say, 'Look, we got to make it here. And we got nobody to help, but we'll do it on our own.' Like Dad said, he said, 'Son, whatever we do, we just got to buckle down and do it. Not look for any frills or anything like that. 'Cause we don't have it and it's not here. We're going to make it on our own.'"

Picking up the pieces of their lives after the 1935 hurricane meant pursuing small goals and keeping expectations to a minimum, Russell said.

"You know, a lot of things you want to blank out," he said. "It's not right, but you want to blank it out, because you can't live yesterday, and you can't live tomorrow until it gets here. Better live today, one day at a time. And that's the only way you could plan it. You couldn't plan anything; you couldn't say, 'I'm going to do this next week.' You had to play it a day at a time, and live it a day at a time."

Russell and his father returned to Islamorada in November 1935. They lived on a boat for about a year until they got a house built.

Russell often wondered why he was still alive, since the moment the Atlantic Ocean suddenly drained off Upper Matecumbe Key and he climbed down off the pile of wreckage that both nearly killed him and saved his life during that awful Monday evening. Except for a stint in the U.S. Army during World War II, he remained in Islamorada. He did well as a cabinetmaker, and he and Laurette raised a daughter.

Russell gave a lot to his community. He attended Matecumbe Methodist Church, which was rebuilt just up the street from the hurricane memorial. He was the driving force in establishing Upper Matecumbe Key's first fire department and rescue squad.

He saw thousands upon thousands of newcomers move into the once remote Keys. He shook his head in disbelief when he heard them say they'd like to experience a hurricane, as though they were talking about a tourist attraction at Walt Disney World. He heard the doomed veterans say the same thing in the summer of 1935, and he warned many of the newcomers about the lethal power of the storms, assuring them that a hurricane is something to be avoided, not experienced.

"People don't stop to realize that once you get so far into one of them, there's nothing you can do," he said. "You're going to ride it out, one way or another. There's no way to get away from it. They say, 'Well, if it gets so bad we'll get in the car and leave.' You just don't do that."

Still, Russell rode out every hurricane that hit the Keys after the 1935 storm. He didn't leave because he felt he might be needed.

Russell was in Islamorada on another sinister September day in 1960 when Hurricane Donna—the most powerful storm to strike the Keys since 1935—hit. Donna, which crossed the Keys on September 8, 1960, resembled the 1935 hurricane in several ways. Besides its incredible strength—at the time it was the fourth-strongest hurricane to strike the United States—it followed a path through the islands that was nearly identical to that of its predecessor.

The steel-and-concrete houses and a school built by the Red Cross easily withstood Donna's fierce blasts. After the worst of the hurricane passed, Russell—who was Islamorada's fire chief—directed the search-and-rescue effort on Upper Matecumbe Key. His experience in the 1935 hurricane was very much on his mind.

"When I took the guys out, this is exactly what I told them—go yell," Russell said. "Yell and scream when you get to a place where there's damaged buildings. Yell. Scream. Somebody might be pinned down, can't get up. And

I had them out doing that when the wind was still howling. I found out that that was the way to do it."

Despite Hurricane Donna's fearsome winds, only four people in the Keys were killed by the storm.

Russell died of complications from Parkinson's on June 19, 2004. He was 85 years old. He was one of the few people who faced a Category 5 hurricane at full roar at landfall with no protection and lived to tell about it.

The beach where the Matecumbe Methodist Church and the Matecumbe Graded School once stood in Islamorada is now part of the Cheeca Lodge, a luxury oceanfront resort. President George H. W. Bush stayed there when he went fishing in the Keys. But the cemetery remains. The 1935 hurricane blew the marble angel off Etta Pinder's grave, but survivors found the statue. Part of the angel's left wing had been broken off, but otherwise the statue was intact. The statue was returned to its pedestal, and it's still there.

A short distance down State Highway 4-A is the building that housed O. D. King's service station and tavern in 1935. The building was heavily damaged by the hurricane, but there was enough of it left to prompt King to repair it, and he built it strong enough to withstand Hurricane Donna 25 years later.

Today King's former service station is the Green Turtle Inn, which opened in 1947. Now, where terrified survivors huddled to escape the hurricane in 1935, tourists enjoy seafood specialties and browse the gift shop for T-shirts and other souvenirs.

Down at the southern tip of Lower Matecumbe Key, where Camp 3 and the ferry landing stood in 1935, there's now a Boy Scout camp and a gated community called Toll Gate Shores. Some of the houses overlook Veterans Key and eight concrete piers protruding from the waters of Florida Bay several hundred yards offshore. The piers—the beginning of the bridge that the veterans were helping build—are the only surviving structure directly linked to the vets. But the Florida Department of Transportation has refused repeated requests to erect a historical marker at the site.

Ed Sheeran directed the workers who set the cofferdams for the piers into Florida Bay, built the concrete forms, lowered the coral blocks into the forms, and poured the concrete. John Ambrose, the talented draftsman from

Louisiana who tempted fate with his sardonic comments about hurricanes, drew a detailed cartoon of the bridge construction work for the July 27, 1935, issue of the *Key Veteran News*. Plans called for dozens of the piers to be built.

But the Labor Day Hurricane of 1935 stopped the construction and the piers were abandoned. Curious boaters who come in close to the piers today can see, just beneath the surface of the water, the corrugated steel sides of the cofferdams, twisted and torn by the action of the massive storm surge that inundated the islands.

Now the old piers are a hangout for cormorants. The long-necked birds perch on the concrete and spread their wings to dry during the day, and they roost there at night. Boaters who happen to be downwind of the piers as they cruise slowly past them can tell instantly that the cormorants have been roosting there for a very long time.

U.S. Weather Bureau officials were stung and deeply angered by criticism from President Roosevelt's top assistant, Harry Hopkins, in the days immediately following the tragedy in the Keys. Hopkins told the Associated Press that the Weather Bureau's forecasts had not communicated the danger the hurricane posed to the Keys and the veterans work camps.

It was an ill-considered remark, coming from someone who knew little or nothing about hurricanes. In fairness to the Weather Bureau, Ray Sheldon and Fred Ghent had been warned that a hurricane—any hurricane—in the Straits of Florida would cause dangerous conditions on the islands. And American Red Cross officials said the advisories were accurate enough to enable them to prepare for the aftermath of the storm.

There was other criticism much sharper than Hopkins's.

"The Weather Bureau has failed," the *Fort Lauderdale Daily News* said in a front-page editorial on September 5, 1935. "That is a blunt statement, but a true one. Something should be done. Something must be done."

The *Miami Daily News* recalled the Weather Bureau's boastful statement back in July that a hurricane would never again sneak up on U.S. shores.

"The much-touted hurricane warning system set up by the Weather Bureau has failed in its first test," the *Daily News* said on September 9.

The comments would become embedded in the Weather Bureau's institutional psyche, and for decades to come, the agency's irritation at criticism of its performance during the Labor Day Hurricane of 1935 would occasionally surface.

The criticism annoyed the forecasters who were on duty in Jacksonville during the deadly storm—Walter Bennett, the meteorologist in charge of the office; Gordon Dunn, an assistant forecaster; and Grady Norton, who recently had been named the Weather Bureau's chief hurricane forecaster.

Norton, an affable Alabamian, became a beloved figure during his long career with the Weather Bureau. His folksy demeanor, soothing Southern drawl, and uncanny ability to explain complex meteorology in simple terms endeared him to the public.

Norton built a reputation for accurate forecasting in the days before Doppler radar and weather satellites. He was awarded the Department of Commerce's Silver Medal for his service.

Norton developed heart problems, however, and his doctor urged him to cut back on his work hours. But when a storm in the Caribbean in October 1954 blew up into fearsome Hurricane Hazel and took aim at the Atlantic Coast, Norton insisted on being at his post.

On October 8, 1954, Norton worked his shift monitoring the fierce storm. Then he went home and said he was very tired. Early the following morning he suffered a stroke and died later that day. He was 60 years old.

The day after his death, *Miami Daily News* reporter Jane Wood Reno—whose daughter Janet would become U.S. attorney general in 1993—wrote that Norton had recently let her in on an intriguing secret about the Labor Day Hurricane of 1935.

Reno said that Norton had told her only a month earlier that he had called Fred Ghent in Jacksonville at three o'clock in the morning on Monday, September 2, 1935, to tell him to get the men out of the Keys. Reno wrote that Norton told her that when the investigations and finger-pointing began after the hurricane, he was told to keep quiet. So he said nothing, she wrote.

Reno repeated her anecdote about Norton in a 1955 story on the 20th anniversary of the Labor Day Hurricane of 1935. In this story, published in the *Miami Daily News* on September 4, 1955, she said Norton called Ghent at "about 3 a.m." and told him "it looked like the hurricane might come in on the keys [sic], better take precautions." She said nothing about Norton specifically telling Ghent to get the veterans off the islands or being told to keep quiet when the investigations began.

The Weather Bureau conducted its own internal investigation of its performance during the hurricane, and the results were outlined in a confidential report dated September 12, 1935. Included in the report was a statement about telephone conversations that meteorologists at several bureau offices had had with FERA officials in the days leading up to the storm's landfall on September 2.

Since the report was classified, it would be seen only by select personnel in the Weather Bureau. If Norton had made a phone call to Ghent telling him to get the men off the islands, Weather Bureau officials certainly would have been aware of it. Such a call presumably would have added much credibility to the Bureau's contention that they had provided adequate warning of the storm's danger. Even if someone had told Norton to keep quiet about the call, there was no reason not to mention it in a confidential internal report that would not be circulated outside the agency. But there was no mention of such a call.

On September 17, 1935, VA investigator David Kennamer and FERA attorney John Abt questioned Dunn and Bennett about their agency's communications with Ray Sheldon and other administrators before the hurricane.

Dunn said the Jacksonville staff had handled countless phone calls seeking information about the hurricane, but the only phone call he'd received from anyone connected with the veterans work program came at around 5 a.m. on Sunday, September 1. He didn't remember the caller's name, only that he identified himself as "a gentleman who represented himself as in charge of the veterans in the Keys."

The caller wanted information about a tropical storm that was headed in their direction. Dunn said he read the latest advisory to the caller, which said that the storm was expected to move through the Straits of Florida. The caller said he'd get the Florida East Coast Railway to send a train to evacuate the men in the camps.

During his testimony before Representative John Rankin's committee in 1936, Fred Ghent said that Ray Sheldon had phoned him in Jacksonville around 5:30 a.m. on Sunday, September 1, to advise him of Key West meteorologist G. S. Kennedy's warning that the storm might be dangerous in the Keys.

After his conversation with Sheldon, Ghent said, he phoned the Weather Bureau office in Jacksonville to ask about the storm advisory.

Neither Dunn nor Bennett mentioned a call by Norton to Ghent in their statements to Kennamer and Abt. But Ernest Carson, a Weather Bureau meteorologist in Miami, testified that he called Ray Sheldon's office at 3:30 a.m. on September 2 to advise the director that high tides and gale-force winds were expected in the Straits of Florida.

During the investigations, detailed telephone logs were compiled that showed every call that went out from or was received by the work camps' administrative office at the Hotel Matecumbe in Islamorada. The phone log was entered into the Congressional Record in 1936 during the House of Representatives' discussion of the bill to compensate families of veterans who'd been killed in the storm.

Similar phone logs and transcripts from FERA offices and other government officials discussing the hurricane tragedy eventually were turned over to the National Archives. None of the files found in the archives mention a phone call from Norton to Ghent.

Norton's heroic stature increased in the years following his death in 1954. He was posthumously awarded the Department of Commerce's Exceptional Service Gold Medal. In 1988 Robert Burpee, who was director of the National Hurricane Center, wrote an article titled "Grady Norton: Hurricane Forecaster and Communicator Extraordinaire" that was published in the journal *Weather and Forecasting*. The article included a section of "Reminiscences" written by people who had worked with Norton. Gordon Dunn, who had been interviewed in 1935 by David Kennamer, wrote about the Labor Day Hurricane of 1935 and the effort to evacuate the vets from the Keys on the train.

Dunn wrote that "the night before Labor Day," Norton "called the WPA office in Miami and issued a warning to evacuate the veterans." Dunn's account differed from Reno's anecdote. Dunn said Norton had called officials in Miami, while Reno said the call had been made to Ghent in Jacksonville.

The log of phone calls during the 24 hours before the hurricane struck the Keys included Carson's call to Sheldon at 3:30 a.m. on Monday, September 2, 1935. Carson was in Miami when he made the call. Phone records and testimony transcripts say that Carson's 3:30 a.m. call was made to Sheldon's office in Islamorada.

In 1993 Jane Wood Reno's anecdote about Norton calling Ghent was included in a collection of her writing published in a posthumous book titled *The Hell With Politics: The Life and Writings of Jane Wood Reno*. The book was edited by her grandson, George Hurchalla.

Reno's 1993 account of the incident differs from her 1954 story in the *Miami Daily News*. In her book she wrote that Norton called Ghent in Jacksonville "before dawn" on September 2. She also wrote that Norton told Ghent that "a hurricane might threaten the Florida Keys that day."

Reno wrote that Ghent responded to Norton's warning by calling Sheldon and instructing him to order the train "when it looks like the hurricane is going to hit the Keys."

Reno said nothing in her book about Norton's superiors ordering him to keep mum about the call.

⸺

Soon after the Labor Day Hurricane of 1935, Iver Olson gave his barometer to the U.S. Weather Bureau to test its accuracy. The meteorologists determined that the instrument was accurate, and that the mark Olson had made on its case corresponded to a barometric pressure reading of 26.35 inches, or 892 millibars. Based on the testing, that reading was accepted as the official low reading of the Labor Day Hurricane of 1935.

It's still the lowest reading ever recorded for a hurricane making landfall in the United States.

More than eight decades after the event, meteorologists are still marveling at the unworldly beast of a storm that struck the Florida Keys on September 2, 1935. In 1999 the Labor Day Hurricane of 1935 was designated the "storm of the century" by the Weather Channel.

The storm is still being studied. Two aspects of that hurricane are especially fascinating and elusive to contemporary science—the very powerful winds generated by the storm, and the rapidity with which those winds developed.

In 2014 a group of meteorologists headed by Chris Landsea of the National Oceanic and Atmospheric Administration used new data from studies of the relationship between lowest barometric pressure readings and maximum wind speeds to reexamine hurricanes that had formed in the Atlantic from 1931 to 1943.

The scientists determined that the Labor Day Hurricane of 1935 was more powerful than first thought. They concluded that the storm's peak sustained winds at landfall were around 184 mph. Before the study the 1935 hurricane's peak winds were thought to have been around 160 mph. At times the hurricane's winds undoubtedly exceeded 200 mph for a few seconds.

The winds were so powerful that NOAA meteorologist Brian Jarvinen, in a study published in 2006, noted that the Labor Day hurricane was off the charts for classifying the intensity of tropical cyclones. "Unequivocally, this hurricane could be a category 6 on the Saffir-Simpson Scale, if the scale provided for a storm higher than a category 5," Jarvinen wrote.

Two storms that were, at least for a while, more powerful than the Labor Day hurricane have formed in the Atlantic since 1935. In 1988, a barometric pressure reading of 26.13 inches, or 888 millibars, was recorded for Hurricane Gilbert as it traversed the northwestern Caribbean. And in 2005, Hurricane Wilma's barometric pressure bottomed out at 26.05 inches, or 882 millibars.

But neither of those hurricanes made landfall while at their peak intensity. The lowest verified reading for the 1935 hurricane was recorded as the storm was making landfall. And had Ed Butters's reading of 26.00 inches, or 880 millibars, been confirmed, the Labor Day storm would still be the most powerful on record for the Atlantic Basin. Unfortunately, Butters was so horrified when he saw the reading that he threw his barometer into the storm, and the accuracy of the instrument could not be confirmed.

The population explosion in the Keys since World War II has created new worries for hurricane forecasters and emergency management officials. In 1935, Ray Sheldon and Fred Ghent had to worry about getting a few hundred people out of the way of a hurricane in an evacuation that would have taken a few hours if it had been carried out. As the end of the second decade of the twenty-first century approaches, about 77,000 people live on the Florida Keys. Getting that many people off the islands to safety takes around three days, if everything goes smoothly.

And while forecasters and emergency management directors have hurricane tracking technology that could only have been dreamed of in Flash Gordon comic strips in 1935, it's a mixed blessing in the age of the internet. Much of the same information that is available to meteorologists is easily available online, and some coastal residents confronting an approaching hurricane make their own interpretation of the data and decide for themselves whether to evacuate or stay put.

"With all the information being provided on the internet, we get more and more tropical meteorologists out there every day. Millions of them," said former Monroe County Emergency Management director Billy Wagner. "I mean, everybody thinks they understand what's going on."

And as we head into the third decade of the twenty-first century, a debate about whether climate change related to human activity might be causing more destructive hurricanes also is raising questions about whether the "act of God" defense that John Abt and John Rankin used to deflect blame for the vets' deaths is still applicable when a powerful hurricane devastates the U.S. coast.

The prospect of another storm similar to the Labor Day Hurricane of 1935 haunts public safety officials in the Keys. Meteorologist Bryan Norcross, hurricane specialist for WPLG-TV in Miami, said the 1935 storm, along with Hurricane Andrew in 1992 and Hurricane Michael in 2018, "are the scariest class of storm."

"They develop quickly near land and continue intensifying as they come ashore," Norcross said.

Besides Hurricane Donna in 1960, other powerful storms have affected the Keys and caused massive damage since the 1935 hurricane.

Hurricane Wilma formed in the Caribbean Sea in mid-October 2005 and underwent a spectacular rapid development. By October 19 it was, for a few hours at least, the most powerful hurricane on record for the Atlantic Basin, which includes the Caribbean Sea and Gulf of Mexico. On that day its barometric pressure dropped to 26.05 inches, or 882 millibars, and its peak winds were around 185 mph.

When Wilma made landfall on Mexico's Yucatan Peninsula on October 21, it had lost some of its intensity but was still a devastating storm with 125 mph winds. From the Yucatan the storm made a right-angle turn like a billiard ball banking off the cushion of a pool table and took aim at Florida.

Wilma's eye stayed offshore as it passed Key West, and the city was spared from its worst winds. But on October 24, 2005, the hurricane sent seawater surging through Key West and the Keys.

Most structures were still standing after Hurricane Wilma passed, but the storm surge flooding put waist-deep water in hundreds of buildings and made homes uninhabitable. Affordable housing—already at a premium before Wilma—was nonexistent after the storm. There was an odd irony in that dilemma. In 1934, Key West turned to tourism because its residents were flat broke and the town was penniless. Seventy-one years later, tourism had created such a demand for housing that the people who maintained order and safety and kept the wheels of commerce turning—cops, firefighters, nurses, waiters and waitresses, cashiers, bartenders—could not afford to live in the Keys. Thousands of people left the islands in the years following Hurricane Wilma.

Still, the lure of the Keys is strong, and by September 2017, the islands' population had returned to its pre-Wilma level. But when the season that Ernest Hemingway described as "a more dangerous summer" arrived that year, newcomers and longtime residents anxiously watched the horizon as one of the most powerful hurricanes on record headed their way.

Its name was Irma.

CHAPTER TWELVE

Time Borrowed from the Wind

In the late summer of 2017, Patrick Garvey was on the verge of accomplishing a goal so unlikely that his attorney had strongly advised him not to take it on.

Garvey, an affable Canadian and former social worker, had set out to restore an overgrown, trash-filled, drug-infested fruit grove on Big Pine Key, about 25 miles up U.S. 1 from Key West. With some careful planning, a modest grant, and some very hard work by Garvey and a crew of volunteers, the old grove—known as Grimal Grove for Adolf Grimal, the eccentric engineer who established it in 1955—was blooming again.

And he was attracting attention. In June a film crew from a PBS affiliate TV station in West Palm Beach had visited the grove to shoot footage for an upcoming broadcast about Garvey's project.

The grove featured exotic fruit trees that Adolf Grimal had collected from all around the world and brought to Big Pine Key. Garvey had coaxed the grove into production and had recently opened a fruit store on U.S. 1 in Big Pine Key.

It was, Garvey acknowledged, a massive project. But things were falling into place. "We were just starting to get that momentum," he said.

On Tuesday, August 29, about 100 people gathered at The Place, a restaurant on Caroline Street in Key West, to watch the TV special about Grimal Grove. Garvey was thrilled by the turnout and all the publicity for his project. He knew that a tropical weather system was rumbling westward across the Atlantic Ocean, but he didn't give it much thought. This was South Florida, after all, and in August and September distant storms at sea are part of the backdrop of living there.

"In the back of my mind there was this little, possible storm," Garvey said. "But I've been living down here for 15 years, and it's hard to take too much thought to it when it's so far out."

Still, the world was hurricane-conscious in late August 2017. Only a few days earlier, Hurricane Harvey had inundated Houston and much of the Gulf Coast with more than five feet of rainfall in some places and blasted the area with peak winds of 130 mph.

Garvey sensed that this new system had the potential to cause trouble for someone. "We knew it was going to be a big one," he said.

This late August system did indeed have the pedigree to become "a big one." It had started its journey from the west coast of Africa near the Cape Verde Islands—a part of the Atlantic that has spawned some of history's worst hurricanes.

A few hours after the gathering in Key West, the unnamed storm's winds reached the threshold for official recognition by the National Hurricane Center in Miami. It became the ninth named storm of the 2017 Atlantic hurricane season and received the NHC's name beginning with "I"—Irma. It's an old-fashioned, meek-sounding name that might be associated with an unmarried, bespectacled aunt who works at the public library and sings in the church choir. But some of the fiercest hurricanes of the early twenty-first century had also received an "I" name.

There was Isabel in 2003, a storm whose peak winds at times approached 200 mph while it was still at sea. Isabel weakened considerably before making landfall on September 18, but it did heavy damage nonetheless from North Carolina to New York.

Hurricane Ivan in 2004 was a true beast of a hurricane whose 165 mph winds did catastrophic damage across the Caribbean Sea and produced measured waves more than 90 feet high in the Gulf of Mexico. Hurricane Ike dealt a crushing blow to Texas in 2008, and Hurricane Irene ripped across The Bahamas before making landfall in North Carolina in 2011.

The storm named Irma quickly began to live up to its fierce ancestry. It would become one of the most intense hurricanes on record to strike the Florida Keys—nowhere near as powerful as the Labor Day Hurricane of 1935 at landfall, but reminiscent of Hurricane Donna, which came ashore at Upper Matecumbe Key on September 10, 1960, with 145 mph winds.

Irma's strength gained momentum. In about 48 hours the storm's peak winds had increased by more than 80 mph. By 8 p.m. on Friday, September 1, Irma's winds exceeded 110 mph. It had become a major hurricane, and the rapidity with which it had strengthened was alarming. Only about one tropical storm in 30 intensifies this quickly.

It was the first of several records the storm would establish.

As Hurricane Irma approached the islands that form the eastern boundary of the Caribbean Sea, its winds cranked up to 145 mph. At 11 p.m. on Monday, September 4, hurricane warnings were issued for Puerto Rico and the U.S. Virgin Islands.

The storm continued to strengthen. And its eye turned slightly, first to the west and then to the west-northwest. The five-day forecast said Irma's eye would not enter the Caribbean but would scrape the Leeward Islands, miss Puerto Rico, and barge across The Bahamas and into the Straits of Florida by Saturday afternoon.

By noon on September 5, Irma's winds had reached 180 mph, and the hurricane's forecast track was moving a little more northward so that an eventual South Florida landfall seemed more likely. Its winds were capable of shoving houses off their foundations and ripping off their roofs—or simply shredding neighborhoods and scattering the lumber and shingles and drywall like sawdust in a summer breeze.

As hurricane edginess crept over millions of Florida residents, radio commentator Rush Limbaugh—broadcasting from his home in Palm Beach—offered a few thoughts about hurricane hysteria.

"So there is a desire to advance this climate change agenda," Limbaugh opined on his broadcast of Tuesday, September 5, "and hurricanes are one of the fastest and best ways to do it. You can accomplish a lot just by creating fear and panic. You don't need a hurricane to hit anywhere. All you need is to create the fear and panic accompanied by talk that climate change is causing hurricanes to become bigger and more dangerous, and you create the panic, and it's mission accomplished, agenda advanced."

Limbaugh's comments outraged many, including Al Roker, a meteorologist and weather anchor for NBC's *Today* show. Roker took to Twitter to blast Limbaugh, saying his remark "borders on criminal."

Around 2 a.m. on Wednesday, September 6, Hurricane Irma's eye crossed the tiny island of Barbuda, once a favorite vacation spot for Princess Diana. The storm's 180 mph winds left little standing. About 95 percent of the island's buildings were damaged or destroyed. The island's schools, both hotels, and its only hospital were smashed. For all practical purposes the island was uninhabitable.

"Barbuda is now literally rubble," Prime Minister Gaston Browne said after the storm had departed. "It is heart-wrenching, absolutely devastating."

The hurricane gave nearby Saint Martin a similar thrashing. An anemometer clocked a gust of 199 mph before the fierce winds disabled it. Trees were torn out of the ground, roots and all, and flung away like weeds plucked from a garden. Cars were picked up, flipped a few times, and dropped. Buildings were simply demolished. Around 60 percent of the buildings on Saint Martin were left uninhabitable.

There's no way of knowing whether Florida governor Rick Scott—who told his staff when he took office in 2011 that they could not make public comments that included the phrases "climate change" or "global warming"— was aware of Limbaugh's comments. But around noon on the day following Limbaugh's radio show, Scott broadcast an urgent appeal to Florida residents to take the hurricane forecasts seriously and get out of harm's way.

"It is life-threatening," Scott said of Hurricane Irma. "This is not a storm you can sit and wait through."

To encourage evacuation, Scott said fees would be suspended on the state's toll roads.

Around the same time, Monroe County Emergency Management officials issued a "mandatory" evacuation order for all Keys residents. There was no penalty for anyone who did not leave. The order was more like a stern warning, but it had an effect.

"By Wednesday, the air in the Keys started to change," said Patrick Garvey. "And people were starting to get a little worried about the whole thing. Every day it started looking like we were more and more vulnerable. My friends started leaving in their RVs and stuff."

Those friends were urging Garvey to come with them. His wife and daughters were visiting his wife's family in Brazil, where they would wait until the storm had passed before returning to Florida.

With his family out of harm's way, Garvey's concerns were more focused on his own safety and protecting his property. He faced the dilemma that always confronts anyone who is in the path of a bad hurricane that is still hundreds of miles away—how do you know that if you leave, you won't be avoiding the storm but walking right into the worst of it.

"I felt confident that I'd survive the storm and come up with a game plan to stay here," Garvey said.

Hurricane Irma's eye passed just to the north of Puerto Rico around 8 p.m. on Wednesday, September 6, and around 4 a.m. the following day the storm center passed north of the island of Hispaniola.

In Florida, preparations for Irma ramped up. The Tampa Bay Rays baseball team was en route to Boston for a weekend series with the Red Sox, and team officials decided to close the team's offices in St. Petersburg so employees could get ready for the storm.

Highways were clogged with northbound traffic, while residents who hadn't evacuated tried to sort through a series of unpleasant choices about staying or going. Some didn't have the money to leave or didn't want to endure the endlessly snarled traffic. Others didn't want to leave because they didn't know when they'd be able to return to their homes.

Among those who did evacuate was Rush Limbaugh, who told his listeners Thursday, September 7 that it would be impossible for him to make his daily broadcast from his studios in his Palm Beach mansion. Limbaugh told his listeners he'd be back on the air the following week, broadcasting "from parts unknown."

Irma had weakened some by Thursday evening, but not much. The storm's peak winds were blowing at around 175 mph when its eye slammed into Turks and Caicos Islands around 7:30 p.m. When Irma departed, the Blue Hills neighborhood on the island of Providenciales was just gone.

Around the time Blue Hills was disintegrating beneath Irma's winds, Charlotte "Charley" Wilson, who owned Date & Thyme Cafe, a small restaurant in Key West, decided to take a break from her hurricane preparation and ride her bike from her home on Fogarty Street to the pier at the foot of White Street.

"I just wanted to cycle out to the pier because something called me down there, to go and just see, to feel and see it," she said.

Key West residents had been scrutinizing five-day forecasts all week. They'd watched Irma's forecast track become more centered on the Keys, and they'd heard the governor urge them to get off the islands. The city was emptying, and the streets were nearly deserted. As Wilson pedaled down White Street, it occurred to her that, with the departure of thousands of people, it was like "a huge weight had been lifted off the island."

"Almost like the island could breathe again," she said. "It was light, and there was a stillness. Many, many people had evacuated."

The city's routines had been forced to a halt. "Our lives had stopped," Wilson said. "Everything had stopped. Doesn't happen very often, unless it's forced."

At the White Street pier, Wilson discovered that her friend Carol Tedesco had been drawn by the same force that had lured her to the ocean's edge for a few moments of contemplation about what lay ahead.

Sunsets in Key West are so routinely spectacular that the city's residents have turned it into a daily excuse for a party. Tourists and locals gather at Mallory Square to watch performers, sample chewy deep-fried conch fritters, sip beers, and hope for a glimpse of the elusive green flash— a green aura that sometimes appears around the sun for a split second as it slides behind the horizon.

A distant hurricane can rearrange the atmosphere and greatly enhance sunsets, and that's partly what drew Wilson and Tedesco to the White Street pier. But as the friends stood on the pier and gazed out at the Atlantic and the departing sun, they saw a sight that was both beautiful and eerie.

"It was very surreal," Tedesco said. "The sea creatures had all come into the shallows. And they were jumping and feeding, and the pelicans were flying low. It felt more unreal than real. Less of this world than of some other."

The elegant lighting of the sunset cast the strangely beautiful scene in luminous, vibrant colors that reminded Tedesco of a Maxfield Parrish painting.

The women watched the sun depart and the agitated sea creatures. They talked about their plans. Both planned to ride out the storm in Key West. They left the pier and went back to their preparations.

Later that night, Governor Rick Scott made another announcement. Around 11 p.m. he ordered all public schools—including colleges and universities—to close from Friday, September 8, to Monday, September 11. His order automatically canceled all college football games in the state that had been scheduled for Saturday, September 9.

University of Florida football coach Jim McElwain was philosophical about the cancellation of the Gators' game against the University of Northern Colorado that had been scheduled for Gainesville. "Sometimes, third down and seven is not the most important thing in life," McElwain said.

Deprived of their football, some Floridians repurposed their team spirit to rally an edgy state looking into the muzzle of a fierce hurricane. In Jacksonville, Lisa Coppedge posted a sign on her Facebook page in the University of Florida's familiar orange and blue school colors. "Go Florida," the post read. "Beat Irma."

The National Football League followed Scott's example and canceled the scheduled game between the Miami Dolphins and Tampa Bay Buccaneers.

Hurricane Irma lost a little of its intensity as it approached The Bahamas, but it still had 155 mph winds when it slammed into Little Inagua Island around 1 a.m. on Friday, September 8.

The storm emerged from The Bahamas Friday afternoon and began re-intensifying as it moved toward Cuba.

In the Keys, residents of Big Pine Key and other islands looked out at sunshine, a partly cloudy sky, and waters that were rippled by a light breeze.

About 50 miles to the northeast in Islamorada, Richie Russell watched a steady caravan of cars streaming northward on U.S. 1.

"There was a mass exodus," Russell said. "But it was fairly orderly."

Still, the traffic was moving very slowly. "Took forever for them to get to Orlando," Russell said. "Florida's Turnpike and the Sunshine Expressway, everything was backed up."

Russell, the nephew of the late Bernard Russell, was athletic director at Coral Shores High School in nearby Tavernier, and lived with his wife and daughter on the bayside of Upper Matecumbe Key. His house was only a few hundred feet from where his ancestors' sturdy storm shelter had stood before it was demolished by the Labor Day Hurricane of 1935. Only about 200 feet away from Russell's home was a house built by another uncle, Floyd Russell, also a Labor Day hurricane survivor.

Floyd Russell had grown up with a profound understanding of the power of the sea. He'd lived with his family in one of the so-called Red Cross houses that the American Red Cross had built for survivors of the Labor Day Hurricane of 1935. In 1960 the houses' foot-thick, steel-reinforced concrete walls had withstood Hurricane Donna, the most powerful storm to strike the Keys since the hurricane of September 2, 1935.

Donna followed a track similar to the 1935 hurricane. But while the 1935 storm had not become a deadly monster until the last minute before its landfall, Donna intensified quickly. As the storm approached the Leeward Islands at the northeastern edge of the Caribbean Sea, its winds reached 160 mph. Donna inflicted massive damage on the islands. The hurricane weakened slightly as it crossed The Bahamas, but it regained power as it bore down on the Keys.

The *Miami News* reported that Donna hit the Keys "like a bomb" on September 10, 1960. Its peak sustained winds were 145 mph, occasionally gusting to as much as 175 mph. A meteorologist at the U.S. Weather Bureau told the *News* that Donna "was releasing energy equivalent to the explosion of a hydrogen bomb every eight minutes."

Donna's eye crossed the islands at Conch Key, about five miles southwest of where the eye of the Labor Day Hurricane of 1935 had crossed the Long Key Fishing Camp.

In 1960 the Florida Keys were no longer the isolated, sparsely populated islands they'd been in 1935. Tourist attractions and housing developments aimed at retirees were beginning to dot the islands. Developers such as Phil Sadowski—a Detroit native who'd built projects in Pensacola and Miami—built Marathon Shores, one of the Keys' earliest housing developments, in the early 1950s.

The Indies House, a swank hotel on Duck Key built by Canadian financier Bryan Newkirk, had opened in December 1959.

Hurricane Donna clobbered Marathon Shores and the Indies House and nearly everything else in its path. The Indies House was uninhabitable. Marathon Shores was leveled.

Adjusted for inflation, Hurricane Donna inflicted almost $8 billion in damages before it dissipated. Building codes and wind-load minimums had not yet been imposed on new construction in the Florida Keys, and many structures built after World War II were destroyed.

But the steel-and-concrete Red Cross houses where Floyd Russell and Bernard Russell now lived withstood the hurricane. It was a lesson Floyd Russell didn't forget when he built his own house in Islamorada in 1973. He repeated the Red Cross houses' formula on a larger scale. His spacious two-story house overlooking Florida Bay had foot-thick concrete walls reinforced by steel. The second story was more than 19 feet above sea level—out of reach of even the 1935 hurricane's deadly storm surge. The roof also was made of reinforced concrete and anchored to the house by steel rods.

Floyd Russell later sold the house and moved to St. Petersburg, but the new owners had assured Richie Russell that he and his family were welcome to ride out any hurricane there.

But while the house had withstood many hurricanes in the 44 years since it had been built, it had been built after Hurricane Donna and never faced a monster storm like Hurricane Irma. Richie Russell decided to call his uncle, now 93 years old, and ask him if he thought he should entrust the lives of his family to the house.

Floyd Russell said the house would withstand the storm. Richie Russell decided to stay put.

A little farther up the coast, Floridians of limited means were trying to find shelter. In Miami Beach, a young man was trying to find a public bus to get his wife and young son to a shelter. Volunteers were driving homeless people to shelters.

Elsewhere, people who didn't own personal computers or cell phones asked strangers to direct them to shelters.

Meanwhile, portable generators, bottled water, and nonperishable food were being sold almost as fast as they could be uncrated and displayed.

The Tampa Bay Rays had three home games against the New York Yankees scheduled at Tropicana Field in St. Petersburg for Monday, September 11, through Wednesday, September 13. But Major League Baseball officials told the team not to return to Florida after its game Sunday in Boston against the Red Sox. Instead, the Rays were told to go to New York, where they'd play their American League rivals, the Yankees, at Citi Field, the home field of the National League New York Mets.

The Rays would be designated the home team, but they wouldn't have much of a home-field advantage when the Yankees were playing only about 10 miles from Yankee Stadium.

Rays' outfielder Steven Souza Jr. said the games against the Yankees were going to be a strange experience. "I was thinking about [the hurricane] this morning," Souza said. "Some people spent their life's savings getting a house in Florida and may never get to go back to it. Stuff can always be replaced, but that's a tragic thing."

Rays' manager Kevin Cash said the storm probably would distract his players.

"It's going to be very eerie on Sunday, if it's projected to hit at that point, and we're in the middle of a ballgame," Cash said. "I'm not sure how people will deal with it. I think a lot of our thoughts will be back at home with our community."

In the Straits of Florida, Hurricane Irma was regaining the strength it had lost crossing The Bahamas. By around 5 p.m. on Friday, September 8, Irma's peak winds were about 155 mph. Forecasters thought it was likely to make landfall Sunday in the Keys as a Category 5 hurricane.

On Big Pine Key, Patrick Garvey was reconsidering his decision to ride out the storm in the islands. "By Friday night, the storm is getting closer and stronger, and you're starting to feel some [storm] bands," he said. "I had a friend from the Coast Guard call me, and he's like, 'Man, get the hell out of there.'"

Garvey started packing to leave the islands, but then changed his mind again. He'd ride out Hurricane Irma in a nearby school that was being opened as a storm shelter.

In Key West, some who had resisted the urge to evacuate earlier were unsettled by the Friday evening forecast and decided to get out. Charley Wilson was among them. Around 10 p.m. she loaded her car and headed up the islands. She'd decided to ride out the storm 200 miles up the Florida coast in Delray Beach.

Florida officials were trying to meet the huge demand for gasoline for people leaving ahead of the hurricane. Tankers were rolling into the state, and Governor Rick Scott ordered that the trucks be escorted to their destinations by the Florida Highway Patrol.

Hurricane Irma's eye touched Cuba around 11 p.m. on Friday, bringing 160 mph winds to Camagüey Province on the island's northern coast. The storm's movement slowed to around 7 mph, and the landmass of Cuba started doing what it's done to so many hurricanes before they've made a run for Florida. Irma's circulation was disrupted, and it began to weaken.

By 5 a.m. Saturday, September 9 the storm's peak winds were down to around 155 mph, and they'd slowed to around 125 mph by 2 p.m.

In Islamorada, Phyllis and Bob Mitchell had been pondering all week whether to ride out the storm in their bayside home or get out. Phyllis Mitchell sat down to jot a few thoughts into a hurricane diary she'd started.

"Constant traffic on highway," she wrote. "People driving down to secure homes, heading north to evacuate. People leaving all week and having more reports of no gas and no place to stay. Call from a friend who evacuated Friday, said he couldn't find a place to stay, long lines in gas stations. He finally got gas and drove 25 hours to find a place to sleep in Tennessee!"

Their friend's experience settled their decision. They were worn out from getting their home ready for the storm anyway. They'd ride out the hurricane in Islamorada.

As soon as it was apparent that Hurricane Irma was likely to head toward the Florida Keys, people of all faiths—as well as people who claimed no faith—made their way to Windsor Lane in Key West, where Our Lady of Lourdes Grotto is tucked into the grounds of The Basilica of Saint Mary Star of the Sea. While traffic backed up with evacuees on U.S. 1 around the corner, they entered the grotto for a few moments of prayer or contemplation. Many of them lit candles.

People have been going to the grotto for nearly a century to seek protection from approaching hurricanes. The shrine was built by Sister Louis Gabriel, who joined the convent at Saint Mary in August 1897.

A few weeks after she joined the convent, Key West was hit by a hurricane. More powerful storms struck the city during the next 22 years, including a storm that devastated the city in 1919.

After the 1919 storm, Sister Mary Louis decided to build a grotto where people could pray for protection whenever a powerful storm was roaming the nearby seas. She dedicated the grotto on her 25th anniversary as a nun in 1922. The sister is said to have declared that Key West would never be hit by the full force of a hurricane so long as the grotto stood.

So far, she's been right. Going to the grotto when a hurricane is near has become deeply ingrained in Key West residents.

In 2004 the state was battered by four major storms between mid-August and late September. A faithful patron of the venerable Green Parrot Bar, which opened on Whitehead Street seven years before Sister Mary Louis arrived in Key West, installed a "hurricane preparedness kit" in the saloon. Its contents were simple—a Saint Jude votive candle, a pack of matches, and printed instructions saying that when a hurricane is near, the user should break the glass, remove the candle and matches, "haul ass to grotto," light the candle, and pray.

Reverend John C. Baker, Rector of The Basilica of Saint Mary's Star of the Sea, held a Mass at the grotto on Saturday. People kept coming throughout the day and into the night, and many candles flickered in the grotto.

Not far away, on Whitehead Street, where author Ernest Hemingway had put up storm shutters and fretted about whether his fishing yacht, the *Pilar*, would make it through the Labor Day Hurricane of 1935, employees of the Ernest Hemingway Home and Museum got the author's former residence ready for Irma. Among their tasks was rounding up 54 cats—many of them descendants of the six-toed felines kept by Hemingway when he lived there in the 1930s—and getting them inside the house's 18-inch-thick stone walls.

The author's granddaughter, actress Mariel Hemingway, urged the museum's general manager, Jacque Sands, to load up the cats and get out. But Sands refused, telling the *New York Times* that she had an obligation to see the property and the cats through the hurricane.

Some of the cats seemed to know that something unusual was happening. When the staff started rounding them up, some of the felines dashed inside.

Although most tourists left Key West, a few stayed behind, and they were roaming the city despite the rainfall and rising wind from the approaching storm.

The Southernmost Point marker—a massive, squat, 12-foot-tall hunk of concrete shaped like a marine buoy and painted with broad, bright multicolored stripes—has been a tourist favorite since the 1980s. Usually when tourists come to the marker that overlooks the Atlantic Ocean at the confluence of South and Whitehead Streets, they look out at a rippled saltwater lake, thanks to the reefs several miles offshore.

But the seas grew steadily more raucous on Saturday, September 8, as storm-driven waves rolled across the reef, barreled toward shore, and broke against a seawall with great foamy eruptions of spray at the Southernmost Point marker.

A steady stream of visitors made their way to the landmark. Some took selfies with the rowdy surf and concrete marker in the background. Others posed or waved at a webcam mounted across the street from the marker. A few were drenched when they turned their backs to the ocean just before a large wave piled into the seawall.

Up the islands in Islamorada, Richie Russell was amazed at the deserted U.S. 1.

"It was like circa 1960," he said. "There was no traffic."

Russell went to visit a friend who lived a couple of miles from his house. He saw only one car—a police cruiser—during his brief trip.

At Big Pine Key, Patrick Garvey was making his final preparations.

Winds from Irma's outer circulation were already clawing at Grimal Grove, and some of the fruit trees were going down. Around 3 p.m. Garvey got his dog and drove to the nearby school being used as a shelter.

There were no restrictions, and the people taking refuge there brought their pets. About 50 people and around 200 animals eventually would ride out the storm there. "It felt like Noah's Ark," Garvey said.

Garvey's neighbor Tim Stanton planned to ride out the hurricane with friends at a True Value Hardware store on Big Pine Key. Stanton, who'd lived on the island for eight years, was born in Cleveland during a snowstorm and came to Big Pine because he "can't stand the cold."

When his father, the late author Will Stanton, moved his family to Pennsylvania, Tim built greenhouses in which his mother grew "mountains of orchids, and passion flowers."

Those memories of his mother's greenhouses and her fondness for tropical flowers came back to him when he saw Big Pine's lush vegetation, and that recollection cemented his bond to the Keys. "I didn't plan on going anywhere else," he said.

Stanton's fondness for the islands is shared by lots of other people. By 2017 more than 77,000 people lived in the Florida Keys. On any given day, thousands of tourists are coming and going in the islands. Housing is at a premium, and affordable housing is almost nonexistent.

Big Pine Key is home to what passes for affordable housing in the Keys, with parks for mobile homes and recreational vehicles.

Stanton had struggled for a while to make ends meet, living modestly in an RV. By the summer of 2017, he'd cobbled together a decent living as a craftsman and entrepreneur. He'd saved enough money to buy a used BMW convertible and made a name for himself fashioning high-quality ukuleles around such unlikely objects as wooden cigar boxes.

On Saturday afternoon Stanton busied himself making final preparations for the storm before joining his friends in the hardware store.

On the peninsula, people who'd stayed behind were also taking care of last-minute details before going to storm shelters. Residents who lived in mobile home parks took a last look as they departed for shelters. Many assumed their homes would be gone when they returned.

Some people did small but vital favors for others. In Tampa, taxi driver Michael Bryant stood in a long line in the heat outside a storm shelter so his rider, a 90-year-old woman, could wait in his taxi while he registered for her.

Others were more lighthearted. Playing off the mounting fear of an impending devastating hurricane, a bar in downtown St. Petersburg called the Iberian Rooster threw an "Irma-geddon" party.

Thick clouds hung over Walt Disney World's Magic Kingdom near Orlando. Park personnel had removed Halloween decorations from Main Street USA and taken down the facades of some of the buildings as a precaution against high winds. Disney officials had already announced that the park would be closing early, and the crowd was a little smaller than usual.

Around 6 p.m. an announcement was made over loudspeakers that the park would close at 9 p.m., and the spectacular lights and fireworks show that usually ended each day's entertainment was canceled.

As the Disney patrons were listening to the announcement, things were getting raucous in the Keys. By 6 p.m. a heavy, wind-driven rain was sweeping across Big Pine Key. But Irma's interaction with land as it moved along

Cuba's northern coast had dragged the storm's peak winds down to about 125 mph. The storm's eye was still raking along the big island's northern coast. It would be a couple of hours before Irma started its inevitable northward turn, and it would lose a little more power.

Shortly after 8 p.m. Irma's movement slowed to around 6 mph and it began the turn. Power was starting to go out in Key West, and Carol Tedesco decided to ride out the hurricane with friends in a 1951-vintage office building on Eaton Street. The concrete-and-steel Art Deco–style building housed an artists' collective. About a dozen people, including a reporter and a photographer from the *Miami Herald*, took shelter there.

The power also was going out in Islamorada, where Phyllis Mitchell was trying to discuss the hurricane and preparations with friends on Facebook. "Being connected to others is very important," she noted in her diary. "When you are not, it is an uneasy situation."

At Big Pine Key the electricity went out shortly after 8 p.m.

By 11 p.m. Irma's eye was pulling away from Cuba. At that moment the storm's center was about 80 miles due south of the Seven Mile Bridge that connects Knights Key and Little Duck Key. The hurricane had not fared well during its trek along Cuba's northern coast. Its winds had dropped to less than 111 mph. But it would have several hours over the warm waters of the Straits of Florida as it churned toward the Keys, and its winds were expected to crank up again as it approached the islands.

Florida residents were glued to their TV screens with a mixture of fascination and dread as they watched around-the-clock coverage of the storm. Hurricane Irma's circulation was now 400 miles wide—wider than the peninsula. The storm's eye was expected to traverse the entire 447-mile length of the state. About 6.4 million people—almost one-third of the state's population—had been ordered to evacuate, and the state's governor had pleaded with them to get out ahead of the storm.

Irma's size and its trek from south to north up the peninsula meant that most of the state would be subjected to high winds and heavy rainfall.

"Florida lives longitudinally," said Jeff Houck, a former *Tampa Tribune* reporter who worked in public relations in Tampa. "Kids go to college north and south. Parents live elsewhere. Grandparents and relatives are sprinkled throughout the state. People have little concept that you can drive for 10 hours in the state and never leave it."

Saturday forecasts warned that Hurricane Irma would plow into the Keys with winds exceeding 130 mph, maintain or increase its strength as it made a short run across a corner of the Gulf of Mexico, and barrel into Naples and the southwest peninsula as a devastating Category 4 storm. Even worse, it was expected to still have winds exceeding 130 mph as it passed near or over Tampa.

Staring at the forecast track brought out a grim sense of humor among some residents. "Tracking Irma is like seeing a drunk driver headed your way," an anonymous reader posted on the website of the *Tallahassee Democrat*.

"It's sort of like waiting for Mike Tyson to hit you," Houck said. "You know it's going to happen. It's just a matter of when."

Hurricane Irma was making the most of its brief trip across the Gulf of Mexico. Its peak winds were strengthening. As its eye drew closer to the Keys, its winds cranked up again to more than 130 mph.

The landfall forecast for Irma's eye—and its most devastating winds— had been nudged to the northeast of Key West. Cudjoe Key and Big Pine Key, about 25 miles from Key West, now were on the bullseye.

Tim Stanton tried to get some sleep at the hardware store on Big Pine Key. But he awakened several times throughout the night. "The wind had been howling," Stanton said. "If you woke up any time during the night it was always windy."

As daybreak approached and Irma's eye came nearer to the Keys, the tenor of the wind changed.

"As the morning went on, it got a little more intense," Stanton said, "and eventually it was just that way for so long, there wasn't so much a lot of gusting. It was just really heavy, consistently high winds. There was just this consistent kind of roar."

Around 7:30 a.m. on Sunday, September 10, Hurricane Irma's eye was approaching landfall. Residents with anemometers at Big Pine Key were clocking winds out of the northeast at 100 mph, and the winds were increasing. The windblown rainfall was horizontal. Irma's full wrath was at the doorstep.

Big Pine Key started going underwater around 9 a.m. The storm surge moved slowly, gradually creeping over the island. Soon Big Pine Key was covered with saltwater, and the winds had increased to more than 110 mph.

Stanton peeked at the storm from the hardware store.

"Right before the eyewall, you could see the surge coming in from the highway," he said.

Soon U.S. 1 was covered in several feet of saltwater. Eventually the surge would nearly cover the shrubbery in front of the hardware store, leaving only a few inches of leaves above the water.

On No Name Key—where the ferry had carried passengers and cars to and from Key West before the Labor Day Hurricane of 1935—Jeremy McQuarter and five friends were riding out Hurricane Irma in a well-constructed concrete house elevated above the island.

McQuarter later told the *South Florida Sun Sentinel* that the house "shook like an earthquake" during the storm. "We had two hours of winds that were 130 mph," McQuarter said.

Around 10 a.m. the winds suddenly died. Hurricane Irma's eye had arrived. The island was still under seawater that nearly covered mailboxes.

On the peninsula, residents who hadn't left the state were going by the thousands to public storm shelters. For at least a few residents, their experiences in storm shelters had a profound effect on them. One would later say that the experience changed her life.

Judith Zaroff, a self-described "healthy 75-year-old woman who leads a relatively insulated and complacent life in a country club development," spent three nights in a shelter in Boca Raton. "What I witnessed there altered many of my preconceived notions of those less fortunate than I," she said.

"Most of my 'shelter-mates' were no strangers to adversity and seemed more prepared for it," Zaroff later wrote in the *South Florida Sun Sentinel*. The people around her "were worried but hopeful, polite and caring," she said.

"I have grown," Zaroff said. "An experience that I feared morphed into one that expanded my view of life and all its people."

In the Keys the winds resumed with renewed fury around noon. Within a few minutes the winds leaped from around 70 mph to more than 120 mph. Irma was back at full blast. On Big Pine Key, residents who'd stayed behind felt their houses shake and vibrate beneath their feet. When they looked out through their high-impact windows, all they could see was a raging white turmoil of storm-driven rain and foamy seawater.

Although Irma's eye was expected to stay on the west coast of the peninsula, the size of the storm meant that the entire state would feel its effects.

Damaging winds already were tearing at the tip of the peninsula. In Miami, two dozen construction cranes towered over the skyline. The rising winds ripped and pulled at them, and finally two of the cranes buckled and came crashing down. The falling cranes caused heavy damage, but no one was injured.

In Fort Lauderdale, cops arrested nine people who'd braved the storm's winds to take advantage of deserted businesses. Security cameras caught them stealing from a pawn shop and a sporting goods store.

Almost three million homes and businesses across Florida had already lost power.

The Sunday morning track forecast for Hurricane Irma showed it going over Tampa Bay around 2 a.m. Monday as a Category 3 hurricane, meaning that its peak sustained winds were expected to be between 111 mph and 130 mph. Forecasters warned that Irma could fling out tornadoes during its long trek up the peninsula, and they expected the state to take a pounding.

Weather Channel forecaster Bryan Norcross warned viewers that Florida had never been threatened by a hurricane like this one before.

"The damaging wind—especially falling trees and power lines—will cover all of the state of Florida, except for the far western panhandle," Norcross posted on his blog.

All along Irma's forecasted path, people made last-minute decisions to leave, or redoubled their efforts to prepare for a bad blow.

Closets and interior windowless rooms were cleaned out and reconfigured as "safe rooms," and stocked with mattresses, flashlights, bottled water, and food for people and pets.

Storm chasers Greg Nordstrom, a meteorology professor at Mississippi State University, and Michael Laca, producer of the website TropMet, were waiting for Hurricane Irma in a parking deck in Naples, about 170 miles southwest of Tampa.

With them were Devin Thomas, a storm-chaser from New York, and Dylan Federico and Brant Beckman, meteorology students at Mississippi State. The storm-chasers settled into a four-story concrete parking deck at the corner of Eighth Street South and Fourth Avenue South in downtown Naples, about four blocks from the Gulf of Mexico.

There wasn't much for anyone to do except wait. Boredom crept in. In Tampa, people went down to the bay to see a bizarre sight—Irma's massive, powerful circulation had pulled the water out of the bay. People were walking around on mud and sand that once had been covered by saltwater. Hundreds of selfies were snapped before police ordered everyone back to shore.

While the peninsula braced for Hurricane Irma, Key West residents ventured from their shelters to see what the storm had done to their city. Candles were still burning in the grotto at The Basilica of Saint Mary's Star of the Sea on Sunday morning. The city had gotten roughed up by Irma, but it could have been much worse. As the dying winds signaled the departure of the storm, Key West's relentless spirit showed itself. A man wearing a black T-shirt, black shorts, and flip-flops and carrying a large American flag picked his way through the debris and downed tree limbs on Eaton Street.

Still, trees were down, cars were damaged, and landmarks altered—or destroyed. A house on Williams Street owned by the late author and poet Shel Silverstein was wrecked by a falling tree. And the side of the Southernmost Point marker that was exposed to wind and storm-driven water had been scrubbed down to the bare concrete.

It was much worse only a few miles up U.S. 1.

Most of the water had receded when Tim Stanton left the hardware store in Big Pine Key to check on his home. But there were still large puddles in low spots. As Stanton walked toward his home, he saw a woman wading through one of the standing puddles stop, reach down, and pick up a large lobster from the water.

The vegetation that had been blasted by wind and soaked by saltwater was already showing the effect. "The leaves that didn't blow right off the trees turned brown," Stanton said. "You could practically see it happen, like, within a couple hours."

As Stanton continued toward his residence, he saw a strange sight—an open coffin, carried out of the showroom of a nearby funeral home and deposited on a street corner.

Stanton discovered that a tree had fallen on his house, and it had been flooded by about 18 inches of water.

He was now homeless.

He went to check on the home of friends whose cottage overlooked the water. They had recently upgraded their house to make it more resistant to a hurricane. Among the improvements was installing storm windows that would stand up to a hurricane's fierce winds.

A house next door that did not have the hardened windows had been gutted by the fierce winds. But when Stanton checked his friends' house, he made a startling discovery. The hurricane-proof windows had been a liability instead of an asset. One of the walls with the special windows had been blown off the cottage and now lay in the backyard. The hurricane-proof windows had stood up to Irma's winds. But while the windows had not given way, the wall could not take the pressure and had finally blown out.

In one Big Pine Key neighborhood, some elevated homes had been smashed and shredded by Irma's winds.

Early damage assessments in the Keys were starting to filter in to emergency management officials, and the news was not good. In addition to the damage at Big Pine Key, there were reports of massive damage on Cudjoe Key and Summerland Key, where the storm's eye had crossed.

Heavy damage also was reported in Islamorada, which had been on the strong side of the storm's circulation. Islamorada resident Bob Lodge said seaweed had been forced through door louvres, and swimming pools were "full of fish and crab, all kinds of sand."

"I make a comparison to Hemingway's comment that it looked like the whole bottom of the sea had gone across Indian Key," Lodge said, recalling the author's statement in his letter to his editor, Maxwell Perkins, after the Labor Day Hurricane of 1935. "This probably was similar to what happened there."

Emergency management officials promised that help would soon be arriving. Giant C-130 cargo planes flown by Air National Guard pilots would be landing two at a time at the airport in Marathon starting Monday, said Monroe County Emergency Management director Martin Senterfitt.

Around 3:30 p.m. Sunday, Irma's eye came ashore on Marco Island, just south of Naples. The storm's peak sustained winds were down to about 115 mph, but the Marco Island Police Department clocked a gust of 130 mph as the eye passed.

Irma's once-massive power continued to diminish. But it was still packing a punch. The eyewall reached the storm-chasers in the parking deck around 3:45 p.m. Sunday.

Storm-chaser Michael Laca estimated the eyewall's sustained winds at about 100 mph. The heavy, wind-driven rain created a near-whiteout around the parking deck, and the chasers could only see a blurred outline of nearby buildings and palm trees being thrashed by the storm.

And the hurricane was not quite finished with its hair-raising winds. Several times as the eyewall passed, the parking deck was blasted with intense gusts that may have reached 140 mph. A mile and a half from the deck, the Naples airport clocked a gust of 142 mph.

A few minutes past 4:30 p.m., a gust that Greg Nordstrom estimated exceeded 130 mph roared past the parking deck. It may have been the weakening hurricane's final fierce blast. A few minutes later, winds started dying down and the sky began lightening.

Irma's weakening lifted spirts farther up the peninsula's coast. In Tampa, Jeff Houck and his family had finished their preparation for the storm. Houck stretched out for a nap.

"Woke up two hours later to a markedly different storm and a house full of happy family," Houck said.

Still, Irma wasn't finished with Florida.

"Sheets of rain pass my window," Houck said. "Oak trees and crepe myrtles bending and bowing in the gusts. We started to empty a walk-in closet for shelter when it was a Cat 4 storm. By the time I awakened, there was no reason to continue.

"The rain has been nonstop for hours as nasty bands swirl through my neighborhood. The house across the street looks like it's in a gas station car wash, the spray is so intense."

While Houck watched Irma's fading wrath, his son Brian—a student at Florida Gulf Coast University in Fort Myers, who was riding out the storm with his parents—exchanged hurricane anecdotes with his friends on Snapchat.

Houck also was monitoring social media commentary on the storm. People clearly were relieved.

"Fascinating to see the change in tone online with reports of the storm weakening," Houck noted. "Proposed drinking games are now appearing. Shots of drones skirting Bayshore Boulevard to show portions of the bay with dry beds. News anchors posting selfies with meteorologists.

"Three hours ago, we were on the verge of cataclysm. Now the storm seems like a courage badge, despite the eye of it not having reached Tampa yet. Yeah, this was the real deal. Every second of it. And it isn't over. This is when people get hurt, thinking it's no big deal. Then they step on downed power lines or take flying debris to the head."

In Bartow, about 45 miles east of Tampa, Bonnie Ley and her partner, Andy Edmund, were riding out the storm in their vintage-1900 house that had stood up to Hurricane Donna in 1960 and Hurricane Charley in 2004. Ley and Edmund didn't think there would be any problem with Irma.

The power went out in Bartow around 10 p.m. Sunday. Around 11:30 p.m. Ley and Edmund heard a terrifying "boom," and water began pouring through the ceiling. Irma's winds had ripped the roof off the house. They put out buckets and pans to catch the water, then waited for the storm's winds to subside some. Around 2:30 a.m. they left the house and moved to a motel.

"I've lived here all my life," Edmund later told the *Tampa Bay Times*. "I've been through a lot of hurricanes, and I've never seen one like this. One that just uprooted trees and dropped them all twisted and snapped."

Irma continued to weaken as it moved up the peninsula. By 8 a.m. Monday, September 11, its winds had dropped to around 70 mph.

In Islamorada, Phyllis Mitchell noted in her hurricane diary, "Extremely hot, bright and sunny, with sounds of generators, soon to turn into (sounds of) chainsaws."

Trees and other vegetation on their property were heavily damaged, but their home was intact. Still, they could not communicate with the outside world. "No one knows we are OK," Mitchell wrote.

Hurricane Irma had cut the Keys' communications with the outside world, but emergency management officials also imposed a quarantine. U.S. 1 was closed. No one would be allowed into the islands until bridges had been checked for damage and at least some debris—including dangerous downed power lines—had been removed from the main highway.

It wasn't long before alarming rumors were circulating, aided and perhaps instigated by social media. Among those rumors:

- The bridge over Snake Creek near Islamorada was damaged and impassable. False.
- The storm surge had washed RVs into canals in Marathon, and bodies would be found in those RVs when they were pulled out of the water. False.
- Coast Guard pilots had seen bodies floating in the surf as they flew above the Keys. False.

Irma's winds were down to around 60 mph as the storm crossed into Georgia early Monday afternoon. Trees began falling on power lines and sometimes going through roofs.

By 8 p.m. Monday, Irma's center was near Albany in southwest Georgia. Its strongest winds were around 50 mph. But they were still doing damage.

In Milledgeville, a picturesque little town with stately old oaks and nineteenth-century homes in the center of Georgia, high winds and rain brought down some of those oaks, which destroyed one of the town's most historic homes.

Thousands were left without power in Georgia.

In Islamorada, Phyllis Mitchell took her dogs for a walk along U.S. 1. She tried to flag down a passing car in hopes that the occupants were leaving the Keys for a place where there was cell phone service that would allow them to call her daughters to tell them their parents were OK.

Mitchell encountered six cars during her 30-minute walk. None stopped, and some roared past her at very high speed. "I'm sure they have their problems," she noted in her diary.

A few hours later, Bob Mitchell flagged down a passing motorist on U.S. 1. The driver accepted a note from Mitchell with his daughters' cell phone numbers. The intense emotional stress of the previous week's ordeal bubbled to the surface. Tears came to the driver's eyes as he read the note. The driver said he'd make the calls when he found cell phone service.

What was left of Hurricane Irma was blowing itself out as it moved across Georgia, took a turn to the northwest, and approached Alabama. By 11 p.m. the storm's top winds were down to about 35 mph.

By Tuesday, September 12, Floridians were trying to get back to their homes, and interstate highways into Florida were jammed.

"If you chose to drive back home Tuesday after evacuating from Irma, you were among thousands of others who faced a frustrating and long trip," the *Tampa Bay Times* wrote. "Traffic jams had already formed by mid-morning and continued throughout the day in Florida and southern Georgia, as millions of evacuated residents flooded back into and through the state in the aftermath of Hurricane Irma."

The *Times* reported that a 150-mile segment of I-75 stretching from the Georgia-Florida border south to Florida's Turnpike was clogged with backed-up traffic.

A few residents were being allowed to return to the Upper Keys. Among the homeowners sorting through the wreckage was former Dallas Cowboys coach Jimmy Johnson, who owned a house in Tavernier. But Johnson didn't want any sympathy for his loss.

"Don't feel sorry for me," Johnson said. "I can rebuild. I have the money. I feel bad for people who lost their house and don't know what to do. Those are the ones to feel sorry for, the ones who need help right now."

Charlotte Wilson was among the Keys residents trying to get back home. She was astonished at what she saw as she drove down the islands to Key West.

"You get away and you go, and then you come back," she said. "Coming down the Keys, it's just devastating. Very sad and shocking."

She saw "lines of trucks" piled high with debris, headed north toward Miami. "Truckload and truckload and truckload, and still piled high."

Although some well-constructed homes on Big Pine Key made it through Hurricane Irma with little or no damage, much of the island was devastated. Many residents were sleeping in the open or in tents as they wondered how they'd rebuild their lives.

Tim Stanton had lost his home and his workshop and tools. He faced a grim existence and a reordering of his priorities. "I've learned a lot of differences between 'want' and 'need,'" he said.

Simply finding a clean source of water was a problem. "You look at ways of collecting rainwater when it comes," he said. "If you see fresh water dripping from anything, you look for ways to collect it.

"I never drank so much coconut water as I did during the first month after the storm. It's a good, clean source. You can count on it being safe."

At times during those first days after the storm, Stanton wondered where he was going to get something to eat. "I suppose if things had gotten desperate enough, I might have learned to develop a taste for iguana," he said.

The weather system that had once been one of the most powerful hurricanes on record was playing out. Now a low-pressure system, the remnants of Irma continued northwestward after crossing Alabama. Around 8 a.m. on Wednesday, September 13, the National Weather Service stopped tracking the system. It had dissipated over southeastern Missouri.

But while Irma was gone, it was still spawning tragedy. In Hollywood, Florida, elderly residents of a nursing home had been sitting in their stiflingly hot rooms for more than two days since Irma had knocked out electrical power and shut down the home's air-conditioning. The temperature in the nursing home eventually reached 99 degrees. After 62 hours of intense heat, three residents died of heat exhaustion on September 13. Nine more eventually died from heat-related causes.

A hospital that never lost power—or air-conditioning—during and after the hurricane was right across the street from the nursing home.

Officials were beginning to get a statistical handle on Irma's damage.

The Federal Emergency Management Agency said 25 percent of the homes in the Florida Keys were destroyed and 65 percent sustained major damage. The *Tampa Bay Times* reported that Hurricane Irma had inflicted about $2.5 billion in lost crops and damaged facilities to the state's agriculture industry. The state's insurers were likely to see a tab of about $6.55 billion to cover property damage claims. And it would probably cost at least $1 billion to restore power to the state's electrical grid.

Hurricane Irma also racked up an impressive list of meteorological firsts. The storm maintained sustained winds of 185 mph for 37 hours—the longest such time on record. It was a Category 5 hurricane for 78 hours. Only one other hurricane—a powerful storm that struck Cuba in 1932—maintained that intensity for that long. And Irma had generated more energy than any Atlantic hurricane on record.

Hurricane Irma had dealt a staggering, historic blow to the Florida Keys. It would take months for the islands just to make a superficial recovery. And with the start of the annual tourism season on the horizon, the islands' businesspeople knew they faced a daunting task of getting the Keys ready for visitors.

In the 85 years since Julius Stone's idea to convert Key West into a tourist attraction, the tourism industry has become the lifeblood of the Florida Keys. Every year, tourism brings about $2.7 billion to the Keys. More than half the workers in the Keys get their paychecks from tourism.

A little normalcy began creeping back into the Keys on Sunday, September 24, when Royal Caribbean International's *Empress of the Seas* cruise ship docked in the Key West harbor. It was the first cruise ship to come to Key West since the hurricane. The ship carried about 880 passengers and around 600 crew members.

The visitors walked down the gangplank into a town that resembled, in some ways, the remote, shabby little town of 1934, when it had cleaned itself up and repackaged itself as a tourist attraction.

Many businesses hadn't removed the plywood from their windows. Tour guides joked about the passengers getting the town all to themselves and apologized for the nearly empty streets.

Still, a few landmarks were open. The Green Parrot had cleaned up and reopened. And Sloppy Joe's, where Ernest Hemingway had hoisted glasses with the boisterous vets 82 years earlier, also had opened.

Key West mayor Craig Cates said he and other political and business leaders had agonized over when to reopen to tourism. Although the city had taken a stiff punch from Irma, it had not suffered nearly the damage as the islands to the north.

"We understand, and we are compassionate about their situation," Cates told the *South Florida Sun-Sentinel*. "But a lot of them work here. We're in this together."

Business and political leaders also were debating—and disagreeing—about whether to cancel Key West's upcoming Fantasy Fest.

The 10-day, R-rated street party showcases the city's traditional fondness for and tolerance of merrymaking that dates back at least to the mid-1930s, when carousing vets rode the train down from the work camps for a weekend of revelry. Behavior that would've gotten them thrown in jail in Miami was more likely to be ignored or only mildly rebuked in Key West.

There were many reasons not to stage the 2017 edition of Key West's unrestrained, uncensored street party that usually brings 50,000 or 60,000 celebrants to the city for 10 days of adult fun.

For starters, U.S. 1 was still a wreck. The road had only recently reopened, and it was still lined with debris and shredded, ruined vegetation. In addition, the workers who took care of tourists were trying to rebuild their own lives, and in many cases were still trying to find places to live.

After some intense debate, the decision was made—Fantasy Fest would go on as scheduled.

"It was a little controversial," conceded festival director Nadene Grossman Orr. "Thirty miles to the north was totally devastated. Some thought it didn't make any sense to go forward with the celebration. It was a tough decision to make."

In the end, getting people back to work—bartenders, servers, hotel workers—was a major factor in the decision.

But another factor also came into play.

"We definitely needed a break to do something fun, silly, creative," Orr said.

And Key West residents felt compelled to let the world know that even one of the most powerful hurricanes on record couldn't destroy the city's irreverent, fun-loving spirit.

The crowd wasn't quite as large as usual, Orr said. But they came.

The event was a signal that Key West was open for business in time for the lucrative winter tourist season. Meanwhile, the massive cleanup continued. By March 2018 there still were signs that a bad hurricane had wracked the Keys. But the visible damage was subtler, at least on U.S. 1.

It was a different story in places just a few blocks off U.S. 1, however. Some neighborhoods on Big Pine Key looked as though Irma had gone through only a few days earlier. And the slow pace of bureaucracy to provide help was more than some could bear. In February 2018 a Big Pine Key resident was told that it would be two years before he would get any help from the Federal Emergency Management Administration. Despondent, he shot his wife and his dog and then shot himself.

One year after Hurricane Irma, the most visible signs of the storm's damage had been either repaired, replaced, or hauled away. But less visible signs of the hurricane still lingered.

"We'll be recovering for years," Monroe County sheriff Rick Ramsay said in November 2018.

Some of the post-Irma problems are nearly identical to those faced after Hurricane Wilma 12 years earlier, Ramsay said. The people who keep the Keys' service-based economy running can't afford to live where they work, and they're leaving.

"We've lost affordable housing," he said. "When they came back, the rent got jacked up. It's hard to recruit people. How do I get people to come back to a hurricane ravaged area? There's a struggle with staffing countywide—teachers, paramedics, nurses, plumbers, electricians. It's a terrible problem, my friend."

Even more unsettling is the fact that, as terrible as Hurricane Irma was, it was not the storm that the Keys has been fearing since 1935. As Floridians watched Irma steadily intensify during its devastating and well-publicized trek from the deep Atlantic past the Caribbean and across The Bahamas and Cuba, they became increasingly more alarmed.

When evacuation orders were issued for the Keys, it didn't take much more than a nudge to get people moving, and those who left had plenty of time to prepare. "People were scared," Ramsay said.

But in October 2018, Keys residents got a frightening look at the hurricane of their nightmares when Hurricane Michael exploded in the Gulf of Mexico and tore into the Florida Panhandle like a buzz saw.

The storm came out of the western Caribbean Sea and became a minimal hurricane as it passed through the Yucatan Channel into the Gulf on October 8. It steadily strengthened, and by noon Eastern Time on Tuesday, October 9 its peak winds were 110 mph.

Its intensification escalated. At 9 p.m. Michael's winds had reached 125 mph, and by midnight, 130 mph.

At 9 a.m. Eastern Time on Wednesday, October 10, the storm was within 50 miles of landfall and its top winds were 145 mph. Even the most powerful hurricanes often lose some intensity when they reach inshore waters, where the water is shallow and usually cooler. But Michael continued strengthening until the moment its eye touched land. Its peak sustained winds were at least 160 mph when it came ashore at Mexico Beach, Florida, around noon on October 10.

"This is really an amazing event," Andrew Dessler, a professor of atmospheric sciences at Texas A&M University, told the *New York Times*. "It really came out of nowhere and really intensified rapidly."

About 120,000 people—far more than live in the Keys—were ordered to evacuate ahead of Hurricane Michael. But the Panhandle evacuees had many routes leading away from the danger area, and that's why watching Hurricane Michael develop as it charged toward landfall made Richie Russell and many other Keys residents uneasy. In only two days, Michael intensified from a tropical storm with peak winds of about 70 mph to a major hurricane with winds exceeding 110 mph.

A mandatory evacuation of the Keys is not ordered unless winds exceeding 110 mph are expected. But a full evacuation of the islands takes three days. So had Hurricane Michael taken aim at the Keys instead of the Panhandle, there wouldn't have been enough time for a mandatory evacuation after the storm reached the threshold for issuing the evacuation order.

"We'd have a difficult time preparing for a storm like that," Richie Russell said. "It was a real curveball."

Alma Pinder Dalton—whose late sister, Laurette, was married to Bernard Russell—was 11 years old when the Labor Day Hurricane of 1935 devastated the Keys. As of November 2018 she was the oldest living survivor of that storm. She still lived in Islamorada, and she did not leave the Keys during Hurricane Irma.

She didn't dispute that Irma was a very bad hurricane. But she wasn't afraid during that storm, and when it was over, her house was still standing. In Dalton's mind, Irma did not compare to the 1935 hurricane, which destroyed her home, leveled her village, and killed so many of her friends.

"I didn't have any idea I'd survive that storm," she said. "Irma didn't even compare to the '35 hurricane and what we went through. I never found any part of the house we lived in after that storm."

And so although three savage hurricanes have pounded the islands and inflicted massive suffering and billions of dollars of damage since the long ago screaming killer of 1935 slaughtered the hapless veterans, the worst-case hurricane for the modern Florida Keys still hasn't happened. To use the phrasing of *St. Petersburg Times* writer Colin Jameson, the crowded islands still may be "living on time borrowed from the wind."

One day, unfortunately, that debt will come due.

NOTES

These notes represent a selection of sources used in the first and second editions of *Storm of the Century: The Labor Day Hurricane of 1935*. More information about the sources can be found at the Florida Keys History and Discovery Center in Islamorada, Florida, and on the center's website, https://www.keysdiscovery.com. Source documents are in the permanent collection of the Jerry Wilkinson Research Library at the Discovery Center and are available to the public.

Prologue: Sunday, September 1, 1935

x. But when the storm crossed Andros Island in The Bahamas: *Prescott* (Arizona) *Evening Courier*, September 2, 1935.

x. On August 31, Grady Norton, the U.S. Weather Bureau's chief hurricane forecaster: *Tallahassee Democrat*, September 1, 1935.

xi. Meanwhile, farmers slaughtered livestock, poured out milk, and burned grain: William Manchester, *The Glory and the Dream: A Narrative History of America, 1932–1972* (Boston and Toronto: Little, Brown and Company, 1973), p. 42.

xi. About two million men roamed the country: William Manchester, *The Glory and the Dream: A Narrative History of America, 1932–1972* (Boston and Toronto: Little, Brown and Company, 1973), p. 20.

xi. The prairie winds whipped the dust into thick, choking clouds: *The Post-Register* (Idaho Falls, ID), April 15, 1935.

xii. But in July 1935, the Weather Bureau had, with considerable fanfare: *The Index-Journal* (Greenwood, SC), July 3, 1935; *Lincoln* (Nebraska) *Sunday Journal and Star*, July 14, 1935; *The Honolulu Advertiser*, July 21, 1935; and others.

xiii. He trusted his own observations and judgment: Testimony of Ed Sheeran, Records Group 69 006.1, Works Progress Administration Selected Records Relating to the 1935 Florida Hurricane, National Archives, College Park, Maryland.

xiii. . . . trying to survive on an average income of $7 a month: "'State of Emergency': Key West in the Great Depression," by Garry Boulard, *Florida Historical Quarterly*, vol. 67, no. 2 (October 1988), p. 169.

xiii. . . . federal officials in charge of the vets camps had created so many regulations: Testimony of Richard Bow, Records Group 69 006.1, Works Progress Administration Selected Records Relating to the 1935 Florida Hurricane, National Archives, College Park, Maryland.

xiii. Sheeran had served as a combat engineer in France during World War I: Author's telephone interview with Edward H. Sheeran (grandson of Ed Sheeran), December 28, 1999.

xiii. A distant hurricane telegraphs its approach in a subtle but unmistakable code: Nathaniel Bowditch, *American Practical Navigator*, vol. 1 (Washington, DC: U.S. Department of Defense, 1977 edition), p. 901–902.

xiv. Months earlier, Sheeran had prepared: Testimony of Ed Sheeran, Records Group 69 006.1, Works Progress Administration Selected Records Relating to the 1935 Florida Hurricane, National Archives, College Park, Maryland.

xiv. As Sheeran worked, horrible memories of a tragedy: "The Wreck of Houseboat No. 4, October 1906," by William H. Saunders, *Tequesta: The Journal of the Historical Association of Southern Florida*, no. 19 (1959), p. 15–21; "Building the Overseas Railway to Key West," by Carlton J. Corliss, *Tequesta: The Journal of the Historical Association of Southern Florida*, no. 13 (1953), p. 16.

xv. But Sheeran was employed by the Florida State Highway Department and didn't have the authority: Testimony of Ed Sheeran, Records Group 69 006.1, Works Progress Administration Selected Records Relating to the 1935 Florida Hurricane, National Archives, College Park, Maryland.

xv. . . . his boss, 45-year-old Ray Sheldon, had decided to take a brief honeymoon in Key West: Testimony of Albert Buck, Records Group 15, Sub-group 5-3, Records of the Veterans Administration, National Archives and Records Administration, Washington, DC.

xv. They rolled out of their bunks and lined up: *Key Veteran News* (Islamorada, FL) cartoon by T. W. Conrad, May 4, 1935.

xvi. But drinking and despondency were serious problems: Author's interview with Bernard Russell, Islamorada, Florida, December 6, 1996, transcript on file at Florida Keys History and Discovery Center, Islamorada, Florida.

xvi. When the crew started pouring concrete for arch number 61: Author's interview with Bernard Russell, Islamorada, Florida, April 12, 1997, transcript on file at Florida Keys History and Discovery Center, Islamorada, Florida.

xvii. . . . "boosted the bloody art of war from bullets and bayonets to long-range high explosives." Donovan Webster, *Aftermath: The Remnants of War: From Landmines to Chemical Warfare—The Devastating Effects of Modern Combat* (New York: Pantheon Books, 1996), p. 4.

xvii. "Retreat?" McCloskey growled: *The Evening Independent* (St. Petersburg, FL), February 10, 1936.

xviii. . . . had entered a new era of perpetual prosperity that would permanently eliminate poverty: *Los Angeles Times*, August 12, 1928.

xviii. In Florida, real estate speculation: T. H. Watkins, *The Great Depression: America in the 1930s* (Boston, New York, Toronto, London: Little, Brown and Company, 1993), p. 35.

xix. "I'm here to see that people don't starve": William Manchester, *The Glory and the Dream: A Narrative History of America, 1932–1972* (Boston and Toronto: Little, Brown and Company, 1973), p. 102.

xix. *Fortune* magazine estimated in 1932: William Manchester, *The Glory and the Dream: A Narrative History of America, 1932–1972* (Boston and Toronto: Little, Brown and Company, 1973), p. 41.

xix. Sports entered a new era when lights were erected: *The Cincinnati Enquirer*, May 25, 1935.

xix. And in August, a struggling bandleader named Benny Goodman: editors of Time-Life Books, *This Fabulous Century, Volume IV, 1930–1940* (New York: Time-Life Books, 1969), p. 230.

xix. Humorist Will Rogers kept Americans chuckling: *Miami Daily News* and many others, November 10, 1932.

xx. More than half the nation's population: William Manchester, *The Glory and the Dream: A Narrative History of America, 1932–1972* (Boston and Toronto: Little, Brown and Company, 1973), p. 38.

xx. A frothy new comedy called *Top Hat*: *The Courier-Journal* (Louisville, KY), September 1, 1935.

xx. . . . the S.S. *Dixie* left its berth in New Orleans and set sail for New York: *Time* magazine, September 16, 1935; *San Francisco Chronicle*, September 6, 1935; *Miami Herald*, October 2, 1935.

xx. . . . a Yale University professor with a fondness for playing poker and the piano: *Wisconsin State Journal* (Madison, WI), September 8, 1935.

xx. . . . a group of young women from Pennsylvania: *The News-Herald* (Franklin, PA), September 3, 1935.

xx. As the ship sailed across the placid waters of the Gulf of Mexico, Charlotte Evans: *Pensacola Journal*, September 4, 1935.

xx. Captain Einar Sundstrom commanded the *Dixie*: *Brooklyn Daily Eagle*, September 4, 1935.

xxi. Hurricane forecasters in Cuba had for some time been an annoyance: Erik Larson, *Isaac's Storm: A Man, a Time, and the Deadliest Hurricane in History* (New York, Toronto, London, etc.: Random House, 1999), p. 9, 102.

xxi. Scorn and criticism were piled high on the Weather Bureau: Erik Larson, *Isaac's Storm: A Man, a Time, and the Deadliest Hurricane in History* (New York, Toronto, London, etc.: Random House, 1999), p. 250.

xxi. Cuban forecasters initially thought the storm that had just crossed The Bahamas: Associated Press/*Palm Beach Post*, September 2, 1935.

xxi. Forecasters at Cuba's Belen Observatory: *Miami Herald*, September 3, 1935.

xxi. Leonard James Povey—"Len" to his friends back in the United States—was known as "El Phenomena": *Miami Herald*, April 11, 1954.

xxi. So he left his home in New Hampshire at the age of 15: *The Boston Globe*, May 28, 1930.

xxii. After his discharge he became a stunt pilot: *The Nashua* (New Hampshire) *Telegraph*, October 17, 1930.

xxii. . . . even bringing a biplane in for a miraculous landing: *Miami Herald*, April 11, 1954.

xxii. . . . the architect of the programs that had given jobs in the Keys to the needy veterans: *Miami Herald*/UPI, September 1, 1935.

xxii. The first session of the 74th Congress: *New York Herald-Tribune*, September 22, 1935.

xxiii. They hit a snag in the last hours: *The Emporia* (Kansas) *Gazette*, August 28, 1935; *The Detroit Free Press*, August 28, 1935.

xxiii. . . . been labeled a "madman" by a U.S. senator: United Press/*Orlando Sentinel*, March 13, 1935.

xxiii. Long dashed out a side door of the Senate chamber: *New York Times*, August 27, 1935.

xxiii. . . . Congress was "a bunch of cowards": Associated Press/*The Salt Lake Tribune*, August 28, 1935.

xxiii. Roosevelt planned to spend several weeks at Hyde Park: *Rochester* (New York) *Democrat and Chronicle*, September 1, 1935.

xxiii. As the election year approached, Roosevelt supporters and campaign strategists: Franklin D. Roosevelt Papers as President, The President's Secretary's File, 1933–1945, Electoral Vote, 1936, Franklin D. Roosevelt Library and Museum, Hyde Park, New York, http://www.fdrlibrary.marist.edu/archives/collections/franklin/?p=collections/findi ngaid&id=502&q=&rootcontentid=139964#id139964.

Chapter 1: A Remote Paradise

1. When Bernard Russell was a boy walking to school: Author's interview with Bernard Russell, Islamorada, Florida, November 17, 1997, transcript on file at Florida Keys History and Discovery Center, Islamorada, Florida.

1. . . . Russell was 16 years old and part of the largest graduating class that Matecumbe Graded School had ever produced: Author's interview with Bernard Russell, Islamorada, Florida, December 6, 1996, transcript on file at Florida Keys History and Discovery Center, Islamorada, Florida.

1. . . . Russell had become friends with schoolmate Laurette Pinder: Author's interview with Alma Pinder Dalton and Laurette Pinder Russell, Islamorada, Florida, November 18, 1997, transcript on file at Florida Keys History and Discovery Center, Islamorada, Florida.

2. . . . but fewer than 1,000 residents inhabited the islands between Key West and the mainland: Viele, John, *The Florida Keys: A History of the Pioneers* (Sarasota, FL: Pineapple Press, 1996), p. 134.

2. At nightfall, Islamorada residents lit their kerosene lanterns: Viele, John. *The Florida Keys: A History of the Pioneers* (Sarasota, FL: Pineapple Press, 1996), p. 132.

2. In 1935 the daily arrival of the southbound passenger train: Author's interview with Bernard Russell, Islamorada, Florida, December 6, 1996, transcript on file at Florida Keys History and Discovery Center, Islamorada, Florida.

2. On most mornings, a few residents were likely to be coming and going at the post office: Author's interview with Bernard Russell, Islamorada, Florida, December 6, 1996, transcript on file at Florida Keys History and Discovery Center, Islamorada, Florida.

2. Bernard Russell, 10 years old at the time: Author's interview with Bernard Russell, Islamorada, Florida, December 6, 1996, transcript on file at Florida Keys History and Discovery Center, Islamorada, Florida.

3. In 1908 writer Ralph Paine described the islands: Frank Oppel and Tony Meisel, eds., *Tales of Old Florida* (Secaucus, NJ: Book Sales Inc., 1987), p. 405.

3. The nearest doctors and dentists: Author's interview with Bernard Russell, Islamorada, Florida, December 6, 1996, transcript on file at Florida Keys History and Discovery Center, Islamorada, Florida.

3. If the wind was against you or the weather suddenly turned bad, the trip could take much longer: Author's interview with Bernard Russell, Islamorada, Florida, December 6, 1996, transcript on file at Florida Keys History and Discovery Center, Islamorada, Florida

3. Over the years Islamorada residents had worn a series of foot trails: Author's interview with Bernard Russell, Islamorada, Florida, November 17, 1997, transcript on file at Florida Keys History and Discovery Center, Islamorada, Florida.

3. In 1935 the number of outhouses far exceeded the number of telephones on Upper Matecumbe Key: Author's interview with Bernard Russell, Islamorada, Florida, November 17, 1997, transcript on file at Florida Keys History and Discovery Center, Islamorada, Florida.

4. The islanders kept a close watch on their cisterns: Author's interview with Bernard Russell, Islamorada, Florida, December 6, 1996, transcript on file at Florida Keys History and Discovery Center, Islamorada, Florida.

4. Living in the middle of the Atlantic meant constantly watching the weather: Author's interview with Bernard Russell, Islamorada, Florida, December 6, 1996, transcript on file at Florida Keys History and Discovery Center, Islamorada, Florida.

4. "My dad lived by the barometer," Bernard Russell said: Author's interview with Bernard Russell, Islamorada, Florida, December 6, 1996, transcript on file at Florida Keys History and Discovery Center, Islamorada, Florida.

4. Despite the isolation and inherent dangers, life on the isolated Keys: Author's interview with Bernard Russell, Islamorada, Florida, December 6, 1996, transcript on file at Florida Keys History and Discovery Center, Islamorada, Florida.

5. Tomato gardens and key lime groves: Author's interview with Bernard Russell, Islamorada, Florida, November 17, 1997, transcript on file at Florida Keys History and Discovery Center, Islamorada, Florida.

5. In the summer of 1935, Reverend Robert Carlson: *Fort Myers News-Press*, September 8, 1935.

5. Many of the pioneers who settled the Keys in the mid-nineteenth century: "Pioneer Cemetery," by Josephine Johnson, *Tequesta: The Journal of the Historical Association of Southern Florida*, no. 51 (1991), p. 29.

5. Islamorada residents lived on or near the beach: Author's interview with Bernard Russell, Islamorada, Florida, November 17, 1997, transcript on file at Florida Keys History and Discovery Center, Islamorada, Florida.

5. Sometimes in the summer, those cooling winds come in the form of a sudden storm: Author's frequent visits to the Florida Keys, 1994–2001.

6. Many had built even sturdier shelters: Author's interview with Bernard Russell, Islamorada, Florida, December 6, 1996, transcript on file at Florida Keys History and Discovery Center, Islamorada, Florida.

6. But the seafaring Conchs complained loudly: Author's interview with Bernard Russell, Islamorada, Florida, December 6, 1996, transcript on file at Florida Keys History and Discovery Center, Islamorada, Florida.

7. Crossing the magnificent bridges: Author's interview with Bernard Russell, Islamorada, Florida, December 6, 1996, transcript on file at Florida Keys History and Discovery Center, Islamorada, Florida.

7. Flagler made several visits to Florida between 1878 and 1883: "Will the Real Henry Flagler Please Stand Up?" by Jaquelin Duggan Mason, *The Historical Association of Southern Florida Update*, vol. 8, no. 1 (February 1981), p. 4.

7. In 1904 Flagler took on a task that seemed impossible: "Building the Overseas Railway to Key West," by Carlton J. Corliss, *Tequesta: The Journal of the Historical Association of Southern Florida*, no. 13 (1953), p. 6.

8. The final tab for the railroad was more than $20 million: *Palm Beach Post*, February 13, 1994.

8. The Conchs knew a storm was rising: "The Wreck of Houseboat No. 4, October 1906," by William H. Saunders, *Tequesta: The Journal of the Historical Association of Southern Florida*, no. 19 (1959), p. 16.

9. "Strong cables were parted like so many cords: *The Daily Miami Metropolis*, October 20, 1906.

9. "It is wreck, wreck, wreck everywhere": *The Daily Miami Metropolis*, October 22, 1906.

10. The furious storm and death toll made a strong impression on Ed Sheeran: Testimony of Edward H. Sheeran to D. W. Kennamer, Miami, Florida, September 13, 1935, Records Group 69 006.1, Works Progress Administration Selected Records Relating to the 1935 Florida Hurricane, National Archives, College Park, Maryland.

10. The first FEC train rolled into Key West in January 1912: *Miami Herald*, January 23, 1912.

10. An Islamorada resident could now be in Key West: Author's interview with Bernard Russell, Islamorada, Florida, December 6, 1996, transcript on file at Florida Keys History and Discovery Center, Islamorada, Florida.

10. In Islamorada a "millionaires row" was created: Author's interview with Bernard Russell, Islamorada, Florida, December 6, 1996, transcript on file at Florida Keys History and Discovery Center, Islamorada, Florida.

11. Ed Butters had also come to the Keys for the first time on a fishing trip: *Miami News*, April 29, 1962.

11. Thomas Edison, who had moved to Fort Myers: *The Fort Myers Press*, March 26, 1924.

11. George Merrick, who created the visionary development of Coral Gables: Arva Moore Parks, *George Merrick: Son of the South Wind* (Gainesville: University Press of Florida, 2015), p. 304.

11. Miami businessman Roland W. Craig: *Miami Herald*, September 11, 1960.

12. People had been coming to Long Key for the fishing: *Miami Herald*, October 10, 1992.

12. Soon after the Key West Extension was completed: *New York Times*, July 1, 1933.

12. A caretaker looked after the expensive amenities: "The Hurricane of August 31 to September 6, 1935," by W. F. McDonald, *Monthly Weather Review*, September 1935, p. 269.

12. A few members of the exclusive fishing club built their own houses: Author's interview with Bernard Russell, Islamorada, Florida, November 17, 1997, transcript on file at Florida Keys History and Discovery Center, Islamorada, Florida; *Miami Herald*, September 7, 1935.

12. . . . who'd been born in Chicago and was formerly known as Daisy Leiter: *Tampa Daily Times*, December 10, 1924.

13. At the same time that the average household income: *The New York Times*, February 3, 2019.

13. Visitors to Long Key included those with names synonymous: *Miami Daily News*, March 11, 1934.

13. The fishing was superb: *Miami Daily News*, January 30, 1935.

13. . . . Grey said he concocted the plots for his novels: *Richmond* (Virginia) *Times-Dispatch*, January 30, 1917.

13. . . . "eternal moan out on the reefs," . . . "always by the glowing, hot colorful day: Zane Grey, *Tales of Fishes* (New York and London: Harper & Brothers Publisher, 1919), p. 85.

14. Hoover insisted that the hard times were only temporary: William Manchester, *The Glory and the Dream: A Narrative History of America, 1932–1972* (Boston and Toronto: Little, Brown and Company, 1973), p. 30; T. H. Watkins, *The Great Depression: America in the 1930s* (Boston, New York, Toronto, London: Little, Brown and Company, 1993), p. 51.

14. When thousands of jobless men started selling apples: T. H. Watkins, *The Great Depression: America in the 1930s* (Boston, New York, Toronto, London: Little, Brown and Company, 1993), p. 63.

14. During the winter of 1931, Hoover insisted: William Manchester, *The Glory and the Dream: A Narrative History of America, 1932–1972* (Boston and Toronto: Little, Brown and Company, 1973), p. 48; T. H. Watkins, *The Great Depression: America in the 1930s* (Boston, New York, Toronto, London: Little, Brown and Company, 1993), p. 56.

14. The industries that had once made Key West prosperous: "'State of Emergency': Key West in the Great Depression," by Garry Boulard, *Florida Historical Quarterly*, vol. 67, no. 2 (October 1988), p. 166.

14. Hoover refused to abandon his staunchly Republican belief: T. H. Watkins, *The Great Depression: America in the 1930s* (Boston, New York, Toronto, London: Little, Brown and Company, 1993), p. 56.

14. As the 1932 election approached: William Manchester, *The Glory and the Dream: A Narrative History of America 1932–1972* (Boston and Toronto: Little Brown and Company, 1973), p. 42.

15. . . . Roosevelt launched his campaign for the White House: *The Index-Journal* (Greenwood, SC), April 8, 1932; *The Philadelphia Inquirer*, April 8, 1932; *Honolulu Star-Bulletin*, March 12, 1932.

15. When he won the Democratic nomination in July: *Detroit Free Press*, July 3, 1932.

15. ... "men and women forgotten in the political philosophy of government": *Chicago Sunday Tribune*, July 3, 1932.

15. The ex-servicemen became more visible during the summer of 1932: *The News Journal* (Wilmington, DE), June 9, 1932.

15. The bonus plan called for each vet to receive about $1,000: T. H. Watkins, *The Great Depression: America in the 1930s* (Boston, New York, Toronto, London: Little, Brown and Company, 1993), p. 98.

15. Some vets on the West Coast started their trip: T. H. Watkins, *The Great Depression: America in the 1930s* (Boston, New York, Toronto, London: Little, Brown and Company, 1993), p. 99.

16. Others moved into a row of abandoned, partially demolished buildings: William Manchester, *The Glory and the Dream: A Narrative History of America, 1932–1972* (Boston and Toronto: Little, Brown and Company, 1973), p. 9.

16. ... wanted Congress to give them a $500 bonus immediately: William Manchester, *The Glory and the Dream: A Narrative History of America, 1932–1972* (Boston and Toronto: Little, Brown and Company, 1973), p. 1.

16. Brigadier General George Mosely proposed: William Manchester, *The Glory and the Dream: A Narrative History of America, 1932–1972* (Boston and Toronto: Little, Brown and Company, 1973), p. 10–11.

16. *The Courier-Journal* of Louisville, Kentucky, was even sharper: *The Courier-Journal* (Louisville, KY), June 7, 1932.

16. By June about 25,000 veterans and their families: William Manchester, *The Glory and the Dream: A Narrative History of America, 1932–1972* (Boston and Toronto: Little, Brown and Company, 1973), p. 1.

16. Their cause was championed by Representative Wright Patman: *The Cincinnati Enquirer*, April 10, 1932; *Statesville* (North Carolina) *Record and Landmark*, April 15, 1932.

16. Representative Hamilton Fish, a Republican from New York, led the opposition: *The Oshkosh* (Wisconsin) *Northwestern*, April 1, 1932.

16. ... "coerced by any groups": *The Evening Sun* (Baltimore, MD), June 13, 1932.

16. On June 15, 1932, the House of Representatives approved Patman's bill: *Chicago Daily Tribune*, June 16, 1932.

16. But two days later the Senate defeated the bill: *Chicago Daily Tribune*, June 17, 1932.

17. ... but a hard-core group of about 8,000 remained: Ted Morgan, *FDR: A Biography* (New York: Simon and Schuster, 1985), p. 356.

17. ... vowing to stay until 1945, if necessary: T. H. Watkins, *The Great Depression: America in the 1930s* (Boston, New York, Toronto, London: Little, Brown and Company, 1993), p. 101.

17. In Las Vegas, Vice President Charles Curtis: *The St. Louis Star and Times*, July 29, 1932; *The Pittsburgh Press*, July 29, 1932.

17. He allowed medical supplies: T. H. Watkins, *The Great Depression: America in the 1930s* (Boston, New York, Toronto, London: Little, Brown and Company, 1993), p. 100.

17. He had the gates to the White House chained shut: William Manchester, *The Glory and the Dream: A Narrative History of America, 1932–1972* (Boston and Toronto: Little, Brown and Company, 1973), p. 1.

17. He ordered that U.S. Army troops be used to evacuate the veterans: William Manchester, *American Caesar: Douglas MacArthur 1880–1964* (Boston and Toronto: Little, Brown and Company, 1978), p. 152.

17. Hoover's instructions stated that the troops: William Manchester. *American Caesar: Douglas MacArthur 1880–1964* (Boston and Toronto: Little, Brown and Company. 1978), p. 152.

17. Newspaper photos of the rout horrified Americans: *The Courier-Journal* (Louisville, KY), July 29–30, 1932; *The Detroit Free Press*, July 29, 1932; and others.

18. One reminder appeared in the March 1933 edition: "The Forgotten Man to His President," by Wilson Follett, *Atlantic Monthly*, March 1933, p. 257.

18. When the moment came for FDR to take the oath of office: Author's visit to Franklin D. Roosevelt Library and Museum, Hyde Park, New York, January 24, 2001.

18. As Roosevelt took the oath of office, banks across the country were failing: T. H. Watkins, *The Great Depression: America in the 1930s* (Boston, New York, Toronto, London: Little, Brown and Company, 1993), p. 122–23.

18. One of the driving philosophies behind FDR's New Deal: "Climbing Out of the Great Depression," by J. Bradford DeLong, Associate Professor of Economics, UCLA, from website http://www.j-bradford-delong.net/tceh/slouch_climb16.html, first accessed September 21, 1999, last accessed June 26, 2018.

19. He improvised, he blundered, he failed often: *The Road to World War II—Part 6—FDR and Hitler—Their Rise to Power*, produced by Anthony Potter Productions, 1978.

19. Among the new agencies . . . was the Federal Emergency Relief Administration: T. H. Watkins, *The Great Depression: xx. America in the 1930s* (Boston, New York, Toronto, London: Little, Brown and Company, 1993), p. 124.

19. Soon after FDR took office, veterans began drifting back into Washington: Kenneth S. Davis, *FDR: The New Deal Years 1933–1937, A History* (New York: Random House, 1979), p. 78–79.

19. . . . . Roosevelt opposed early payment of the veterans' bonus: T. H. Watkins, *The Great Depression: America in the 1930s* (Boston, New York, Toronto, London: Little, Brown and Company, 1993), p. 130.

Chapter 2: Forgotten Men

21. On the evening of July 7, 1935, a violent thunderstorm: *Key Veteran News* (Islamorada, FL), July 13, 1935.

21. "Shacks creaked and canvas billowed and cracked," he wrote: *Key Veteran News* (Islamorada, FL), July 13, 1935.

22. The Conchs feared and respected the powerful storms: Author's interview with Bernard Russell, Islamorada, Florida, December 6, 1996, transcript on file at Florida Keys History and Discovery Center, Islamorada, Florida.

22. Still others had been wounded in a less obvious: *The Arizona Legion News* (Phoenix, AZ), March 12, 1933.

23. The first fight erupted as soon as the vets drew their first pay in early November 1934: Glenn Robertson, letter to unnamed recipient, Records Group 69 006.1, Works Progress Administration Selected Records Relating to the 1935 Florida Hurricane, National Archives, College Park, Maryland.

23. The sober, hardworking Conchs looked on: Author's interview with Bernard Russell, December 6, 1996, Islamorada, Florida, transcript on file at Florida Keys History and Discovery Center, Islamorada, Florida.

23. As the nineteenth century drew to a close, Key West was Florida's largest city: "'State of Emergency': Key West in the Great Depression," by Garry Boulard, *Florida Historical Quarterly*, vol. 67, no. 2 (October 1988), p. 168.

23. The marine salvaging industry: "'State of Emergency': Key West in the Great Depression," by Garry Boulard, *Florida Historical Quarterly*, vol. 67, no. 2 (October 1988), p. 169.

23. By the late 1920s Key West was on the skids: "'State of Emergency': Key West in the Great Depression," by Garry Boulard, *Florida Historical Quarterly*, vol. 67, no. 2 (October 1988), p. 169.

24. A promising young writer named Ernest Hemingway: James McLendon, *Papa Hemingway in Key West* (Key West, FL: Langley Press, 1990), p. 22.

24. By the summer of 1934 the city faced a bond debt of $5 million: "'State of Emergency': Key West in the Great Depression," by Garry Boulard, *Florida Historical Quarterly*, vol. 67, no. 2 (October 1988), p. 166.

24. On July 1, 1934, Key West and Monroe County leaders passed joint resolutions: "'State of Emergency': Key West in the Great Depression," by Garry Boulard, *Florida Historical Quarterly*, vol. 67, no. 2 (October 1988), p. 166.

25. "I knew it didn't mean a thing," Stone said: "'State of Emergency': Key West in the Great Depression," by Garry Boulard, *Florida Historical Quarterly*, vol. 67, no. 2 (October 1988), p. 171.

25. "I got away with it because we were so far off: "'State of Emergency': Key West in the Great Depression," by Garry Boulard, *Florida Historical Quarterly*, vol. 67, no. 2 (October 1988), p. 173.

25. In 1929 Stone, who held a doctorate in organic chemistry: *Orlando Morning Sentinel*, April 25, 1935.

25. By August 1934 the PWA had hired about 675,000 workers: *The Baltimore Sun*, August 12, 1934.

25. Stone predicted Key West would become "the Bermuda of Florida": *Miami Daily News*, July 5, 1934.

26. Stone also hired public relations specialist M. E. Gilfond: *Miami Daily News*, November 16, 1934.

26. He put the credibility and prestige of the New Deal on the line: *New York Times*, August 12, 1934.

26. . . . Stone told a Miami radio audience: Transcript, "Program of the Florida Emergency Relief Administration Over Station WIOD," Miami, Friday, August 24, 1934, 7:00 p.m., A Fifteen-Minute Radio Address by Julius F. Stone Jr., Administrator,

Records Group 69 006.1, Works Progress Administration Selected Records Relating to the 1935 Florida Hurricane, National Archives, College Park, Maryland.

26. The *Miami Daily News* reported that between mid-December: *Miami Daily News*, March 28, 1935.

26. "With a scratch of my pen I started this work in Key West: *The Tampa Tribune*, April 7, 1935.

26. Stone and other Florida ERA officials wanted to make it quicker: *Miami Daily News*, October 18, 1934.

27. "Give a man a dole and you save his body: "Along the 'American Way': The New Deal's Work Relief Programs for the Unemployed," by William W. Bremer, *The Journal of American History*, vol. 62, no. 3 (December 1975), published by the Organization of American Historians, p. 637.

28. The first men sent to the Keys would be housed: *The Leader-Enterprise* (Homestead, FL), November 30, 1934.

28. B. M. Duncan, a state highway department engineer: *The News-Leader* (Homestead, FL), November 30, 1934; R. M. Porter, "Strike at the Veterans' Work Camps, Florida," memorandum to a "Mr. Baker," March 9, 1935, Records Group 69 006.1, Works Progress Administration, Selected Records Relating to the 1935 Florida Hurricane, National Archives, College Park, Maryland.

28. In early November 1934 about 50 vets: *Key Veteran News* (Islamorada, FL), March 25, 1935.

28. They included Jimmy Conway, a former professional boxer: *The Miami Metropolis*, January 31, 1920.

29. He'd made some money in the ring: *Key Veteran News* (Islamorada, FL), August 17, 1935.

29. He'd also done two hitches in the peacetime army: Find A Grave website, www.findagrave.com/memorial/106978671, accessed July 9, 2018.

29. Arthur Mewshaw, an attorney in Charlotte: *Key Veteran News* (Islamorada, FL), July 6, 1935; Associated Press/*Asheville* (North Carolina) *Citizen-Times*, August 12, 1930.

29. John T. McNulty was a former actor: *Key Veteran News* (Islamorada, FL), August 17, 1935.

29. Bill Hendren had been a high school principal: *Key Veteran News* (Islamorada, FL), June 22, 1935; University of North Carolina General Alumni Association, *2015 Alumni Directory of the University of North Carolina* (Chesapeake, VA: Harris Connect LLC, 2015), p. A1126.

29. Other veterans had worked at large newspapers: *Key Veteran News* (Islamorada, FL), June 8, 1935.

29. "There were flies," said Albert Keith: Testimony of Albert Keith, Records Group 69 006.1, Works Progress Administration Selected Records Relating to the 1935 Florida Hurricane, National Archives, College Park, Maryland.

30. In a brief report, Close noted that camp sanitation was "terrible": Memo, E. J. Close to W. H. Green, November 17, 1934, Records Group 69 006.1, Works Progress Administration Selected Records Relating to the 1935 Florida Hurricane, National Archives, College Park, Maryland.

30. On December 3 William H. D. : Transcript of meeting of Ed Neff, Colonel G. S. Robinson, and W. H. D. Hinchman, December 3, 1934, Records Group 69 006.1, Works Progress Administration Selected Records Relating to the 1935 Florida Hurricane, National Archives, College Park, Maryland.

31. On Christmas Eve, Albert Keith wrote a letter: Letter, Albert C. Keith, Islamorada, Florida, to "The Attorney General," Washington, DC, December 24, 1934, Records Group 69 006.1, Works Progress Administration Selected Records Relating to the 1935 Florida Hurricane, National Archives, College Park, Maryland.

31. On New Year's Eve, 1934: *The Boston Globe*, January 1, 1935.

31. A few days later, Daniel A. Hobart: Associated Press/*The Morning Call* (Allentown, PA), January 3, 1935.

31. Brightly colored signs with the slogan "Help to All Who Help Themselves": Copy of sign reading "Help to All Who Help Themselves," Records Group 69 006.1, Works Progress Administration Selected Records Relating to the 1935 Florida Hurricane, National Archives, College Park, Maryland.

31. African American women in Key West were encouraged: *Key West Citizen*, December 11, 1934.

31. Gilfond and his staff, which included talented graphic artists: *Key West*, a booklet produced by the Florida Emergency Relief Administration in Key West, Florida, 1934, Records Group 69 006.1, Works Progress Administration Selected Records Relating to the 1935 Florida Hurricane, National Archives, College Park, Maryland.

32. About 40,000 tourists visited Key West during the 1934–1935 season: Stuart McIver, *Hemingway's Key West* (Sarasota, FL: Pineapple Press, 1993), p. 61.

32. Even Dizzy Dean, the star pitcher: *Miami Herald*, December 11, 1934.

32. No one had bothered to confer with Ernest Hemingway: "The Sights of Whitehead Street: A Key West Letter," by Ernest Hemingway, *Esquire* magazine, April 1935.

32. Hemingway made light of the intrusions: "The Sights of Whitehead Street: A Key West Letter," by Ernest Hemingway, *Esquire* magazine, April 1935.

32. . . . anti–New Deal Republican who despised Julius Stone: Stuart McIver, *Hemingway's Key West* (Sarasota, FL: Pineapple Press, 1993), p. 59.

32. When Florida ERA leaders decided in early 1935: Stuart McIver, *Hemingway's Key West* (Sarasota, FL: Pineapple Press, 1993), p. 55.

32. The author bought 19,000 of them for $38: *Key West Citizen*, April 22, 1937.

32. By early February 1935 about 600 men were living in the Upper Keys: *Miami Daily News*, February 3, 1935.

33. "They had to rush to get up tents of any description: Testimony of Hubert Nichols, Records Group 69 006.1, Works Progress Administration Selected Records Relating to the 1935 Florida Hurricane, National Archives, College Park, Maryland.

33. Rufus Johnson, who'd lived on the islands for more than 50 years: Testimony of Rufus Johnson, Records Group 69 006.1, Works Progress Administration Selected Records Relating to the 1935 Florida Hurricane, National Archives, College Park, Maryland.

33. Johnson warned one administrator about putting the camps: Testimony of Rufus Johnson, Records Group 69 006.1, Works Progress Administration Selected Records Relating to the 1935 Florida Hurricane, National Archives, College Park, Maryland.

34. By late February the men in Camp 3 had formed: Letter, Perry A. Fellows, Washington, to Julius Stone, Miami, March 2, 1935, Records Group 69 006.1, Works Progress Administration Selected Records Relating to the 1935 Florida Hurricane, National Archives, College Park, Maryland.

34. On February 25 the men in Camp 3 went on strike: *Miami Daily News*, March 2, 1935.

34. The strike and the presence of the National Guard: *Miami Daily News*, March 2, 1935.

35. Two days later the veterans returned to work: *Miami Daily News*, March 4, 1935.

35. "I considered [Cutler] rather an exceptional person: Testimony of Paul Vander Schouw, Records Group 69 006.1, Works Progress Administration Selected Records Relating to the 1935 Florida Hurricane, National Archives, College Park, Maryland.

36. . . . said Cutler was "a very nervous sort of fellow" who "imagines things": Testimony of Robert Aldrich Ayer, Records Group 69 006.1, Works Progress Administration Selected Records Relating to the 1935 Florida Hurricane, National Archives, College Park, Maryland.

36. Stone said that 25,000 veterans eventually would be sent to the Keys: *Palm Beach Post*, March 16, 1935; *The Courier-Journal* (Louisville, KY), March 16, 1935.

36. Florida officials and residents were horrified: *Sarasota Tribune*, March 17, 1935; *Fort Myers News Press*, March 17, 1935.

37. . . . the *Washington Post* published two stories by Edward Folliard: *Washington Post*, March 24, 1935, and March 25, 1935.

37. "You have another good man down there now: Letter, Joseph Hyde Pratt to W. H. D. Hinchman, March 25, 1935, Records Group 69 006.1, Works Progress Administration Selected Records Relating to the 1935 Florida Hurricane, National Archives, College Park, Maryland.

37. But before going he delivered speeches: *Key Veteran News* (Islamorada, FL), March 30, 1935.

38. Bernard Russell, who was 16 in 1935, recalled that one day: Author's interview with Bernard Russell, Islamorada, Florida, April 12, 1997, transcript on file at Florida Keys History and Discovery Center, Islamorada, Florida.

38. The postmaster was troubled by the frequent drunkenness: Testimony of John A. Russell, Records Group 69 006.1, Works Progress Administration Selected Records Relating to the 1935 Florida Hurricane, National Archives, College Park, Maryland.

38. "Every payday was just a big spree": Testimony of Hubert Campbell Nichols to H. W. Farmer, September 17, 1935, Homestead, Florida, Records Group 69 006.1, Works Progress Administration Selected Records Relating to the 1935 Florida Hurricane, National Archives, College Park, Maryland.

38. "We always had boom days then: Testimony of Dr. Lassiter Alexander, Records Group 69 006.1, Works Progress Administration Selected Records Relating to the 1935 Florida Hurricane, National Archives, College Park, Maryland.

39. Ghent, an Alabama native, had lived in Florida: Florida Hurricane Disaster, Hearings Before the Committee on World War Veterans' Legislation, House of Representatives, 74th Congress, Second Session, on H.R. 9486 (Washington, DC: U.S. Government Printing Office, 1936), p. 285.

39. . . . who'd served in the U.S. Navy during World War I: Florida Hurricane Disaster, Hearings Before the Committee on World War Veterans' Legislation, House of Representatives, 74th Congress, Second Session, on H.R. 9486 (Washington, DC: U.S. Government Printing Office, 1936), p. 285.

39. Ghent's superiors in Florida weren't as impressed: Testimony of Conrad Van Hyning, Records Group 69 006.1, Works Progress Administration Selected Records Relating to the 1935 Florida Hurricane, National Archives, College Park, Maryland.

40. Work had scarcely begun on Camp 5: "Day letter" from W. H. D. Hinchman to Ghent, April 8, 1935, Records Group 69 006.1, Works Progress Administration Selected Records Relating to the 1935 Florida Hurricane, National Archives, College Park, Maryland.

40. In an April 9 letter to Pratt, Ghent pointed out: Letter, F. B. Ghent, Islamorada, Florida, to Colonel Joseph Hyde Pratt, Atlanta, April 9, 1935, Records Group 69 006.1, Works Progress Administration Selected Records Relating to the 1935 Florida Hurricane, National Archives, College Park, Maryland.

40. The storm—which nearly leveled the city—was so fierce: *Miami Herald*, October 17, 1996.

41. During a lengthy April 24 meeting with the vets, Ghent commented: Minutes of Meeting/7:45 to 10:45 P.M. April 24, 1935/Veterans Rehabilitation Camp No. 3/ Islamorada, Florida, Records Group 69 006.1, Works Progress Administration Selected Records Relating to the 1935 Florida Hurricane, National Archives, College Park, Maryland; *Key Veteran News* (Islamorada, FL), April 27, 1935.

41. On May 13 the National Guard troops were withdrawn: *Key Veteran News* (Islamorada, FL), May 18, 1935.

41. "Now, the men didn't pay much attention to rules": Testimony of Loring Scott, Records Group 69 006.1, Works Progress Administration Selected Records Relating to the 1935 Florida Hurricane, National Archives, College Park, Maryland.

42. "They seem to be glad to have these men come to Key West": Transcript of meeting of Ed Neff, Colonel G. S. Robinson, and W. H. D. Hinchman, December 3, 1934, Records Group 69 006.1, Works Progress Administration Selected Records Relating to the 1935 Florida Hurricane, National Archives, College Park, Maryland.

42. In the saloons of Key West, Ernest Hemingway was happy: Stuart McIver, *Hemingway's Key West* (Sarasota, FL: Pineapple Press, 1993), p. 67.

42. They'd block the railroad tracks with logs: Author's interview with Bernard Russell, Islamorada, Florida, April 12, 1997, transcript on file at Florida Keys History and Discovery Center, Islamorada, Florida.

42. The vets' behavior tried the patience: Author's interview with Bernard Russell, Islamorada, Florida, April 12, 1997, transcript on file at Florida Keys History and Discovery Center, Islamorada, Florida.

42. Homestead librarian Lily Bow—whose son Lawrence Bow: *Key Veteran News* (Islamorada, FL), August 3, 1935; *The Leader-Enterprise* (Homestead, FL), September 6, 1935.

43. Joseph Huau got busy setting up volleyball courts: Testimony of J. H. Huau, Records Group 69 006.1, Works Progress Administration Selected Records Relating to the 1935 Florida Hurricane, National Archives, College Park, Maryland.

43. A smattering of former professional baseball players: *Key Veteran News* (Islamorada, FL), May 18, 1935.

43. . . . the *Key Veteran News* reported on its front page: *Key Veteran News* (Islamorada, FL), May 18, 1935.

44. "Mr. Ghent said, 'We have trains waiting for you in Miami: Testimony of Clyde McCain, Records Group 69 006.1, Works Progress Administration Selected Records Relating to the 1935 Florida Hurricane, National Archives, College Park, Maryland.

44. On June 6 Loflin sent a letter to Ghent: Letter, Scott Loflin to Fred Ghent, June 6, 1935, Records Group 69 006.1, Works Progress Administration Selected Records Relating to the 1935 Florida Hurricane, National Archives, College Park, Maryland.

45. . . . said the vets were doing "wonderful work on the bridge project": Testimony of Junius T. Wigginton, Records Group 69 006.1, Works Progress Administration Selected Records Relating to the 1935 Florida Hurricane, National Archives, College Park, Maryland.

46. But fitting the men into daily work routines wasn't easy: Testimony of Hubert Campbell Nichols, Records Group 69 006.1, Works Progress Administration Selected Records Relating to the 1935 Florida Hurricane, National Archives, College Park, Maryland.

46. Sheeran assigned the vets to clear brush on shore: Testimony of Ed Sheeran, Records Group 69 006.1, Works Progress Administration Selected Records Relating to the 1935 Florida Hurricane, National Archives, College Park, Maryland.

46. But Hubert Nichols, who worked under Sheeran, said it was "just impossible": Testimony of Hubert Campbell Nichols, Records Group 69 006.1, Works Progress Administration Selected Records Relating to the 1935 Florida Hurricane, National Archives, College Park, Maryland.

46. "About the middle of June, the mosquitoes were so bad: Testimony of Loring Scott, Records Group 69 006.1, Works Progress Administration Selected Records Relating to the 1935 Florida Hurricane, National Archives, College Park, Maryland.

47. Recently [it] got so I could not get work: Testimony of Ira Hatch, Records Group 69 006.1, Works Progress Administration Selected Records Relating to the 1935 Florida Hurricane, National Archives, College Park, Maryland.

47. Barometers have been around for hundreds of years: Nathaniel Bowditch, *American Practical Navigator*, vol. 1 (Washington, DC: U.S. Department of Defense, 1977 edition), p. 845–846.

48. Carson's Miami office was responsible for monitoring conditions: Testimony of Ernest Carson, Records Group 69 006.1, Works Progress Administration Selected Records Relating to the 1935 Florida Hurricane, National Archives, College Park, Maryland.

48. A hurricane in the northern hemisphere rotates counterclockwise: Felix M. Cornell and Allan C. Hoffman, eds. *American Merchant Seaman's Manual* (New York: Cornell Maritime Press, 1942), p. 442–43.

49. Sailors refer to this part of a hurricane: Harry A. Baldridge and Austin M. Knight, *Modern Seamanship* (New York: D. Van Nostrand Company, Inc., 1930), p. 913.

50. Yet the Weather Bureau had still boasted that no hurricane: *Honolulu Star Advertiser, The Index-Journal* (Greenville, SC), *Lincoln* (Nebraska) *Sunday Journal and Star,* and others, July 3–July 14, 1935.

50. Ray W. Sheldon was a Massachusetts native: Application for Marriage License CJ#10302, Ray Wakefield Sheldon, State of Florida Office of Vital Statistics, Dade County, Miami, Florida, August 26, 1935, copy on file at Florida Keys History and Discovery Center, Islamorada, Florida.

50. Sheldon's wife had died unexpectedly in November 1934: *Fort Lauderdale Daily News* and others, November 1, 1934.

50. . . . he planned to get married again: Application for Marriage License, Ray Wakefield Sheldon and Gayle L. Colvert, Dade County, Florida, August 26, 1935, copy on file at Florida Keys History and Discovery Center, Islamorada, Florida.

51. "I found that advice or constructive criticism: Testimony of John Good, Records Group 69 006.1, Works Progress Administration Selected Records Relating to the 1935 Florida Hurricane, National Archives, College Park, Maryland.

51. "I thought Mr. Sheldon was the type that wouldn't listen: Testimony of Wilbur E. Jones, Records Group 69 006.1, Works Progress Administration Selected Records Relating to the 1935 Florida Hurricane, National Archives, College Park, Maryland.

51. F. E. Simpson, a veteran at the South Carolina camp, fired back: *Key Veteran News* (Islamorada, FL), August 31, 1935.

52. . . . Conrad Van Hyning learned in Washington: Testimony of Conrad Van Hyning, Records Group 69 006.1, Works Progress Administration Selected Records Relating to the 1935 Florida Hurricane, National Archives, College Park, Maryland.

52. On the afternoon of August 12, a discouraged Fred Ghent: Testimony of Fred Ghent, Records Group 69 006.1, Works Progress Administration Selected Records Relating to the 1935 Florida Hurricane, National Archives, College Park, Maryland.

53. A few hours before he had to catch his train, Ghent met Van Hyning: *Jacksonville Journal,* October 2, 1935.

53. On August 16 WPA administrator Harry Hopkins announced: *New York Times,* August 16, 1935.

53. On August 26 Ray Sheldon married Gayle Colvert: Marriage License 13170, Central Bureau of Vital Statistics, State of Florida, Dade County, Miami, Florida, copy on file at Florida Keys History and Discovery Center, Islamorada, Florida.

53. At 11:15 Friday morning, camp officials started handing out pay envelopes: Testimony of Louis Maloney, Records Group 69 006.1, Works Progress Administration Selected Records Relating to the 1935 Florida Hurricane, National Archives, College Park, Maryland.

54. Albert Davis, the barber at Camp 1: Testimony of Albert V. Davis, Records Group 69 006.1, Works Progress Administration Selected Records Relating to the 1935 Florida Hurricane, National Archives, College Park, Maryland.

54. "Conditions remain unsettled and slightly squally: Appendix A. Advisories Issued by the U.S. Weather Bureau, Florida Hurricane Disaster, Hearings Before the Committee on World War Veterans' Legislation, House of Representatives, 74th Congress, Second Session, on H.R. 9486 (Washington, DC: U.S. Government Printing Office, 1936), p. 101–102.

54. The newspaper tried to buck up its readers' sagging spirits: *Key Veteran News* (Islamorada, FL), August 31, 1935.

54. "Every day we hear discussion and dissertation: *Key Veteran News* (Islamorada, FL), August 31, 1935.

55. "Tropical disturbance of small diameter but considerable intensity: Appendix A. Advisories Issued by the US. Weather Bureau, Florida Hurricane Disaster, Hearings Before the Committee on World War Veterans' Legislation, House of Representatives, 74th Congress, Second Session, on H.R. 9486 (Washington, DC: U.S. Government Printing Office, 1936), p. 101–102.

Chapter 3: A Wind Stirs in the Atlantic

57. At 11 a.m. on Saturday, August 31, 1935, the surface temperature: *Miami Daily News*, August 31, 1935.

58. In Homestead two sisters, Myrtle and Sarah Hodge: *The Leader-Enterprise* (Homestead, FL), September 6, 1935.

58. In Islamorada, Rita Berteau, the 14-year-old daughter: List of Casualties, Hurricane of September 2, 1935, compiled by American Red Cross, on file at Monroe County Public Library, Key West, Florida; *The Leader-Enterprise* (Homestead, FL), September 6, 1935.

58. On Saturday, August 31, Bascom Grooms Jr., 13, was trying to squeeze: Author's telephone interview with Bascom Grooms Jr., January 12, 2000, transcript on file at Florida Keys History and Discovery Center, Islamorada, Florida.

58. Her impulsive marriage on August 21, 1934, to Lieutenant (j.g.) George Palmer: *Miami Daily News*, August 22, 1934.

59. But Rosalind Grooms Palmer didn't take herself or her looks: Author's telephone interview with Bascom Grooms Jr., January 12, 2000, transcript on file at Florida Keys History and Discovery Center, Islamorada, Florida.

59. In July the couple visited a photographer's studio in Miami: Author's copies of photos and documents from Bascom Grooms Jr., December 2, 2002, Key West, Florida, now part of collection at Florida Keys History and Discovery Center, Islamorada, Florida.

59. . . . Rosalind sat down at her typewriter to bang out a note: Author's copies of photos and documents from Bascom Grooms Jr., December 2, 2002, Key West, Florida, now part of collection at Florida Keys History and Discovery Center, Islamorada, Florida.

61. This advisory was waiting for Cutler: Florida Hurricane Disaster, Hearings Before the Committee on World War Veterans' Legislation, House of Representatives, 74th

Congress, Second Session, on H.R. 9486 (Washington, DC: U.S. Government Printing Office, 1936), p. 183.

61. "These men who didn't leave the camp: Testimony of John Good, Records Group 69 006.1, Works Progress Administration Selected Records Relating to the 1935 Florida Hurricane, National Archives, College Park, Maryland.

61. By Saturday afternoon the storm advisories had gotten the attention: *Miami Daily News*, August 31, 1935.

61. . . . author Ernest Hemingway put down his pencil and settled into a chair: *Miami Herald*, October 6, 1985; Stuart McIver, *Hemingway's Key West* (Sarasota, FL: Pineapple Press, 1993), p. 69.

61. . . . but the courses of brick were not straight. They rose and fell slightly: Author's visit to Ernest Hemingway Home and Museum, Key West, Florida, June 4, 1997.

62. But he was jolted out of his self-satisfaction when a small headline: *Key West Citizen*, August 31, 1935.

62. He pulled out his barometer and storm chart: Stuart McIver, *Hemingway's Key West* (Sarasota, FL: Pineapple Press, 1993), p. 64.

62. . . . the S.S. *Dixie* was leaving its berth in the New Orleans harbor: *Time* magazine, September 6, 1935; *San Francisco Chronicle*, September 6, 1935.

62. The *Dixie* had been scheduled to sail from New Orleans at 11 a.m.: *Miami Tribune*, September 6, 1935.

62. Sundstrom grew up in the small seaport of Brunswick, Georgia: *Los Angeles Times*, September 4, 1935.

63. The *Dixie* was the flagship: *Lloyd's Register of Shipping, 1935-36*, vol. 1 (London: The Society of Lloyd's, 1935); *Record of the American Bureau of Shipping* (Chicago: The Lakeside Press, R.R. Donnelly & Sons).

64. Florence Steiler, a passenger from San Francisco: *San Francisco Examiner*, September 6, 1935.

64. Among the teachers was Grace Nichols: *San Francisco Chronicle*, September 4, 1935.

64. A few were traveling with small but precious personal items: *Sunday News* (Sunday edition of the *New York Daily News*), September 8, 1935.

64. Ed Sheeran had planned to spend the Labor Day weekend: Testimony of E. H. Sheeran, Records Group 69 006.1, Works Progress Administration Selected Records Relating to the 1935 Florida Hurricane, National Archives, College Park, Maryland.

65. At 9:30 p.m. Saturday, the U.S. Weather Bureau bulletin: Florida Hurricane Disaster, Hearings Before the Committee on World War Veterans' Legislation, House of Representatives, 74th Congress, Second Session, on H.R. 9486 (Washington, DC: U.S. Government Printing Office, 1936), p. 183.

66. Throughout the day the sound of banging hammers: Testimony of Tony Lapinski, Records Group 69 006.1, Works Progress Administration Selected Records Relating to the 1935 Florida Hurricane, National Archives, College Park, Maryland.

67. M. E. Gilfond, who was now in charge of Florida ERA operations: Florida Hurricane Disaster, Hearings Before the Committee on World War Veterans' Legislation, House of Representatives, 74th Congress, Second Session, on H.R. 9486 (Washington, DC: U.S. Government Printing Office, 1936), p. 428.

68. One sign of the approach of a hurricane is the long, rhythmic swells: Author's interview with U.S. Coast Guard Warrant Officer David Umberger, Buxton, North Carolina, March 3, 1999.

68. When the swells arrive at a coastline: Author's interview with U.S. Coast Guard Warrant Officer David Umberger, Buxton, North Carolina, March 3, 1999.

68. If the direction from which the swells approach the beach does not change: Author's interview with U.S. Coast Guard Warrant Officer David Umberger; Buxton, North Carolina; March 3, 1999.

68. But local fishermen noticed the swells: Testimony of Thomas F. Lannon, Records Group 69 006.1, Works Progress Administration Selected Records Relating to the 1935 Florida Hurricane, National Archives, College Park, Maryland.

68. Barometers also usually indicate the approach of a hurricane: Nathaniel Bowditch, *American Practical Navigator*, vol. 1 (Washington, DC: U.S. Department of Defense, 1977 edition), p. 901–902.

69. "We all hoped it would blow the mosquitoes away: Testimony of Fred Bomer Jr., Records Group 69 006.1, Works Progress Administration Selected Records Relating to the 1935 Florida Hurricane, National Archives, College Park, Maryland.

69. After the service they chatted briefly about the bad weather: Author's interview with Alma Pinder Dalton and Laurette Pinder Russell, Islamorada, Florida, November 18, 1997, transcript on file at Florida Keys History and Discovery Center, Islamorada, Florida.

69. At Lower Matecumbe Key, Cardy Bradford: *Miami Herald*, October 6, 1985.

69. The Weather Bureau issued another advisory: Florida Hurricane Disaster, Hearings Before the Committee on World War Veterans' Legislation, House of Representatives, 74th Congress, Second Session, on H.R. 9486 (Washington, DC: U.S. Government Printing Office, 1936), p. 184.

70. "I knew that Sam was very concerned: Testimony of Captain Ed Butters, Records Group 69 006.1, Works Progress Administration Selected Records Relating to the 1935 Florida Hurricane, National Archives, College Park, Maryland.

71. Paul Jeans, editor of Miami Beach's: Paul G. Jeans, *Tropical Disturbance: The Story of the Making of the Miami Tribune* (Miami, published as an insert of the *Miami Tribune* edition of April 4, 1937).

72. "A Hearst newspaper is like a screaming woman: W. A. Swanberg, *Citizen Hearst: A Biography of William Randolph Hearst* (New York: Galahad Books, 1961), p. 351.

72. In Miami, Jeans worked for publisher Moe Annenberg: "Newspapers of America's Last Frontier," by Jeanne Bellamy, *Tequesta: The Journal of the Historical Association of Southern Florida*, no. 12 (1952), p. 14.

72. Annenberg amassed his own fortune: "Newspapers of America's Last Frontier," by Jeanne Bellamy, *Tequesta: The Journal of the Historical Association of Southern Florida*, no. 12 (1952), p. 14; Nixon Smiley, *Knights of the Fourth Estate: The Story of the* Miami Herald (Miami: E.A. Seemann Publishing Co., 1974), p. 129.

73. The Weather Bureau's Sunday morning advisory: Narrative of MAS Activities Before, During and Following the September 2 Hurricane, 1935, Records Group 26.651, "Wrecks, Fires, Floods, etc.," Records of the U.S. Coast Guard, General

Correspondence, 1910–1935, National Archives and Records Administration, Washington, DC.

73. Around 11 a.m. Lieutenant William L. Clemmer: Narrative of MAS Activities Before, During and Following the September 2 Hurricane, 1935, Records Group 26.651, "Wrecks, Fires, Floods, etc.," Records of the U.S. Coast Guard, General Correspondence, 1910–1935, National Archives and Records Administration, Washington, DC.

74. By noon, the driver Cutler had sent to Miami: Testimony of Eugene A. Pattison, Records Group 69 006.1, Works Progress Administration Selected Records Relating to the 1935 Florida Hurricane, National Archives, College Park, Maryland.

74. Lieutenant Clemmer was back in the skies: Narrative of MAS Activities Before, During and Following the September 2 Hurricane, 1935, Records Group 26.651, "Wrecks, Fires, Floods, etc.," Records of the U.S. Coast Guard, General Correspondence, 1910–1935, National Archives and Records Administration, Washington, DC.

75. But the sight of the big Coast Guard seaplane: Testimony of Melton Jarrell, Records Group 69 006.1, Works Progress Administration Selected Records Relating to the 1935 Florida Hurricane, National Archives, College Park, Maryland.

75. Cutler told Ghent that there were indications: Testimony of John Good, Records Group 69 006.1, Works Progress Administration Selected Records Relating to the 1935 Florida Hurricane, National Archives, College Park, Maryland.

75. In Islamorada Postmaster John Russell: Testimony of John A. Russell to D. W. Kennamer and H. W. Farmer, Miami, Florida, September 14, 1935, Records Group 69 006.1, Works Progress Administration Selected Records Relating to the 1935 Florida Hurricane, National Archives, College Park, Maryland.

76. The veteran was fascinated by the prospect: Florida Hurricane Disaster, Hearings Before the Committee on World War Veterans' Legislation, House of Representatives, 74th Congress, Second Session, on H.R. 9486 (Washington, DC: U.S. Government Printing Office, 1936), p. 248.

76. . . . another advisory was released from the Weather Bureau: Florida Hurricane Disaster, Hearings Before the Committee on World War Veterans' Legislation, House of Representatives, 74th Congress, Second Session, on H.R. 9486 (Washington, DC: U.S. Government Printing Office, 1936), p. 184.

77. "The majority of us thought they would go ahead: Testimony of D. A. Malcolm, Records Group 69 006.1, Works Progress Administration Selected Records Relating to the 1935 Florida Hurricane, National Archives, College Park, Maryland.

77. Scientists do not fully understand: Author's telephone interview with meteorologist Chris Landsea, January 7, 2000.

77. Scientists are still trying to figure out: Author's telephone interview with meteorologist Chris Landsea, January 7, 2000.

78. At sunset John Dombrauski: Testimony of John Dombrauski, Records Group 69 006.1, Works Progress Administration Selected Records Relating to the 1935 Florida Hurricane, National Archives, College Park, Maryland.

79. Still, officials in Isabela des Augua: *New York Times*, September 2, 1935; *Havana Post*, September 3, 1935.

79. At Lower Matecumbe Key, Ed Sheeran's crew: Testimony of Ed Sheeran, Records Group 69 006.1, Works Progress Administration Selected Records Relating to the 1935 Florida Hurricane, National Archives, College Park, Maryland.

79. Thinking that he was speaking to Sheldon, Carson read: Testimony of Ernest Carson, Records Group 69 006.1, Works Progress Administration Selected Records Relating to the 1935 Florida Hurricane, National Archives, College Park, Maryland.

80. As Sheldon was about to retire for the night: Testimony of Eugene A. Pattison, Records Group 69 006.1, Works Progress Administration Selected Records Relating to the 1935 Florida Hurricane, National Archives, College Park, Maryland.

80. At 3:30 a.m. on Monday, the phone rang again: Testimony of Ernest Carson, Records Group 69 006.1, Works Progress Administration Selected Records Relating to the 1935 Florida Hurricane, National Archives, College Park, Maryland.

80. Albert Buck, the foreman at Camp 5: Testimony of Albert S. Buck, Records Group 69 006.1, Works Progress Administration Selected Records Relating to the 1935 Florida Hurricane, National Archives, College Park, Maryland.

80. Seventeen-year-old Laurette Pinder looked out: Author's interview with Alma Pinder Dalton and Laurette Pinder Russell, Islamorada, Florida, November 18, 1997, transcript on file at Florida Keys History and Discovery Center, Islamorada, Florida.

81. Buck decided to go to the Hotel Matecumbe: Testimony of Albert S. Buck, Records Group 69 006.1, Works Progress Administration Selected Records Relating to the 1935 Florida Hurricane, National Archives, College Park, Maryland.

81. A few minutes later Buck, the Camp 5 foreman: Testimony of Albert S. Buck, Records Group 69 006.1, Works Progress Administration Selected Records Relating to the 1935 Florida Hurricane, National Archives, College Park, Maryland.

81. And he ordered O. D. King: Testimony of O. D. King, Records Group 69 006.1, Works Progress Administration Selected Records Relating to the 1935 Florida Hurricane, National Archives, College Park, Maryland.

82. Perry Fellows, an administrative assistant for the WPA: Florida Hurricane Disaster, Hearings Before the Committee on World War Veterans' Legislation, House of Representatives, 74th Congress, Second Session, on H.R. 9486 (Washington, DC: U.S. Government Printing Office, 1936), p. 547.

82. The headline read "Hurricane Heads Toward Florida": *Washington Post*, September 2, 1935.

82. In Tavernier young Bascom Grooms Jr. waited: Author's telephone interview with Bascom Grooms Jr., January 12, 2000, transcript on file at Florida Keys History and Discovery Center, Islamorada, Florida.

82. . . . . *Miami Daily News* reporter William Johns picked up his phone: *New York Times*, September 5, 1935.

83. Meanwhile in Washington, Perry Fellows decided: Florida Hurricane Disaster, Hearings Before the Committee on World War Veterans' Legislation, House of Representatives, 74th Congress, Second Session, on H.R. 9486 (Washington, DC: U.S. Government Printing Office, 1936), p. 547.

83. Fellows briefed Williams about the story: Florida Hurricane Disaster, Hearings Before the Committee on World War Veterans' Legislation, House of Representatives,

74th Congress, Second Session, on H.R. 9486 (Washington, DC: U.S. Government Printing Office, 1936), p. 547.

83. Fellows got on the phone: Florida Hurricane Disaster, Hearings Before the Committee on World War Veterans' Legislation, House of Representatives, 74th Congress, Second Session, on H.R. 9486 (Washington, DC: U.S. Government Printing Office, 1936), p. 547

83. Van Hyning decided to call M. E. Gilfond: Florida Hurricane Disaster, Hearings Before the Committee on World War Veterans' Legislation, House of Representatives, 74th Congress, Second Session, on H.R. 9486 (Washington, DC: U.S. Government Printing Office, 1936), p. 425.

83. In the Straits of Florida, the *Dixie* had rounded Key West: *The Literary Digest*, September 14, 1935.

83. The regularly scheduled flight from Havana to Miami: *Prescott (Arizona) Evening Courier*, September 2, 1924.

83. Meanwhile, Cuban meteorologists told the Associated Press: Associated Press/ *Prescott (Arizona) Evening Courier*, September 2, 1935.

83. At the makeshift veterans hospital near Snake Creek, Elmer Darty: Testimony of Elmer Darty, Records Group 69 006.1, Works Progress Administration Selected Records Relating to the 1935 Florida Hurricane, National Archives, College Park, Maryland.

84. Around 10:30 a.m. Sheldon spoke with Ernest Carson: Testimony of Ernest Carson, Records Group 69 006.1, Works Progress Administration Selected Records Relating to the 1935 Florida Hurricane, National Archives, College Park, Maryland.

84. M. E. Gilfond finally got a telephone line: Florida Hurricane Disaster, Hearings Before the Committee on World War Veterans' Legislation, House of Representatives, 74th Congress, Second Session, on H.R. 9486 (Washington, DC: U.S. Government Printing Office, 1936), p. 425.

84. "I told Mr. Gilfond we were watching the barometer: Florida Hurricane Disaster, Hearings Before the Committee on World War Veterans' Legislation, House of Representatives, 74th Congress, Second Session, on H.R. 9486 (Washington, DC: U.S. Government Printing Office, 1936), p. 460.

84. We were sitting around talking: Testimony of Jacob Herbert, Records Group 69 006.1, Works Progress Administration Selected Records Relating to the 1935 Florida Hurricane, National Archives, College Park, Maryland.

85. . . . Pan American's big seaplane bounced across: American Legion Digest of Minutes, National Executive Committee Meetings, St. Louis, Missouri, September 22 and 26, 1935, Exhibit B, by Watson B. Miller, p. 21.

85. . . . the pilot reported seeing heavy, dark clouds: Associated Press/*Prescott* (Arizona) *Evening Courier*, September 2, 1935.

85. . . . where he bumped into Paul Vander Schouw: Testimony of Paul Vander Schouw, Records Group 69 006.1, Works Progress Administration Selected Records Relating to the 1935 Florida Hurricane, National Archives, College Park, Maryland.

86. Meanwhile, Lawrence Bow, the former assistant camp administrator: Testimony of Richard Lawrence Bow, Records Group 69 006.1, Works Progress Administration

Selected Records Relating to the 1935 Florida Hurricane, National Archives, College Park, Maryland.

86. "This thing looks bad to me: Testimony of Paul Vander Schouw, Records Group 69 006.1, Works Progress Administration Selected Records Relating to the 1935 Florida Hurricane, National Archives, College Park, Maryland.

87. "I was glad to get out of there": Testimony of Paul Vander Schouw, Records Group 69 006.1, Works Progress Administration Selected Records Relating to the 1935 Florida Hurricane, National Archives, College Park, Maryland.

Chapter 4: It's Blowing Like Hell Down Here

90. In winds blowing at hurricane force—74 mph: *Los Angeles Times*, August 26, 1992.

91. The 160-ton locomotive needed to get up steam before the train could leave: Author's telephone interview with C. E. Spear, retired locomotive mechanic, North Carolina Transportation Museum, October 12, 1998.

92. At Tavernier young Bascom Grooms Jr.: Author's telephone interview with Bascom Grooms Jr., January 12, 2000, transcript on file at Florida Keys History and Discovery Center, Islamorada, Florida.

93. . . . caretaker and Weather Bureau observer James E. Duane Jr. clutched his barometer: "The Hurricane of August 31 to September 6, 1935," by W. F. McDonald, *Monthly Weather Review*, September 1935, p. 270.

93. At 2 p.m. Duane's barometer read 28.90: "The Hurricane of August 31 to September 6, 1935," by W. F. McDonald, *Monthly Weather Review*, September 1935, p. 270.

94. The wind was beginning to unnerve Fern: Fern Butters, unpublished manuscript, "Fern's account of the '35 hurricane," undated, copy provided by her granddaughter-in-law Gayle Butters of Gainesville, Florida, October 2000, copy on file at Florida Keys History and Discovery Center, Islamorada, Florida.

94. . . . FEC engineer J. J. Haycraft answered his ringing telephone: *Miami Daily News*, September 5, 1935.

97. Cuban meteorologists were determined to find: *Havana Post*, September 2, 1935; *Miami Herald*, *St. Petersburg Times*, *Orlando Morning Sentinel*, September 23, 1935.

97. . . . and climbed into an American-made Curtiss P-6S "Hawk": Email exchanges with Neal Martin Dorst, 2015–2018, research meteorologist with Hurricane Research Division, National Oceanic and Atmospheric Administration, Miami.

97. "It appeared to be a cone-shaped body of clouds: *Miami Herald*, *St. Petersburg Times*, *Orlando Morning Sentinel*, September 23, 1935.

98. Duane took another barometric pressure reading: "The Hurricane of August 31 to September 6, 1935," by W. F. McDonald, *Monthly Weather Review*, September 1935, p. 270.

98. "Along about supper time the wind: Testimony of Jacob Herbert, Records Group 69 006.1, Works Progress Administration Selected Records Relating to the 1935 Florida Hurricane, National Archives, College Park, Maryland.

98. "We got uneasy about four o'clock,": Testimony of John Dombrauski, Records Group 69 006.1, Works Progress Administration Selected Records Relating to the 1935 Florida Hurricane, National Archives, College Park, Maryland.

99. In Miami, engineer Haycraft grasped the handle: *Miami Daily News*, September 5, 1935.

99. "I instructed Mr. Pepper to make haste: Testimony of B. E. Davis, Records Group 69 006.1, Works Progress Administration Selected Records Relating to the 1935 Florida Hurricane, National Archives, College Park, Maryland.

100. O. D. King, the motor pool supervisor: Testimony of O. D. King, Records Group 69 006.1, Works Progress Administration Selected Records Relating to the 1935 Florida Hurricane, National Archives, College Park, Maryland.

100. At about 5:15 p.m. the evacuation train: *Miami Daily News*, September 4, 1935.

100. Branch's plan was to run this configuration: George Branch, in a letter to his daughter, Frances Jane Bloodworth, September 15, 1935, copy on file at Florida Keys History and Discovery Center, Islamorada, Florida.

101. "The old Atlantic was kissing our feet: George Branch, in a letter to his daughter, Frances Jane Bloodworth, September 15, 1935, copy on file at Florida Keys History and Discovery Center, Islamorada, Florida.

101. Conditions improved a little: George Branch, in a letter to his daughter, Frances Jane Bloodworth, September 15, 1935, copy on file at Florida Keys History and Discovery Center, Islamorada, Florida.

101. The men were finishing their meal when Ed Butters: Testimony of Ed Butters, Records Group 69 006.1, Works Progress Administration Selected Records Relating to the 1935 Florida Hurricane, National Archives, College Park, Maryland.

102. "The ship was hammered by such waves: Associated Press/*Standard-Sentinel* (Hazelton, PA), September 6, 1935.

102. . . . caught in the hurricane's dangerous semicircle: Author's interview with U.S. Coast Guard Warrant Officer Dave Umberger, Buxton, North Carolina, March 3, 1999.

103. "We heard the wind: Associated Press/*The Gettysburg* (Pennsylvania) *Times*, September 6, 1935.

104. "We'd been telling ourselves how much better: Testimony of Leroy J. McMullen, Records Group 69 006.1, Works Progress Administration Selected Records Relating to the 1935 Florida Hurricane, National Archives, College Park, Maryland.

104. "Nearly everybody ran: Testimony of James B. Lindley, Records Group 69 006.1, Works Progress Administration Selected Records Relating to the 1935 Florida Hurricane, National Archives, College Park, Maryland.

104. G. C. Sain, the timekeeper at Camp 3: Testimony of G. C. Sain, Records Group 69 006.1, Works Progress Administration Selected Records Relating to the 1935 Florida Hurricane, National Archives, College Park, Maryland.

106. . . . store owner Cardy Bradford was talking on the phone: *Miami Herald*, October 6, 1985.

106. "Just as I got outside the door: Testimony of Gay M. Postell, Records Group 69 006.1, Works Progress Administration Selected Records Relating to the 1935 Florida Hurricane, National Archives, College Park, Maryland.

106. John Dombrauski and Adam Rambowski made a couple of stops: Testimony of John Dombrauski, Records Group 69 006.1, Works Progress Administration Selected

Records Relating to the 1935 Florida Hurricane, National Archives, College Park, Maryland.

107. Aboard the train, George Branch and his crew: George Branch, in a letter to his daughter, Frances Jane Bloodworth, September 15, 1935, copy on file at Florida Keys History and Discovery Center, Islamorada, Florida.

107. Down at Long Key, James Duane's barometer: "The Hurricane of August 31 to September 6, 1935," by W. F. McDonald, *Monthly Weather Review*, September 1935, p. 270.

107. Nearby, Mallie K. Pitman: Testimony of Mallie K. Pitman, Records Group 69 006.1, Works Progress Administration Selected Records Relating to the 1935 Florida Hurricane, National Archives, College Park, Maryland.

108. The train was moving at about 40 mph: George Branch, in a letter to his daughter, Frances Jane Bloodworth, September 15, 1935, copy on file at Florida Keys History and Discovery Center, Islamorada, Florida.

Chapter 5: In the Heft of the Hurricane

109. George Branch kept the train between himself and the howling wind: George Branch, in a letter to his daughter, Frances Jane Bloodworth, September 15, 1935, copy on file at Florida Keys History and Discovery Center, Islamorada, Florida.

109. As Mallie Pitman neared the railroad track: Testimony of Mallie Pitman, Records Group 69 006.1, Works Progress Administration Selected Records Relating to the 1935 Florida Hurricane, National Archives, College Park, Maryland.

110. . . . a few more veterans and some Windley Key residents: *Miami Daily News*, September 4, 1935.

110. Branch returned to the locomotive: George Branch, in a letter to his daughter, Frances Jane Bloodworth, September 15, 1935, copy on file at the Florida Keys History and Discovery Center, Islamorada, Florida.

110. When James Duane Jr. recorded his 7 p.m. barometer reading: "The Hurricane of August 31 to September 6, 1935," by W. F. McDonald, *Monthly Weather Review*, September 1935, p. 270.

110. The size of the surge is directly related: Author's telephone interview with meteorologist Chris Landsea, January 7, 2000.

111. A few Islamorada residents had gathered at the home of Reverend Robert Carlson: *Fort Myers News-Press*, September 8, 1935.

111. The needle kept plunging, and by 7:45 p.m.: Testimony of Ed Butters, Records Group 69 006.1, Works Progress Administration Selected Records Relating to the 1935 Florida Hurricane, National Archives, College Park, Maryland.

112. Meanwhile, George Outland had tired of playing the piano: United Press/*The South Bend Tribune*, September 8, 1935.

113. "The sound was horrible, even above the roar: Associated Press/*Standard-Sentinel* (Hazelton, PA), September 6, 1935.

113. Sheldon and Olin Perdue climbed down: George Branch, in a letter to his daughter, Frances Jane Bloodworth, September 15, 1935, copy on file at Florida Keys History and Discovery Center, Islamorada, Florida.

113. "The hotel sounded like it was going: Fern Butters, unpublished manuscript, "Fern's account of the '35 hurricane," undated, copy provided by her granddaughter-in-law Gayle Butters of Archer, Florida, copy on file at Florida Keys History and Discovery Center, Islamorada, Florida.

114. In the Russell family's storm shelter: Author's interview with Bernard Russell, Islamorada, Florida, December 6, 1996, transcript on file at Florida Keys History and Discovery Center, Islamorada, Florida.

115. Sheldon was very glad to see the train: Testimony of Olin Perdue, Records Group 69 006.1, Works Progress Administration Selected Records Relating to the 1935 Florida Hurricane, National Archives, College Park, Maryland.

115. "I guess those damn boxcars: George Branch, in a letter to his daughter, Frances Jane Bloodworth, September 15, 1935, copy on file at Florida Keys History and Discovery Center, Islamorada, Florida.

116. At the Russells' storm shelter, John Russell had made: Author's interview with Bernard Russell, Islamorada, Florida, December 6, 1996, transcript on file at Florida Keys History and Discovery Center, Islamorada, Florida.

116. When a storm surge makes landfall, giant breaking waves: Author's telephone interview with meteorologist Chris Landsea, January 7, 2000.

117. In the train's smoking car, reporter William Johns: *Miami Daily News*, September 4, 1935.

117. In the baggage car the wind carried away: George Branch, in a letter to his daughter, Frances Jane Bloodworth, September 15, 1935, copy on file at Florida Keys History and Discovery Center, Islamorada, Florida.

117. The surging water also pushed over the boxcar: Author's telephone interview with Wilbur Jones, May 3, 2002.

118. . . . Bernard Russell plunged into the watery, howling darkness: Author's interview with Bernard Russell, Islamorada, Florida, December 6, 1996, transcript on file at Florida Keys History and Discovery Center, Islamorada, Florida.

118. "The chief topic was death: Associated Press/*The Cincinnati Enquirer*, September 6, 1935.

118. "All the while, the ship was rolling badly: Associated Press/*The Cincinnati Enquirer*, September 6, 1935.

119. Islamorada resident Jimmy Woods took shelter: *Miami Herald*, August 31, 1997.

119. "We had constant flashes of sheet lightning: Fern Butters, unpublished manuscript, "Fern's account of the '35 hurricane," undated, copy provided by her granddaughter-in-law Gayle Butters of Archer, Florida, copy on file at Florida Keys History and Discovery Center, Islamorada, Florida.

119. The Pinders gathered near the back door: Author's interview with Alma Pinder Dalton and Laurette Pinder Russell, Islamorada, Florida, November 18, 1997, transcript on file at Florida Keys History and Discovery Center, Islamorada, Florida.

120. . . . Ed Butters stationed himself at the door of the bus: Fern Butters, unpublished manuscript, "Fern's account of the '35 hurricane," undated, copy provided by her granddaughter-in-law Gayle Butters of Archer, Florida, copy on file at Florida Keys History and Discovery Center, Islamorada, Florida.

120. . . . Carlson grabbed an ax and started hacking away at the ceiling: *Orlando Sentinel*, August 3, 1975.

120. John Conway, another Camp 1 veteran: Testimony of John Conway, Records Group 69 006.1, Works Progress Administration Selected Records Relating to the 1935 Florida Hurricane, National Archives, College Park, Maryland.

122. James Lindley, who had escaped the wreckage: Testimony of James B. Lindley, Records Group 69 006.1, Works Progress Administration Selected Records Relating to the 1935 Florida Hurricane, National Archives, College Park, Maryland.

122. Arthur Mewshaw half waded and half swam: Testimony of Arthur W. Mewshaw, Records Group 69 006.1, Works Progress Administration Selected Records Relating to the 1935 Florida Hurricane, National Archives, College Park, Maryland.

122. "All my buildings on the east side: Testimony of Roland Craig, Records Group 69 006.1, Works Progress Administration Selected Records Relating to the 1935 Florida Hurricane, National Archives, College Park, Maryland.

122. "We could hear this wave out there: Testimony of Ben E. Davis, Records Group 69 006.1, Works Progress Administration Selected Records Relating to the 1935 Florida Hurricane, National Archives, College Park, Maryland.

124. At 9:10 p.m. the torrential rains: "The Hurricane of August 31 to September 6, 1935," by W. F. McDonald, *Monthly Weather Review*, September 1935, p. 270.

124. At Craig Key, Roland Craig ventured down the railroad trestle: Records Group 69 006.1, Works Progress Administration Selected Records Relating to the 1935 Florida Hurricane, National Archives, College Park, Maryland.

124. . . . Fern Butters stood in chest-deep seawater: Fern Butters, unpublished manuscript, "Fern's account of the '35 hurricane," undated, copy provided by her granddaughter-in-law Gayle Butters of Archer, Florida, copy on file at Florida Keys History and Discovery Center, Islamorada, Florida.

125. As the water receded, Bernard Russell discovered: Author's interview with Bernard Russell, Islamorada, Florida, December 6, 1996, transcript on file at Florida Keys History and Discovery Center, Islamorada, Florida.

125. Elizabeth Pinder and her daughter Dolores: Author's interview with Alma Pinder Dalton and Laurette Pinder Russell, Islamorada, Florida, November 18, 1997, transcript on file at Florida Keys History and Discovery Center, Islamorada, Florida.

125. Ed Butters heard calls for help: Fern Butters, unpublished manuscript, "Fern's account of the '35 hurricane," undated, copy provided by her granddaughter-in-law Gayle Butters of Archer, Florida, copy on file at Florida Keys History and Discovery Center, Islamorada, Florida.

126. At Craig Key, Roland Craig and Jack Crow: Testimony of Roland Craig, Records Group 69 006.1, Works Progress Administration Selected Records Relating to the 1935 Florida Hurricane, National Archives, College Park, Maryland.

126. Not far away, Iver Olsen had pulled his small, sturdy boat: "Lowest Barometer Reading in the Florida Keys Storm of September 2, 1935," by W. F. McDonald, *Monthly Weather Review*, October 1935, p. 295.

126. Bascom Grooms Jr. ignored the deluge: Author's telephone interview with Bascom Grooms Jr., January 12, 2000, transcript on file at Florida Keys History and Discovery Center, Islamorada, Florida.

127. Leo Moran, a veteran from Philadelphia, watched as the strain: Testimony of Leo Moran, Records Group 69 006.1, Works Progress Administration Selected Records Relating to the 1935 Florida Hurricane, National Archives, College Park, Maryland.

127. Harry Gaskins, a veteran from New Bern, North Carolina: Testimony of Harry Gaskins, Records Group 69 006.1, Works Progress Administration Selected Records Relating to the 1935 Florida Hurricane, National Archives, College Park, Maryland.

128. Albert Christie, a veteran from Detroit, was trying to protect: Testimony of Albert Christie, Records Group 69 006.1, Works Progress Administration Selected Records Relating to the 1935 Florida Hurricane, National Archives, College Park, Maryland.

128. Lassiter Alexander, a physician who worked at the hospital: *The Boston Globe*, September 4, 1935.

128. In Islamorada, George Branch and the others: George Branch, in a letter to his daughter, Frances Jane Bloodworth, September 15, 1935, copy on file at Florida Keys History and Discovery Center, Islamorada, Florida

130. At Camp 1, Lloyd Fichett crawled from the wreckage: Testimony of Lloyd Fichett, Records Group 69 006.1, Works Progress Administration Selected Records Relating to the 1935 Florida Hurricane, National Archives, College Park, Maryland.

130. Charles Van Vecten, who had been visiting friends: Testimony of Charles W. Van Vecten, Records Group 69 006.1, Works Progress Administration Selected Records Relating to the 1935 Florida Hurricane, National Archives, College Park, Maryland.

130. In Islamorada, Bernard Russell followed the voice: Author's interview with Bernard Russell, Islamorada, Florida, December 6, 1996, transcript on file at Florida Keys History and Discovery Center, Islamorada, Florida.

130. At Camp 5, Melton Jarrell: Testimony of Melton Jarrell, Records Group 69 006.1, Works Progress Administration Selected Records Relating to the 1935 Florida Hurricane, National Archives, College Park, Maryland.

131. Around midnight Ernest Hemingway got out of bed: Stuart McIver, *Hemingway's Key West* (Sarasota, FL: Pineapple Press 1993), p. 66.

131. At about 12:15 a.m. Tuesday, Captain Sundstrom got his: *Washington Post*, September 4, 1935.

132. George Branch estimated that the winds: George Branch, in a letter to his daughter, Frances Jane Bloodworth, September 15, 1935, copy on file at Florida Keys History and Discovery Center, Islamorada, Florida.

132. Ray Sheldon spent the night in the locomotive: Testimony of Ray Sheldon, Records Group 69 006.1, Works Progress Administration Selected Records Relating to the 1935 Florida Hurricane, National Archives, College Park, Maryland.

132. Around 2 a.m. the winds peaked at 45 mph: *Miami Daily News*, September 5, 1935.

132. Ernest Hemingway watched his boat until about 5 a.m: Stuart McIver, *Hemingway's Key West* (Sarasota, FL: Pineapple Press 1993), p. 67.

Chapter 6: A Terrible Sunrise

134. John Russell had been badly injured: Author's interview with Bernard Russell, Islamorada, Florida, December 6, 1996, transcript on file at Florida Keys History and Discovery Center, Islamorada, Florida.

134. William Johns, the *Miami Daily News* reporter: *Miami Daily News*, September 4, 1935.

135. The departing hurricane blew over a scene: Federal Writers' Project American Guide Series, "Photographs Taken on Florida Keys after Hurricane, September 2, 1935," by Conrad Van Hyning, compiled by Phillis T. Bird, Miami, February 25, 1936, P. K. Yonge Library of Florida History, University of Florida George A. Smathers Libraries, Gainesville, Florida.

135. The ship, the *Leise Maersk*, had been picked up by a giant wave: Report to U.S. Department of Commerce, Bureau of Navigation and Steamboat Inspection, Office of Local Inspectors, Jacksonville, Florida, from Richard Mortensen, master of Danish steamer S.S. *Leise Maersk*, September 6, 1935, from personal papers of Rae Sheldon Cummings, Vero Beach, Florida, December 14, 2002, copy on file at Florida Keys History and Discovery Center, Islamorada, Florida.

136. A puppy crouched next to one of the piles: *Miami Daily News*, September 5, 1935.

137. "I would rather face machine-gun fire: *Palm Beach Post*, September 4, 1935.

137. "The wind shrieked and howled: Fern Butters, unpublished manuscript, "Fern's account of the '35 hurricane," undated, copy provided by her granddaughter-in-law Gayle Butters of Archer, Florida, copy on file at Florida Keys History and Discovery Center, Islamorada, Florida.

137. Bertram Pinder appeared and asked Ed Butters: Fern Butters, unpublished manuscript, "Fern's account of the '35 hurricane," undated, copy provided by her granddaughter-in-law Gayle Butters of Archer, Florida, copy on file at Florida Keys History and Discovery Center, Islamorada, Florida.

138. In some places the scouring force of the storm surge: Author's interview with Bernard Russell, Islamorada, Florida, December 6, 1996, transcript on file at Florida Keys History and Discovery Center, Islamorada, Florida.

141. W. H. Depperman, a passenger aboard the *Platano*: *The Evening Sun* (Baltimore), September 4, 1935.

Chapter 7: Just a Catastrophe

143. The road into the islands was a battered pathway: *Miami Daily News*, September 4, 1935.

144. Edward Kettner, a 58-year-old bus driver: *Palm Beach Post*, September 4, 1935.

144. Roy Hurley and the women from Key West: Testimony of Roy R. Hurley, Records Group 69 006.1, Works Progress Administration Selected Records Relating to the 1935 Florida Hurricane, National Archives, College Park, Maryland.

145. In Miami, Elizabeth Bradford had been worried sick: *Miami Herald*, October 6, 1985.

145. By mid-afternoon Roy Hurley and his three companions: Testimony of Roy R. Hurley, Records Group 69 006.1, Works Progress Administration Selected Records Relating to the 1935 Florida Hurricane, National Archives, College Park, Maryland.

146. The first rescue boat brought: *The Boston Globe*, September 4, 1935.

147. At Dinner Key the Coast Guard was preparing: U.S. Coast Guard Official Dispatch, September 3, 1935, from Commander, Jacksonville Division to Coast Guard Headquarters and Commandant, Seventh Naval District, Records Group 26.651, "Wrecks, fires, floods, etc.," Records of the U.S. Coast Guard, General Correspondence, 1910–1935, National Archives, Washington, DC.

147. By Tuesday night Homestead was swamped: *Redland District News* (Homestead, FL), September 6, 1935.

147. . . . Fred Ghent talked by telephone: *The Boston Globe*, September 4, 1935.

148. . . . Bernard and Clifton Russell climbed out of the overturned train car: Author's interview with Bernard Russell, Islamorada, Florida, December 6, 1996, transcript on file at Florida Keys History and Discovery Center, Islamorada, Florida.

148. The stench summoned blowflies: Email exchanges with Dr. Dean Hawley, Department of Pathology and Laboratory Medicine, Indiana University School of Medicine, 1998–2000.

149. Soon Bernard, John, and Clifton Russell would learn: Author's interview with Richie Russell, Islamorada, Florida, March 13, 2018, transcript on file at Florida Keys History and Discovery Center, Islamorada, Florida.

149. Two people who got through the roadblock: Testimony of Ben E. Davis, Records Group 69 006.1, Works Progress Administration Selected Records Relating to the 1935 Florida Hurricane, National Archives, College Park, Maryland.

149. One of the most haunting pictures was a *Miami Herald* portrait of eight-year-old Robert Adams: *Miami Herald*, September 4, 1935.

150. Newsreel cameramen descended on the Coast Guard air station: Narrative of MAS Activities Before, During and Following the September 2 Hurricane, 1935, Records Group 26.651, "Wrecks, Fires, Floods, etc.," Records of the U.S. Coast Guard, General Correspondence, 1910–1935, National Archives and Records Administration, Washington, DC.

150. The *Miami Herald* cautiously reported that 25 to 100 were dead: *Miami Herald*, September 4, 1935.

150. The *Miami Daily News* published a list: *Miami Daily News*, September 4, 1935.

150. "Death Toll on Keys Over 700": *Miami Beach Daily Tribune*, September 4, 1935.

151. . . . the *Washington Post*'s lead story said 100 were dead: *Washington Post*, September 4, 1935.

151. But Coast Guard reports: Narrative of MAS Activities Before, During and Following the September 2 Hurricane, 1935, Records Group 26.651, "Wrecks, Fires, Floods, etc.," Records of the U.S. Coast Guard, General Correspondence, 1910–1935, National Archives and Records Administration, Washington, DC.

151. . . . George Andrews, a Federal Emergency Relief Administration engineer in Washington: Digest of telephone conversation between Mr. Unkridge [*sic*], Assistant to Conrad Van Hyning, State Emergency Relief Administrator, Jacksonville, Florida, and

Mr. Andrews, September 4, 1935, Records Group 69 006.1, Works Progress Administration Selected Records Relating to the 1935 Florida Hurricane, National Archives, College Park, Maryland.

151. "It looks bad," Porter warned Andrews: Digest of telephone conversation between Mr. R. Marvin Porter, Regional Engineer, Miami, Florida, and Mr. Andrews, September 4, 1935, Records Group 69 006.1, Works Progress Administration Selected Records Relating to the 1935 Florida Hurricane, National Archives, College Park, Maryland.

151. "What is the number of the known or estimated dead?": Digest of telephone conversation between Mr. Lawrence Westbrook and Mr. Marvin Porter, September 4, 1935, Records Group 69 006.1, Works Progress Administration Selected Records Relating to the 1935 Florida Hurricane, National Archives, College Park, Maryland.

151. Meanwhile, Stephen Early, one of FDR's secretaries: Telephone conversation between Mr. Westbrook and Mr. McIntyre, The White House, September 4, 1935, Records Group 69 006.1, Works Progress Administration Selected Records Relating to the 1935 Florida Hurricane, National Archives, College Park, Maryland.

152. "I've been talking to Mr. Early and General Hines": Telephone conversation between Mr. Westbrook and Mr. McIntyre, The White House, September 4, 1935, Records Group 69 006.1, Works Progress Administration Selected Records Relating to the 1935 Florida Hurricane, National Archives, College Park, Maryland.

152. Meanwhile, U.S. Coast Guard Lieutenant William Clemmer: Narrative of MAS Activities Before, During and Following the September 2 Hurricane, 1935, Records Group 26.651, "Wrecks, Fires, Floods, etc.," Records of the U.S. Coast Guard, General Correspondence, 1910–1935, National Archives and Records Administration, Washington, DC.

154. George Branch was among the survivors: George Branch, in a letter to his daughter, Frances Jane Bloodworth, September 15, 1935, copy on file at Florida Keys History and Discovery Center, Islamorada, Florida.

155. By Wednesday afternoon word reached Fern and Ed Butters: Fern Butters, unpublished manuscript, "Fern's account of the '35 hurricane," undated, copy provided by her granddaughter-in-law Gayle Butters of Archer, Florida, October 2000, copy on file at Florida Keys History and Discovery Center, Islamorada, Florida.

155. At Jackson Memorial Hospital a young woman sat in a wheelchair: *Miami Daily News*, September 5, 1935.

156. The passengers put on life jackets, and *Dixie* crew members: Associated Press/ *Indianapolis Star*, September 6, 1935.

157. . . . W. M. Pepper Jr., editor of the *Gainesville Daily Sun*: Associated Press/*Oakland Tribune*, September 5, 1935.

157. Farther inland, winds toppled trees in Gainesville: *Palm Beach Post*, September 5, 1935.

157. The hurricane dealt a savage blow to poor, sparsely populated Taylor County: *Palm Beach Post*, September 7, 1935, and September 9, 1935.

160. As soon as conditions permitted Wednesday, the Florida East Coast Railway: George Branch, in a letter to his daughter, Frances Jane Bloodworth, September 15, 1935, copy on file at Florida Keys History and Discovery Center, Islamorada, Florida.

Chapter 8: An Act of God

161. The *Tribune's* front page had all a tabloid editor could hope for: *Miami Beach Daily Tribune*, September 5, 1935.

161. The *Washington Post* of September 5, 1935, reported that as many as 500 people: *Washington Post*, September 5, 1935.

162. Reporters risked their necks: *Editor & Publisher* magazine/*The Racine Journal-Times*, September 11, 1935.

162. Around 8 a.m. Thursday a Coast Guard patrol boat cast off from Lower Matecumbe Key: Narrative of MAS Activities Before, During and Following the September 2 Hurricane, 1935, Records Group 26.651, "Wrecks, Fires, Floods, etc.," Records of the U.S. Coast Guard, General Correspondence, 1910–1935, National Archives and Records Administration, Washington, DC.

162. "The stench was something that made men turn and leave: "Special Field Report to Colin Herrle," by John L. Teets, American Red Cross field representative, September 20, 1935, Florida Collection, Helen Wadley Branch Library, Islamorada, Florida.

163. David Sholtz had had enough: "Special Field Report to Colin Herrle," by John L. Teets, American Red Cross field representative, September 20, 1935, Florida Collection, Helen Wadley Branch Library, Islamorada, Florida.

163. The press also was squabbling: U.S. Coast Guard Official Dispatch from Commander, New York Division to Coast Guard Headquarters, Records Group 26.651, "Wrecks, fires, floods, etc.," Records of the U.S. Coast Guard, General Correspondence, 1910–1935, National Archives, Washington, DC.

165. Westbrook found his most useful—and imaginative—informant in Julius Stone: Transcript of telephone conversation between Mr. Westbrook and Mr. Stone, Miami, Florida, September 5, 1935, Records Group 69 006.1, Works Progress Administration Selected Records Relating to the 1935 Florida Hurricane, National Archives, College Park, Maryland.

167. Meanwhile, Federal Emergency Relief Administration engineer George Andrews: Digest of telephone conversation between Mr. Unkridge [*sic*] and Mr. Andrews, September 5, 1935, Records Group 69 006.1, Works Progress Administration Selected Records Relating to the 1935 Florida Hurricane, National Archives, College Park, Maryland.

168. . . . Lawrence Westbrook drafted a statement exonerating Florida ERA officials: Testimony by Lawrence Westbrook, Records Group 69 006.1, Works Progress Administration Selected Records Relating to the 1935 Florida Hurricane, National Archives, College Park, Maryland.

168. "Our information from the weather reports showed: Associated Press/*The Palm Beach Post* and others, September 6, 1935.

168. Alexander J. Mitchell, the retired director of the Florida Weather Service: *St. Petersburg Times*, September 7, 1935.

169. When the rains reached Virginia, the James River: Associated Press/*The Virginian-Pilot* (Norfolk, VA), September 7, 1935.

169. E. F. Arrington, a farmer near Danville, Virginia, had to battle a twister: Associated Press/*Norfolk* (Virginia) *Landmark*, September 6, 1935 and September 7, 1935.

169. . . . a tornado killed Mrs. Preston Simanski and her daughter-in-law: Associated Press/*The Staunton* (Virginia) *News-Leader*, September 7, 1935.

169. The storm was still battering the East Coast when an angry Governor David Sholtz: "Special Field Report to Colin Herrle," by John L. Teets, American Red Cross field representative, September 20, 1935, Florida Collection, Helen Wadley Branch Library, Islamorada, Florida.

170. . . . the storm continued its destruction in New Bern, North Carolina: *The Virginian-Pilot* (Norfolk, VA), September 7, 1935.

170. Around 5 a.m. Friday, attorney Thomas A. Williams: Associated Press/*The Staunton* (Virginia) *News-Leader*, September 7, 1935

170. . . . floodwaters were running through the streets of towns in Delaware, and on Maryland's Eastern Shore: Associated Press, September 7, 1935.

171. "We are dead tired," Pusey told local reporters: *The Daily Mail* (Hagerstown, MD), September 7, 1935.

171. Three crewmen aboard a Pennsylvania Railroad freight train in Delaware: *Wilmington* (Delaware) *Morning News*, September 7, 1935.

171. "With surprising suddenness, the tropical hurricane swept away: Associated Press/ *The Virginian-Pilot* (Norfolk, VA), September 7, 1935.

172. "Lay Vets' Deaths to Neglect," blared the *Tribune* headlines: *Chicago Daily Tribune*, September 6, 1935.

173. "Florida Burning Dead": *New York Daily News*, September 6, 1935.

174. Sholtz met with reporters: *St. Petersburg Times*, September 7, 1935.

174. In Washington, WPA director Harry Hopkins: UP/*Great Falls* (Montana) *Tribune*, September 6, 1935.

174. "Everybody seems to have done what they thought: AP/*Reno* (Nevada) *Gazette-Journal*, September 6, 1935.

174. "Grady C. Lewis, Concord Mechanic: *Charlotte Observer*, September 6, 1935.

175. . . . "Portsmouth Man Probable Victim: *The Virginian-Pilot* (Norfolk, VA), September 6, 1935.

175. *The Bee* of Danville, Virginia noted: *The Bee*, September 9, 1935.

175. President Roosevelt, at his home in Hyde Park, New York, probably saw: *The Poughkeepsie* (New York) *Eagle-News*, September 6, 1935.

175. "Plans that make no allowance: *Washington Post*, September 6, 1935.

175. ". . . it is simply nonsensical to impute the blame for the disaster: *New Orleans Item*, September 7, 1935.

175. The *Tampa Daily Times* called Hopkins's statements: *Tampa Daily Times*, September 7, 1935.

175. When the Weather Bureau gives warning of a hurricane: *Pensacola News*, September 7, 1935.

176. ". . . in the still unsettled question of why the evacuation of the veterans was delayed: *The Virginian-Pilot* (Norfolk, VA), September 8, 1935.

176. The Sunday edition of the *Miami Beach Daily Tribune* again shrieked: *Miami Beach Daily Tribune*, September 8, 1935.

176. On Sunday, September 8, *Chicago Sunday Tribune* reporter Spearman Lewis: *Chicago Sunday Tribune*, September 8, 1935.

177. "The bodies were considerably swollen: Testimony of Arthur P. Bilsbrough, Records Group 69 006.1, Works Progress Administration Selected Records Relating to the 1935 Florida Hurricane, National Archives, College Park, Maryland.

178. During stops along the way, some got off long enough to buy local newspapers: *Des Moines* (Iowa) *Tribune*, September 7, 1935.

178. . . . 11-year-old Eleanor Shields of Philadelphia: *Des Moines* (Iowa) *Tribune*, September 7, 1935; *Warren* (Pennsylvania) *Times-Mirror*, September 7, 1935.

178. . . . Ben Grill searched the crowd: *Sunday News* (Sunday edition of *New York Daily News*), September 8, 1935.

178. Ida Flatow and Ann Cinder, also teachers from Brooklyn: *New York Post*, September 7, 1935.

178. Eight-year-old Herbert Shprentz of Brooklyn: *New York Post*, September 7, 1935.

178. Frank Belcher, the opera-singer-turned-Broadway tobacconist: *New York Daily News*, September 8, 1935.

179. At 6:15 p.m. ranks of soldiers, sailors, Coast Guardsmen, and veterans: "Programs for Ceremonial at Bayfront Park Sunday Night, September 8, 1935," Records Group 15, Sub-group 5-3, Records of the Veterans Administration, National Archives and Records Administration, Washington, DC; *Miami Daily News*, September 8, 1935.

180. "On the hurricane-swept Florida keys has been enacted: *The Sunday Star* (Washington, DC), September 8, 1935.

181. Williams had arrived in Florida: *The Atlanta Constitution*, September 8, 1935.

181. "It is impossible for us to reach the conclusion: *The Atlanta Constitution*, September 8, 1935.

181. Around 8 p.m. Long: *The Atlanta Constitution*, September 9, 1935.

182. The Greater Miami Ministerial Association: *Miami Daily News*, September 12, 1935.

182. Charles Clark, acting director of the U.S. Weather Bureau, was defending: U.S. Department of Agriculture memorandum from acting director Charles C. Clark regarding U.S Weather Bureau activities during hurricane of September 2, 1935, September 9, 1935, from files of Historic Preservation Society of Upper Keys, Tavernier, Florida, copy on file at Florida Keys History and Discovery Center, Islamorada, Florida.

183. On September 11, Hines told his staff: Letter, Frank T. Hines, Administrator of Veterans Administration, Washington, DC, to D. W. Kennamer, Washington, DC, September 11, 1935, Records Group 15, Sub-group 5-3, Records of the Veterans Administration, National Archives and Records Administration, Washington, DC.

Chapter 9: Regret to Inform You

184. One of those telegrams was delivered: Records Group 15, Sub-group 5-3, Records of the Veterans Administration, National Archives and Records Administration, Washington, DC.

184. A telegram also was sent to Betty Neel: Records Group 15, Sub-group 5-3, Records of the Veterans Administration, National Archives and Records Administration, Washington, DC.

185. ... 30 of the 48 states: U.S. Department of Labor, St. Petersburg, Florida, Bulletin #3, September 1935, Records Group 15, Sub-group 5-3, Records of the Veterans Administration, National Archives and Records Administration, Washington, DC.

185. A delivery boy went to 440 Senator Street: Records Group 15, Sub-group 5-3, Records of the Veterans Administration, National Archives and Records Administration, Washington, DC.

187. Soon after he returned to Key West, Hemingway—who had no use for Franklin Roosevelt: "Who Murdered the Vets? A Firsthand Report on the Florida Hurricane," by Ernest Hemingway, *New Masses*, vol. 16, no. 12 (September 17, 1935), p. 9–10.

188. The *Chicago Daily Tribune* also was taking aim: *Chicago Daily Tribune*, September 12, 1935.

189. At the U.S. Weather Bureau, acting director Charles Clark: U.S. Department of Agriculture, Weather Bureau Special and Confidential Report on Hurricane August 31–September 6, 1935, report dated September 12, 1935, Records Group 27, Records of the U.S. Weather Bureau, National Archives and Records Administration, College Park, Maryland.

190. At last the VA director got a radiogram: Radiogram, from Dunkelberger, New York, to A. D. Hiller, Assistant Administrator, Veterans Administration, Washington, DC, September 10, 1935, Records Group 15, Sub-group 5-3, Records of the Veterans Administration, National Archives and Records Administration, Washington, DC.

190. The general had Kennamer's orders: Letter, Frank Hines, Administrator of the Veterans Administration, Washington, DC, to D. W. Kennamer, Washington, DC, September 11, 1935, Records Group 15, Sub-group 5-3, Records of the Veterans Administration, National Archives and Records Administration, Washington, DC.

190. David Kennamer's brother Thomas had served in the Alabama state legislature: *The Montgomery Advertiser*, September 29, 1938.

190. Kennamer arrived in Miami: Letter, D. W. Kennamer, McAllister Hotel, Miami, Florida, to Sam Jared, Chief of Investigative Division, Veterans Administration, Washington, DC, September 12, 1935, Records Group 15, Sub-group 5-3, Records of the Veterans Administration, National Archives and Records Administration, Washington, DC.

190. Kennamer and Farmer then met with John Abt: Letter, D. W. Kennamer, McAllister Hotel, Miami, Florida, to Sam Jared, Chief of Investigative Division, Veterans Administration, Washington, DC, September 12, 1935, Records Group 15, Sub-group 5-3, Records of the Veterans Administration, National Archives and Records Administration, Washington, DC.

190. Abt said he knew nothing about it: Letter, D. W. Kennamer, McAllister Hotel, Miami, Florida, to Sam Jared, Chief of Investigative Division, Veterans Administration, Washington, DC, September 12, 1935, Records Group 15, Sub-group 5-3, Records of the Veterans Administration, National Archives and Records Administration, Washington, DC.

191. He had quickly looked over some of the transcripts: Letter, D. W. Kennamer, McAllister Hotel, Miami, Florida, to Sam Jared, Chief of Investigative Division, Veterans Administration, Washington, DC, September 12, 1935, Records Group 15,

Sub-group 5-3, Records of the Veterans Administration, National Archives and Records Administration, Washington, DC.

191.... Kennedy said in a second interview that he told Sheldon the Keys might be in danger: Testimony of G. S. Kennedy, Records Group 69 006.1, Works Progress Administration Selected Records Relating to the 1935 Florida Hurricane, National Archives, College Park, Maryland.

191. General Hines sent a letter to Hopkins on Saturday, September 14: Letter, Frank T. Hines, Administrator, Veterans Administration, Washington, DC, to Harry L. Hopkins, Administrator, Federal Emergency Relief Administration, Washington, DC, September 14, 1935, Records Group 15, Sub-group 5-3, Records of the Veterans Administration, National Archives and Records Administration, Washington, DC.

191. Williams scolded Abt and told the lawyer: Telephone call to Mr. Abt, Florida, September 14, 1935, from Aubrey Williams, Records Group 69 006.1, Works Progress Administration Selected Records Relating to the 1935 Florida Hurricane, National Archives, College Park, Maryland.

192. "Wire prompt report of all circumstances: Telegram, Sam Jared, Veterans Administration Director of Investigations, Washington, DC, to D. W. Kennamer, McAllister Hotel, Miami, Florida, September 14, 1935, Records Group 15, Sub-group 5-3, Records of the Veterans Administration, National Archives and Records Administration, Washington, DC.

192. Kennamer asked Abt where he could find Sheldon: Letter, D. W. Kennamer, Miami, Florida, to Sam Jared, Chief of Investigation Division, Veterans Administration, Washington, DC, September 15, 1935, Records Group 15, Sub-group 5-3, Records of the Veterans Administration, National Archives and Records Administration, Washington, DC.

192. "We were afraid because it was in our area: Testimony of John A. Russell, Records Group 69 006.1, Works Progress Administration Selected Records Relating to the 1935 Florida Hurricane, National Archives, College Park, Maryland.

193. The investigators went to the Florida ERA offices in Miami: Letter, D. W. Kennamer, Miami, Florida, to Sam Jared, Chief of Investigation Division, Veterans Administration, Washington, DC, September 15, 1935, Records Group 15, Sub-group 5-3, Records of the Veterans Administration, National Archives and Records Administration, Washington, DC.

194. Sheldon was edgy, and didn't want to talk to Kennamer and Farmer unless Abt: Letter, D. W. Kennamer, Miami, Florida, to Sam Jared, Chief of Investigation Division, Veterans Administration, Washington, DC, September 15, 1935, Records Group 15, Sub-group 5-3, Records of the Veterans Administration, National Archives and Records Administration, Washington, DC.

194. Kennamer tried to ease Sheldon's concerns: Letter, D. W. Kennamer, Miami, Florida, to Sam Jared, Chief of Investigation Division, Veterans Administration, Washington, DC, September 15, 1935, Records Group 15, Sub-group 5-3, Records of the Veterans Administration, National Archives and Records Administration, Washington, DC.

194. Ayer told Kennamer that he had repeated the advisory exactly: Testimony of Robert Aldrich Ayer, Records Group 69 006.1, Works Progress Administration Selected

Records Relating to the 1935 Florida Hurricane, National Archives, College Park, Maryland.

194. Sheldon told the VA investigators that there had been so much "passing the buck": Letter, D. W. Kennamer, Miami, Florida, to Sam Jared, Chief of Investigation Division, Veterans Administration, Washington, DC, September 15, 1935, Records Group 15, Sub-group 5-3, Records of the Veterans Administration, National Archives and Records Administration, Washington, DC.

194. . . . Kennamer sent a letter to Sam Jared: Letter, D. W. Kennamer, Miami, Florida, to Sam Jared, Chief of Investigation Division, Veterans Administration, Washington, DC, September 15, 1935, Records Group 15, Sub-group 5-3, Records of the Veterans Administration, National Archives and Records Administration, Washington, DC.

197. Captain Harry Farmer dug up evidence contradicting the rumors: Testimony of Paul Pugh, Records Group 15, Sub-group 5-3, Records of the Veterans Administration, National Archives and Records Administration, Washington, DC.

197. . . . Sheldon had said Kennedy suggested he return to the Keys: Testimony of G. S. Kennedy, Records Group 69 006.1, Works Progress Administration Selected Records Relating to the 1935 Florida Hurricane, National Archives, College Park, Maryland.

198. Kennamer also noticed Sheldon's habit of ignoring advice: Confidential Report of Investigation re. Florida Hurricane Disaster, made by D. W. Kennamer, October 30, 1935, Records Group 15, Sub-group 5-3, Records of the Veterans Administration, National Archives and Records Administration, Washington, DC.

198. Sheldon told Kennamer that if the train had arrived: Confidential Report of Investigation re. Florida Hurricane Disaster, made by D. W. Kennamer, October 30, 1935, Records Group 15, Sub-group 5-3, Records of the Veterans Administration, National Archives and Records Administration, Washington, DC.

198. "No one was more sympathetic with the veterans: Confidential Report of Investigation re. Florida Hurricane Disaster, made by D. W. Kennamer, October 30, 1935, Records Group 15, Sub-group 5-3, Records of the Veterans Administration, National Archives and Records Administration, Washington, DC.

198. The answer, he decided, was because there had been friction and pettiness: Confidential Report of Investigation re. Florida Hurricane Disaster, made by D. W. Kennamer, October 30, 1935, Records Group 15, Sub-group 5-3, Records of the Veterans Administration, National Archives and Records Administration, Washington, DC.

199. During Ed Butters's testimony to John Abt in Miami: Testimony of Ed Butters, Records Group 69 006.1, Works Progress Administration Selected Records Relating to the 1935 Florida Hurricane, National Archives, College Park, Maryland

199. "Sam, there has been quite a little talk been heard: Testimony of Sam Cutler, Records Group 69 006.1, Works Progress Administration Selected Records Relating to the 1935 Florida Hurricane, National Archives, College Park, Maryland.

199. When Camp 3 superintendent Ben Davis was questioned: Testimony of Ben Davis, Records Group 69 006.1, Works Progress Administration Selected Records Relating to the 1935 Florida Hurricane, National Archives, College Park, Maryland.

200. During the testimony of Junius Wigginton: Testimony of Junius T. Wigginton, Records Group 69 006.1, Works Progress Administration Selected Records Relating to the 1935 Florida Hurricane, National Archives, College Park, Maryland.

200. Sheldon's presence—and his questioning—during the testimony: Confidential Report of Investigation re. Florida Hurricane Disaster, made by D. W. Kennamer, October 30, 1935, Records Group 15, Sub-group 5-3, Records of the Veterans Administration, National Archives and Records Administration, Washington, DC.

201. A group of local African American men: Photo showing African American men removing debris from wreckage of house, photo from the Jerry Wilkinson Research Library at the Florida Keys History and Discovery Center, Islamorada, Florida.

201. On September 18 rescue workers found 11 corpses: *Miami Herald*, September 19, 1935.

201. That same day, workers discovered Ben Davis's 1934 Dodge: *Key West Citizen*, September 18, 1935.

201. A passing boater discovered Rosalind Grooms Palmer's body: *Key West Citizen*, September 21, 1935; *Miami Daily News*, September 21, 1935.

201. One of the storm's fierce gusts shoved O. D. King's car: Testimony of O. D. King, Records Group 69 006.1, Works Progress Administration Selected Records Relating to the 1935 Florida Hurricane, National Archives, College Park, Maryland.

202. Reverend Robert Carlson lost his struggle: *Fort Myers News-Press*, September 14, 1935.

202. His wife's body was found: *Fort Myers News-Press*, September 14, 1935.

202. On September 10 the crew of a Coast Guard cutter from Biloxi, Mississippi: U.S. Coast Guard Official Dispatch, September 10, 1935, from USCG *Triton* to USCG *Nemesis* and Commandant, Jacksonville Division, Records Group 26.651, "Wrecks, Fires, Floods, etc.," Records of the U.S. Coast Guard, General Correspondence, 1910–1935, National Archives, Washington, DC.

203. The body of Sarah Hodge—who'd gone with her sister Myrtle: *The Leader-Enterprise* (Homestead, FL), November 22, 1935.

203. On French Reef, salvagers had gotten the *Dixie* ready to refloat: *Miami Daily News*, September 19, 1935.

203. On September 30 the Merritt-Chapman & Scott tug *Relief*, with the battered *Dixie* in tow: *Sunday News* (Sunday edition of *New York Daily News*), September 29, 1935.

203. On October 1, Sundstrom walked into the offices: Report of Casualties and Violations of Steamboat Laws, October 2, 1935, Records Group 41, Bureau of Marine Inspection and Navigation, Steamboat Inspection Service Headquarters Records, Card Reports of Casualties and Violations Investigated, 1911–1935, National Archives, Washington, DC.

203. Sundstrom told the board he knew there was a storm: *New York Daily News*, October 2, 1935.

204. This time Florida ERA supervisors were taking no chances: *Miami Daily News*, September 29, 1935.

204. The legionnaires quickly decided they'd conduct their own investigation: Associated Press/*The Tampa Tribune* and others, October 6, 1935.

204. The hurricane had destroyed about 40 miles of track: *Miami Daily News*, October 2, 1935.

205. Melton, Whitlock, and Jones went straight to the auditorium of Key West High School: *Tampa Daily Times*, October 12, 1935.

205. From there the investigators went to Tallahassee: *St. Petersburg Times*, October 16, 1935.

206. . . . FEC workers arrived in Islamorada to start salvage work: *Miami Daily News*, October 14, 1935.

206. Six days later on November 5: Letter, John J. Abt to D. W. Kennamer, November 5, 1935, Records Group 69 006.1, Works Progress Administration Selected Records Relating to the 1935 Florida Hurricane, National Archives, College Park, Maryland.

Chapter 10: For the Record

209. On the morning of April 2, 1936, Ray Sheldon was talking about hurricanes: Florida Hurricane Disaster, Hearings Before the Committee on World War Veterans' Legislation, House of Representatives, 74th Congress, Second Session, on H.R. 9486 (Washington, DC: U.S. Government Printing Office, 1936), p. 143.

210. On January 3, 1936—the first day of the new session of Congress—Rankin introduced a bill: Congressional Record, Proceedings and Debates of the Second Session of the 74th Congress of the United States of America, Vol. 80, Part 1, January 3, 1936, to January 29, 1936, p. 1936.

210. As a lawyer, Rankin knew how to selectively present facts to steer a jury: Author's interview with Chester M. "Bo" Morgan, Professor of History, Delta State University, December 20, 2001; letter to author from Robert J. McAfee, attorney, McCotter, McAfee & Ashton, PLLC, New Bern, North Carolina, January 14, 2002, copies on file at the Florida Keys History and Discovery Center, Islamorada, Florida.

211. Rogers had been sniping at Rankin and Roosevelt Administration officials: Congressional Record, Proceedings and Debates of the Second Session of the 74th Congress of the United States of America, Vol. 80, Part 3, February 19, 1936, to March 10, 1936, p. 2705.

211. . . . Rogers asked the camps administrator if he could have loaded the veterans: Florida Hurricane Disaster, Hearings Before the Committee on World War Veterans' Legislation, House of Representatives, 74th Congress, Second Session, on H.R. 9486 (Washington, DC: U.S. Government Printing Office, 1936), p. 143.

212. "Mr. Sheldon, right there," Rankin said, "what was the attitude: Florida Hurricane Disaster, Hearings Before the Committee on World War Veterans' Legislation, House of Representatives, 74th Congress, Second Session, on H.R. 9486 (Washington, DC: U.S. Government Printing Office, 1936), p. 144.

212. Patman asked Sheldon whether the Russell family left the Keys: Florida Hurricane Disaster, Hearings Before the Committee on World War Veterans' Legislation, House of Representatives, 74th Congress, Second Session, on H.R. 9486 (Washington, DC: U.S. Government Printing Office, 1936), p. 181.

213. Rogers had insisted that Rankin call Fecteau: Florida Hurricane Disaster, Hearings Before the Committee on World War Veterans' Legislation, House of Representatives,

74th Congress, Second Session, on H.R. 9486 (Washington, DC: U.S. Government Printing Office, 1936), p. 469.

213. "Now, you were down there," Rankin said to Fecteau: Florida Hurricane Disaster, Hearings Before the Committee on World War Veterans' Legislation, House of Representatives, 74th Congress, Second Session, on H.R. 9486 (Washington, DC: U.S. Government Printing Office, 1936), p. 486.

213. "I want to put myself in the condition of those people down there": Florida Hurricane Disaster, Hearings Before the Committee on World War Veterans' Legislation, House of Representatives, 74th Congress, Second Session, on H.R. 9486 (Washington, DC: U.S. Government Printing Office, 1936), p. 487.

214. When John Jacob Rogers died suddenly in 1925, she entered a special election: *The Boston Globe*, June 17, 1925 and July 1, 1925.

214. She was exactly the kind of woman: Author's telephone interview with David Sansing, Professor Emeritus of History, University of Mississippi, June 22, 1999.

214. Rankin, a Democrat, represented Mississippi's First District: Office of the Clerk, U.S. House of Representatives, Historical Election Statistics, Election Statistics 1920 to Present, Statistics of the Congressional and Presidential Election of November 2, 1920.

214. He'd grown up in rural Itawamba County in northeastern Mississippi: *The Clarion-Ledger* (Jackson, MS), November 28, 1960.

214. Rankin graduated from the University of Mississippi's law school in 1910: *The Clarion-Ledger* (Jackson, MS), November 28, 1960.

215. "Yes," the clerk replied, "I got it copied down during a burst of silence: Author's telephone interview with David G. Sansing, PhD, Professor Emeritus of History, University of Mississippi, June 17, 1999.

215. . . . and so he established a political relationship with FDR: Author's telephone interview with Chester M. "Bo" Morgan, Professor of History, Delta State University, February 8, 2001.

215. Rankin asked FDR to stay neutral in the contest for Speaker: Letter, John Rankin to President Roosevelt, December 1, 1932, Folder PPF 2650, Franklin D. Roosevelt Library and Museum, Hyde Park, New York.

215. Roosevelt responded with a letter saying he'd comply: Letter, Franklin Roosevelt to John Rankin, January 27, 1933, Folder PPF 2650, Franklin D. Roosevelt Library and Museum, Hyde Park, New York.

215. Senator George Norris of Nebraska was an ardent supporter of making cheap electricity: *The Pittsburgh Press*, February 20, 1936.

215. FDR took up Norris's cause almost immediately: Franklin D. Roosevelt, *On Our Way* (London: Faber & Faber Limited, 1934), p. 57.

216. More than 40,000 people gathered in Harrodsburg, Kentucky: *The Courier-Journal* (Louisville, KY), November 17, 1934.

217. Rankin—who'd also gone to bat for FDR's tax plan: John Rankin, letter to President Roosevelt, June 25, 1935, Folder PPF 2650, Franklin D. Roosevelt Library and Museum, Hyde Park, New York; "President Roosevelt's Tax Program" (script), delivered over National Broadcasting Company, June 24, 1935, Folder PPF 2650, Franklin D. Roosevelt Library and Museum, Hyde Park, New York.

217. On January 9 the House of Representatives passed a bill approving early payment, and the Senate followed the next day: *Boston Evening Globe*, January 10, 1936.

218. Adding to the Democrats' anxiety was a worrisome political poll: *Detroit Free Press*, *The Brooklyn Daily Eagle*, *The Los Angeles Times*, *The Philadelphia Inquirer*, and others, January 25, 1936.

218. . . . the House approved a resolution offered by Representative J. Hardin Peterson: Congressional Record, Proceedings and Debates of the Second Session of the 74th Congress of the United States of America, Vol. 80, Part 1, January 3, 1936, to January 29, 1936, p. 33.

218. The following day, Representative Edith Nourse Rogers sent a letter to General Frank Hines: Letter, Representative Edith Nourse Rogers, Washington, DC, to General Frank Hines, Administrator, Veterans Administration, Washington, DC, January 4, 1936, Records Group 15, Sub-group 5-3, Records of the Veterans Administration, National Archives and Records Administration, Washington, DC.

218. . . . when voters had nearly thrown them out of Washington: Office of the Clerk, U.S. House of Representatives; Historical Election Statistics, Election Statistics 1920 to Present, Statistics of the Congressional and Presidential Election of November 6, 1934. A hurricane that had killed more than 250 veterans because their New Deal–appointed bosses: Letter to author from Robert J. McAfee, attorney, McCotter, McAfee & Ashton, PLLC, New Bern, North Carolina, January 14, 2002, copy now on file at Florida Keys History and Discovery Center, Islamorada, Florida.

219. In the five elections in which she'd defended her seat: Office of the Clerk, U.S. House of Representatives, Historical Election Statistics, Election Statistics 1920 to Present, Statistics of the Congressional and Presidential Election of November 2, 1926; Statistics of the Congressional and Presidential Election of November 6, 1928; Statistics of the Congressional and Presidential Election of November 4, 1930; Statistics of the Congressional and Presidential Election of November 8, 1932; Statistics of the Congressional and Presidential Election of November 6, 1934; all accessed at http://history.house.gov/Institution/Election-Statistics/Election-Statistics.

219. Rankin won his first term in the House in 1920 with a staggering 96 percent of the votes: Office of the Clerk, U.S. House of Representatives, Historical Election Statistics, Election Statistics 1920 to Present, Statistics of the Congressional and Presidential Election of November 2, 1920; Statistics of the Congressional and Presidential Election of November 8, 1932; both accessed at http://history.house.gov/Institution/Election-Statistics/Election-Statistics.

219. In late February Rogers received a response to her request for information: Letter, General Frank Hines, Administrator, Veterans Administration, Washington, DC, to Representative Edith Nourse Rogers, Washington, DC, February 24, 1936, Records Group 15, Sub-group 5-3, Records of the Veterans Administration, National Archives and Records Administration, Washington, DC.

219. Rogers was infuriated and immediately fired back: Letter, Representative Edith Nourse Rogers to General Frank Hines, Administrator, Veterans Administration, February 25, 1936, Records Group 15, Sub-group 5-3, Records of the Veterans Administration, National Archives and Records Administration, Washington, DC.

220. That same day on the floor of the House of Representatives, Rogers took an indirect jab: Congressional Record, Proceedings and Debates of the Second Session of the 74th Congress of the United States of America, Vol. 80, Part 3, February 19, 1936, to March 10, 1936 (Washington, DC: U.S. Government Printing Office, 1936), p. 2705.

220. On February 25, VA director Hines sent another letter to Rogers: Letter, General Frank Hines, Administrator, Veterans Administration, Washington, DC, to Representative Edith Nourse Rogers, Washington, DC, February 25, 1936, Records Group 15, Sub-group 5-3, Records of the Veterans Administration, National Archives and Records Administration, Washington, DC.

220. Rogers was still angry a day later when Wilcox presented the appropriations amendment: Congressional Record, Proceedings and Debates of the Second Session of the 74th Congress of the United States of America, Vol. 80, Part 3, February 19, 1936, to March 10, 1936 (Washington, DC: U.S. Government Printing Office, 1936), p. 2886.

221. On March 25, 1936, Rankin got permission from the House of Representatives to subpoena witnesses: Congressional Record, Proceedings and Debates of the Second Session of the 74th Congress of the United States of America, Vol. 80—Part 4, March 11, 1936, to March 31, 1936 (Washington, DC: U.S. Government Printing Office, 1936), p. 4324.

221. Later that day Rankin talked to a reporter for the *New York Times*: *New York Times*, March 26, 1936.

222. At 10 a.m. on Thursday, March 26, 1936: Florida Hurricane Disaster, Hearings Before the Committee on World War Veterans' Legislation, House of Representatives, 74th Congress, Second Session, on H.R. 9486 (Washington, DC: U.S. Government Printing Office, 1936), p. 1.

222. "They had plenty of notice, and I want to fix the responsibility": Telegram, J. Hardin Peterson to Harry Hopkins, September 4, 1935, Records Group 69 006.1, Works Progress Administration Selected Records Relating to the 1935 Florida Hurricane, National Archives, College Park, Maryland.

222. McFarlane said he'd found "no culpable or criminal negligence: Florida Hurricane Disaster, Hearings Before the Committee on World War Veterans' Legislation, House of Representatives, 74th Congress, Second Session, on H.R. 9486 (Washington, DC: U.S. Government Printing Office, 1936), p. 4.

225. He would allow some witnesses with little knowledge of relevant facts to make statements that couldn't possibly be verified: Letter to author from Robert J. McAfee, attorney, McCotter, McAfee & Ashton, PLLC, New Bern, North Carolina, January 14, 2002, copy on file at Florida Keys History and Discovery Center, Islamorada, Florida.

226. Or perhaps because he was a first-term Republican: Office of the Clerk, U.S. House of Representatives, Historical Election Statistics, Election Statistics 1920 to Present, Statistics of the Congressional and Presidential Election of November 6, 1934.

226. . . . . Rankin interrupted with a barbed reference to President Hoover's 1932 fiasco: Florida Hurricane Disaster, Hearings Before the Committee on World War Veterans' Legislation, House of Representatives, 74th Congress, Second Session, on H.R. 9486 (Washington, DC: U.S. Government Printing Office, 1936), p. 442.

226. "If you had been one of those soldiers and they left you the selection of the place: Florida Hurricane Disaster, Hearings Before the Committee on World War Veterans' Legislation, House of Representatives, 74th Congress, Second Session, on H.R. 9486 (Washington, DC: U.S. Government Printing Office, 1936), p. 37.

227. "If a ship that was well equipped with the proper instruments: Florida Hurricane Disaster, Hearings Before the Committee on World War Veterans' Legislation, House of Representatives, 74th Congress, Second Session, on H.R. 9486 (Washington, DC: U.S. Government Printing Office, 1936), p. 38.

227. "The minute you put a group of detached men anywhere near a city: Florida Hurricane Disaster, Hearings Before the Committee on World War Veterans' Legislation, House of Representatives, 74th Congress, Second Session, on H.R. 9486 (Washington, DC: U.S. Government Printing Office, 1936), p. 55.

227. "What do you consider the standard of health conditions in the camp: Florida Hurricane Disaster, Hearings Before the Committee on World War Veterans' Legislation, House of Representatives, 74th Congress, Second Session, on H.R. 9486 (Washington, DC: U.S. Government Printing Office, 1936), p. 66.

228. "The only feature of these camps that I can think of that was at all unsettling: Florida Hurricane Disaster, Hearings Before the Committee on World War Veterans' Legislation, House of Representatives, 74th Congress, Second Session, on H.R. 9486 (Washington, DC: U.S. Government Printing Office, 1936), p. 67.

228. Aubrey Williams told the committee that Florida officials were: Florida Hurricane Disaster, Hearings Before the Committee on World War Veterans' Legislation, House of Representatives, 74th Congress, Second Session, on H.R. 9486 (Washington, DC: U.S. Government Printing Office, 1936), p. 447.

228. Williams defended the no-fault conclusion he presented in his report: Florida Hurricane Disaster, Hearings Before the Committee on World War Veterans' Legislation, House of Representatives, 74th Congress, Second Session, on H.R. 9486 (Washington, DC: U.S. Government Printing Office, 1936), p. 456.

228. Edith Nourse Rogers told Williams his hastily completed report: Florida Hurricane Disaster, Hearings Before the Committee on World War Veterans' Legislation, House of Representatives, 74th Congress, Second Session, on H.R. 9486 (Washington, DC: U.S. Government Printing Office, 1936), p. 449.

229. "Your administration had jurisdiction of these men in 1932": Florida Hurricane Disaster, Hearings Before the Committee on World War Veterans' Legislation, House of Representatives, 74th Congress, Second Session, on H.R. 9486 (Washington, DC: U.S. Government Printing Office, 1936), p. 450.

229. "Mr. Chairman, I would say that the procedure followed by the committee: Florida Hurricane Disaster, Hearings Before the Committee on World War Veterans' Legislation, House of Representatives, 74th Congress, Second Session, on H.R. 9486 (Washington, DC: U.S. Government Printing Office, 1936), p. 363.

230. Rogers asked Ijams if he thought everything possible had been done: Florida Hurricane Disaster, Hearings Before the Committee on World War Veterans' Legislation, House of Representatives, 74th Congress, Second Session, on H.R. 9486 (Washington, DC: U.S. Government Printing Office, 1936), p. 387.

230. Ijams said he "did not go into that end of it": *Florida Hurricane Disaster, Hearings Before the Committee on World War Veterans' Legislation, House of Representatives*, 74th Congress, Second Session, on H.R. 9486 (Washington, DC: U.S. Government Printing Office, 1936), p. 388.

230. Fred Ghent, who had landed a new federal job in Washington: *Florida Hurricane Disaster, Hearings Before the Committee on World War Veterans' Legislation, House of Representatives*, 74th Congress, Second Session, on H.R. 9486 (Washington, DC: U.S. Government Printing Office, 1936), p. 284; *Jacksonville Journal*, October 2, 1935.

230. Ghent said that since he had given the railroad 32 hours' notice: *Florida Hurricane Disaster, Hearings Before the Committee on World War Veterans' Legislation, House of Representatives*, 74th Congress, Second Session, on H.R. 9486 (Washington, DC: U.S. Government Printing Office, 1936), p. 296.

230. Ghent told the committee that his expectations: *Florida Hurricane Disaster, Hearings Before the Committee on World War Veterans' Legislation, House of Representatives*, 74th Congress, Second Session, on H.R. 9486 (Washington, DC: U.S. Government Printing Office, 1936), p. 296.

230. . . . he refused a request from FEC officials to reimburse them for travel: *Florida Hurricane Disaster, Hearings Before the Committee on World War Veterans' Legislation, House of Representatives*, 74th Congress, Second Session, on H.R. 9486 (Washington, DC: U.S. Government Printing Office, 1936), p. 359.

231. . . . Edith Nourse Rogers discovered she'd been working at an even greater disadvantage: *Florida Hurricane Disaster, Hearings Before the Committee on World War Veterans' Legislation, House of Representatives*, 74th Congress, Second Session, on H.R. 9486 (Washington, DC: U.S. Government Printing Office, 1936), p. 403.

231. On Saturday, May 9, representatives of the Veterans of Foreign Wars and the American Legion: *Florida Hurricane Disaster, Hearings Before the Committee on World War Veterans' Legislation, House of Representatives*, 74th Congress, Second Session, on H.R. 9486 (Washington, DC: U.S. Government Printing Office, 1936), p. 589, 591.

231. Taylor told Rankin that he'd brought copies of the American Legion's full report: *Florida Hurricane Disaster, Hearings Before the Committee on World War Veterans' Legislation, House of Representatives*, 74th Congress, Second Session, on H.R. 9486 (Washington, DC: U.S. Government Printing Office, 1936), p. 589.

232. Edith Nourse Rogers tried to get Rankin to call witnesses from the American Legion: *Florida Hurricane Disaster, Hearings Before the Committee on World War Veterans' Legislation, House of Representatives*, 74th Congress, Second Session, on H.R. 9486 (Washington, DC: U.S. Government Printing Office, 1936), p. 590.

232. Rogers made a motion to call an American Legion witness: *Florida Hurricane Disaster, Hearings Before the Committee on World War Veterans' Legislation, House of Representatives*, 74th Congress, Second Session, on H.R. 9486 (Washington, DC: U.S. Government Printing Office, 1936), p. 590.

232. "Mr. Chairman, the VFW did have a special committee: *Florida Hurricane Disaster, Hearings Before the Committee on World War Veterans' Legislation, House of Representatives*, 74th Congress, Second Session, on H.R. 9486 (Washington, DC: U.S. Government Printing Office, 1936), p. 591.

233. On June 1, 1936, Rankin's bill to compensate the dependents: Congressional Record, Proceedings and Debates of the Second Session of the 74th Congress of the United States of America, Vol. 80, Part 8, May 28, 1936, to June 6, 1936, p. 8609.

233. "I feel that there was gross negligence": Congressional Record, Proceedings and Debates of the Second Session of the 74th Congress of the United States of America, Vol. 80, Part 8, May 28, 1936, to June 6, 1936, p. 8610.

233. "I ask every member of the House: Congressional Record, Proceedings and Debates of the Second Session of the 74th Congress of the United States of America, Vol. 80, Part 8, May 28, 1936, to June 6, 1936, p. 8610.

233. "I am delighted to have the membership: Congressional Record, Proceedings and Debates of the Second Session of the 74th Congress of the United States of America, Vol. 80, Part 8, May 28, 1936, to June 6, 1936, p. 8611.

234. "I saw the technical rules of evidence: Congressional Record, Proceedings and Debates of the Second Session of the 74th Congress of the United States of America, Vol. 80, Part 8, May 28, 1936, to June 6, 1936, p. 8612.

234. Perhaps they had decided it just wasn't worth the effort: Author's telephone interview with Chester M. "Bo" Morgan, Professor of History, Delta State University, Cleveland, Mississippi, December 20, 2001.

234. The bill to compensate the veterans' dependents was passed: Congressional Record, Proceedings and Debates of the Second Session of the 74th Congress of the United States of America, Vol. 80, Part 8, May 28, 1936, to June 6, 1936, p. 8615.

Chapter 11: The Illusion of Remoteness

236. On September 7, 1936—Labor Day Monday—Bascom Grooms Sr. and his family were returning to Key West: Author's telephone interviews with Bascom Grooms Jr., January 12, 2000, and December 18, 2000, transcript on file at Florida Keys History and Discovery Center, Islamorada, Florida.

237. As they approached the spot where the car carrying Rosalind had left the highway: Author's telephone interview with Bascom Grooms Jr., January 12, 2000, transcript on file at Florida Keys History and Discovery Center, Islamorada, Florida.

237. Bertram Pinder moved his family back to Islamorada: Author's interview with Alma Pinder Dalton and Laurette Pinder Russell, Islamorada, Florida, November 18, 1997, transcript on file at Florida Keys History and Discovery Center, Islamorada, Florida.

237. The flooding had carried away much of the thin layer of topsoil: Author's interview with Bernard Russell, Islamorada, Florida, December 6, 1996, transcript on file at Florida Keys History and Discovery Center, Islamorada, Florida.

237. Every so often during the years after the hurricane of 1935, Alma, Dolores, and Laurette Pinder found odd personal reminders: Author's interview with Alma Pinder Dalton and Laurette Pinder Russell, Islamorada, Florida, November 18, 1997, transcript on file at Florida Keys History and Discovery Center, Islamorada, Florida.

238. Amid the dozens of pleas federal officials received from distraught relatives: Letter, December 4, 1935, Amanda Ambrose, 2176 Cherokee St., Baton Rouge, Louisiana, to "War Department," Washington, DC, Records Group 69 006.1, Works Progress

Administration Selected Records Relating to the 1935 Florida Hurricane, National Archives, College Park, Maryland.

238. The card for John Ambrose has only a single brief notation: "Missing unaccounted for 9/28/35": Records Group 15, Subgroup 5-3, Records of the Veterans Administration, National Archives and Records Administration, Washington DC.

239. Abt's name popped up again in 1963: United States, Warren Commission & Associated Press, *The Official Warren Commission Report on the Assassination of President John F. Kennedy* [S.l.], Associated Press, vol. 10, p. 116, testimony of John J. Abt, April 17, 1964.

243. . . . took possession of her father's documents when her mother died in 1976: Author's interview with Rae Sheldon Cummings, Vero Beach, Florida, December 14, 2002, transcript on file at Florida Keys History and Discovery Center.

244. He recovered enough to take a long summer vacation: *Palm Beach Post*, June 8, 1952.

244. By the spring of 1937, the *Daily Tribune* of Miami Beach had moved into a beautiful new Art Deco–style office building: Paul G. Jeans, *Tropical Disturbance: The Story of the Making of the Miami Tribune* (Miami, published as an insert of the *Miami Tribune* edition of April 4, 1937), p. 2.

244. In his estimation only the *Tribune* had had the courage: Paul G. Jeans, *Tropical Disturbance: The Story of the Making of the Miami Tribune* (Miami, published as an insert of the *Miami Tribune* edition of April 4, 1937), p. 2–3.

245. . . . "impressed as perhaps nothing else could have upon the community the value and importance of honest, accurate reporting": Paul G. Jeans, *Tropical Disturbance: The Story of the Making of the Miami Tribune* (Miami, published as an insert of the *Miami Tribune* edition of April 4, 1937), p. 45.

245. On April 18, 1937, Jeans was returning from a trip to Tallahassee: Associated Press/ *New York Times*, *Atlanta Constitution*, and many others.

245. Jeans's sudden death ended Moe Annenberg's dream: "Newspapers of America's Last Fontier," by Jeanne Bellamy, *Tequesta: The Journal of the Historical Association of Southern Florida*, no. 12 (1952), p. 15.

245. The *Trib* then began a crusade to change Florida law to prohibit unrestricted grazing: *Miami Tribune*, April 20, 1937.

246. On a clear, hot day in mid-November 1937, nine-year-old Faye Marie Parker: *Miami Daily News*, November 15, 1937.

247. Although Cuban strongman Fulgencio Batista had a reputation: *Greenville* (S.C.) *News*, July 8, 1984.

247. He was briefly an inspector: *Dunkirk* (N.Y.) *Evening Observer*, July 11, 1938.

247. Povey was still capable of surprises: *St. Louis Post-Dispatch*, January 10, 1938.

247. In 1939 Povey became a vice president: *Greenville* (S.C.) *News*, July 8, 1984.

247. After the war Povey helped found: *Greenville* (S.C.) *News*, July 8, 1984.

247. Povey's knack for escaping: *Fort Lauderdale News*, August 3, 1965.

248. Povey moved to Highlands, North Carolina: *Greenville* (S.C.) *News*, July 8, 1984.

248. Lieutenant William Clemmer was awarded: *Miami Daily News*, May 19, 1936.

248. On July 15, 1939, Clemmer: *Life* magazine, July 15, 1939.

248. He'd performed a very risky night landing: *Miami Daily News*, February 21, 1936.

249. A month later he'd gone to the aid: *Miami Daily News*, March 23, 1936.

249. In July 1936 Clemmer had once again landed: *Miami Daily News*, July 25, 1937.

250. On February 18, 1939, the president and his entourage: *Miami Daily News*, February 18, 1939.

250. Ed Sheeran became an engineer: *Miami Daily News*, December 29, 1951.

250. On a Monday in 1946, Sheeran, as usual, arose around 4 a.m.: Author's telephone interview with Edward H. Sheeran (grandson of Ed Sheeran), December 28, 1999.

251. "He was too involved with his job to be bothered: Author's telephone interview with Edward H. Sheeran (grandson of Ed Sheeran), August 21, 1998.

251. Death arrived for Sheeran: *Miami Daily News*, December 29, 1951; Certificate of Death, Edward H. Sheeran, December 28, 1951, State of Florida, Office of Vital Statistics, Certified Copy, February 2, 2002.

251. President Harry Truman started coming to Key West: *Miami Daily News*, November 22, 1946.

251. By December 1951 Truman had visited Key West 10 times: Numerous visits to Harry S Truman Little White House Museum, Key West, Florida 1994–2000.

251. Authors Elizabeth Bishop and Tennessee Williams bought houses in Key West: Stephen Nichols, *A Chronological History of Key West* (Key West, FL:, Key West Images of the Past, 1989), p. 43.

251. . . . he still visited Key West occasionally: *Key West Citizen*, December 21, 1940; June 7, 1941; September 13, 1947; June 15, 1953; November 12, 1959.

252. "The old town is too small for the present flow of visitors: *The New Yorker*, December 15, 1951.

252. Between 1978 and 1985 the former FEC bridges that had been converted for automobile traffic: *Miami Herald*, September 1, 1985.

253. The city became the theme for a new amusement park in Orlando: *Tallahassee Democrat*, October 12, 1995.

253. In January 1968 Mathias von Brauchitsch, a writer and television producer in Pittsburgh: Letter, Mathias von Brauchitsch to John Radowich, Information Service, Veterans Administration, January 23, 1968, Records Group 15, Sub-group 5-3, Records of the Veterans Administration, National Archives and Records Administration, Washington, DC.

253. Von Brauchitsch's request was passed on to Manuel Mota: Memorandum, Manuel Mota, Special Investigator, Veterans Administration, to Assistant Director for Investigation, Veterans Administration, February 15, 1968; Memorandum, Howard Bernstein, General Counsel to Director, Investigation and Security Service, Veterans Administration, March 21, 1968, Records Group 15, Sub-group 5-3, Records of the Veterans Administration, National Archives and Records Administration, Washington, DC.

253. In his memo of February 26, 1968, Retew said he'd found "documents: Memorandum, W. L. Retew Jr. to Director, Investigation and Security Service, Veterans Administration, Records Group 15, Sub-group 5-3, Records of the Veterans Administration, National Archives and Records Administration, Washington, DC.

254. In a March 26, 1968, letter to von Brauchitsch: Letter, W. L. Retew Jr. to Mathias von Brauchitsch, March 26, 1968, Records Group 15, Sub-group 5-3, Records of the Veterans Administration, National Archives and Records Administration, Washington, DC.

256. Archivist Kate Snodgrass said Rankin left very few documents: Author's telephone conversation with archivist Kate Snodgrass at National Archives in Washington, DC, February 13, 2003.

258. On a warm afternoon in mid-November 1997: Author's visit with Bernard Russell, Islamorada, Florida, November 17, 1997, transcript on file at Florida Keys History and Discovery Center, Islamorada, Florida.

259. "Those memories of what happened: Author's interview with Bernard Russell, Islamorada, Florida, April 12, 1997, transcript on file at Florida Keys History and Discovery Center, Islamorada, Florida.

259. "I can remember being so numb: Author's interview with Bernard Russell, Islamorada, Florida, April 12, 1997, transcript on file at Florida Keys History and Discovery Center, Islamorada, Florida.

259. "You didn't have time to dwell on it": Author's interview with Bernard Russell, Islamorada, Florida, April 12, 1997, transcript on file at Florida Keys History and Discovery Center, Islamorada, Florida.

260. Except for a stint in the U.S. Army: Author's interview with Bernard Russell, Islamorada, Florida, November 17, 1997, transcript on file at Florida Keys History and Discovery Center, Islamorada, Florida.

260. Russell was in Islamorada on another sinister September day in 1960: Author's interview with Bernard Russell, Islamorada, Florida, December 6, 1996, transcript on file at Florida Keys History and Discovery Center, Islamorada, Florida.

263. He was awarded the Department: "Grady Norton: Hurricane Forecaster and Communicator Extraordinaire," by Robert W. Burpee, *Weather and Forecasting*, Volume 3, Number 3, September 1988, p. 248.

263. On October 8, 1954, Norton worked his shift: "Grady Norton: Hurricane Forecaster and Communicator Extraordinaire," by Robert W. Burpee, *Weather and Forecasting*, Volume 3, Number 3, September 1988, p. 254.

263. Reno said that Norton had told her: *Miami Daily News*, October 10, 1954.

263. Reno repeated her anecdote about Norton in a 1955 story: *Miami Daily News*, September 4, 1955.

264. Dunn said the Jacksonville staff had handled: Statement of Walter Bennett and Gordon Dunn, Records Group 69 006.1, Works Progress Administration Selected Records Relating to the 1935 Florida Hurricane, National Archives, College Park, Maryland.

264. . . . Fred Ghent said that Ray Sheldon had phoned him in Jacksonville: Florida Hurricane Disaster, Hearings Before the Committee on World War Veterans' Legislation, House of Representatives, 74th Congress, Second Session, on H.R. 9486 (Washington, DC: United States Government Printing Office, 1936), pp. 353.

265. The phone log was entered into the Congressional Record in 1936. Congressional Record, Proceedings and Debates of the Second Session of the 74th Congress of the United States of America, Vol. 80, Part 8, May 28, 1936, to June 6, 1936, pp. 8613–8615.

265. He was posthumously awarded: *Miami Daily News*, May 26, 1955.

265. In 1993 Jane Wood Reno's anecdote about Norton: Hurchalla, George (editor), *The Hell With Politics: The Life and Writings of Jane Wood Reno* (Atlanta: Peachtree Publishers, 1994), p. 49.

265. The Weather Bureau conducted its own internal investigation: U.S. Department of Agriculture Weather Bureau Special and Confidential Report on Hurricane, August 31–September 6, 1935; report is dated September 12, 1935, Records Group 27, Records of the U.S. Weather Bureau, National Archives and Records Administration, College Park, Maryland.

266. Soon after the Labor Day Hurricane of 1935, Iver Olson : "Lowest Barometer Reading in the Florida Keys Storm of September 2, 1935," by W. F. McDonald; *Monthly Weather Review*, October 1935, p. 295.

266. In 2014 a group of meteorologists headed by Chris Landsea: "A Reanalysis of the 1931-43 Atlantic Hurricane Database," by Chris Landsea, Andrew Hagen, William Bredemeyer, Cristina Carrasco, David A. Glenn, Adrian Santiago, Donna Strahan-Sakoskie, and Michael Dickinson, published in *Journal of Climate*, Volume 27, August 2014, available online at https://www.aoml.noaa.gov/hrd/Landsea/landsea-et-al-jclimate-2014.pdf, p. 6114 (Author's note: The authors of this study express the reanalyzed peak winds of the Labor Day Hurricane of 1935 at 160 knots per hour. This is equivalent to 184 miles per hour).

266. Unequivocally, this hurricane could be a category 6: "Storm Tides In Twelve Tropical Cyclones (Including Four Intense New England Hurricanes)," by Brian R. Jarvinen, published by the National Hurricane Center, Miami, Florida, 2006, p. 54. Available online at https://www.aoml.noaa.gov/hrd/Landsea/12Tides.pdf.

267. With all the information being provided on the internet: Author's telephone interview with Billy Wagner, January 9, 2002.

268. They develop quickly near land: Author's email exchange with Brian Norcross, November 1, 2018.

Chapter 12: Time Borrowed from the Wind

269. In the late summer of 2017, Patrick Garvey was on the verge: Author's interview with Patrick Garvey, Big Pine Key, Florida, March 14, 2018, transcript on file at Florida Keys History and Discovery Center, Islamorada, Florida.

270. It had started its journey from the west coast of Africa: John P. Cangialosi, Andrew S. Latto, and Robbie Berg, *National Hurricane Center Tropical Cyclone Report: Hurricane Irma, 30 August–12 September 2017* (National Hurricane Center, 2018), p. 2.

271. . . . its winds cranked up to 145 mph: National Hurricane Center website, "Irma Graphics Archive: 3-day Forecast Track and Watch/Warning Graphic," https://www.nhc.noaa.gov/archive/2017/IRMA_graphics.php?product=3day_cone_with_line, last accessed December 17, 2018.

271. The hurricane's forecast track was moving a little more northward: National Hurricane Center website, "Irma Graphics Archive: 3-day Forecast Track and Watch/Warning Graphic," https://www.nhc.noaa.gov/archive/2017/IRMA_graphics.php?product=3day_cone_with_line, last accessed December 17, 2018.

272. As hurricane edginess crept over millions of Florida residents: *Palm Beach Post*, September 8, 2017; *Orlando Sentinel*, September 7, 2017, and September 9, 2017; Transcript of the Rush Limbaugh show, "My Analysis of the Hurricane Irma Panic," broadcast September 5, 2017, downloaded from https://www.rushlimbaugh.com/daily/2017/09/05/my-analysis-of-the-hurricane-irma-panic/?utm_source=CNN+Media%3A+Reliable+Sources&utm_medium=email&utr, last accessed December 28, 2018.

272. Around 2 a.m. on Wednesday, September 6: John P. Cangialosi, Andrew S. Latto, and Robbie Berg, *National Hurricane Center Tropical Cyclone Report: Hurricane Irma, 30 August–12 September 2017* (National Hurricane Center, 2018), p. 3.

272. "Barbuda is now literally rubble," Prime Minister Gaston Browne: *The Telegraph* (London), September 7, 2017.

272. . . . they could not make public comments that included the phrases "climate change" or "global warming": *USA Today/Herald Times Reporter* (Manitowac, WI), September 17, 2017.

272. "It is life-threatening," Scott said: *Florida Governor Rick Scott Discusses Plans For Hurricane Irma*, YouTube video posted September 6, 2017, https://www.youtube.com/watch?v=rMsO7CYU_Hk, last accessed December 17, 2018.

272. "By Wednesday, the air in the Keys started to change": Author's interview with Patrick Garvey, Big Pine Key, Florida, March 14, 2018, transcript on file at Florida Keys History and Discovery Center, Islamorada, Florida.

273. Hurricane Irma's eye passed just to the north of Puerto Rico: "Timeline: Hurricane Irma's progress to monster storm," *USA Today* website, https://www.usatoday.com/story/news/2017/09/10/timeline-hurricane-irma-fluctuating-strgrowing-stronger-weaker-crashed-into-caribbean-islands-florid/651421001, September 10, 2017, last accessed December 23, 2018.

273. The Tampa Bay Rays baseball team was en route: *Tampa Bay Times*, September 13, 2017.

273. Highways were clogged with northbound traffic: Diary of Phyllis Mitchell, Islamorada, Florida; author's interview with Richie Russell, Islamorada, Florida, March 13, 2018, transcript on file at Florida Keys History and Discovery Center, Islamorada, Florida.

273. Among those who did evacuate was Rush Limbaugh: *Washington Post*, September 8, 2017, https://www.washingtonpost.com/news/the-fix/wp/2017/09/06/rush-limbaughs-dangerous-suggestion-that-hurricane-irma-is-fake-news/?utm_term=.cd1130e233a3, last accessed December 28, 2017.

273. Irma had weakened some by Thursday: "Timeline: Hurricane Irma's progress to monster storm," *USA Today* website, https://www.usatoday.com/story/news/2017/09/10/timeline-hurricane-irma-fluctuating-strgrowing-stronger-weaker-crashed-into-caribbean-islands-florid/651421001, September 10, 2017, last accessed December 23, 2018; National Hurricane Center website, "Irma Graphics Archive: 3-day Forecast Track and Watch/Warning Graphic," https://www.nhc.noaa.gov/archive/2017/IRMA_graphics.php?product=3day_cone_with_line, last accessed December 17, 2018.

273. Around the time Blue Hills was disintegrating: Author's interview with Carol Tedesco and Charlotte Wilson, Key West, Florida, March 6, 2018, transcript on file at Florida Keys History and Discovery Center, Islamorada, Florida.

274. . . . Wilson discovered that her friend Carol Tedesco: Author's interview with Carol Tedesco and Charlotte Wilson, Key West, Florida, March 6, 2018, transcript on file at Florida Keys History and Discovery Center, Islamorada, Florida.

274. Sunsets in Key West are so routinely spectacular: Author's visits to Key West, Florida, 1993 to 2018.

274. "It was very surreal," Tedesco said: Author's interview with Carol Tedesco and Charlotte Wilson, Key West, Florida, March 6, 2018, transcript on file at Florida Keys History and Discovery Center, Islamorada, Florida.

274. Later that night, Governor Rick Scott: *Tampa Bay Times*, September 8, 2017.

274. University of Florida football coach Jim McElwain: *Sun-Sentinel* (Fort Lauderdale, FL), September 14, 2017.

274. In Jacksonville, Lisa Coppedge posted a sign: Facebook post of Lisa Coppedge, used with permission.

275. The National Football League followed Governor Scott's example: *Orlando Sentinel*, September 7, 2017.

275. Hurricane Irma lost a little of its intensity: *USA Today* website, https://www.usa today.com/story/news/2017/09/10/timeline-hurricane-irma-fluctuating-strgrowing-stronger-weaker-crashed-into-caribbean-islands-florid/651421001, September 10, 2017, last accessed December 23, 2018.

275. In the Keys, residents of Big Pine Key: YouTube video, *In the Eye of a Hurricane/Irma Survivors*, https://www.youtube.com/watch?v=Jl6CXnJkY4A&t=164s, produced by Livin' the Keys Life, last accessed January 27, 2017.

275. About 50 miles to the northeast in Islamorada, Richie Russell: Author's interview with Richie Russell, Islamorada, Florida, March 13, 2018, transcript on file at Florida Keys History and Discovery Center, Islamorada, Florida.

275. As the storm approached the Leeward Islands: National Hurricane Center website, "Irma Graphics Archive: 3-day Forecast Track and Watch/Warning Graphic," NOAA website https://www.nhc.noaa.gov/archive/2017/IRMA_graphics.php?product=3day_cone_with_line, last accessed December 25, 2018.

275. The *Miami News* reported that Donna hit the Keys "like a bomb": *Miami News*, September 11, 1960.

276. Developers such as Phil Sadowski: *Palm Beach Post*, January 27, 1957; *Orlando Sentinel*, April 9, 1961.

276. The Indies House, a swank hotel on Duck Key: *Miami News*, November 13, 1959, and December 6, 1959.

276. Hurricane Donna clobbered Marathon Shores: *Miami News*, September 11, 1960.

276. But the steel-and-concrete Red Cross houses: Author's interview with Richie Russell, Islamorada, Florida, March 13, 2018, transcript on file at Florida Keys History and Discovery Center, Islamorada, Florida.

277. In Miami Beach a young man was trying to find a public bus: *Tampa Bay Times*, September 10, 2017.

277. Elsewhere, people who didn't own personal computers or cell phones: *Tampa Bay Times*, September 10, 2017.

277. Meanwhile, portable generators, bottled water: *Tampa Bay Times*, September 15, 2017.

277. The Tampa Bay Rays had three home games: *Tampa Bay Times*, September 9, 2017.

277. Rays' outfielder Steven Souza Jr. said the games: *Tampa Bay Times*, September 9, 2017.

277. Rays' manager Kevin Cash said the storm: *Tampa Bay Times*, September 9, 2017.

277. In the Straits of Florida, Hurricane Irma was regaining the strength: National Hurricane Center website, "Irma Graphics Archive: 3-day Forecast Track and Watch/Warning Graphic," NOAA website, https://www.nhc.noaa.gov/archive/2017/IRMA_graphics.php?product=3day_cone_with_line, last accessed December 28, 2018.

277. On Big Pine Key, Patrick Garvey was reconsidering: Author's interview with Patrick Garvey, Big Pine Key, Florida, March 14, 2018, transcript on file at Florida Keys History and Discovery Center, Islamorada, Florida.

278. In Key West, some who had resisted the urge to evacuate: Author's interview with Carol Tedesco and Charlotte Wilson, Key West, Florida, March 6, 2018, transcript on file at Florida Keys History and Discovery Center, Islamorada, Florida.

278. Florida officials were trying to meet the huge demand for gasoline: *Palm Beach Post*, September 8, 2017.

278. Hurricane Irma's eye touched Cuba: National Hurricane Center website, "Irma Graphics Archive: 3-day Forecast Track and Watch/Warning Graphic," https://www.nhc.noaa.gov/archive/2017/IRMA_graphics.php?product=3day_cone_with_line, last accessed December 28, 2018.

278. By 5 a.m. Saturday the storm's peak winds: National Hurricane Center website, "Irma Graphics Archive: 3-day Forecast Track and Watch/Warning Graphic," https://www.nhc.noaa.gov/archive/2017/IRMA_graphics.php?product=3day_cone_with_line, last accessed December 28, 2018.

278. In Islamorada, Phyllis and Bob Mitchell: Diary of Phyllis Mitchell, Islamorada, Florida; author's interview with Richie Russell, Islamorada, Florida, March 13, 2018, transcript on file at Florida Keys History and Discovery Center, Islamorada, Florida.

278. As soon as it was apparent that Hurricane Irma was likely to head toward the Florida Keys: Author's telephone interview with Zulema Pradas, secretary of The Basilica of Saint Mary Star of the Sea, Key West, Florida, August 15, 2018, transcript on file at Florida Keys History and Discovery Center, Islamorada, Florida.

279. People have been going to the grotto for nearly a century: *Miami Herald*, September 27, 1998.

279. A faithful patron of the venerable Green Parrot Bar: Green Parrot Bar website, https://www.greenparrot.com/colbys-official-green-parrot-hurricane-preparedness-kit, last accessed January 27, 2017.

279. Reverend John C. Baker, Rector of The Basilica: Author's telephone interview with Zulema Pradas, secretary of The Basilica of Saint Mary Star of the Sea, Key West, Florida, August 15, 2018, transcript on file at Florida Keys History and Discovery Center, Islamorada, Florida.

279. Not far away, on Whitehead Street: *Tampa Bay Times*, September 19, 2017.

279. The author's granddaughter, actress Mariel Hemingway: *New York Times*, September 11, 2017.

279. Some of the cats seemed to know: *Tampa Bay Times*, September 19, 2017.

280. Although most tourists had left Key West: Live from Key West Southernmost Webcam, accessed September 8–September 15, 2017, http://southernmostpointwebcam.com.

280. But the seas grew steadily more raucous on Saturday, September 8: Live from Key West Southernmost Webcam, accessed September 8–September 15, 2017, http://southernmostpointwebcam.com.

280. Up the islands in Islamorada, Richie Russell: Author's interview with Richie Russell, Islamorada, Florida, March 13, 2018, transcript on file at Florida Keys History and Discovery Center, Islamorada, Florida.

280. Winds from Irma's outer circulation were already clawing: Author's interview with Patrick Garvey, Big Pine Key, Florida, March 14, 2018, transcript on file at Florida Keys History and Discovery Center, Islamorada, Florida.

280. Garvey's neighbor Tim Stanton planned to ride out: Author's interview with Tim Stanton, Big Pine Key, Florida, March 14, 2018, transcript on file at Florida Keys History and Discovery Center, Islamorada, Florida.

281. By 2017 more than 77,000 people lived in the Florida Keys: *Miami Herald*, September 13, 2018.

281. Stanton had struggled for a while to make ends meet: Author's interview with Tim Stanton, Big Pine Key, Florida, March 14, 2018, transcript on file at Florida Keys History and Discovery Center, Islamorada, Florida.

281. In Tampa, taxi driver Michael Bryant: *Tampa Bay Times*, September 10, 2017.

281. . . . a bar in downtown St. Petersburg called the Iberian Rooster: *Tampa Bay Times*, September 10, 2017.

281. Park personnel had removed Halloween decorations: YouTube video, *Hurricane Irma Prep Live Stream at the Magic Kingdom—Walt Disney World*, https://www.youtube.com/watch?v=hpFhxjvxQxk&t=334s, last accessed January 27, 2019.

281. Around 6 p.m. an announcement was made over loudspeakers: YouTube video, *Hurricane Irma Prep Live Stream at the Magic Kingdom—Walt Disney World*, https://www.youtube.com/watch?v=hpFhxjvxQxk&t=334s, last accessed January 27, 2019.

281. . . . things were getting raucous in the Keys: Author's interview with Patrick Garvey, Big Pine Key, Florida, March 14, 2018, transcript on file at Florida Keys History and Discovery Center, Islamorada, Florida.

282. Shortly after 8 p.m. Irma's movement slowed: National Hurricane Center website, "Irma Graphics Archive: 3-day Forecast Track and Watch/Warning Graphic," https://www.nhc.noaa.gov/archive/2017/IRMA_graphics.php?product=3day_cone_with_line, last accessed December 28, 2018.

282. . . . Carol Tedesco decided to ride out the hurricane with friends: Author's interview with Carol Tedesco and Charlotte Wilson, Key West, Florida, March 6, 2018, transcript on file at Florida Keys History and Discovery Center, Islamorada, Florida.

282. The power also was going out in Islamorada: Diary of Phyllis Mitchell, Islamorada, Florida; author's interview with Richie Russell, Islamorada, Florida, March 13, 2018, transcript on file at Florida Keys History and Discovery Center, Islamorada, Florida.

282. At Big Pine Key the electricity was lost: YouTube video, *In the Eye of a Hurricane/ Irma Survivors*, https://www.youtube.com/watch?v=Jl6CXnJkY4A&t=164s, produced by Livin' the Keys Life, last accessed January 27, 2017.

282. By 11 p.m. Irma's eye was pulling away: National Hurricane Center website, "Irma Graphics Archive: 3-day Forecast Track and Watch/Warning Graphic," https://www .nhc.noaa.gov/archive/2017/IRMA_graphics.php?product=3day_cone_with_line, last accessed December 28, 2018.

282. The hurricane had not fared well: National Hurricane Center website, "Irma Graphics Archive: 3-day Forecast Track and Watch/Warning Graphic," https://www .nhc.noaa.gov/archive/2017/IRMA_graphics.php?product=3day_cone_with_line, last accessed December 28, 2018.

282. Hurricane Irma's circulation was now 400 miles wide: *Tampa Bay Times*, September 12, 2017.

282. The storm's eye was expected to traverse: *Tampa Bay Times*, September 12, 2017.

282. About 6.4 million people: *The Daily Item* (Sunbury, PA) and many others, September 10, 2017.

282. "Florida lives longitudinally," said Jeff Houck: Author's email exchanges with Jeff Houck, Tampa, Florida, September 9–11, 2017. Houck's comments were posted by the author on the National Geographic website as "Live-blogging Hurricane Irma," from September 9, 2017, to September 20, 2017, https://blog.nationalgeographic. org/2017/09/09/live-blogging-hurricane-irma.

282. Saturday forecasts warned that Hurricane Irma would plow: "Hurricane and Tropical Cyclones," Weather Underground website, https://www.wunderground.com/ hurricane, accessed repeatedly from September 5, 2017, to September 15, 2017.

283. "Tracking Irma is like seeing a drunk driver: *Tallahassee Democrat*, September 10, 2017.

283. "It's sort of like waiting for Mike Tyson: Author's email exchanges with Jeff Houck, Tampa, Florida, September 9–11, 2017. Houck's comments were posted by the author on the National Geographic website as "Live-blogging Hurricane Irma," from September 9, 2017, to September 20, 2017, https://blog.nationalgeographic.org/2017/09/09/ live-blogging-hurricane-irma.

283. Hurricane Irma was making the most of its brief trip: National Hurricane Center website, "Irma Graphics Archive: 3-day Forecast Track and Watch/Warning Graphic," https://www.nhc.noaa.gov/archive/2017/IRMA_graphics.php?product=3day_cone_ with_line, last accessed December 28, 2018.

283. The landfall forecast for Irma's eye: "Hurricane and Tropical Cyclones," Weather Underground website, https://www.wunderground.com/hurricane, accessed repeatedly from September 5, 2017, to September 15, 2017.

283. Tim Stanton tried to get some sleep: Author's interview with Tim Stanton, Big Pine Key, Florida, March 14, 2018, transcript on file at Florida Keys History and Discovery Center, Islamorada, Florida.

283. Residents with anemom[...] at Big Pine Key: National Hurricane Center website, "Irma Graphics Archive: 3-d[...] recast Track and Watch/Warning Graphic," https://www.nhc.noaa.gov/archive/2[...] IRMA_graphics.php?product=3day_cone_with_line, last accessed December 28, 2[...]

283. Big Pine Key started go[...] nderwater: Author's interview with Tim Stanton, Big Pine Key, Florida, March 14, [...], transcript on file at Florida Keys History and Discovery Center, Islamorada, F[...]a.

283. Stanton peeked at the st[...] Author's interview with Tim Stanton, Big Pine Key, Florida, March 14, 2018, tran[...]t on file at Florida Keys History and Discovery Center, Islamorada, Florida.

284. On No Name Key—wh[...]e ferry had carried passengers: *South Florida Sun Sentinel* (Fort Lauderdale), Septe[...] 14, 2017.

284. Around 10 a.m. the win[...] ddenly died: YouTube video, *In the Eye of a Hurricane/Irma Survivors*, www.youtube[...]/watch?v=Jl6CXnJkY4A&t=98s, produced by Livin' the Keys Life, last accessed J[...]y 6, 2019.

284. Judith Zaroff, a self-desc[...] "healthy 75-year-old woman: *South Florida Sun Sentinel* (Fort Lauderdale), Septe[...] 14, 2017.

284. In the Keys the winds re[...]d with renewed fury: YouTube video, *In the Eye of a Hurricane/Irma Survivors*, htt[...]www.youtube.com/watch?v=Jl6CXnJkY4A&t=98s, produced by Livin' the Keys L[...]st accessed January 6, 2019.

284. Although Irma's eye was [...]cted to stay on the west coast: National Hurricane Center website, "Irma Graphi[...]chive: 3-day Forecast Track and Watch/Warning Graphic," https://www.nhc.n[...]v/archive/2017/IRMA_graphics.php?product=3day_cone_with_line, last accessed [...]mber 28, 2018.

284. In Miami, two dozen co[...]tion cranes: *South Florida Sun Sentinel* (Fort Lauderdale), September 20, 2017.

285. In Fort Lauderdale, cops [...]ted nine people: *South Florida Sun Sentinel* (Fort Lauderdale), September 11, 2017.

285. Almost three million ho[...]d businesses: *Tampa Bay Times*, September 11, 2017. The Sunday morning track for[...]: National Hurricane Center website, "Irma Graphics Archive: 3-day Forecast Track[...]Watch/Warning Graphic," https://www.nhc.noaa .gov/archive/2017/IRMA_gra[...].php?product=3day_cone_with_line, last accessed December 28, 2018.

285. Weather Channel forecas[...]ryan Norcross warned: Bryan Norcross podcast, September 10, 2017, posted at [...]-blogging Hurricane Irma" on National Geographic website, https://blog.nationalg[...]phic.org/2017/09/09/live-blogging-hurricane-irma, September 10, 2017.

285. In Tampa, people went d[...]o the bay to see a bizarre sight: *Tampa Bay Times*, September 11, 2017.

285. . . . Key West residents ver[...]d from their shelters: Author's email exchanges with Carol Tedesco in Key West, Fl[...], September 10–16, 2017.

285. Candles were still burning [...]hor's telephone interview with Zulema Pradas, secretary of The Basilica of Saint M[...]Star of the Sea, Key West, Florida, August 15, 2018, transcript on file at Florida Key[...]story and Discovery Center, Islamorada, Florida.

286. As the dying winds signaled the departure: Author's email exchanges with Carol Tedesco in Key West, Florida, September 11–12, 2017.

286. Most of the water had receded when Tim Stanton left: Author's interview with Tim Stanton, Big Pine Key, Florida, March 14, 2018, transcript on file at Florida Keys History and Discovery Center, Islamorada, Florida.

286. In one Big Pine Key neighborhood, elevated homes: Author's visits to Big Pine Key, Florida, March 7, 2018.

287. Early damage assessments in the Keys: *Tampa Bay Times*, September 12, 2017; September 13, 2017; September 16, 2017.

287. Giant C-130 cargo planes: *South Florida Sun Sentinel* (Fort Lauderdale), September 12, 2017.

287. Around 3:30 p.m. Sunday, Irma's eye came ashore: *USA Today*, September 10, 2017.

287. Irma's once-massive power continued to drain: National Hurricane Center website, "Irma Graphics Archive: 3-day Forecast Track and Watch/Warning Graphic," https://www.nhc.noaa.gov/archive/2017/IRMA_graphics.php?product=3day_cone_with_line, last accessed December 28, 2018.

287. Storm-chaser Michael Laca estimated: Author's email exchanges with Michael Laca, August 24, 2018.

287. Several times as the eyewall passed, the parking deck was blasted: *USA Today*, September 10, 2017.

287. . . . a gust that Greg Nordstrom estimated: Livestream of Hurricane Irma's landfall at Naples, Florida, September 10, 2017, https://www.pscp.tv/w/1DXGyOaWrbgxM?f bclid=IwAR3QV8Lx3QlRi8UBgPu4pfEAsWx0_jULn0VilG8ZDUeG9DeiVbLgk-2kfrS4, last accessed January 7, 2019

288. In Tampa, Jeff Houck and his family: Author's email exchanges with Jeff Houck, Tampa, Florida, September 9–11, 2017. Houck's comments were posted by the author on the National Geographic website as "Live-blogging Hurricane Irma," from September 9, 2017, to September 20, 2017, https://blog.nationalgeographic.org/2017/09/09/live-blogging-hurricane-irma.

288. In Bartow, about 45 miles east of Tampa, Bonnie Ley and her partner: *Tampa Bay Times*, September 12, 2017.

289. Irma continued to weaken: National Hurricane Center website, "Irma Graphics Archive: 3-day Forecast Track and Watch/Warning Graphic," https://www.nhc.noaa.gov/archive/2017/IRMA_graphics.php?product=3day_cone_with_line, last accessed December 28, 2018.

289. In Islamorada, Phyllis Mitchell noted in her hurricane diary: Diary of Phyllis Mitchell, Islamorada, Florida, transcript on file at Florida Keys History and Discovery Center, Islamorada, Florida.

289. . . . emergency management officials also imposed a quarantine: *Tampa Bay Times*, September 13, 2017.

289. The bridge over Snake Creek: *South Florida Sun Sentinel* (Fort Lauderdale), September 12, 2017.

289. The storm surge had washed RVs into canals: Author's phone interview with Monroe County sheriff Rick Ramsay, November 1, 2018.

289. Coast Guard pilots had seen bodies floating: Author's phone interview with Monroe County sheriff Rick Ramsay, November 1, 2018.
289. Irma's winds were down to around 60 mph: National Hurricane Center website, "Irma Graphics Archive: 3-day Forecast Track and Watch/Warning Graphic," https://www.nhc.noaa.gov/archive/2017/IRMA_graphics.php?product=3day_cone_with_line, last accessed December 28, 2018.
289. By 8 p.m. Monday, Irma's center was near Albany: National Hurricane Center website, "Irma Graphics Archive: 3-day Forecast Track and Watch/Warning Graphic," https://www.nhc.noaa.gov/archive/2017/IRMA_graphics.php?product=3day_cone_with_line, last accessed December 28, 2018.
290. In Islamorada, Phyllis Mitchell took her dogs: Diary of Phyllis Mitchell, Islamorada, transcript on file at Florida Keys History and Discovery Center, Islamorada, Florida.
290. Mitchell encountered six cars: Diary of Phyllis Mitchell, Islamorada, Florida, transcript on file at Florida Keys History and Discovery Center, Islamorada, Florida.
290. What was left of Hurricane Irma: National Hurricane Center website, "Irma Graphics Archive: 3-day Forecast Track and Watch/Warning Graphic," https://www.nhc.noaa.gov/archive/2017/IRMA_graphics.php?product=3day_cone_with_line, last accessed December 28, 2018.
290. By Tuesday, September 12, Floridians were trying: *Tampa Bay Times*, September 13, 2017.
290. "If you chose to drive back home Tuesday: *Tampa Bay Times*, September 13, 2017.
290. The *Times* reported that a 150-mile segment: *Tampa Bay Times*, September 13, 2017.
290. Among the homeowners sorting through the wreckage was former Dallas Cowboys coach: *South Florida Sun Sentinel* (Fort Lauderdale), September 15, 2017.
290. Charlotte Wilson was among the Keys residents: Author's interview with Carol Tedesco and Charlotte Wilson, Key West, Florida, March 6, 2018, transcript on file at Florida Keys History and Discovery Center, Islamorada, Florida.
291. . . . much of the island was devastated: Author's interviews with Patrick Garvey and Tim Stanton, March 14, 2018; author's visits to Big Pine Key, March 2, 2018, and March 14, 2018.
291. Tim Stanton had lost his home and his workshop: Author's interview with Tim Stanton, March 14, 2018, transcript on file at Florida Keys History and Discovery Center, Islamorada, Florida.
291. The weather system that had once been: National Hurricane Center website, "Irma Graphics Archive: 3-day Forecast Track and Watch/Warning Graphic," https://www.nhc.noaa.gov/archive/2017/IRMA_graphics.php?product=3day_cone_with_line, last accessed December 28, 2018.
291. In Hollywood, Florida, elderly residents of a nursing home: *Tampa Bay Times*, September 14, 2017, and December 31, 2018.
291. A hospital that never lost power: *Tampa Bay Times*, September 14, 2017.
291. The Federal Emergency Management Agency said 25 percent of the homes: *South Florida Sun Sentinel* (Fort Lauderdale), September 20, 2017.
292. Hurricane Irma also racked up an impressive list: *Tampa Bay Times*, September 11, 2017.

292. Every year, tourism brings about $2.7 billion: *Tampa Bay Times*, October 1, 2017.

292. A little normalcy began creeping back into the Keys on Sunday: *South Florida Sun Sentinel* (Fort Lauderdale), September 25, 2017; *Florida Today*, September 25, 2017.

292. The Green Parrot had cleaned up: *Palm Beach Post*, September 28, 2017.

292. Key West mayor Craig Cates said he and other political and business leaders: *Florida Today*, September 25, 2017.

293. "It was a little controversial," conceded festival director: Author's telephone interview with Nadene Grossman Orr, Key West, Florida, August 17, 2018.

293. By March 2018 there still were signs that a bad hurricane: Author's visit to Florida Keys, March 2018.

294. In February 2018 a Big Pine Key resident was told that it would be two years: Author's telephone interview with Monroe County sheriff Rick Ramsay, November 1, 2018, transcript on file at Florida Keys History and Discovery Center, Islamorada, Florida.

294. "We'll be recovering for years": Author's telephone interview with Monroe County sheriff Rick Ramsay, November 1, 2018, transcript on file at Florida Keys History and Discovery Center, Islamorada, Florida.

294. Its intensification escalated: "Hurricane Michael Tropical Cyclone Update, 1 AM CDT Wed Oct 10 2018," National Hurricane Center, Miami, Florida, from the National Hurricane Center website, https://www.nhc.noaa.gov/archive/2018/al14/al142018.public_a.014.shtml, last accessed January 28, 2018.

294. At 9 a.m. Eastern Time on October 10, the storm was: "Hurricane Michael Tropical Cyclone Update, 9 AM CDT Wed Oct 10 2018," National Hurricane Center, Miami, Florida, from the National Hurricane Center website, https://www.nhc.noaa.gov/archive/2018/al14/al142018.update.10101355.shtml, last accessed January 28, 2019.

295. "This is really an amazing event": *New York Times*, October 11, 2018.

295. Hurricane Michael became the fourth most: *National Hurricane Center Tropical Cyclone Report, Hurricane Michael (AL142018)*, by John L. Beven II, Robbie Berg, and Andrew Hagen, April 19, 2019, p. 1; Report available at https://www.nhc.noaa.gov/data/tcr/AL142018_Michael.pdf, accessed April 19, 2019.

295. About 120,000 people—far more than live in the Keys: *Palm Beach Post*, October 10, 2018; *South Florida Sun Sentinel* (Fort Lauderdale), October 10, 2018.

"We'd have a difficult time preparing for a storm like that": Author's interview with Richie Russell, Islamorada, Florida, March 13, 2018, transcript on file at Florida Keys History and Discovery Center, Islamorada, Florida.

295. As of November 2018 she was the oldest living survivor: Author's interview with Richie Russell, Islamorada, Florida, March 13, 2018, transcript on file at Florida Keys History and Discovery Center, Islamorada, Florida.

295. "I didn't have any idea I'd survive that storm": Author's telephone interview with Alma Pender Dalton, October 7, 2018, transcript on file at Florida Keys History and Discovery Center, Islamorada, Florida.

Select Bibliography

The sources listed below represent a selection of sources consulted during the research for the first and second editions of *Storm of the Century: The Labor Day Hurricane of 1935.*

Books and Pamphlets

Barnes, Jay. *Florida's Hurricane History.* Chapel Hill: University of North Carolina Press, 1998.

Best, Gary Dean. *FDR and the Bonus Marchers, 1933–1935.* Westport, CT: Praeger, 1992.

Bowditch, Nathaniel. *American Practical Navigator*, vol. 1. Washington, DC: Defense Mapping Agency Hydrographic/Topographic Center, 1984.

Bramson, Seth. *The Greatest Railroad Story Ever Told: Henry Flagler & the Florida East Coast Railway's Key West Extension.* Charleston, SC: The History Press, 2011.

Burnett, Gene M. *Florida's Past: People and Events that Shaped the State.* Sarasota, FL: Pineapple Press, 1986.

Chambers, Clarke A., ed. *The New Deal at Home and Abroad, 1929–1945.* vol. 8 of *Sources in American History*, ed. George H. Knoles. New York: The Free Press, 1965.

Daniels, Roger. *The Bonus March: An Episode of the Great Depression.* Westport, CT: Greenwood Publishing Co., 1971.

Davies, Pete. *Inside the Hurricane: Face to Face with Nature's Deadliest Storms.* New York: Henry Holt and Company, 2000.

Dean, Love. *Lighthouses of the Florida Keys.* Key West, FL: Historic Florida Keys Foundation, Inc., 1992.

Douglas, Marjorie Stoneman. *Hurricane.* New York: Rhinehart, 1958.

Dunn, Gordon E., and Banner I. Miller. *Atlantic Hurricanes.* Baton Rouge: Louisiana State University Press, 1960.

Emanuel, Kerry. *Divine Wind: The History and Science of Hurricanes.* New York: Oxford University Press, 2005.

Emery, Edwin. *The Press and America: An Interpretive History of Journalism.* Englewood Cliffs, NJ: Prentice-Hall, 1962.

Gallagher, Dan. *Pigeon Key and the Seven-Mile Bridge 1908–1912.* Marathon, FL: Pigeon Key Foundation, Inc., 1995.

Hotchner, A. E. *Papa Hemingway: A Personal Memoir.* New York: Random House, 1955.

Junger, Sebastian. *The Perfect Storm: A True Story of Men Against the Sea.* New York: W.W. Norton & Company, 1997.

Kaufelt, Lynn Mitsuko. *Key West Writers and their Houses.* Sarasota, FL: Pineapple Press and Fort Lauderdale, FL: Omnigraphics, Inc., 1986.

Knight, Austin M., revised by Harry A. Baldridge. *Knight's Modern Seamanship.* New York: D. Van Nostrand Company, 1930.

Knowles, Thomas Neil. *Category 5: The 1935 Labor Day Hurricane.* Gainesville: The University Press of Florida, 2009.

Knowles, Thomas Neil. *Long Key: Flagler's Island Getaway for the Rich & Famous*. Gainesville: University Press of Florida, 2014.

Kobal, John. *Gotta Sing Gotta Dance: A History of Musicals*. New York: Exeter Books; distributed by Bookthrift, 1983.

Larson, Erik. *Isaac's Storm: A Man, a Time, and the Deadliest Hurricane in History*. New York: Crown Publishers, 1999.

Lisio, Donald J. *The President and Protest: Hoover, Conspiracy, and the Bonus Riot*. Columbia: University of Missouri Press, 1974.

Manchester, William. *The Glory and the Dream: A Narrative History of America—1932–1972*, vol. 1 & 2. Boston and Toronto: Little, Brown and Company, 1973–1974.

McIver, Stuart B. *Dreamers, Schemers and Scalawags*. Sarasota, FL: Pineapple Press, 1994.

———. *Hemingway's Key West*. Sarasota, FL: Pineapple Press, 1993.

McLendon, James. *Papa Hemingway in Key West*. 3rd ed. Key West, FL: Langley Press, 1993.

Murphy, George, ed. *The Key West Reader: The Best of Key West's Writers 1830–1990*. Key West, FL: Tortugas Ltd., 1989.

Niedhauk, Charlotte Arpin. *Charlotte's Story*. Lower Sugarloaf Key, FL: Laurel & Herbert, 1973.

O'Sullivan, Maurice, and Jack C. Lane. *The Florida Reader: Visions of Paradise from 1530 to the Present*. Sarasota, FL: Pineapple Press, 1991.

Opel, Frank, and Tony Meisel, eds. *Tales of Old Florida*. Secaucus, NJ: Castle, a division of Book Sales Inc., 1987.

Parks, Pat. *The Railroad That Died at Sea: The Florida East Coast's Key West Extension*. Key West, FL: Langley Press, Inc., 1968.

Roosevelt, Franklin D. *On Our Way*. London: Faber & Faber Limited, 1934.

Schlesinger, Arthur M. Jr. *The Coming of the New Deal: The Age of Roosevelt*. Boston: Houghton-Mifflin Company, 1958.

Sloan, Bill. *"I Watched a Wild Hog Eat My Baby!": A Colorful History of Tabloids and Their Cultural Impact*. Amherst, NY: Prometheus Books, 2001.

Smiley, Nixon. *Knights of the Fourth Estate: The Story of the Miami Herald*. Miami: E.A. Seemann Publishing Co., 1974.

Smith, Richard Norton. *The Colonel: The Life and Legend of Robert R. McCormick, 1880–1955*. Boston: Houghton-Mifflin Co., 1997.

Standiford, Les. *Last Train to Paradise: Henry Flagler and the Spectacular Rise and Fall of the Railroad That Crossed an Ocean*. New York: Crown Publishers, 2002.

Swanberg, W. A. *Citizen Hearst: A Biography of William Randolph Hearst*. New York: Galahad Books, 1996.

Tufty, Barbara. *1001 Questions Answered About Hurricanes, Tornadoes, and Other Natural Air Disasters*. New York: Dodd, Mead & Co., 1970; New York: Dover Publications, Inc., 1987.

Viele, John. *The Florida Keys: A History of the Pioneers*. Sarasota, FL: Pineapple Press, 1996.

Journals and Periodicals

"Report of Special Investigating Committee, Florida Hurricane Disaster." *Digest of Minutes*, National Executive Committee Meeting, *American Legion* magazine, November 1936.

Bellamy, Jeanne. "Newspapers of America's Last Frontier." *Tequesta: The Journal of the Historical Association of Southern Florida*, no. 12 (1952).

Boulard, Garry. "'State of Emergency': Key West in the Great Depression." *Florida Historical Quarterly*, vol. 67, no. 2, October 1988.

Bremer, William W. "Along the 'American Way': The New Deal's Work Relief Programs for the Unemployed." *The Journal of American History* 62, no. 3 (1975): 636–52.

Burt, Al. "Fury in the Keys." *Tropic* magazine, August 20, 1978.

Cox, Merlin G. "David Sholtz: New Deal Governor of Florida." *Florida Historical Quarterly*, vol. 43, no. 2, October 1964.

Davis, Elmer. "New World Symphony." *Harper's Magazine*, May 1935.

Gentry, Richard E. "Early Families of Upper Matecumbe." *Tequesta: The Journal of the Historical Association of Southern Florida*, no. 34 (1974).

Hemingway, Ernest. "The Sights of Whitehead Street: A Key West Letter." *Esquire* magazine, April 1935.

———. "Who Murdered The Vets?" *New Masses* magazine, September 17, 1935.

Jeans, Paul. "Tropical Disturbance: The Story of the Making of the Miami Tribune." *Miami Tribune*, April 4, 1937.

McDonald, W. F. "Lowest Barometer Reading in the Florida Keys Storm of September 2, 1935." *Monthly Weather Review*, October 1935.

———. "The Hurricane of August 31 to September 6, 1935." *Monthly Weather Review*, September 1935.

Mitchell, Charles L. "The West Indian Hurricane of September 14–22, 1926." *Monthly Weather Review*, October 1926.

Painton, Fred C. "Rendezvous with Death." *American Legion* magazine, November 1935.

Rovers, Richard. "End of the Line." *The New Yorker*, December 15, 1951.

Weightman, R. Hanborn. "West Indian Hurricanes of August 1928." *Monthly Weather Review*, October 1928.

Saunders, William H. "The Wreck of Houseboat No. 4, October 1906." *Tequesta: The Journal of the Historical Association of Southern Florida*, no. 19 (1959).

Websites

www.rice.edu/fondren/woodson/exhibits/wac/rogers.html: Edith Nourse Rogers biography by Dorothy M. Brown.

www.indo.com/distance/: a website maintained by Darrell Kindred that provides a link to a navigation computer.

INDEX

Abernathy, Rep. Tom, 256
Abt, John J., 190–91, 194,
    198, 267
  Butters's testimony
    to, 199
  and communist party,
    239–40
  conversation with
    Williams, 191–92
  and Ghent's
    testimony, 200
  hurricane report by,
    240–41, 242, 243
  and Kennamer, 190–91
  questions Weather
    Bureau, 264
  on Rankin, 256
  report by, 206, 254, 255
Adams, Robert, 149–50
Advocate and Activist:
    Memoirs of an
    American Communist
    Lawyer (Abt), 240
Aitcheson, F. L., 89, 90
Albury, Capt. Charles, 74,
    76, 202
Albury, Maj. William,
    147, 205
Alexander, Dr. Lassiter, 38,
    128, 136
U.S.S. *Alligator,* 1
Alligator Reef Lighthouse, 1
Ambrose, John, 21–22, 47,
    121, 238
  comments on hurricane,
    54–55
  vets bridge project,
    261–62
Ambrose, Mrs. Amanda, 238
American Expeditionary
    Force. *See* World War
    I, American forces in
American Legion,
    investigation by,
    204–6, 231

American Red Cross, 261
Andrews, George, 151,
    167–68
Andros Island. *See* Bahamas,
    The
Annenberg, Moe, 72,
    244, 245
Arrington, E. F., 169
Astaire, Fred, xx
Atlantic Ocean, surface
    temperature of, 56
  See also hurricanes
Atlantis (research ship), 248
Auden, W. H., xi
Ayer, Robert, Jr., 36, 80,
    81, 194

Baggs, Leila, 86
Bahamas, The, xxi
  Hurricane Irma in, 271,
    275, 277
  Labor Day hurricane in,
    x, 58
  water temperature of,
    56–57
Baker, L. H., 202
Baker, Rev. John C., 279
Baker, William, 141
Barbuda, hurricane on,
    271–72
barometers, 47–48, 68, 69
Barringer, Clarence, 182
Batista, Col. Fulgencio, xxi,
    xxii, 247
Beckham, J. R., 130–31, 146
Beckman, Brant, 285
Bee, The, on Morris's
    death, 175
Beery, Wallace, 126
Beganske, Andrew, 185
Belcher, Anna, 64, 178
Belcher, Frank, 64, 178
Belgrano, Frank, Jr., 159
Bennett, Walter, 263, 264
Berteau, Paul, 58

Berteau, Rita, 58, 203
Biggers, L. Garland, 187
Big Pine Key, 269, 281
  Hurricane Irma in, 275,
    282, 283, 284, 286–87,
    291, 293–94
  See also Garvey, Patrick
Bilsbrough, Arthur, 177
Bird, Preston, 146
Bishop, Elizabeth, 251
Boatmen, Edgar, 110
Bomer, Fred, Jr., 69
Booth, Ruth, 202
Boring, Arthur, 152
Bow, Lawrence, 42–43, 205
  on hurricane's
    position, 86
  Stone on, 228
  and vets' work camp, 28,
    29, 30, 31, 34, 35, 36
Bow, Lily, 42–43
Bradford, Cardy, 69, 106
Bradford, Carson, 106
Bradford, Elizabeth, 145,
    147, 149
Branch, George, 91, 99, 100,
    101, 128–29, 160
  in hurricane, 107, 108,
    109, 110, 115–16, 117,
    128–29
  hurricane's aftermath,
    154–55
Britton, Jack, 28
Broderick, Lawrence, 175
Brown, Arthur, 205
Brown, Willard K., 162
Browne, P.M. Gaston, 272
Bruce, Toby, 32, 61
Bryant, Michael, 281
Buck, Albert, 80, 81
Buckley, Charles, 222
Buffett, Jimmy, 252
Bunnell, Gifford, 149
Burk, Harry, 178
Burpee, Robert, 265

Bush, Pres. George H.
    W., 261
Butters, Charles, 94,
    114, 137
Butters, Chester, 103
Butters, Ed, 11, 40, 70, 101,
    199, 250
    in hurricane, 94, 98, 103,
        111–12, 113, 114,
        120, 125
    in 1926 hurricane, 93
    hurricane's aftermath,
        137, 155, 236
    storm's barometric
        reading, 267
Butters, Fern, 11, 40,
    236, 250
    in hurricane, 93, 94, 103,
        113–14, 119, 124–25
    hurricane's aftermath,
        137, 155
Butters, Jack, 94, 98, 103
Byrum, J. L., 90–91

Calman, Cal, 64
Calusa Indians, 12
Cape Sable (Fl), 152–53
Caribee Colony, 11, 138
Carlisle, Pete, 129
Carlson, Maude, 5, 111,
    120, 202
Carlson, Rev. Robert E., 5,
    111, 120
    death of, 202, 213, 237
Carpenter, William, 222
Carson, Ernest, 48, 70, 85
    call to Sheldon, 84,
        264, 265
    Duane's report to,
        196–97
    Tribune's comments
        on, 161
    weather advisories of,
        79, 80
Cash, Kevin, 277
Cates, Craig, 292
Cedar Key (Fl), 157

Chambers, Anna R.,
    102, 113
Cheeca Lodge, 261
Chicago Daily Tribune,
    154, 176
    on veterans' deaths,
        172, 188
Chiles, Sen. Lawton, 254–55
Christie, Albert, 128
Cinder, Ann, 178
Civilian Conservation Corps
    (CCC), 20
Clark, Charles C., 168, 182
    report by, 189–90
Clark, O. W., 229–30
Clark, William, 105
Clemmer, Lt. William L.,
    148, 173
    death of, 248–49
    and hurricane warnings,
        73–75
    search for survivors,
        152–54
Clifford, Jack, 120
Close, E. J., 30
Coast Guard. See U.S. Coast
    Guard
Coffin, A. M., 186
Coleman, Sheriff Dave, 162,
    163, 170
Collar, Charles, 145,
    147, 149
Colvert, Gayle. See Sheldon,
    Gayle
Connery, William, Jr., 222
Conway, Jimmy, 28–29, 104,
    128, 185
Conway, John, 120, 185
Coolidge, Pres. Calvin,
    xviii, 190
Coppedge, Lisa, 274
Courier-Journal, on veterans'
    march, 16
Craig, Roland W., 11, 60, 67
    in hurricane, 90, 122,
        124, 126
    on hurricane's
        position, 71

Crow, Jack, 67, 90, 122, 126
Cuba
    forecasters in, xxi
    Hurricane Irma in, 278
    hurricane nears, 79, 83,
        96, 97
Cummings, Rae
    Sheldon, 243
Curtis, Vice-Pres.
    Charles, 17
Cutler, Ray, 207
Cutler, Sam, 34, 47, 50, 60,
    76, 97, 241
    and bridge project, 35–36
    and evacuation train,
        75, 77
    and hurricane advisory,
        61, 70, 71
    Kennamer's opinion
        of, 198
    meeting with Carson, 48
    meeting with Sheeran, 74
    and rescue train, xv,
        131, 132
    testimony of, 199
    and Vander Schouw, 85,
        86–87

Daily Miami Metropolis,
    1906 hurricane, 8, 9
Daily Tribune, 71,
    72–73, 244
Dalton, Alma Pinder,
    295–96
Darty, Elmer, 83, 96
Daugherty, Thomas A., 187
Davis, Albert, 54
Davis, Ben, 135, 195, 199
    and evacuation train, 92,
        98–99
    in hurricane, 122, 123
Day, Henry, 146
Dean, Dizzy, 32
DeKlein, William, 155
Depperman, W. H., 141
Digest Literary, The, 218
Dixie, S.S., xx, 63, 83, 257
    departure of, 62

hurricane hits, 94–95, 97, 102–3, 112–13, 118–19, 131–32
in hurricane's aftermath, 156, 161, 162
hurricane's damage to, 139–40, 140–41, 144, 243
proximity to hurricane, 85
rescue of, 131–32, 178, 203
towed to New York, 203
See also Sundstrom, Capt. Einar
Dombrauski, John, 78, 98, 106
Duane, James, Jr., 12, 93, 98, 140, 150
after hurricane, 196–97
in hurricane, 107, 110, 123, 124, 125–26, 129–30, 132
Dubin, Al, 20
Dumas, Marie, 138
Dumas, Wade, 138
Duncan, B. M., 28, 33, 34, 35, 36, 64, 228
highway project of, 29–30
and Sheeran, 91, 92, 142
Duncan, James, 103
Dunn, Gordon, 263, 264
article on hurricane, 265

Eagle, Joe, 222
Early, Stephen, 151, 158–59
investigation into vets' deaths, 189
on veterans' deaths, 173
Edison, Thomas, 11, 236
Editor & Publisher magazine, 162
Edmund, Andy, 288–89
Edwards, Willard, 172
El Occidente (ship), 141

Empress of the Seas (cruise ship), 292
Engel, Albert Joseph, 222, 226, 233
Evans, Charlotte, xx

Farmer, Capt. Harry, 159, 160, 173
investigation by, 197
meetings with Russell and Sheldon, 192, 193–94
meeting with Kennamer, 190–91
Fecteau, Joseph, 40, 90, 213
Federal Emergency Management Agency, on Hurricane Irma, 291
Federal Emergency Relief Administration (FERA), 19, 164, 168, 254
Federico, Dylan, 285
Felker, Edward, 186
Fellows, Perry, 82, 83
Fish, Rep. Hamilton, 16
Fitchett, Lloyd, 100, 130
Flagler, Henry Morrison, 6, 7–8, 204
railroad bridges of, 252–53
Flatow, Ida, 178
Fletcher, Duncan, 188
Florida
1919, 1926, 1928 hurricanes in, 50, 123–24
Emergency Response Administration, 167, 168
Hurricane Irma in, 272–75
1935 hurricane warnings in, 69–70
Overseas Highway in, 249–50

real estate boom in, xviii
See also specific places in
Florida East Coast Railway (FEC), 2, 21, 160, 249
bankruptcy of, 23–24, 204–5
and evacuation train, 165, 206, 230, 231
hurricanes damage to, 40
Key West Extension, xiv, 7–8, 10
logo of, 12
Florida Keys, x, 2, 3–14, 204
in 1960, 276
bridges on, 252–53
canal at Lower Matecumbe Key, xiv
current population of, 267
history of hurricanes in, 40, 166
Hurricane Donna in, 252, 260–61, 275–76
1906 hurricane in, xiv, 8–10, 40
Hurricane Irma in, 268, 270–75, 276, 281, 282–89, 291, 292
Hurricane Michael in, 294–95
Labor Day hurricane in, xiii, 81, 88, 100, 143–60, 162
population growth in, 250, 251–52
2017 population of, 281
railroad in, 6–8, 10
reefs off, 68
in 1930s, 1, 3
Sept. 2, 1935, 81
storm surge in, 111
veterans work camps in, xiv, xv–xvi, xviii–xix, 13–14, 20, 21, 22
See also Key West (FL)
Folds, Dennis, 204
Follett, Wilson, 18

Folliard, Edward T., 36, 37, 52
Forbes, Charles, 151
Ford, Charles, 163–64
Forster, Rudolph, 188
Fort Lauderdale Daily News, on Weather Bureau, 262
Fortune magazine, on unemployment, 14
Fox, Abraham, 33
Frankfurter, Felix, 17
Frazier, John L., xii
French, John, 196
French, Monto, 196
Fritchmann, Mrs. L. A., 103

Gabriel, Sister Louis, 40, 279
Gaddis, P. I., 78
Gainesville (Fl), hurricane's impact in, 157
Galveston (TX), hurricane in, xxi
Gamble, J. E., 99
Gamble, Maggie, 169
Garvey, Patrick, 269–70, 272, 277–78, 280
Gaskins, Harry, 127
Gatun (ship), 141
Gehrig, Lou, 13
Georgia, Hurricane Irma in, 289
Ghent, Fred, xv, 51, 58, 62, 77, 96, 213
  Abt's conclusion on, 240–41
  call from Sheldon, 67
  call to Sheeran, 64
  and Cutler's call, 75
  and evacuation train, 84, 87–88, 89, 106, 124, 131, 132, 231, 265
  in hurricane's aftermath, 143, 145–46, 147, 164–65

inspecting veterans' camp, 33, 34
  Kennamer's opinion of, 198, 199, 206, 208, 242
  McFarlane's comments on, 223
  meeting with Van Hyning, 52–53
  in Rankin's hearing, 230
  and Sheldon's report, 157–58
  statement of, 191
  testimony of, 264
  vets opinion of, 196
  and Weather Bureau's forecasts, 262, 263
  Westbrook's questions of, 164–65
  working with veterans, 39, 40, 41, 43–45, 46
Gilfond, M. E., 67, 83, 84
  and Key West's economy, 26, 31
  on Sheldon's testimony, 198
  testimony of, 205
Gold Diggers of 1933 (film), 20
Good, John, 51, 61, 75, 76, 77
Goodman, Benny, xix
Grant, W. J., 9
Grapes of Wrath, The (Steinbeck), xi
Gray, Joseph, 222
Great Depression, xi
Great War. *See* World War I, xvi, xvii–xviii, 14
Green Turtle Inn, 261
Grey, Zane, 13
Griffin, Oscar D., 196
Grill, Ben, 178
Grill, Goldie, 178
Grimal, Adolf, 268
Griswold, Glenn, 222

Grooms, Bascom, Jr., 58, 59, 82, 92–93, 126, 237
Grooms, Bascom, Sr., 58
  after the hurricane, 236–37
Gross, Ben, 257
Grosskopf, Albert, 187

Halleck, Charles, 222
Hallihan, J. P., 168
Hamilton, Frank, 187
Hampden-Sydney College, 169
Hardaker, William, 79, 100
Harding, Pres. Warren, xviii
Harper, Herbert, 149
Hartridge, Earle, 9
Hatch, Ira, 47
Haycraft, J. J., 94, 99, 100, 101
  in hurricane, 109, 110, 112, 115
Hearst, Mrs. William Randolph, 13
Hearst, William Randolph, 71, 72
The Hell With Politics: The Life and Writings of Jane Wood Reno (Reno), 265
Hemingway, Ernest, 24, 61–62, 251, 268, 287, 292
  drinking with veterans, 42
  Home and Museum of, 279
  in hurricane, 66, 126–27, 131, 132–33, 154
  and Key West tourism campaign, 32
  on veterans deaths, 187–88
Hemingway, Pauline Pfeiffer, 24, 251
Hendren, Bill, 29
Herbert, Jacob, 84, 98

Hilbun, Joseph, 186
Hiller, A. D., 210
Hinchman, William, 30, 36–37
Hines, Gen. Frank, 151, 186, 206, 211, 242
  investigation plan of, 188, 189, 190, 191, 192
  memo from Clark, 229, 230
  and Rogers, 218, 219, 220, 221
  and veterans' deaths, 158, 159
  and Williams' report, 182, 183, 229
Hobart, Daniel A., 31
Hodge, Myrtle, 58, 203
Hodge, Sarah, 58, 203
Hoeppel, John, 222
Hoover, Pres. Herbert, xviii, xix, 13, 14, 15
  attitude towards veterans, 16, 17, 226
Hopkins, Harry, xix, 15, 27, 53, 83, 152, 220
  and Abt's report, 240, 242
  heads Public Works Administration (PWA), 25
  in hurricane's aftermath, 166, 168
  and Kennamer, 191
  meeting with Hines, 188
  Peterson's telegram to, 222
  on veterans' relocation, 36
  on veterans supervision, 174
  on Weather Bureau's forecasts, 262
Hotel Matecumbe, 40, 236, 250
  after hurricane, 137
  hurricane hits, 113–14
Houck, Brian, 288

Houck, Jeff, 282, 283, 288
Houston, John, 222
Howe, Louis, 15, 27, 31, 39
Huau, Joseph, 43
Hurchalla, George, 265
Hurley, Roy, 143–45, 147
Hurley, W. C., 170
Hurricane Andrew, 93, 124, 268, 295
Hurricane Camille, 93, 295
Hurricane Donna, 252, 260–61, 268, 270, 275–76
Hurricane Fran, 93
Hurricane Gilbert, 267
Hurricane Harvey, 270
Hurricane Hazel, 263
Hurricane Ike, 270
Hurricane Irene, 270
Hurricane Irma, 268, 270–75, 276–80, 281–94
Hurricane Isabel, 270
Hurricane Ivan, 270
Hurricane Michael, 268, 294–95
hurricanes
  1906, xiv, 8–10
  approach of, 68–69
  barometric pressure in, 47–48, 93
  and climate change, 271
  in Florida, 1920s, 50
  formation of, 56–58
  storm surges landfall, 110–11, 116–17
  and Straits of Florida, 48–49
  winds in, 90
  See also Labor Day Hurricane, 1935; specific hurricanes
Hurricane Wilma, 267, 268
Hyde, Lady Marguerite, 12

Ijams, Col. George E., 159, 160, 163, 165, 169, 173, 181
  and Abt's report, 242
  burial of veterans and memorial service, 169, 176–77, 179
  in Rankin's hearing, 230
Ingraham, Mary, 202–3
Ingraham, Robert, 202
Ireland, Edgar, 171
Islamorada (FL), 2, 5, 10, 48
  hurricane hits, 119, 130–31, 137, 156, 236
  Hurricane Irma in, 287, 290
  Matecumbe Club in, 10–11
  memorial to hurricane in, 246
  National Guard troops in, 34
  post office in, 258
  today, 261
  train station in, 111

Jackson, R. G., 124
Jameson, Colin, 252, 296
Jared, Sam, 191, 192, 194
Jarrell, Melton, 75, 130
Jarvinen, Brian, 266
Jeans, Paul, 71–72, 73, 150, 161, 244–45
  See also Miami Beach Daily Tribune
Johns, William, 3, 82, 100, 142, 146, 198
  in hurricane, 110, 117, 134–35
Johnson, Jimmy, 290
Johnson, Leo, 136
Johnson, Rufus, 8, 33
Jones, Catesby A. R., 204, 205, 223, 224, 231
Jones, Wilbur, 51, 117, 132

Karpus, Joseph, 185

Keith, Albert, 29, 31, 32
Kelly, Thomas, 246–47
Kennamer, David, 183,
190, 265
on hurricane tragedy,
241–42, 253
interview with
Russell, 212
investigation by, 195, 197,
198–201, 206–8, 229,
230, 231, 264
meeting with Abt,
190–91
meeting with Russell,
192–93
meeting with Sheldon,
193–94
report by, 207, 222,
253–54, 255
Kennamer, Thomas,
190–91, 192
Kennedy, Gerald S., 62, 65,
66, 164, 264
statement of, 191
testimony of, 197,
198, 205
Kettner, Edward, 144
Keys. See Florida Keys; Key
West (FL)
Key Veteran News, 21, 37, 42,
43, 238
on Ghent, 39
Key West Citizen, 61, 62, 65
Key West (FL), 2, 7
depression in, 14
economy of, 23–26, 217
Fantasy Fest in, 293
growth of, 251–53
highway to, 26–28,
29–31, 249–50
1919 hurricane in,
40, 123
Hurricane Irma in, 273,
274–75, 278–80.,
285–86, 290–91
Hurricane Wilma in, 268

Labor Day hurricane in,
62, 65–68, 126
Our Lady of Lourdes
Grotto in, 278–79
railroad to, 6, 10
tourism campaign for,
31–32, 292
See also Florida Keys
King, O. D., 81, 100,
201, 261
Knight, John, 245
Koleser, Andrew, 185, 186
Kreitzburg, Elmer, 104,
141, 184
Kreitzburg, Theresa, 184

Labor Day Hurricane, 1935
aftermath of, 134–42,
143–60
barometric pressure of,
123–24, 266, 267
congressional hearings
on, 209–13
on the East Coast,
169–71
hits the Keys, 100, 110
hits veterans' camp,
120–23, 124, 127–29
path of, 75
"rapid deepening" of,
77–78
Sept. 2, 1935, 81, 82
storm surge of, 110–11,
116–17
in Straits of Florida, 66
strength of, 266, 268,
270, 295
Laca, Michael, 285, 287
La Guardia, Fiorello, 172
Lake Okeechobee, 1928
hurricane, 50
Landon, Alf, 218, 238
Landsea, Chris, 266
Lapinski, Tony, 66–67
Laycock, John, 85, 95, 102
Lee, Joshua, 222
Lee, Robert B., 103

Leise Maersk (ship),
135–36, 243
Leiter, Daisy. See Hyde,
Lady Marguerite, 12
Lewis, Grady C., 174
Lewis, Spearman, 154, 176
Ley, Bonnie, 288
Limbaugh, Rush, 271,
272, 273
Limon (ship), 141
Lindley, James B., 104, 122
Literary Digest, The, 255
poll by, 238–39
Lodge, Bob, 287
Loflin, Scott, 44, 206
Long, Sen. Huey, xxiii,
181–82, 216–17
Long Key (FL)
after hurricane, 140
hurricane hits, 107, 110,
124, 129
1906 hurricane in, 8–9
Long Key Fishing Camp,
12–13, 132
Long Key Viaduct, 12
Loper, Dave, 127
Loper, Elva, 127
Lowe, Col. Thomas, 195
Lower Keys, 5
See also Florida Keys
Lower Matecumbe Key, xiv,
28, 90
bridge from, 45
hurricane's aftermath in,
154, 162–63
today, 261
veterans' camp on, 39–40
See also Florida Keys
Lowkis, Eugene, 145
Lydon, Joseph M., 103

MacArthur, Gen. Douglas,
17, 226
MacDonnell, George N., 85
Maggesen, Fritz, 90, 121,
123, 138–39
Malcolm, D. A., 76, 77

Mallory Steamship
    Lines, 23
Malone, Frank, 162
Maloney, Dep. Sheriff Louis,
    54, 101, 103
    in hurricane, 117, 132
Mariel Hemingway, 279
Marine, Charlie, 171
Matecumbe Club, 10–11
Matecumbe Graded
    School, 135
McCain, Clyde, 44
McCloskey, Col. Manus, xvii
McComb, Everett, 224
McCormick, Col. Robert,
    154, 172
McDonald, Father
    Alfred, 156
McDonald, Stewart, 172
McElwain, Jim, 274
McFarlane, Howard,
    222–23, 225, 231
McIntyre, Marvin, 151–52,
    165, 186
McLean, Charles, 52
McMullen, Leroy J., 104
McNulty, John T., 29
McQuarter, Jeremy, 284
McRea, Capt. C. D., 141
Melton, Quimby, 204, 205,
    206, 223, 224, 231
Merrick, George, 11
Mewshaw, Arthur, 29, 122
Meyer, Karl, 255
Miami Beach Daily Tribune,
    71, 72–73, 244
    hurricane coverage, 147,
        150–51, 161, 162, 176
Miami Beach (Fl), 1926
    hurricane in, 50,
        124, 209
Miami Daily News, 71
    hurricane coverage,
        61, 150
    on Norton, 263
    on Stone's plan, 26

on veterans' fate, 139,
    142, 143
on Weather Bureau,
    262, 263
Miami (FL), 1926 hurricane
    in, 50, 209
Miami Herald, 244
    hurricane coverage of,
        149–50
    and *Tribune,* 71
Miami News, on Hurricane
    Donna, 275–76
Miami Tribune, 244, 245
Middle Keys, 5
    See also Florida Keys
Miller, Victor, 72, 245
Mitchell, Alexander J., 168
Mitchell, Bob, 278, 290
Mitchell, Phyllis, 278, 282,
    289, 290
Moberg, Rev. Carl, 179
Monroe County (ship),
    121–22
Moore, Willis, xxi
Moran, Bugs, 72
Moran, Leo, 127
Morr, Bertha, 245
Morr, Edward, 245
Morris, Nan, 175
Morris, Owen Hughes, 175
Morse, Anthony, 187
Moseley, Brig. Gen. George,
    16, 27
Mosley, Zack, 247
Mota, Manuel, 253
Moten, Etta, 20

Neel, Betty, 184
Neel, John T., 184
Newfoundland, hurricane
    in, x
Newkirk, Bryan, 276
New Orleans Item, on
    Weather Bureau, 175
New York Daily News, on
    veterans' deaths, 173
New York Times

Gilfond's article for, 26
    on Hopkins, 53
    on vets' work program,
        52, 53
Nichols, Grace, 64
Nichols, Hubert, 33, 38, 46
Nobel, Alfred, xvii
No Name Key, Hurricane
    Irma on, 284
Norcross, Bryan, 268,
    269, 285
Nordstrom, Greg, 285, 287
Norris, Sen. George, 215
Norton, Grady, x, xi, 263,
    264, 265–66

O'Bannion, Dion, 72
Ollier, V. M., 39
Olsen, Lt. Carl, 148, 150,
    151, 154, 163, 173
Olson, Iver, 126, 266
On Our Way (Roosevelt), 216
Orr, Nadene Grossman, 293
O'Ryan, Edward, 194
O'Shaughnessy, P. J., 246
O'Sullivan, Maureen, 126
Oswald, Lee Harvey, 240
Outland, George, 112, 113
Overseas Railroad, 6–7, 8

Paine, Ralph, 3
Palmer, Lt. George, 58–59
Palmer, Rosalind Grooms,
    58–60, 99, 100, 101,
        126, 135
    brother of, 92–93
    death of, 236, 237
    in hurricane, 201–2,
        236, 237
Pan American Airways
    seaplane, 83, 85
Parker, Edney, 135, 140
Parker, Faye Marie, 246
Patman, Rep. Wright, 16,
    212, 213
    on Rankin's committee,
        222, 224, 226–27, 232

Pattison, Eugene, 71, 74, 80
Pearson, Drew, 256
Pearson, Herron, 222
Pegler, Arthur James, 72
Pegler, Westbrook, 72
Pemburn, Charles, 186–87
Pensacola News, on Weather
    Bureau, 175–76
Pepper, Claude, 59
Pepper, George, 59, 99, 100,
    101, 126, 135
    death of, 201–2, 236, 237
Pepper, W. M., Jr., 157
Perdue, Loretta, 103
Perdue, Olin, 94, 113, 115,
    116, 117
Perdue, Pete, 103
Perkins, Frances, 18
Perkins, Maxwell, 287
Pershing, Gen. John, xvii
Pervis, Jones, 86, 103,
    106, 112
Peterson, Rep. J. Hardin,
    152, 218, 221
    testimony of, 222, 223,
    224, 225
Pigeon Key (FL), 1906
    hurricane in, 9
Pinder, Alma, 237–38
Pinder, Bertram, 119,
    137, 237
Pinder, Dolores, 120,
    125, 237
Pinder, Elizabeth, 125, 137
Pinder, Etta, 5, 261
Pinder, Evanette, 119–20
Pinder, Laurette, 1, 80, 237,
    238, 258
Pinder, Russell, 120
Pitman, Mallie K., 107,
    109–10
Pitt, Gladstone, 195
Platano S.S., 141
Plumley, Charles, 222
Pooser, A. I., 90–91
Porter, Marvin, 34–35, 151,
    152, 167, 168, 170

Postell, Gay M., 106
Poughkeepsie-Eagle, on
    veterans' deaths, 175
Povey, Capt. Leonard J., xxi–
    xxii, 247–48
    flight of, 96, 97–98, 99
Powell, Adam Clayton, 256
Pratt, Joseph Hyde, 33, 34,
    35, 37
Public Works
    Administration
    (PWA), 25
Puerto Rico, x, 271
Pugh, Paul, 197
Pusey, Reba, 171

Racing Form, 72
Rambowski, Adam, 98, 106
Ramsay, Rick, 294
Rankin, John, 267
Rankin, Rep. John, 214–15,
    219, 220, 235,
    255–56, 264
    and Abt, 240
    bill by, 218
    hearings on hurricane,
    209–11, 212–13,
    221–35, 243, 255–56
    and TVA, 216, 217
Redkey, Henry, 195
Reed, Chauncey, 222
Reno, Janet, 263
Reno, Jane Wood, 263,
    265–66
Retew, W. L., Jr., 253–54
Rice, Millard, 232
Risk, Charles, 222, 233, 234
Roberts, Ruby, 203
Robertson, Glenn, 23
Robinson, Col. G. S., 28,
    30, 42
Rockefeller, John D., 7
Rogers, Ginger, xx
Rogers, John Jacob, 214, 220
Rogers, Rep. Edith Nourse,
    213, 214, 218, 256
    letter to Hines, 219–21

questioning Sheldon,
    211–12
    in Rankin's hearings, 222,
    224–26, 228–34
    report on hearings,
    233, 234
Rogers, Will, xix–xx
Roker, Al, 271
Roosevelt, Pres. Franklin
    D., xix, xxii, xxiii–xiv,
    13, 15
    1933 bills by, 18–19
    briefing on
    hurricane, 150
    criticism of over veterans,
    152, 186–88
    in 1936 election, 238
    election of, 17–18
    and Hopkins, 25
    and Kennamer's report,
    254, 255
    and Key West highway
    plan, 25, 27–28,
    31, 250
    Literary Digest poll
    on, 218
    and Rankin, 215
    relationship with
    veterans, 19–20,
    159, 210
    and TVA, 215–16, 217
    on veterans' deaths, 169,
    172–73, 175
    Williams' report to,
    180–81
Roosevelt I Knew, The
    (Perkins), 18
Rovers, Richard, 251
Rowena (ship), 121, 123,
    138–39
Russell, Bernard, 1, 2, 4, 38,
    275, 276, 295
    after hurricane, 258–61
    death of mother, 202
    in hurricane, 114–15,
    116, 118, 125, 130

in hurricane's aftermath, 134, 148–49
Russell, Clifton, 2, 130, 134
in hurricane's aftermath, 148–49
Russell, Dep. Sheriff T. F., 127
Russell, Emma, 202
Russell, Floyd, 275, 276
Russell, John, 2, 6, 38, 42, 149
in hurricane, 114, 115, 116, 130, 134
hurricane shelter of, 75–76
meeting on vets' deaths, 192–93
on veterans' danger, 212, 213
Russell, Laurette Pinder, 260, 295
Russell, Richie, 275, 276, 280, 295

Sadowski, Phil, 276
Sain, G. C., 104–5
Saint Lucie (steamboat), 9
Saint Martin, hurricane on, 272
Sanders, Jared, Jr., 222
Sands, Jacque, 279
Sanquist, O. A., 246
Saunders, Bra, 154
Saunders, William, 8, 9
Sauter, Herman, 246
Sauthoff, Harry, 222, 225, 233, 234
Scott, Gov. Rick, 272, 274, 278
Scott, Loring, 41–42, 46–47
Senison, George, 105, 137
Senterfitt, Martin, 287
Severeid, Eric, 19
Sheeran, Ed, xiii–xv, 45–46, 64–65, 67–68, 73
Abt's conclusion on, 241

and American Legion investigation, 205
car accident of, 250–51
and 1906 hurricane, 10
hurricane's aftermath, 139, 141–42
on hurricane's strength, 91–92, 101, 122, 201
meeting on storm, 70, 74, 76–77, 79
and tanker car, 84–85
vets' bridge project, 261–62
Sheldon, Gayle, 60, 65, 74, 76, 96, 243
Sheldon, Ray, 58, 60, 65, 66
on ferry, 74, 75
McFarlane's comments on, 223
Sheldon, Ray W., 50–51, 53, 79, 96–97, 103, 111
Abt's conclusion on, 240–41
after hurricane, 139, 141, 142, 242–44
and American Legion investigation, 205
call to Ghent, 264
call to Kennedy, 65–66
on evacuating veterans, 78, 80, 81, 89, 99, 101
and evacuation train, 106
before House Committee, 209, 211–12
in hurricane, 113, 115, 117, 132, 133
on hurricane's arrival, 91–92
and hurricane shelters, 235
Kennamer's opinion of, 197, 198–99, 200, 206, 207, 208, 242
Kennedy's advice for, 191
marriage of, 53, 58

meeting on hurricane, 76–77
meeting with Kennamer and Farmer, 193–94
questions to witnesses, 199–200
report of, 157–58
on Sept. 2, 1935, 81, 82, 84, 87, 88
testimony of, 197–98
and veterans' work program, xv
vets opinion of, 196, 197
and Weather Bureau's advisory, 192, 262
Sherman, George, 121, 136
Shields, Eleanor, 178
Sholtz, Gov. David, 24–25, 34, 163, 169–70, 173, 174
and American Legion investigation, 205
Shprentz, Freda, 178
Shprentz, Herbert, 178
Shprentz, Isidore, 178
Silverstein, Shel, 285
Simanski, Mrs. Preston, 169
Simmons, Sen. Furnifold, 29
Simpson, F. E., 52
Smith, Carlton, 170
Smith, Sam, 170
Snodgrass, Kate, 256
Souza, Steven, Jr., 277
Spanish American War, 14
Spira, Dora, 156
Spitz, Marjorie, 116
Spitz, Raymond, Jr., 116
Stanton, Tim, 280–81, 283, 285, 291
Stanton, Will, 280–81, 283
Starnes, Joe, 222
Steiler, Florence, 64, 76, 87, 156
in hurricane, 95, 113, 118
on hurricane's damage, 139
Steinbeck, John, xi

Stoddard, J. C., 173
Stone, Julius, 25–27, 31, 168,
239, 292
hurricane as "act of
God," 181
publicity campaign of, 36
in Rankin's hearing, 226,
227–28
and veterans' camp, 28,
32, 34, 35
and Westbrook, 165–66
Straits of Florida, 48
1935 hurricane, 66,
69, 88
hurricane hits, 88
Hurricane Irma in, 277
See also Florida Keys
Sullivan, Sully, 154
Sunday Star, veterans' eulogy
in, 180
Sundstrom, Capt. Einar, xx–
xxi, 62–63, 76, 131,
141, 227
fame of, 257
in hurricane, 94, 95,
102–3, 112, 118
on storm's position, 85
testimony of, 203–4
Sweeting, Etta Parker, 89–90

Tallahassee Democrat, on
Stone's plan, 26
Tampa Bay (Fl), impact of
hurricane on, 157
Tampa Bay Rays, 277
Tampa Bay Times, on
Hurricane Irma, 290,
291–92
Tampa Daily Times, on
Weather Bureau, 175
Tannehill, Ivan, 49
Taylor, Col. John Thomas,
231, 232
Tedesco, Carol, 274, 282
Teets, John, 162, 163, 170
Tennessee Valley Authority,
25, 215–16

Thomas, Devin, 285
Thompson, David W., 170
Thompson, Edith, 247
Thompson, J. Rodney,
185–86
Thompson, Sheriff Karl, 34,
35, 147
Thompson, William, 87
Torricelli, Evangelista, 47
Treger, Henry, 95, 131, 257
Truman, Pres. Harry, 251
Tugwell, Henry, 182
Turner, Nathaniel, 169

United States
in 1935, xix–xx
Great Depression in, xi,
xvi, 14–15, 18–19
hurricanes in, 1935, x,
xi–xii
1920s in, xviii
74th Congress in,
xxii–xxiv
veterans march on D.C.,
15–17
in World War I, xvi–xviii
Unkrich, R. G., 51, 52,
151, 167
Upper Keys, 3, 5
hurricane approaches,
69–70, 71
hurricane in, 88, 89, 134
1935 thunderstorm in, 21
See also Florida Keys
Upper Matecumbe Key, 1,
3, 153
after the hurricane, 236
damage in, 135, 136
Hurricane Donna in, 270
Labor Day Hurricane in,
115, 117–18, 125, 153
U.S. Coast Guard
and hurricane
advisory, 73
rescue efforts of, 147
U.S. Virgin Islands, 271
U.S. Weather Bureau, 158

in 1935, xii, 4
advisories on hurricane,
65, 69–70, 73, 76,
78–79, 82, 88, 99
Clark's report on, 189
and Cuban forecasters,
xxi
equipment of, 220
on Hurricane Donna,
275–76
hurricane investigation
by, 263–65
on hurricane's
strength, 140
hurricane warnings of,
49–50, 164–65, 167,
168, 171
reaction to criticism,
262–63
support for after
hurricane, 175–76
and Williams's
report, 182

Vander Schouw, Paul, 35, 45,
85–86, 86–87
Van Hyning, Conrad, 166,
194, 213
and American Legion
investigation, 205
evacuation of veterans,
83, 84
Kennamer's report and
opinion of, 198, 199,
206, 207, 208, 242
meeting with Sholtz, 170
opinion of Ghent, 39
and veterans' work
program, 51, 52, 53
Van Ness, Dorothy, 146
Van Ness, Laura, 146
Van Vecten, Charles, 130
Van Zandt, James E., 187
veterans
American Legion
investigation of
deaths, 204–6

bridge project of, 261–62
at Camp Foster, 195–96
camps closing, 53–54
deaths of and hurricane's
    aftermath, 136–37,
    138, 147–48, 151–52,
    154, 158, 161–62, 166,
    171–78, 246
details of deaths of,
    253–56
drunkenness of, 22–23,
    37–39, 40–41, 42, 52
evacuation of, 84, 87–88,
    89, 90, 92, 96, 98,
    100–101, 107–8,
    110, 111
housing and camps of,
    xv–xvi, 13–14, 21,
    27–31, 32–37, 39–40,
    43–44
in hurricane, 61, 70–71,
    104–6, 120–23, 124,
    127–28, 130, 132
hurricane evacuation
    plans for, 44–45, 51
and hurricane warnings,
    74–75
investigation into deaths
    of, 184–201
and Key West highway
    project, 27–31, 32
march on Washington,
    15–17, 19–20
memorial service for,
    179–80
and mosquitoes, 46–47
relationship with
    Ghent, 41
storm warning, 54–55, 75
work program, xvi, 45, 46,
    51–52

Veterans Administration,
    notifications of
    victims' families,
    184–85
Veterans Key, 261
Veterans of Foreign Wars,
    investigation by, 231
Virginia, impact of 1935
    hurricane in, 169
Virginian-Pilot, on
    storm, 175
von Brauchitsch, Mathias,
    253, 254

Wagner, Billy, 267
Wakeman, Rev. F. A., 118
Walker, Will, 99
Wallace, Henry, 182, 189
Warman, Stanley, 127
Warren, Cecil, 162
Washington Post
    hurricane coverage of, 82,
        151, 161–62
    on veterans' deaths, 175
    on veterans' march, 16
    on veterans' work
        program, 36, 37
Waters, R. V., 179
Weather Bureau. See U.S.
    Weather Bureau
Webster, Donovan, xvi–xvii
Weiss, Carl, 181–82
Weiss, Hymie, 72
Westbrook, Col. Lawrence,
    151, 152, 166,
    168, 189
    and Ghent, 164–65
Wheatley, Mollie, 171
Whitlock, W. E., 204, 205,
    223, 224, 231
Wigginton, Junius, 45,
    81, 200

Wilcox, Rep. Mark, 220,
    226–27, 235
Wilkinson, Jerry, 258
Williams, Aubrey, 83, 165,
    166, 174, 198, 200,
    240, 242
    conversation with Apt,
        191–92
    in Rankin's hearing, 226,
        228–29
    report by, 180–81,
        182, 187, 188, 191,
        220, 223, 229, 231,
        253–54, 255
    and Sheldon, 194
Williams, Tennessee, 251
Williams, Thomas A., 170
Wilson, Charley, 278
Wilson, Charlotte,
    273–74, 290
Winchell, Walter, 256
Wise, Lt. Col. Frederick, xvii
Woods, Jimmy, 119
Woods, Ruth, 119, 125
Woodward, Lt. Col. M.
    R., 38
World War I, American
    forces in, xvi, xvii–
    xviii, 14
Worley, George, 181,
    197, 205
Wright, J. G., 195, 196

Young, Robert, 126

Zaroff, Judith, 284